CONSCIENTIOUS OBJECTOR TO THE *APARTHEID* ARMY

T0414115

CONSCIENTIOUS OBJECTOR TO THE *APARTHEID* ARMY

PETER GRAHAM MOLL

ISBN: 979-8-35094-188-3 (print)
ISBN: 979-8-35094-189-0 (eBook)

In grateful memory of my friends who gave me advice prior
to my trials, 1977-1979

Dot Cleminshaw
Rev. Robert 'Rob' J.D. Robertson
Rev. (later Bishop) David Russell
Owen and Dora Tudor
Professor Francis Wilson

Contents

Foreword by Rev. Dr. James Cochrane

This intimate memoir tells the extraordinary story of Peter Moll, a conscientious objector to service in the *apartheid* South African military in the late 1970s. What makes it extraordinary is not that Peter was or is unique, some kind of heroic figure that ordinary people cannot match. Rather, it is the way it takes the reader through the rich and revealing journey of Peter's mind and spirit as he moved from unquestioned initial service in the army to rejecting its authority over him as he came to realise how great the injustice of its role in South Africa was.

From one point of view, yes, Peter's consistent and persistent stand, once he had taken it, could be described as heroic. But … pay close attention to what kept Peter going, and it could also be your, or my story. Anywhere.

The core of the book is Peter's arrest and incarceration in the military Detention Barracks (first Wynberg, Cape Town, then Voortrekkerhoogte, Pretoria) for a year from 1979 to 1980, much of it in solitary confinement. As he tells this story, Peter invites you into the gradual development of his own sense of what is right and good, wrong and evil. This was no easy journey.

Peter begins his story by locating his own upbringing as a White South African, tracing the experience of Whiteness in "church, school, residential areas, the labour market, public transport and public services." He introduces the reader into one of the most useful, brief accounts I have seen for anyone to understand how White South Africa functioned in those years, how easy it was for young white people—especially young men drafted into the *apartheid* military—to accept the way things were as perfectly normal.

This includes the bubble of complicity engendered by a conservative form of Christianity that intrinsically, if not overtly, legitimated the injustices that flowed from the structure of domination that the *apartheid* state and its collaborating institutions represented. It is in this context that Peter writes about his 'Damascus Road experience.' This took place, following the student uprisings that began in Soweto on 16 June 1976, in a fraught conference of organisationally segregated Evangelical Christian student groups in Pietermaritzburg. Black Christians present there were no longer happy to be segregated or subservient.

In the confrontation between White and Black students that ensued, Peter realised with full force that the South African state's anti-Communist propaganda he had internalised, sustained by many of his own church's views, really functioned to conceal the struggle for racial justice in South Africa. He writes, when it dawned on him that the society in which he lived was riven by

"a thicket of lies. [government / military explanations] …[that] it became impossible to promote my interests or those of my family/clan/group/race by means of the lie of racism."

Throughout his story, the complicity of faith becomes palpable; but so, too, does its role in shaping Peter to take a different path, to re-read his own tradition to find it not just wanting but necessary. Here is no easy rejection of his faith tradition; rather, a deep searching for the well-springs of mercy and justice, for generosity and humanity, that lie in its roots. Peter himself embodies this as he writes of what was a harrowing and harmful experience, "I bear no resentment against anyone involved in this account. I had and have no axe to grind."

A key part of Peter's narrative that shapes the middle chapters is his experience of incarceration and confinement. Again, the extraordinary dimensions appear, this time in the finely detailed accounting of what it was like to deal with the frequent arbitrariness of prison authorities, the cruelties and illegalities that were a regular occurrence on the part of their behaviour, how other 'normal' prisoners or arrestees interacted with each other and with Peter, what he needed in order to deal with days of isolation and poor or no meals, and—remarkably—how it was possible in the midst of all this to study Hebrew, Greek, French, German and even Spanish while reading other books in between, notably, the Bible. At times, one feels almost there with Peter, figuring out how to cope, how to remain human, and how even to act in ways that might humanise those who inflicted insult or injury in their incomprehension of why a young man would take the stance Peter did.

Drawing on rich archival sources, as well as his own memories and records, this memoir is full of valuable detail. For historians, also for those he names, this is important.

The book consists of three major elements: the first, often gripping, is on how Peter came to be a conscientious objector; the second is on his treatment and experiences in a year of imprisonment in the Detention Barracks, much of it in solitary confinement; the third provides a record of those details and documents that Peter wants to share more widely, which includes selected letters and a listing of all conscientious objectors, their rationale, and their first court dates going from 1977 to 1992.

Peter's narrative is not just moving; it is in a sense the story of anyone who has had to break free of the straightjackets of authority, political or religious, that allow for injustice to thrive, in order to find and follow the moral foundations that offer hope for all of humanity. What he offers to us is both an entrée into a time capsule of a particular form of resistance to *apartheid* in South African when it was at its height, a recognition of how this informs the present for anyone anywhere in the world whose moral sensibilities are offended by widespread injustice, and an invitation into the future for all who hold to the vision of a just and healed society.

Jim Cochrane
Emeritus Professor, University of Cape Town
Cape Town, April 2023

Abbreviations

ANC	African National Congress
AWOL	Absent Without Leave
CALS	Centre for Applied Legal Studies at the University of the Witwatersrand
CI	Christian Institute
COSAWR	Committee on South African War Resistance (in London)
COSG	Conscientious Objector Support Group
CPSA	Church of the Province of Southern Africa (viz. Anglican).
DB	Detention Barracks
ds.	Dominee (minister in the Dutch Reformed Church)
ECC	End Conscription Campaign
ECC Coll.	ECC Collection (either at the Library of the University of Cape Town or the Library of the University of the Witwatersrand)
ICJ	International Court of Justice
Lt.	Lieutenant
NUSAS	National Union of South African Students
Nathan Coll.	Nathan Collection at the Library of the University of Cape Town
OC	Officer Commanding
ouman, pl. *oumanne*	Old man (men) in Afrikaans, referring to certain of the longer-term inmates
PAC	Pan Africanist Congress

Rob. Coll.	R.J.D. Robertson Collection at the library of the University of the Witwatersrand
SACC	South African Council of Churches
SADF	South African Defence Force, up to 1993
SAIRR	South African Institute of Race Relations
SAIRR Coll.	SAIRR Collection at the Library of the University of the Witwatersrand
SALDRU	South African Labour and Development Research Unit at the University of Cape Town
SAMRAF	South African Military Refugee Aid Fund in New York
SANDF	South African National Defence Force, from 1994
SANNC	South African Native National Congress
SCA	Students' Christian Association
SCA/SCO Coll.	The Students' Christian Association / Students' Christian Organisation Collection at the University of Cape Town
SCM	Students' Christian Movement
Sgt.	Sergeant
SWAPO	South West Africa People's Organisation
TSD	Technical Stores Depot (as in 84 TSD, Grahamstown)
UCCSA	United Congregational Church of Southern Africa

UCT	University of Cape Town
UN	United Nations
Wits	University of the Witwatersrand
YMCA	Young Men's Christian Association (at the University of Cape Town)

CONSCIENTIOUS OBJECTOR
TO THE *APARTHEID* ARMY

Introduction

This book explains why I became a conscientious objector during the period 1977 to 1979, describes the conditions of my imprisonment in the Detention Barracks from 1979 to 1980, and outlines some of the consequences of my opting for conscientious objection. In the process I document the key events, such as the three convictions that led to my detention and the ten summary courts-martial for refusing to obey military orders. I have aimed for this work to be accurate and factual, so it can serve as a historical document and a reference in respect of my case. To make it readable, I stripped out most of the footnotes and hundreds of pages of detailed references in the press to the 56 conscientious objectors (1977-1993). If you, the reader, wish to pursue this research I can make the original files available to you.

I also wish to recognise the many people who supported me in my most need, and thus have included a list of names of letter writers, vigil attendees and visitors, and have added an index. There are no doubt some omissions owing to military censorship and disorganisation; I apologise for any remaining lapses. If I missed you, the reader, please let me know, and I shall recognise you in the next edition. (You can contact me by reconstituting my address as follows. The first letter of my first name (p), then my surname (moll), then an important year (1980), followed by the 'at' sign, then the first letter of my middle name (g), then the word for postage (mail), then a dot, and then the common ending (com). Thus my address has exactly 19 characters. I have deliberately made this long-winded so as to prevent web spiders and advertisers from locating my particulars.)

I bear no resentment against anyone involved in this account. I had and have no axe to grind. I remained on good terms with the staff at the Detention Barracks after my release. After Richard Steele's release, he and I went together to visit the Detention Barracks and collect all remaining postage items in February 1981. While travelling in Latin America in 1981, I collected all the foreign stamps I could and sent envelopes-full to Staff-Sergeant Marais, and also to Sergeant-Major Els whose son was a collector. I am on excellent terms with a theology student who came to visit in August 1980, and who three decades later turned out to be much more than a student ... but see the main text for the full story. I would like to meet up again with Corporal Gebhardt and Lieutenants Spriestersbach and Smith if I could locate them.

It is, however, hard to tell the story without occasionally shaking my head, marvelling at the bureaucratic incompetence, and intoning *"Swak, Piketberg!"* The origin of this humorous Afrikaans expression meaning, literally, "Weak, Piketberg!" is that the Dominee (minister) of Piketberg in the Western Cape had a long night of boozing after which he tried to stagger home, only to come to land in a dug grave in the cemetery alongside the church, where he slept. At daybreak he suddenly awoke, seeing the sun with clouds and feeling a breeze. "The Rapture!" he cried. "Glory be! Christ has come again to raise the dead. Ah, to be among the chosen!" He looked around to see if his parishioners had been resurrected but saw only sullen tombs. "No more chosen ones? Poor show, Piketberg!"

Sources that aided the memory include my own collection of documents and newspaper cuttings, augmented by the collection of my mother, Beryl Maureen Moll (1931-2020), and a similar collection of my cousin Richard Steele (his mother, Mrs. Dorothy Winifred Steele, and my mother were sisters); and a two-hour recording I did in February 1981 at the suggestion of

Professor Francis Wilson, recalling the key events of the previous year. I made occasional use of many other documents such as the Truth and Reconciliation Commission Final Report (1998) and my own submission thereto (Moll, 1997); a thesis about the Conscientious Objector Support Groups by Connors (2007); a history of St. Anthony's United Church by Rev. Rob Robertson (1999); Hale's works about Baptist ethics (2000, 2009); SAMRAF (1979); legal treatises such as that of Berat (1989); the history of the End Conscription Campaign by Jones (2013); the accounts of the Voortrekkerhoogte Detention Barracks by Kaempf (2002), Yeats (2005) and Budge (2013); and other papers and letters. For a sense of perspective about prison conditions in South Africa in general, I consulted Chikane (2009), Isaacs (2010), Kathrada (2004), Lewin (1989) and Mandela (1994).

Thanks are due to several individuals who went to libraries or churches to obtain documents for me: Hannah Cuaterno, Caleb Manikam, Simon Hyslop and Anne Clarkson. Thanks are also due to the staff of the Library of the University of the Witwatersrand, the Library of the University of Cape Town, the National Library (Pretoria and Cape Town campuses), and the Archives of the Baptist Union housed at the Baptist Theological College in Johannesburg. I am indebted to Rev. Corin Mathews for facilitating access to the Library of the University of the Witwatersrand. I thank the Alan Paton Will Trust for permission to use Alan Paton's poem *Caprivi Lament* (granted on 20 June 2023). I am grateful also for the kind assistance of Douglas Bax, Jen Beck, Rod Botsis, Jim and Renate Cochrane, John Child, Walter and Brenda Coxon, Anton Eberhard, Cheryl Gammon, Allen Goddard, John de Gruchy, Stephen Granger, Peter Hathorn, Wilma Jakobsen, Marian Loveday, Chris Marais, Terence Moll, Adrian Paterson, Richard Steele and Trevor Webster. I thank my brother Terence Moll and my sister Jen

Beck in particular for help with editing. I remain responsible for all remaining errors.

References to source libraries are frequently introduced so that anyone wishing to verify or research these matters further may do so quickly. The references are done as in this example: 'Wits, Rob. Coll., A2558-15.8' means the Library of the University of the Witwatersrand, the R.J.D. Robertson Collection, accession number A2558-15.8. The abbreviations for libraries and collections may be found in the list of abbreviations and acronyms.

Chapter 1. Baptist origins and my 'Damascus Road experience'

Question. *Apartheid* is now 30 years in the past. We all know it was evil, and Nelson Mandela was so great a man that he brought the nation together and won the Nobel Peace Prize. Surely, anybody with a scrap of honour would have refused to join the South African army in a war against Mandela's party, the African National Congress (ANC)? Is it not obvious that any and every person of good will should have resisted *apartheid* and the *apartheid* army?

Answer. No. If you were brought up in 'white' South Africa in the 1960s and 1970s, it was not obvious that you should resist *apartheid* and its army. The obvious thing for an 18-year-old boy finishing high school in 1973 was to get his military service over and done with, and then focus on getting a job, studying further, building relationships and living a 'normal' life.

I shall try to explain, from the perspective of a white boy growing up in the 1960s and 1970s, why the usual tendency was for white people to support the army even if they found some aspects of *apartheid* to be distasteful or immoral. The key element of my childhood and boyhood was that we lived in a white society: church, school, residential areas, the labour market, public transport and public services.

Church

My father was a magistrate (judge) and so we moved between villages or towns every three to five years. I was born in Pretoria. We spent some months in Lusikisiki in the Transkei, and then moved to Whittlesea, Alice, Lady Frere, East London, and finally Umtata (today Mthatha). My father's work had to do with administration of these towns and deciding court cases, in all instances involving black people. Nevertheless, we lived in our own, insulated, white world. For us, a key element was church and specifically the Baptist church.

My family and our cousins were staunch Baptists, stemming from our German origins. My great-great-grandfather Franciscus Xaverius Moll (1825-1889) became a mercenary in the British German Legion in 1856. The Crimean War ended before he could be deployed, and rather than go home, he decided to take the British offer to go to the Cape Colony as a military settler, arriving there in 1857. He was baptised by a lay pastor, Christian Friedrich Sandow, on 19 July 1863 in the Yellowwood River near Frankfort. His family became one of the mainstays of the Frankfort Baptist Church until the 1960s.

Many of his descendants remained within the Baptist tradition. When my family lived in the Eastern Cape and the Transkei, we always attended the closest Baptist church. In Lady Frere we attended the local Methodist church but drove to the Queenstown Baptist Church once per month. All the members of both churches were white; there were no black or coloured members. All the ministers were white. Sometimes, for special events, visitors came from coloured Baptist churches; for instance, we heard some testimonies and sermons from Rev. Malvory Peffer, a coloured minister who had earned his diploma at the Baptist College in Johannesburg. He was pastor of a coloured Baptist church in North End, East London, with a fine sense of humour amidst his oratory. Baptist youth events in King William's Town and Grahamstown were attended only by young white people. White members of Baptist churches in the Eastern Cape never observed people of other races in positions of authority such as deacon or minister.

De facto segregation of Baptist churches had multiple causes. The Group Areas Act of 1950 defined residential areas as 'white', 'coloured', 'Indian' or 'African'. There were cultural and language differences, particularly between the African members and the others. There was a certain amount of segregation in ministerial training: while white, coloured and Indian pastors were trained at the Baptist College in Johannesburg, black pastors were trained at the Baptist Bible Institute at Fort White near King William's Town (now Qonce). The Baptist Union itself was partially segregated: white, coloured and Indian churches became members of the Baptist Union, but African churches were grouped together in the Baptist Convention, which in turn had representation in the Baptist Union.

Most important, however, was that segregation had become part of our lives without our even needing to reflect on it. It never occurred to me, as I was involved with the Young People's meetings, that we might ever get together with young coloured or African Baptists. The fact that the Baptist Union was led by white people was never, to my knowledge, raised as a problem. To be separate was 'normal.' As a result, white Baptists did not hear from coloured, Indian and African Baptists how the latter were being hurt and humiliated by *apartheid*.

One of the prime tasks of Baptists was evangelism, that is, the winning of new converts. This preoccupation had a long history. Rev. Carl Hugo Gutsche (1843-1926), one of the founders of the German branch of the Baptist church in the Cape Colony, used the slogan 'every Baptist a missionary'. From his time forth, evangelism crowded out social justice and assistance to the poor. In the Baptist church one was expected to be deeply involved. One went through a conversion in one's teens, which was followed by baptism at which a verbal testimony was given, often in a highly emotional manner since the audience was large and the person being baptised was not skilled in public speaking. One then became a member of the church.

At the Cambridge Baptist Church in East London one was expected to be present at the morning and the evening services on Sundays, as well as the Sunday School hour before the morning service, the Young People's meeting on Friday evenings, the Bible Study run by the pastor on Wednesday evenings, and a prayer meeting before the service on Sunday evenings. There was a Sunday School picnic on Ascension Day. There were evangelistic missions run at Cambridge during the June/July or December/January vacations, typically running over a week; when there was no mission at Cambridge I took part in similar evangelistic endeavours at other venues such as City Baptist in East London, the CSSM (Children's Special Service Mission) in King William's Town and a Baptist church in Port Elizabeth. The Baptist church adherents became our circle of friends. Young people were expected to go out with other Baptist young people, and marriage to anyone outside the church was discouraged.

Some Baptists took positions of prominence. For instance, Rev. Andrew William van den Aardweg, a Baptist pastor, became a chaplain in the SADF (South African Defence Force) in 1966, rising to Colonel and Assistant Chaplain-General of the Air Force in 1974 and to Brigadier in 1983. For young white Baptist men facing an army call-up, it was easy to conclude that the army was on God's side because there were full-time, uniformed Baptist chaplains with rank. In addition to being preoccupied with evangelism, the white Baptist churches regarded themselves as apolitical. Racial discrimination and *apartheid* were rarely discussed. The ethical approach focused on individual ethics, which were readily found in the New Testament by a selective reading. For instance, "The fruit of the Spirit is love, joy, peace, patience, kindness, goodness, faithfulness, gentleness, and self-control: against such there is no law" (Galatians 5:22-23). Social ethics were not entirely absent. Among the key social ethics was to abide by the law. One was to obey the government which, to Christian South Africa, was divinely instituted: "Everyone must submit to governing authorities. For all authority comes from God, and those in positions of authority have been placed there by God. So those who rebel against authority are rebelling against what God has instituted, and they will be punished" (Romans 3:1-2). Of course among the laws to be obeyed was the military call-up.

The Baptist Church, at that time and in that place, acted as a theological straitjacket. The essential Baptist way of salvation was to be converted and believe in Jesus' atoning sacrifice, and then to seek to live a life of personal purity and work as a missionary in one's private capacity. Social ethics were rarely discussed. I did not realise it at the time, but in order to make progress in social ethics—and to respond in a thoughtful way to my repeated army call-ups—I needed to be liberated from the Baptist straitjacket.

Education

The schools were a key part of our white world. I attended primary school in Alice and Lady Frere and then high school at Selborne College in East London. All the pupils were white. In Alice some were Afrikaans-speaking and in Lady Frere most were, because it was a farming village where Afrikaners predominated; at Selborne almost all the pupils were English-speaking. All the teachers at the three schools were white. The only blacks present were labourers on the grounds, cleaners for the classrooms, sometimes construction workers, and ice cream vendors.

Selborne College was academically focused and had a number of excellent teachers. Though the school was required to be strictly apolitical, the groundwork for my later development was laid there as I learned how to think independently and to express my analyses and opinions clearly in writing and speech. History and English were particularly important in this process. My English teacher, Mr. Trevor Webster, encouraged me to read novels such as Alan Paton's *Cry, the Beloved Country*, Aldous Huxley's *Brave New World*, Daphne du Maurier's *Rebecca* and George Orwell's *1984*. I was enraptured by Tennyson's poem *Ulysses* in which the king, tiring of doling out "unequal laws to a savage race," declares his love of travel and discovery, even at the risk of shipwreck. He wishes to "drink life to the lees". His final word before departure is that he is determined "to strive, to seek, to find, and not to yield." I remember as clear as a bell when Mr. Webster said, "Note the power of this climax!" and read out that last iambic pentameter, striking the beats with his right hand.

History lessons were the story of the European settlers of South Africa, from Jan van Riebeeck in 1652 to the Second World War, again and again over our twelve years' schooling. The carefully selected syllabi had much fine detail about, for instance, Wolraad Woltemade (c. 1708-1773) and his rescue of 14 sailors from a shipwreck using his horse. The tale went thus: first there were the doughty Dutch settlers, then the British in 1820, and then the German in 1856. The settlers gradually expanded along the Eastern seaboard, and some embarked on the Great Trek to the north. There followed the Anglo-Boer War and the creation of the Union of South Africa in 1910. It was not the history of the varied peoples of the southern tip of Africa but the Settlers' Hall of Fame.

For the Matric history course, covering standards eight to ten (the equivalent of grades ten to twelve), we were given two textbooks: Fowler and Smit (1965) and Boyce (1965). The former reflected the syllabus and propounded the government's view, and we had to study it with the greatest care. The book was replete with buzzwords reflecting the settlers' one-sided views. The Xhosas in the Eastern Cape conducted "raiding parties" (p. 262f) and "stole" cattle, "invaded" (p. 265) in a "large horde" (p. 270), and their chiefs "fomented trouble" (p. 271). Whereas the settlers were "trekboers" who "recovered" their cattle; they were "hardy pioneers" who "opened up" the Eastern Cape (p. 264).

The Boyce textbook had fewer settler buzzwords and gave a fairer assessment of the conflicts between the settlers and the Xhosas in the early nineteenth century. For instance, Boyce declared that the annexation of the Suurveld had no legal basis, so "the Europeans were really the aggressors and not the Xhosa" (p. 135), and acknowledged that Governor Grey's policy of encouraging European settlement in British Kaffraria "squeezed the Native population into areas too small to support them" (p. 334). Nevertheless the Boyce textbook, too, was a history of the settlers, driven by the need to conform to the syllabus set by the Cape Education Department. Stuck at the back of both books were brief chapters about 'The Indians', 'The Coloureds' and 'The Bantu.' It is shocking on rereading these chapters to find that they were filled with minute detail about the many schemes, political, economic and educational, that the settler governments had granted them. There was not even an attempt at writing a history of *all* of South Africa, integrating the settlers' stories with those of the indigenous peoples.

Plenty of material was available for the historian's use, e.g. Sol Plaatje's *Native Life in South Africa* (1916), Edward Roux's *Time Longer Than Rope* (1948) and Albert Luthuli's *Let My People Go* (1962). Carefully omitted from the syllabus was anything that demonstrated capability or leadership by the indigenous peoples of South Africa. There was no mention of Clements Kadalie (c. 1896-1951) who in the 1920s created the largest trade union in South Africa, the Industrial and Commercial Union. The syllabus, and these two textbooks, had nothing about the founding in 1912 of the South African Native National Congress, the predecessor to the African National Congress. This omission is the more glaring because the SANNC was formed on account of many grievances such as the creation of the Union in 1910 that excluded black leadership, and the Land Act of 1913 that awarded just seven percent of the country's land area to 78 percent of the population. The textbooks have much information about the Union and about the Land Act but the response of the black population was omitted with surgical precision.

In their attempt to justify the actions of the SA government, Fowler and Smit even stooped to making misleading statements. They quoted a decision by the International Court of Justice that South Africa was not under a legal obligation to submit South West Africa to the Trusteeship Council. In fact this was one of four key decisions in the Advisory Opinion of the International Court of Justice taken on 11 July 1950, which were as follows: the Union of South Africa must submit reports to the supervisors, the United Nations and the ICJ; the UN Charter provided a means by which the Territory of South West Africa could be brought under the Trusteeship system; the Union of SA was not under a legal obligation to submit South West Africa to the Trusteeship Council; and the Union of South Africa had no right unilaterally to change the status of South West Africa, viz. to incorporate it as a fifth province in the Union of South Africa. The tenor of this Advisory Opinion was to bring South West Africa under the supervision of the UN and the ICJ and to prevent its incorporation in South Africa. But Fowler and Smit misleadingly quoted without context from the Opinion to give the impression to its teenage readers that South Africa was acting within its rights by treating South West Africa as a fifth province of the Union.

The history syllabus of the Cape Education Department sought to reinforce what we saw around ourselves, namely a white man's world.

Fortunately at Selborne College there was more. Mr. Roger Goodwin taught us the history of South Africa and of modern Europe—the French Revolution, the revolts of 1830 and 1848, nationalism in the 19th century, the Third Reich—which enabled me later to think critically about *apartheid* and the military. Mr. Goodwin permitted me to use his own notes from university history studies about Nazi Germany. I recall one lesson in which Mr. Goodwin told us to put our books aside. Since we were then studying Henri de Saint-Simon and Karl Marx, he proposed we discuss the question: Should people possess private property or should they not? Divergent opinions were voiced and the boys proceeded to defend them. The Arts Society—chaired by Nico Yiangou and assisted by Mr. Trevor Webster—invited Mr. Knowledge M.N. Guzana, leader of the opposition in the Transkei, to speak to the College when I was in my final year of school in 1973. He described the ills of *apartheid* and the discrimination that black people suffered, making a case for a nonracial South Africa in which dialogue and negotiation would replace confrontation and conflict. As secretary of the Arts Society, I closed off the proceedings by thanking Mr. Guzana, briefly summarising what he had said, and commenting to the assembled teachers, boys and parents: "Mr. Guzana has presented us with the challenge of ending racism. I think this is a challenge to us, the new generation."

I was in matric when we had a special visit from a former teacher at Selborne, Mr. Clyde Broster. He assembled all the would-be matriculants in the main hall and read the poem *Triumphal March* by T.S. Eliot. It was all very puzzling at first, with descriptions of what seemed to be a pompous Roman triumphal march, mixed in with listings of 20th century weaponry, and with bits of conversation among the observers who eat sausages. "What on earth would be the point of all this?" Broster asked. No one, not even Gordon Springett, who always won the English and History prizes, attempted an interpretation. Without handing it to us on a plate, for that was not Selborne College's way, Broster said, "Read the poem again. Listen to the noise and watch the spectacle. Where are the noise and spectacle *interrupted*?"

Now some tentative hands went up, one of the boys (not I!) plumping for the phrase "The natural wakeful life of our Ego is a perceiving."

"Yes," said Broster. "And now, reread the poem and interpret it in the light of this 'perceiving.'" It became clear to me that this poem was written by a sceptic who likened a modern military parade to an ancient Roman triumphal march, and dismissed both as excessive and ridiculous, whence the humour at the end about young Cyril shouting "Crumpets" in church. It was acceptable at Selborne to ask questions and to rouse one's own scepticism, as Clyde Broster had artfully done.

There was never a debate about 'separate development vs. equal development' or '*apartheid* vs. integration'. Some teachers would have been delighted to arrange this but punishment would have been swift. Occasionally some genuine moral feeling would shine through the clouds. Mr. D. Neil Emslie, our class master in standard six (the equivalent of grade eight in the USA) mentioned to us at the beginning of the year when textbooks and notebooks were being handed out that he had that morning seen black children clutching coins standing in line to buy school books—which we got for free. I have never forgotten the look on his face and the pang of guilt that I felt as a child of twelve.

At Selborne College, Assembly was held every weekday morning except Wednesdays. A hymn was sung and a prayer said. One of the hymns, John Bunyan's *Who Would True Valour See*, made an impression for the force of the poetry and the vigour of its folk song melody arranged by Ralph Vaughan Williams:

Who would true Valour see
Let him come hither;
One here will Constant be,
Come Wind, come Weather;
…
Then Fancies fly away,
He'l fear not what men say,
He'l labour Night and Day,
To be a Pilgrim.

Those thoughts were to stick with me: to have courage is to act fearlessly, regardless of what people say.

There were more influences during the critical high school years. My elder brother Douglas came back from Rhodes University in the late 1960s with new political ideas. The government was spending ten times as much on each white child's education, he said, as on each black child. Black people were being removed by force from land they had occupied for generations. Above all, he said, there were 20 million people in South Africa; it was not fair that only the three million whites had the vote. Our father was not impressed.

Residential areas

In all the places we lived in when I was a boy—Whittlesea, Alice, Lady Frere, East London and Umtata—our house was in a 'white' area, except for Umtata where after about 1976 black people started to move in. In Alice we lived at the Residency, the house of the Magistrate. Official letters to my father were addressed to 'Mr. T.A. Moll, the Residency, Alice'. The house overlooked the railway station, a prestigious place to be in those days. Somehow we grew accustomed to the deafening sound of the steam engines. The plot was 1.15 acres in size and included a tennis court. Over the road to the east lived Mrs. McGillivray. On the same block of Odendaal and Stocks Streets, to the west, lived Dr. MacVicar, who said he wished he could have been born forty years later, so as to marry my sister Jen, who was such a charming child. I was not charming for I was scared stiff of his needles. Any ache or pain had a ready solution: an injection. I learned that complaining about earaches and whatnot to my mother was not worth it because the resulting injection would be worse. Further to the east lived Professor Greene of the English department at the University of Fort Hare. His daughter Fiona was in my class at school and her sister Claire was a year younger, and we were all taught in the same classroom. Diagonally opposite to the south lived the McLeods, whose sons Peter and Rodney were my schoolmates.

It was a white society. We saw black women who offered their labour as domestic servants, and we sometimes saw beggars; often we saw Xhosa boys who used to drive herds of cattle along the road between us and the railway station. One of our nannies was Agnes Ndibaza, whom my mother first hired when we lived in Whittlesea. She moved with us to Alice and to Lady Frere, and also worked for my parents years later in Umtata. Kind and affectionate with children, she taught us English nursery rhymes such as *Ring a Ring o' Roses* and *London's Burning*. My sister Jen reminded me that Agnes taught her and me to sing the latter in the bath together as small children, in Xhosa:

Umzi watsha, umzi watsha,	The house is burning (2X)
Khangela phaya, khangela phaya,	Look outside (2X)

Umlilo! Umlilo!	Fire! (2X)
Galel' amanzi, galel' amanzi.	Pour on water (2X)

She played a large role in bringing us up since my mother was preoccupied with the infants Terence and later Brenda, and with managing the chicken run, the weeding and watering of the shrub garden, and with church activities.

In Lady Frere, similarly, we lived at the Residency on the north-eastern side of the town. The village was occupied by white people—at the most 200 of them. During the late 1960s the government was gradually buying up properties with an eye to the eventual 'independence' of the Transkei in accordance with the theory of grand *apartheid*. When we lived in the village, just a handful of businesses had been taken over by black people. The black population of the district was far more numerous than the white. Black people lived in 'locations' on the outskirts of the village and in rural areas where the main activities were subsistence farming and cattle-herding, funded by the remittances of migrant workers.

We mixed with other white children, most of them Afrikaans-speaking. There was an annual sports day when children from neighbouring towns—Ida, Cala, Dordrecht, Indwe and Qamata—would come to compete in field events culminating in the '880', a half-mile run. All were white. My mother taught English for a time at the Fremantle High School, a boarding school for Xhosa boys. The Xhosa people we encountered—apart from our nannies—had little education and rudimentary or no English, e.g. men looking for odd jobs and beggars. There were a few exceptions such as Mr. Pengca who spoke very good English and had had a tertiary education, and who worked in the magistrate's office. Social contacts between the races were limited.

Despite the unashamed racism of many white people we encountered, my parents always insisted that we treat everyone, including black people, with respect. We were never to use the standard terms of abuse when referring to them. "Love your neighbour as yourself" (Mark 12:31), they said.

My parents made efforts to bridge the cultural gap by learning Xhosa. They started with a textbook that came with long-playing records. Then they bought the Lumko Xhosa Self-Instruction Course by the Lumko Institute, and attended the Institute, seven miles south of Lady Frere, for evening instruction by the expert Fr. J. Riordan. Both became proficient. I was fortunate enough to be taken by my mother to Lumko during the June-July holiday in 1968 for a crash course in Xhosa. There was a language laboratory with huge reel-to-reel tapes, enabling one to listen and copy, while Fr. Riordan selectively monitored through headphones and helped students in difficulty. This was the 'new technology' of the day, and seemed awfully grand to me. Often we stayed there for most cf the day, absorbing this extraordinary language.

Xhosa is quite unlike anything that European ears are attuned to. With three basic clicks (the q, the c and the x) that are combined with other sounds, often onomatopoeically, plus an implosive b, profuse nasalisation, and a scratching sound at the back of the throat written kr, it is forceful, expressive and vivid. Compare the onomatopoeic words for scratch: German has 'kratzen,' which is quite good, but anodyne compared with the Xhosa 'krakra.' Exactitude in pronunciation is called for: *bhala* (with an explosive b) is to write, while *bala* (implosive b) is to count. The t can be aspirated (th) or palatal (t) sounding almost like a d, thus *thatha* (take) vs. *tata* (father). There are tones as in Chinese; Xhosa has three, the high, the low and the falling. These can deliver widely different meanings. *Ithanga* is pumpkin, *ithanga* is thigh, and *ithanga* is a kraal. The verb forms with special beginnings and endings could have been designed by a scientist for their precision. The language is agglutinative like Icelandic, meaning that the subject, verb, object, adverbs and tense indicators are all run together in long 'words' that come naturally to native speakers.

There are countless expressions that convey images and ideas powerfully and efficiently. Consider the alternatives for 'hushing something up'. The English 'hushing' is not bad, being onomatopoeic. Its force is exceeded by the Afrikaans 'doodswyg' (kill by silence) but both are impotent compared with the Xhosa *'bek' ingca'* or *'bek' ingca kulondawo'*, meaning 'grow grass over the place' suggesting a murder that one covers up by burying the corpse and growing grass over it.

So as a youngster of twelve—thanks to the kindness and forethought of my mother—I had the unusual opportunity to learn how difficult the language is, but also how beautiful and resounding it can be. Learning this extraordinary language gave me a new respect for the people who spoke it. This was one of the many experiences that laid the foundations for my later development. Had it not been for what I observed and experienced in faraway Lady Frere in the western Transkei, I wonder whether I would have been intellectually and emotionally ready for my 'Damascus Road experience' in 1976.

In East London, we first lived in the suburb of Vincent and then in Bonnie Doon (Nahoon), both of which were designated white by the Group Areas Act. Black people were allowed to stay only if they were domestic servants and had rooms with a family in the area; otherwise there was a night-time curfew for blacks. Most black people lived in Mdantsane, 14 miles by road north-west of East London centre, and commuted by bus. One result of these measures was that living standards were correspondingly lower for black people. From their wages— already lower on account of their poorer education and labour market discrimination—they had to pay much more for transport to work.

Labour market, public services

Further segregation occurred in the labour market. In the towns we lived in, all public officials were white, from the mayor to the bus drivers. In firms the management and skilled positions were occupied by whites, and the labouring and unskilled positions by blacks. Plenty of academic economic studies have presented evidence of labour market discrimination. Young white people graduating from university could normally be assured of good jobs that would frequently involve managerial duties early on, and carried excellent career prospects.

Public services such as the Post Office were carefully segregated. Even a tiny branch of the Post Office like those in Rosebank and in Mowbray, Cape Town, had two entrances, one for whites and the other for everyone else. The buses in East London were for whites only or for blacks only, with one exception: blacks could mount a 'white' bus but could take only one of the five seats in the rearmost row. In Cape Town there was a little more integration in that the buses were double-deckers, where whites sat on the lower floor and blacks on the upper. The trains were either completely segregated by race or had coaches that were segregated. Conscription to the military was enforced from 1952 onwards,[1] but only for white men, while people of other races could volunteer to join the Permanent Force but did so only in small numbers. In the Eastern Cape where I was posted in 1974 there were a few coloured servicemen. I worked alongside one coloured corporal

---

[1] There was a ballot system from 1952 to 1966, so that not all men liable for service were actually called up. New legislation in 1967 provided for universal service instead of the ballot (Callister, 2007).

at 84 TSD (Technical Stores Depot, Grahamstown). He was deeply resentful about the privileges that white people enjoyed, in the military and outside, and made his views plain to conscripts like myself. I could not disagree with him about the privileges he named.

The 'plausibility structure,' censorship and propaganda

As a child and a teenager one does not appreciate all the many historical, economic and political forces that have combined to create the outcomes in wealth and social status that one observes. Quite the contrary: one's observations of wealth and status become what the sociologist Peter Berger called a 'plausibility structure.' Because these enormous differentials of wealth and status are obvious to our eyes, they convey an illusion of permanence and tend to create their own justification. A child's mind may naturally conclude that the white people worked harder, or were more advanced in the first place. Then there are the self-serving observers who note that white people paid more tax from their higher incomes than did black people, and that whites were keeping the whole system going by paying for and running the police, the army and the civil administration.

Just as important as the 'plausibility structure' was the fact that my family, like most of the families and friends we encountered, was either conservative or apolitical. We went through life without reflecting carefully about political events in the country. We did not link up *apartheid* and the occasional skirmishes at South Africa's northern border. We did not derive cause and effect from discrimination in government spending and income differentials. We did what most people do most of the time: we got on with our lives, our relationships, our activities and our careers as best we could.

The trump card used by the government to shore up support for the military was that South Africa was defending

Christianity from communism. The government contended that the outside forces—principally the ANC, the PAC and SWAPO—were acting as surrogates for the Soviet Union and Eastern Germany which sought to seize South Africa's mineral wealth. They would proceed to impose communism on the country and—so the rationale went—outlaw all religious activity; hence all religious people, irrespective of their political views, liberal or conservative, were morally obliged to support the armed forces.

This argument, repeated *ad nauseum* by government and military spokespersons and on the government-controlled radio and television, was cleverly backed up by censorship. There was no alternative privately owned radio or television station in South Africa that might have presented a different point of view. There was vigorous debate in the English-language press, but censorship was rife. It was not possible to report on the conditions inside prisons or in any military operational area, unless specific permission was granted by the government. It would have been very difficult, if not impossible, to conduct debates in print about the true nature of the wars of the SADF, because this would involve writing about proscribed organisations and banned individuals. Furthermore, in 1974 a law was passed forbidding anyone to encourage someone to resist the military call-up, with a maximum penalty of six years' imprisonment or a fine of R5,000 or both. In short, the government created an information void and then proceeded to fill it with its self-serving propaganda.

It was surprising how many people who should have known better drank in this toxic Kool-Aid. The famed writer of *Cry, the Beloved Country*, Dr. Alan Paton, delivering the Hoernlé Memorial Lecture to the conference of the Institute of Race Relations in July 1979, also raised the question of whether it was worthwhile to fight for *apartheid*:

Is South Africa worth fighting for? Can young white men go in good conscience to the border, to fight against men who almost without exception are black, and who believe that they have a duty to liberate this country from its present rulers, and in particular from the oppression of its racial laws? … In 1979 many of our young white people argue that they would in fact be fighting for the National Party, and for the maintenance of those racial laws which many of them find indefensible (Paton, 1979:12).

Then came the answer, which for Paton was uncharacteristically laden with *non sequiturs*:

There is … only one decent reason for going to the border and that is to fight for the chance to make this a more just society. I would go there because I do not want to be liberated by the Cubans and the Russians. I would go there because I want the chance for the white people of this country to liberate themselves.

To summarise, the reasons that most white people supported the army were as follows. The near-complete segregation of white people from people of other races made for a lack of sympathy and understanding. Sharp inequality of incomes stemmed from poor black education, labour market inequalities and vast disparities in government spending, but most white people did not know or did not care because their interests were well served. Censorship prevented white people from knowing about opposition movements and from linking up the injuries of *apartheid* with the resultant civil war. Loads of propaganda convinced them that they had to send soldiers to fight for their religious freedom.

* * *

I was required to enter the army on 9 January 1974 after completing matric, the final year of high school. I had encountered no guidance about social ethics or the ethics of the military or conscientious objection. I did basics at 1 Maintenance Unit at Lenz, south of Johannesburg, was then moved to Services School in Pretoria, then the Eastern Province Command in Port Elizabeth for three days, and then spent the remainder of the year at 84 TSD (Technical Stores Depot) in Grahamstown. I did what I was told and was released on 7 January 1975. After this I was required to do a certain number of 'camps' which might be anything from three weeks to three months in length.

In 1975 I started a B.Business Science (Actuarial) degree at the University of Cape Town, with a full scholarship from the insurance company the Old Mutual. In return I would be required to work for the firm for at least four years after graduating, or have to repay the bursary. I attended the Claremont Baptist Church. At the university I joined the Students' Christian Association (SCA) which was a conservative evangelical institution with individual and social ethics similar to those of the Baptist church, and a similar emphasis on evangelism that crowded out social assistance. As of this time I was a conformist: while not having any particular belief about *apartheid*, I performed my military duties without demur, fell in with the prevailing 'anti-communist' doctrine, devoted myself to Baptist and conservative evangelical causes, and got on with my studies and career. Paul of Tarsus called himself a 'Hebrew of the Hebrews' (Philippians 3:5); I was a 'Baptist of the Baptists', having studied large parts of the New Testament off by heart, and spending my university vacations on Baptist church missions in East London, Umtata and elsewhere. Nevertheless, through the SCA there began a process of broadening my personal experience and thinking that soon led to my becoming a conscientious objector.

Another conscientising experience was offered by the Young Men's Christian Association at the university, which brought me into contact with orphaned boys at the Ruby Adendorff home in Claremont in 1975. At a YMCA meeting in February 1975 Stephen Granger invited us to attend a briefing session at the orphanage and to volunteer some hours on Saturday afternoons through the year, entertaining the children. Kate Stavrou, a student from Baxter Hall at the University of Cape Town, and I were assigned a group of five boys between ten and twelve years of age. It was an opportunity to learn a great deal about their social circumstances and their needs. They were extremely talkative. Their every word was aimed at grasping our attention. We played ball games, and we had some success with chequers. I wanted to read them stories but on only one occasion did I succeed, since they were mostly too restless. We visited regularly for that year and on one occasion borrowed the orphanage's Kombi to take them for a *braaivleis* at the Tokai Forest. Entertaining them was feasible for Kate and myself, but I quickly came to realise that owing to their deprived backgrounds they would have great difficulty following a serious course of study at school.

In late 1975 I attended a symposium at Stellenbosch involving Christian students from the University of the Western Cape, the University of Cape Town and the University of Stellenbosch. There I encountered discussions about black consciousness and black theology that started to fill in gaps in my social outlook.

On 16 June 1976 began the Soweto uprising when tens of thousands of school children took to the streets to protest the introduction of Afrikaans as a medium of instruction. That is, Afrikaans was to be the medium of instruction for mathematics and social studies, while English was to continue as the medium for general science and practical subjects such as woodwork. The introduction of Afrikaans was resented because it was seen as the language of the oppressor, and English was preferred, being the more common language in commerce and industry. A mass rally was organized. The police responded with live bullets. Official numbers indicated 23 dead children that day; estimates by local people were much higher.

The citizen force unit to which I had been assigned, Cape Flats Commando, placed me on eight-hour standby. By way of background: every Commando member was issued with uniforms, boots and a R1 rifle upon entry, in my case in March 1975, and had to have the rifle locked up somewhere safely. For me, this was in a cupboard in my room at Leo Marquard Hall. We were not issued with any ammunition. When placed on standby in 1976, I had to be ready to show up at the unit the same day if called upon. We were not informed what use would be made of us. It was obvious, however, that this would have been to patrol the townships or put down demonstrations or marches. I realised I might be required to shoot people that I knew as personal friends. Fortunately for me, the unit was not activated despite the growing unrest.

My 'Damascus Road' experience

A few days later I attended the annual Students' Christian Association (SCA) Intervarsity Conference at the University of Pietermaritzburg. It was colourfully entitled 'Contending with Horses,' quoting Jeremiah 12:5. The guest speakers were Bishop David Gitari of the Anglican church at Embu, Kenya, and Rev. Michael Cassidy of the evangelistic organisation Africa Enterprise, based in Pietermaritzburg. A total of 161 students registered.

We learned that the African, coloured and Indian people attending, who were from the sister organisation SCM (Students' Christian Movement) at the University of the Western Cape and the University of Natal Westville, were not permitted to sleep in the same living quarters as the white students were, on the university campus in Pietermaritzburg. Instead their lodgings were some ten miles away. They were upset about this because they had collected over R400 to support the trip, and had faced the disapproval of the student organisations and even, according to the official SCA account, faced the threat of disaffiliation of the SCM. They felt the discrimination in sleeping quarters to be a betrayal: the conference organisers had compromised with *apartheid*.

It was decided to split the Conference up into groups by university or college origin, where the matter would be discussed and each group would try to put itself into the shoes of the black, coloured and Indian students. Group after group urged the black, coloured and Indian students to stay. The latter were undeterred, and called a parallel meeting to discuss the matter and explain to the rest of us why they intended to leave. I and a dozen other white students attended the meeting. The other 150 students did not. It was a painful encounter because it was obvious that we had let the SCM students down and that the organisers of the conference had tolerated racial discrimination in lodging.

At the same conference I attended the meetings of the theology students where one of the discussions dealt with the armed conflict on the borders of South Africa and of Namibia.[2] Rev. Michael Cassidy joined in, as did the Old Testament

---

[2] South West Africa became known as Namibia when the General Assembly of the United Nations changed its name by Resolution 2372 (XXII) of 12 June 1968.

scholar Deryck C.T. Sheriffs, then doing his doctorate and working as travelling secretary for the SCA in the Eastern Province. Someone raised the issue: there are young white men in the SADF, and on the other side there are young black men who are unable to express themselves through the ballot box and who have been treated as second-class citizens. I realised with a shock that this war that the government had always claimed was a war of Christian South Africa against communist powers, and a war in defence of the right to freedom of worship, was nothing of the sort. Instead, it was a civil war, a war of brother against brother.

Young black men had left the country because they were frustrated: for decades black people in Namibia and South Africa had tried every peaceful alternative to gain equal rights, and had been beaten, jailed, tortured and shot. Right then I became a conscientious objector in principle. The Students' Christian Association had unwittingly delivered my Damascus Road experience. I needed to think differently about the politics of South Africa. It was no longer possible for me to be a Christian in my own cocoon, separating my religious life from my physical, political and economic life. I was shocked and disappointed that the sort of Christianity I had been brought up on had not focused on any of the wrongdoing of *apartheid*. I could no longer participate in military training camps since that was active participation in the system of oppression. No longer a conformist, I had become a zealous opponent of that critical element of South African polity, namely the use of the SADF to back up *apartheid*.

I sought to fill in the gaps of traditional Baptist thinking by reading far and wide. My B.Bus.Sc. studies helped thanks to the Economics II course which had a section on labour economics with Dr. Johann Maree as lecturer. He had had years of experience in working with labour unions. This was my first introduction to the history of labour struggles in South Africa. It was an opportunity to ponder the mechanisms by which racial discrimination persisted in labour markets despite the predictions of economic theory that discriminating firms would be out-competed by fair-hiring firms.

In the latter half of 1976 I started attending meetings arranged by the Students' Representative Council (SRC), some of them being focused on detention, whereby the police could hold prisoners incommunicado, and deaths in detention. A large demonstration against detention was organised by students from the drama department. Students were called upon to boycott classes for the day to sit on the steps of Jameson Hall where they listened to speeches and sang songs such as "We Shall Overcome." A metal basin was placed on a pedestal in the middle of the road in front of 'Jammie,' with heavy oil in it belching out smoke. Someone read over the loudspeaker the very long list of detainees, including of course Steve Biko, each name followed by the words "Come with me", evoking a policeman in the act of detaining. While this was going on, students in the audience of many hundreds were invited, as a symbol of their resistance to *apartheid* and to arbitrary detention, to take a scissors and cut a substantial tuft of hair from their forehead, and to throw it into the metal basin where it burnt blacker still. It was an emotional moment as student after student took the scissors and performed the act. Many women participated, thereby ruining their fringes.

I read in the newspapers[3] about Bill Anderson who in 1976 left for London, a year after doing his military service, and there denounced the torture by the SADF in Namibia and Angola. He said he had witnessed torture during his national service, and

---

[3] e.g. 'Students retell tale of "torture,"' *Natal Mercury*, 29 September 1976. (SAIRR Coll, ZA HPRA AD1912A-S236.5.)

asserted that SADF soldiers beat and burned prisoners of war from SWAPO and the Popular Movement for the Liberation of Angola (MPLA). Furthermore, he said that the SADF had tortured and killed civilians in Ovamboland during a security sweep code named 'Operation COBRA' between November 1975 and June 1976. He gave speeches in the UK and the USA, and testified before the United Nations (Collins, 1995: 42; Amnesty International, 1982; Grundy, 1983: 117).

In addition to my actuarial studies, in 1976 I did correspondence courses in missiology and church history with the University of South Africa, which helped to relativise the 'truth' of the traditional Baptist position, particularly on social ethics. I attended the Missiology Society conference at the University of Pretoria in February 1977 about liberation theology and the discussions between theologians and Marxists. I was sceptical about such a *rapprochement*, but this exposure to different ideas helped me to broaden my understanding of theological social ethics. Specifically, the church cannot afford to ignore the moral failures of the government—even if the government vows to safeguard the freedom of religion— because the church's silence comes to mean assent. I devoured Alfredo Fierro's *The Militant Gospel* and Gustavo Gutierrez's *A Theology of Liberation*, and many books about social ethics such as Sydney Bailey's *Prohibitions and Restraints in War*, Dietrich Bonhoeffer's *The Cost of Discipleship* and his *Letters and Papers from Prison*, ed. Eberhard Bethge.

I came across the statement about conscientious objection by the South African Council of Churches, at its meeting at Hammanskraal in 1974.[4] Proposed by Rev. Douglas Bax and

---

[4] The SACC Resolution taken at its National Conference, August 1974, is reproduced in full in *South African Outlook Special Issue: War, Peace and Conscience*, vol. 104, no. 1239 (August 1974). Page 121. Wits, Rob. Coll., A2558-15.8.

seconded by Rev. Beyers Naudé, it reminded its member Churches that the taking up of arms was justifiable, if at all, only in order to fight a "just war." It noted that South African society was "fundamentally unjust and discriminatory" and that this violence of *apartheid* constituted the primary, institutionalised violence that provoked the counter-violence of the ANC, the PAC and other organisations. Hence it challenged the Churches' members to "consider whether Christ's call to take up the cross and follow Him in identifying with the oppressed does not ... involve becoming conscientious objectors." The government's response was to pass the Defence Further Amendment Act, no. 83 of 1974, which made it illegal to encourage refusal of military service, on pain of a fine of R5,000 or six years' imprisonment or both.

I was much influenced by Henry David Thoreau's essay *On Civil Disobedience* (1849). He practiced a token act of civil disobedience—refusing to pay the poll tax and spending a night in jail—as his way of protesting slavery and the Mexican-American War. He protested the latter because President Polk had ordered the army to provoke a skirmish with Mexico, which it did by massing heavily armed troops on the border, inducing the Mexican army to attack. Then Polk was able to argue that American blood had been shed on American soil, justifying a war on Mexico. By the end of the war (1846-1848) the USA was able to seize California and New Mexico—which had been Polk's objective in the first place.

Thoreau's essay convinced me that it was not moral to think, as so many people told me, 'my country right or wrong.' Rather one should independently evaluate, to the best of one's ability, the moral standing of every war in which one's country participates. One should participate in such wars only if one is convinced that the country is on the side of right. If not, one would be justified in protesting in some way.

I was fortunate to be able to take a trip to England during the university vacation in June/July 1977, thanks to a very cheap APEX flight arranged through the National Union of South African Students. I spent three weeks in London and discovered the truth of the adage that 'he who is tired of London is tired of life.' After days of wonderment at the British Museum and the British Library, and attending free Shakespeare plays at Regent Park, I visited the ANC office in London three times. I had conversations each time, and on the third visit spent several hours with an older gentleman 'Solly Smith' (his *nom de guerre*, not his real name). I found it hard to reconcile myself to the idea that the ANC might use violence against the South African regime, since this seemed to me unrealistic. However, there was no gainsaying that the authorities had blocked off every possible means for black people to express their political views.

I bought and read a pile of issues of the ANC mouthpiece *Sechaba*, which was banned in South Africa. I suspected that the ANC received assistance from East Germany and the Soviet Union, and became more suspicious still when my interlocutors in London denied this outright. My encounter with the ANC did not lead to any continuing contact, but it did convince me that this was not a front organisation of the Soviet Union as the South African government alleged, but a real organisation representing real people with the genuine cause of national liberation. Few white people in South Africa were ever able to come into contact with the ANC in this way. This was one of the key experiences that convinced me the war the SADF was waging was nothing more than a civil war.

My first encounter with the Assistant Chaplain-General of the Air Force, Colonel (Rev.) Andrew van den Aardweg, was at the house of my aunt, Beryl Daphne Webb, in Pretoria, in February 1977. She invited several relatives in the area, including my sister Jen, my cousin Richard Steele, and Chaplain van den Aardweg as a family friend, and others. Around the *braaivleis* that evening the Chaplain told us proudly about the advances of the SA troops into Angola, boasting that they were overlooking the lights of Luanda. Richard and I sharply demurred, each of us explaining our reasons for being conscientious objectors. Chaplain van den Aardweg's response should have been to say, as a Baptist minister, that he might disagree with our views but supported our right to say them, because, as it is put in the 1689 Baptist Confession of Faith, "God alone is Lord of the conscience … and the requiring of an absolute and blind obedience is to destroy liberty of conscience and reason also."[5] On that evening, however, the Chaplain made his best effort to defend the army's right to invade Angola and to persuade us not to be conscientious objectors.

Meanwhile a member of the Students' Christian Association, Stephen Hofmeyer, heard that I was thinking seriously of conscientious objection. He circumspectly told me about Anton Adriaan Eberhard of Port Elizabeth, who was then studying for a BA with the University of South Africa, and who was thinking similarly. I wanted to know Anton's motives for resisting the call-up and the length of sentence he was anticipating. Anton's friend Lucia Thesen, then in Cape Town, served as the go-between. She came one windy night to my room at University House (University of Cape Town) to drop off Anton's reply to my questions, in an unmarked manila envelope. One had to be careful in those times to avoid the attentions of the security police. I was encouraged to note that Anton's motives were similar to mine in that he believed *apartheid* was wrong and that the military was upholding it. After having done his initial service in 1970 (Jones, 2013) he was called up for a three-month

---

[5] See https://www.the1689confession.com/1689/chapter-21 , chapter 21.

military camp[6] to start on 24 January 1977.[7] He refused, writing to his officer commander:

> I believe the current system of government to be totally unjust. Not only does it not govern with the consent of the majority of the people in South Africa, but it is only able to maintain its position through violence, as was clearly demonstrated during the recent country-wide riots. My sympathies are almost wholly with those of the black people of this country who daily suffer indignity, insults, poverty, lack of opportunities and freedom because of the selfish policies of the present government. Black people look upon the army as epitomising and sustaining the oppression they suffer. I am thus unable to participate at all in the army. It is my belief that the present government has no right to remain in power and any organisation which enables it to do so, cannot be supported.[8]

I was later to learn that Anton was tried on 13 December 1977 in a magistrate's court in Port Elizabeth, defended by Advocate L.S. Melunsky. He pled guilty. He stated to the court that his refusal to report was based on his interpretation of the scriptures, adding "I am a committed … Christian. I attend church regularly." He was found guilty and was sentenced on 14 December 1977 to twelve months' detention, of which ten months were suspended for five years. This was an unusually harsh sentence for a first offender. He was taken by train to Voortrekkerhoogte near Pretoria, where the Detention Barracks were located. There he served the two months, and was released

---

[6] SAMRAF (1979:16). Note that UNCAA and COSAWR (1989) says he refused a three-*week* camp.

[7] 'Christian won't go into army', *Rand Daily Mail* (14 December 1977). The article was reproduced in full in: *South African Outlook* vol. 108, no. 1287 (September 1978), p. 142. Wits, Rob. Coll., A2558-15.8.

[8] This excerpt from the statement was obtained from Anton by private communication on 13 June 2022.

in early February 1978. He was placed in the blocks with the ordinary military offenders (not the Jehovah's Witnesses). He wore the brown overalls but rejected the 'staaldak' (steel helmet) and the military boots, and refused military orders, on the grounds that his very imprisonment was due to refusal of military orders (Robertson, 1999:205). He neither did things at the double nor did he undergo physical training as punishment. At mealtimes the soldiers lined up in a squad, the Jehovah's Witnesses lined up on their own, and Anton stood alone.[9] He initially spent some weeks in solitary confinement but after that was mostly left alone. He was a member of St. Anthony's United Church in Mayfair, Johannesburg, from 1977 to 1979 and the minister of the church, Rev. Rob Robertson, visited him three times at the Detention Barracks, and went to welcome and photograph him when he was discharged from the Detention Barracks in February 1978 (Robertson, 1999:198).

Students of the Catholic Society at UCT, some of them living at Kolbe House in Rondebosch, were interested in my arguments about conscientious objection. Trish Murray, Rory and Dermot Gogarty, Andy Smail, Aneene Dawber and others from time to time engaged me in long discussions and asked me to speak at their meetings, many of which were at Kolbe House in Rondebosch. Together with them I went out to the informal settlement at Modderdam in Bellville South, which was razed by bulldozers with police assistance in August 1977. I was horrified. For me that was the final straw. How can I go and defend this whole system when this is being done at home? Through the Catholic students I met Rev. David Russell, an Anglican priest, who had pastoral responsibility for the Crossroads informal settlement. Many a discussion ensued,

---

[9] Letter from Rev. Rob Robertson to the lawyer Patrick Bracher of Port Elizabeth on 7 January 1978. Wits, Rob. Coll., A2558-9.8.

about justice in South Africa, about the repression exercised by the police, and about the role of the military. I often went to see him at his office in one of the back rooms of a meeting hall of St. Saviour's Anglican Church in Claremont, Cape Town. There we discussed the various papers that I wrote. David became a good friend. He was later to officiate at my marriage in 1984.

Through David I met Mrs. Dot Cleminshaw who worked as his assistant at St. Saviour's. She and I also spent much time in discussion. Her background in the Civil Rights League came in very useful because she knew an enormous amount about South African politics and her work had brought her in contact with many people. She had drafted a paper about conscientious objection—probably the first of its kind in South Africa—for the Study Project on Christianity in an Apartheid Society (SPRO-CAS) in 1972.[10] Her contribution to the publicity about my conscientious objection was to prove very valuable.

Other people who helped me think my way through the issues were Richard Steele (my cousin, also a student at UCT), Professor Francis Wilson (Economics Department, UCT) and Rev. Dr. Jim Cochrane (Religious Studies Department, UCT). Among my puzzles was this: Is this matter of conscription into the *apartheid* army important enough that I should take on the burden of a possible jail sentence? Or is the matter of conscientious objection a personal question, best solved by a personal solution such as moving to one of the 'bantustans' or seeking refugee status in the UK? They were convinced that it was much more than a personal matter. Richard introduced me to the Christian Institute which he had joined and convinced me to read its literature. Jim presciently stressed that if I felt in the

---

[10] *SPRO-CAS 2 Background paper: 6. Conscientious Objection.* Christian Institute, Braamfontein, Transvaal, n.d., A SPRO-CAS Background Paper prepared by Dot Cleminshaw. 4 pages. Wits, Rob. Coll., A2558-15.1.

1970s that *apartheid* was morally indefensible, in a few years' time the military role in preserving *apartheid* would be far more obvious and even less morally defensible. He predicted that before long young white conscripts like myself would be deployed in and around the townships to quell demonstrations. Francis insisted that the issue of conscientious objection was not only personal but also central to the moral and political debates of the time. A government that called itself Christian was appealing to anti-communist notions to persuade white people of the rightness of its cause; but if a Christian conscript were to stand up and say that the SADF was not defending Christianity from communism, but was in the business of preserving *apartheid*, it would strike at the moral spinal cord of the supremacist system and initiate a process of rethinking throughout the country.

In August 1977 I received a call-up for 1-19 December 1977, which, we were told, would likely be extended to three months so that we could serve at the 'grens'—the border, then the northern border of Namibia. We were told to be in possession of a signed and valid will. I contacted Captain J. Moolenschot, the acting Officer Commanding (OC) of my assigned Civilian Force unit, Cape Flats Commando, to request an interview at which I wished to explain my position about conscientious objection. I was granted the interview on 3 October 1977. I presented the OC with a short position paper and explained that *apartheid* was fundamentally unjust and that the war that the SADF was fighting on its borders was a civil war. I was not willing to participate in fighting for *apartheid* or training to that end. I would be willing, though, to do work of social assistance or upliftment under civilian direction. Major Moolenschot was surprisingly pleasant about this. He listened patiently to what I had to say but it was clear that he earnestly believed that the SADF was defending the country against foreign aggression at the border. He assumed that I was afraid, as he put it, of 'snuffing it,' but assured me that this was very unlikely. He concluded by reminding me that either I would have to go to the border or I would go to jail.

Meanwhile, we learned in September of the murder of the black consciousness leader Steve Biko in prison. I attended an impassioned speech by his friend Donald Woods, editor of the *Daily Dispatch*, who toured the country with the message that Biko had died of a grisly battering by the police, not a hunger strike as had been alleged by the Minister of Justice and Police, Jimmy Kruger.

I arranged a meeting with Rev. Theo Kotze of the Christian Institute (CI) in September 1977. I showed him an early draft of my rationale for conscientious objection. He read it through and urged me to bring out the theological arguments at greater length. He reminded me that as a committed Baptist and chairman of the Students' Christian Association at the university, I had thought about these matters in moral and theological terms from the start. I was grateful for this advice and proceeded to further writing of my statement. I arranged to visit him again on Wednesday 19 October 1977, directly after my English Poetry I examination which was from nine in the morning to one in the afternoon. The exam done, I walked down from the university campus to the CI building in Mowbray, only to discover it surrounded by police vehicles. The CI and its key staff including Theo had been banned[11] that very day, along with many Black Consciousness organisations and activists. I did not

---

[11] 'Banning' in South Africa was somewhat similar to house arrest. The person was typically not allowed to speak to more than two individuals at once, could not attend public meetings, could not go outside his/her magisterial district without permission from the police, had to be at home from sundown to sunrise, and could not publish anything in the press.

manage to see Theo to show him the improved version of my rationale for conscientious objection.

A fellow student of mine in the B.Bus.Sc. degree, Jeff Cohen, suggested I read Martin Luther King's *Letter from Birmingham Jail* (16 April, 1963). I was grateful for the timeous hint. The background to the book was that black leaders in Birmingham (in the state of Alabama in the south of the USA) had called for marches against racial segregation. The authorities promptly declared all marches and protests illegal. The marches went ahead anyway, and King participated. He was arrested and imprisoned. In the book King explained his position: the authorities had made 'normal' means of protest against racism almost impossible by declaring marches and sit-ins illegal, and so black people were left with no alternative but to deliberately disobey unjust laws. King insisted that this be done in a non-violent way, which meant finding the facts about injustice; seeking to negotiate with the instigator of the injustice; and then if the attempts to negotiate led nowhere, one was to take 'direct action.'

King's ideas seemed to fit my situation perfectly. I had tried to negotiate with the SADF about doing a non-military alternative to military service, and had achieved nothing. The time had come to take direct action in the form of openly disobeying the call-up, and being prepared to face the consequences.

My parents tried their best to dissuade me from becoming a conscientious objector. They first tried the line that Christians should obey the government, according to Romans 13, "Let everyone be subject to the governing authorities, for there is no authority except that which God has established ... Consequently, whoever rebels against the authority is rebelling against what God has instituted, and those who do so will bring judgment on themselves." Then they tried the hoary old argument about the defence of Christianity against communism. They enlisted the support of a family friend, Rev. Aubrey Phipson, a missionary with the Baptist Missionary Society. Rev. Phipson and his wife lived at the time in Umtata and sometimes played golf with my father and my brother Terence. My mother hurried Rev. Phipson and me to the dining room to talk privately. I explained in a sentence or two why I was a conscientious objector. To his credit, Rev. Phipson immediately said that he recognised that I was sincere and determined, and did not want to interfere.

I reminded my parents that they had always taught me to be honest and never to tell a lie. They had brought me up with a Christian ethic, as best they knew how. And now this same Christian ethic, applied to the circumstances that I faced, required me to continue to be honest and never to tell a lie, which meant that I had to acknowledge the evils of *apartheid* and abhor any attempt by the military to preserve it.

My father was frustrated. He was a magistrate, then at the pinnacle of his career as Regional Magistrate of the Transkei. He thought as a man of the law. Once he told me, in utter exasperation, that "[t]here *is* no such thing as conscientious objection!" By this he meant that there was no provision for conscientious objection in the laws about conscription. My parents were, of course, primarily concerned for my psychological and physical welfare, and for my career prospects, all of which might be ruined by a jail sentence.

I did not relish the prospect of a stay in the Detention Barracks, but having been in the army for a year I knew what the institution was like and I doubted that I would be psychologically harmed. About physical harm I could not be sure since from time to time men died in the Detention Barracks. While in the army I had heard of harsh physical treatment of Detention Barracks inmates, but was determined to go ahead anyway. Whilst I had been partially prepared for the Detention Barracks because I had been in the army for twelve months in 1974, and had done a three-week camp in 1975 and various weekend-long 'shoots' with the Cape Flats Commando, I sought to prepare myself further by reading books about prison experiences: Dostoevsky's *House of the Dead*, Solzhenitsyn's *One Day in the Life of Ivan Denisovich*, *The First Circle*, and *The Gulag Archipelago*, Koestler's *Darkness at Noon*, and Dickens' *Little Dorrit*.

Chapter 2. Trials in December 1977 and September 1979

In November 1977 I again requested, in writing, a non-military alternative to military service. This time I added that if this were not granted, I would refuse to obey the call-up for 1 December 1977. The letter is reproduced in the section of original documents.

I was issued with a summons to appear in the Wynberg Magistrate's Court on 27 December 1977. Friends rallied around in the days leading up to the trial. I had an invitation from Dermot Gogarty and his family in Rondebosch to come to dinner. Liz Thomas kindly invited me to lunch with the family on Christmas Day before the case; and so I met her parents, Edmund Maclachlan 'Mac' and Mary St. Clair Thomas. I was staying at a friend's house in Rondebosch when, on the day before the court case, I heard a knock at the door at 7.30 a.m. It turned out to be Victor Pearce and a student friend from University House. Victor was associated with the Methodist church in Rosebank. A gentleman of retirement age, he conducted a ministry of speaking and praying with young men in the university residences, invariably at the crack of dawn. Most male members of the Students' Christian Association and the Young Men's Christian Association had had an early-morning visit from 'Vic' at some point in their student careers. How very kind of Victor that was, on 26 December 1977. He took me and the student friend to an upscale restaurant at Stuttaford's in Claremont where we had breakfast and prayed.

Through Owen Tudor, a friend from Claremont Baptist Church, I managed to arrange for Professor Johan Hendrik van Rooyen, then a visiting professor of law at the University of

Cape Town, to represent me. Some friends from the Catholic Society at the University of Cape Town attended the trial. The magistrate presiding was Mr. H. van Wyk. Professor van Rooyen advised me to plead guilty and to explain that this was a matter of conscience for me. I was sentenced to three months' jail suspended for five years. I had been lucky: Anton Eberhard had been held in the Detention Barracks for two months for a similar 'offence' just days before. I did not know it at the time, but the first political objector, the Afrikaner poet Johan van Wyk, had on 26 September 1977 been given a sentence similar to mine: 15 months suspended for three years. He was later discharged from military duty due to psychological vulnerability.[12]

I continued to work on my rationale for conscientious objection. After my graduation from the B.Bus.Sc. (Actuarial) degree in 1978, I had many discussions with close relatives, with members of the Students' Christian Association and the Catholic Society, and with Rev. David Russell among others, and brought out two papers that summarised my findings more thoroughly.[13] With the help of several volunteers from the Catholic Society, and with the kind intervention of Rev. David Russell, I was able to produce 300 copies of both of these papers on the trusty Gestetner duplicator at the Institute of Race Relations in Mowbray. I distributed these to friends, family, student societies, church ministers and newspapers all over the country. (Later during my court case of 4 December 1979, it emerged that both papers were in the possession of the SADF.)

As before, I argued on the basis of just war theory that a Christian can go to war only, if at all, in support of a just war.

---

[12] See Appendix H for details about Johan van Wyk.

[13] Moll (1978b) and Moll (1979a). The first of these is reproduced in the section of original documents.

One of the key requirements for a just war, in Augustine, Aquinas, de Victoria and Calvin was to have a just cause, typically defence against aggression or retrieval of stolen property. Calvin cited expansive grounds for a just war, including repressing sedition, assisting the oppressed, and punishing evil actions:

> It is sometimes necessary for kings and states to take up arms in order to execute public vengeance. On this basis we may judge wars lawful which are so undertaken. For if power has been given them to preserve the tranquillity of their subjects, repress the seditious movements of the turbulent, assist those who are violently oppressed, to punish evil deeds—can they use it more opportunely than in repressing the fury of him who disturbs both the ease of individuals and the common tranquillity of all, who excites seditious tumult, and perpetrates acts of violent oppression and gross wrongs? If it becomes them to be the guardians and maintainers of the laws, they must repress the attempts of all alike by whose criminal conduct the discipline of the laws is impaired.[14]

The Spanish theologian Franciscus de Victoria (c. 1483-1546), the chair of theology at the University of Salamanca, was critical of the treatment by the Spanish colonisers of the indigenous people of south America, because he said the latter were the rightful owners of their property. Deploying the standard 'just war' criteria led him to argue that there was no basis for war against the indigenous peoples. He examined what the common person should do if the war is manifestly unjust. He insisted that,

---

[14] John Calvin, *Institutes* IV.20.11.

It is essential for a just war that an exceedingly careful examination be made of the justice and causes of the war and that the reasons of those who on grounds of equity oppose it be listened to.[15]

Furthermore, contended de Victoria,

If a subject is convinced of the injustice of a war, he ought not to serve in it, even on the command of his prince ... The proofs and tokens of the injustice may be such that ignorance would be no excuse even to subjects ... who have no place or audience in the prince's council or the public council.[16]

Thus in de Victoria's view, if the common person finds, after an "exceedingly careful examination," that the war is manifestly unjust, s/he should refuse to serve in it. Using modern language, one should be a conscientious objector to participation in all unjust wars.

I discovered the considerable resources of the Baptist communion in respect of conscience and participation in war. I had not learned of these during my childhood and youth; it seemed to me that they had been forgotten. The *First London Baptist Confession of Faith* (1644) states, in the Conclusion:

But if any man shall impose upon us anything that we see not to be commanded by our Lord Jesus Christ, we should in His strength, rather embrace all reproaches and tortures of men, to be stript of all outward comforts, and if it were possible, to die a thousand deaths, rather than to do anything against the least tittle of the truth of God, or against the light of our own consciences.[17]

---

[15] de Victoria (1964), article 21.

[16] *Ibid.*, articles 22 to 26.

[17] https://en.wikisource.org/wiki/1644_Baptist_Confession_of_Faith .

The *Second London Baptist Confession* (1689), which was republished in 1855 by the renowned preacher Charles Haddon Spurgeon (1834-1892), states:

> God alone is Lord of the conscience, and has left it free from the doctrines and commandments of men which are in any thing contrary to his word, or not contained in it. So that to believe such doctrines, or obey such commands out of conscience, is to betray true liberty of conscience; and the requiring of an implicit faith, an absolute and blind obedience, is to destroy liberty of conscience and reason also …
>
> It is lawful for Christians to accept and execute the office of a magistrate when called thereunto; in the management whereof, as they ought especially to maintain justice and peace, according to the wholesome laws of each kingdom and commonwealth, so for that end they may lawfully now, under the New Testament, wage war upon just and necessary occasions.[18]

Those early Baptists would wage war only "upon just and necessary occasions". By implication, it was not possible for a Christian to wage an unjust war. Furthermore, to be considered 'just' the war also had to be 'necessary', indicating that among the criteria for justice was that the war be the last resort. The only person who can make the judgment of whether the war is just or unjust is the individual. The stab of conscience is not biddable. Conscience is neither mediated by priests nor administered by governments. Since "God alone is Lord of the conscience," the Christian must decide in liberty without being forced into "absolute and blind obedience". To do otherwise, namely to do something against one's conscience, would be worse than "to die a thousand deaths."

---

[18] Chapters 21 and 24 of the Baptist Confession of 1689. Available at https://www.the1689confession.com/ .

Hence I came to understand that as a Baptist I had to make an informed judgment about the war the SADF was waging, without fear or favour, and that in making such judgment I was exercising the right of the Christian to freedom of conscience.

An example I used for an *un*just war was the invasion of Poland by Hitler's Wehrmacht in September 1939, which quickly led to the Second World War. Correspondingly, an example I used of a *just* war was that of the Allied side in defeating Hitler's military. It would be hard to find anyone today, except for extremist neo-Nazis, who does not believe that Hitler's military had to be defeated. One shudders to think of the human cost if Hitler had been victorious: the six million Jews (and Roma, Sinti, gays and communists) murdered would have been but the first fruits of Nazi depredations in Europe, Africa and elsewhere, not to mention the civilian victims of the endless wars the Nazi military would have waged.

Next was to make an "exceedingly careful examination" (de Victoria) of the justice or otherwise of the war the SADF was fighting. I considered *apartheid* fundamentally unfair because it was based on a racist ordering of society in which white people enjoyed political power and privilege at the expense of black people. The Land Act of 1913 allocated only seven percent of the country's land for occupation by blacks who were 78 percent of the population. There were similar gross inequities in access to education, to health care, to agricultural extension (training for farmers), to government jobs, and to infrastructure such as roads and railways. In the 1950s Prime Minister Hendrik Verwoerd came up with the notion of 'separate development' or 'good neighbourliness' when seeking to justify the National Party government's racially discriminatory policies before the international community. The key element of 'separate development' was that black people would be allowed to have the vote in the 'homelands' or bantustans, while being excluded from all political processes in 'white' South Africa.

Apartheid was the primary violence that drove black people to seek redress by turning to armed opposition outside the country. After the Sharpeville massacre of April 1960, the African National Congress (ANC) and Pan-Africanist Congress (PAC) were banned and their leaders thrown in prison. 'Banning' in this context meant that the organisations were outlawed. The role of the SADF was to protect the *apartheid* system by fending off attacks by the military wings of the ANC and PAC. Hence I felt I could no longer be part of the SADF in any way because it was defending an unjust system.

Another influence on my thinking at this time was visiting the Crossroads informal settlement and meeting people there through various church connections, both Anglican and Baptist. Rev. David Russell kindly arranged for me to stay for four days over the Easter weekend of 1979 at the house in Crossroads of one of his parishioners, a Mrs. Sylvia Mtulu and her family. I ate their simple fare and helped fetch water from the water-point 200 metres away. It was an immersion programme that taught me a great deal about how ordinary people lived and the challenges that they faced with employment, housing, travel, crime and so on. I had to make do with my broken Xhosa because Mrs. Mtulu's English was limited.

This visit in turn led to my visiting Crossroads of a Saturday afternoon many times. At one household I regularly gave lessons in arithmetic and accounting to the children. I learned directly and personally the circumstances that had led to the development and spread of this informal housing community. Some people had been there for ten years or more, having left the Transkei or Ciskei in search of better employment in Cape Town. Others had moved in desperation to find better medical services for their children. Moving from rural areas to the cities was illegal because the government had decreed that people of African descent should remain in the 'homelands' and be tolerated in the cities only upon specific permission as recorded in the so-called 'dompas,' which was granted on the basis of employment in specific fields only, and for only a limited period of time. It was a system of internal passports such as was pursued in the Soviet Union at the time and is still enforced in China. If black people were found in the cities without a valid 'dompas' they risked a fine and/or imprisonment, to be followed with being placed on a train back to the relevant 'homeland'. Economists found, using Monte Carlo models, that because wages in rural areas were so low, it was worthwhile for one to break the law by moving to an urban job, even if one were arrested by the police and fined or imprisoned, and then sent back.

I quickly learned from these Xhosa-speaking Crossroads residents that they had moved to Cape Town because that was the way they could best improve their life chances, despite the non-existent infrastructure in the informal settlement, the thick mud when it rained, the common crime (typically theft) to which they fell victim, and the harassment by the police. On one of my visits to Crossroads I was accompanied by Ron Begbie whom I had met at the Treverton Baptist youth conference in Natal in 1975. That Sunday it happened to be raining but we took the bus to Lansdowne anyway, and saw Crossroads in a way that few outsiders did: enveloped in mud deep enough to cover one's shoes. We talked a little with Mrs. Mtulu. That visit alone was a profoundly conscientising experience. Those people were just ordinary people like ourselves, with the same desires and needs; the difference was that they had had the bad luck to be born in rural Transkei or Ciskei in a country whose government was much more interested in staving off political opponents (read: black people) and in keeping the cities as 'white' as possible, than in providing good education, health, open labour markets and security from crime to the whole population.

During 1979 I did Religious Studies III at the University of Cape Town. Part of this was a module on Marxism and existentialism. I was particularly impressed by a careful reading of Helmut Gollwitzer's *The Christian Faith and the Marxist Critique of Religion* (1970). My perception then was that the Marxists were asking the right questions, even if they did not have all the right answers. Gollwitzer's approach helped me to gradually shed the suspicions I had about Marxist influences in the liberation movements. The course included study of the Lutheran theologian Dietrich Bonhoeffer, who for his resistance to the Nazi regime was jailed in 1943 and hanged in 1945. Etched on my memory is an evening that about 15 students— including Glenda Emslie (later Stewart) and Michelle Rundle (later Granger)—spent at Dr. John de Gruchy's house in Rosebank, when he showed slides about Bonhoeffer's life and times. We were impressed at how many times Bonhoeffer, theologian and professor at the Finkenwalde Seminary, was photographed in informal sessions with his students: sitting in a circle with them in the woods, or walking down a country road with students on either side. We reflected that John's approach was similar: he met his students in the classroom but also in his own home. What a way to learn about those tumultuous times, about Bonhoeffer's extraordinary courage, and his composure before his jailers.

After Johan van Wyk, Anton Eberhard and myself in 1977, the next non-peace-church conscientious objector to be tried and sentenced was Edric Gorfinkel. I knew Edric well from the Students' Christian Association at the University of Cape Town. He was a student of drama. Edric, Su Rhodes and Brian Notcutt put on a number of productions for the SCA including a rendition of a play *Go Down, Moses*. He refused to do a military camp after failing to obtain the status of non-combatant. In May 1978 at the Bellville court, he explained to the magistrate his religious pacifist persuasions, stressing his unwillingness to be involved in violence, and stating that *apartheid* was a violent system. The magistrate noted that Edric had conscientious objections, but complained that there also seemed to be some "political motives." The court found Edric guilty of failing to report for service and sentenced him to a fine of R30. Edric subsequently travelled in Ecuador and Brazil for a year, and went into exile in Zimbabwe.

I continued to try to persuade the army to allow me to do a non-military alternative to military service. I made another written request on 25 October 1978. The reply from the military was that I would stay on the strength of the unit and attend camps, but do so in a non-combatant role (such as medical staff). In June 1979 I tried again, with the help of my mother who found that the Cicira Training College (for teachers) in Umtata was in need of a mathematics teacher. I could have applied for the position and made a valuable contribution to mathematics education at the College. She even persuaded the Secretary of Education of the Transkei, Mr. T.M. Mbambisa, to request of the army that I do my national service as a teacher of mathematics. All to no avail.

Meanwhile, without my knowledge, my father had written to Major-General Neil Webster, Head of Resources, on 24 May 1979, asking that the army leave me alone for the good of both parties. He predicted, accurately, that their threats of prosecution would not induce me to return to soldiering. The official reply from the Chief of the Army was that I should report for duty, whereupon I could be offered a role as a non-combatant, failing which I would be prosecuted.

I should stress the point made repeatedly already: I did not initiate this cat-and-mouse game. It was the army that was pursuing me like the hound of heaven. My father gave the army a face-saving way of quashing the entire matter. For instance, the army could have assigned me to an inactive unit such as the former Transkei Commando, and told me to teach mathematics in Transkei colleges or schools, intimating that if I left matters there all would be well, but that if I raised my voice about conscientious objection again I would be called up and brought to book. The army turned down the opportunity and ploughed ahead with further call-ups. The evidence now at my disposal shows that the army had a concerted approach of trying dissuasion using the chaplaincy, and influencing the media.

In April 1979 I wrote an article, 'My country, right or wrong?' for the Christian student newspaper *Comment* at the University of Cape Town. I noted that during the seventies the idea of 'my country right or wrong' had become unpopular, and that more and more South African men were leaving the country to avoid their call-ups, or were evading by supplying false addresses, or were refusing outright and going to prison. I referred to a survey of readers by the newspaper *The World*, with the question, 'Would you fight for South Africa if we were invaded from Angola?' Of the 244 black people who participated, 204 or 83 percent, replied in the negative. The reasons for not fighting included such objections as that such an invasion would be a 'white man's war', and that most blacks would have little to defend.

On 3 May 1979 I received a letter, out of the blue, from a Permanent Force Chaplain called Rev. Sydney Harold Arthur Middlemost, an Anglican priest then assigned to the South African Cape Corps in Eersterivier, Cape Town. How had he found my name, learned of my intention to be a conscientious objector, and discovered my address and phone number? I cannot be sure, but I suspect that as a Permanent Force Chaplain he had been drawn into a plan by the SADF to get me to 'turn.'

His letter attempted to persuade me that the SADF was fighting a just war:

> The next point which needs clearing up is that 'liberation' is two very different things: 1) It is a beautiful theory, And 2) When applied in practice in a sinful world, it always goes viciously wrong. Let us accordingly ask very carefully, 'What does the fire look like, BEFORE we jump out of the frying pan?'
>
> I recently had the privilege of touring the operational area in S.W.A./Namibia, and saw at close quarters what 'liberation' really looks like. It does people good to come down out of the Ivory Towers of Pure Theory, and see the Flesh at work. To me, 'liberation' stinks of fear (did you know that fear can be smelt?), blood, rotting flesh, faeces and stale urine, sometimes mixed with the acrid smell of TNT, and the musical jangle of spent AK47 cartridges. And the vast majority of the victims are black. The only 'liberation' here is 'all-the-way-to-the-Pearly-Gates-in-one-bang.' Just remember. too that it was a 'liberation' regime that killed Archbishop Luwum.[19] Even Hitler's Nazi party was a 'liberation' regime, wresting power in order to 'free' the German people from their bondage to crippling war reparations.
>
> Remember too that although this country has its Crossroads and its Robben Island, most of the 'liberated' countries ARE Crossroads and Robben Islands. Most of them had to be 'liberated' to discover what true oppression, poverty, and hopelessness really are. There is an ancient Chinese curse which says quite simply, 'May you have an interesting day today.' I believe it can very accurately be updated to a modern African curse which says equally simply, 'May you live to see liberation.'

---

[19] Janani Luwum (c. 1922-1977) was the Archbishop of the Church of Uganda. He protested against the killing of opponents by the Idi Amin regime of Uganda. He was accused of treason and arrested. The next day it was announced that he had died in a car crash. When his body was returned to his family, however, it was riddled with bullets. Archbishop Luwum is recognised by the Anglican Church as a martyr.

I am not trying to defend Apartheid and all that goes with it, but we would be irresponsible to refuse to admit that there are worse things. And liberation is one of them—especially for Blacks.

I could never fight a war to 'maintain white supremacy in an oppressionist society,' but I have no difficulties about a war to keep 'liberation' out of this country. Such a war, I believe, is just. In refusing to fight in such a war, are you not in fact aiding the advancement of 'liberation'?

In the evening of 20 June 1979, Chaplain Rev. Middlemost even came to my humble digs at 'Lynden,' Avenue Road, Mowbray, to pursue his argumentation. He had the usual pat answers for my every argument. For instance, I noted that the SADF had no right to be in Namibia in the first place, on account of United Nations Security Council Resolution 264 of 20 March 1969, which declared that "the continued presence of South Africa in Namibia is illegal and contrary to the principles of the Charter and the previous decisions of the United Nations and is detrimental to the interests of the population of the Territory and those of the international community."[20] He answered that the United Nations had no authority in the matter, which was one internal to South Africa.

In May 1979 I wrote an article, 'The Christian response to military service,' in *Varsity*, a student publication at the University of Cape Town.[21] I discussed the commonest positions adopted by various churches: the 'pacifist' position; the 'militarist' position that advocates obedience to any call-up irrespective of the nature of the war; and the 'just war' position which has it that a Christian may fight in a just war and that s/he has a personal responsibility to decide whether the particular war is just or not using a standard set of criteria.

---

[20] See the full resolution at http://unscr.com/en/resolutions/264 .
[21] Wits, SAIRR Coll., ZA HPRA AD1912A-S236.9.

I gave talks about conscientious objection whenever possible, and participated in discussions with friends and interested people. Some of these were at Kolbe House to the Catholic Students' Society of the University of Cape Town. One of these was to an audience of about 30 at The Loft community in Germiston. Situated on the Simmer and Jack mining property, and run by Tony Russell, The Loft had a rambling house with offices and bedrooms for boarders. The organisation promoted Reformed theology with a social conscience and cultivated links with theologians at the University of Potchefstroom. At this meeting I met for the first time Rev. Rob Robertson, the minister of St. Anthony's United Church in Mayfair, Johannesburg. Rev. Robertson was to play a major role in my subsequent stand as a conscientious objector.

I published an article in *Contours of the Kingdom* (May-June issue 1979), the magazine of The Loft. Entitled 'To be a soldier or not to,'[22] the chief argument was that the war of the SADF was a civil war; it was a myth "that the war we are fighting is a defensive war, that we are protecting Christianity, that we are guarding this our bastion of democracy; when in fact we are fighting to retain our interest, to dictate our terms, and to keep control." I argued that the solution for South Africa could not be a military one but a political, social and economic one. The problem was that the SADF was being used to forestall social change. While I would have fought in the Second World War against Nazi Germany, I was morally bound to refuse to be part of the SADF. This issue was banned by the Publication Control Board for the following reasons: "The Committee considers this article to be extremely dangerous. It casts doubt on the authority of the State, and encourages resistance to the authorities in a way

---

[22] Wits, Rob. Coll., A2558-9.13.

that undermines the military readiness of the Republic of South Africa."[23]

I published an article, 'Thinking no', in the June 1979 edition of the *National Student* magazine of the National Union of South African Students. I put forward the case that the war in which the SADF was engaged was a civil war, and "defending the present society was essentially defence of a system which guaranteed benefits for whites but not for blacks." This was among the articles that persuaded the Publications Control Board to ban *National Student* in perpetuity because it was "calculated to discourage South Africans from doing military service and demoralise the South African Defence Force, ... to cast doubt on the cause for which South African soldiers are fighting and harm South African morale, ... undermining the South African defence effort."[24]

I wrote a letter to *The Star* on 24 July 1979 entitled 'Is SA worth fighting for?'[25] Then I wrote to the *Cape Times* on 26 July 1979 in response to a certain Dr. Andre Schulman's letter asserting that South Africa was morally defensible because *apartheid* was diminishing in degree and scope. I responded that 'grand *apartheid*' was not changing fundamentally and that this was the primary violence that had provoked the civil war.

This letter to the *Cape Times* galvanised the military into action. It emerged later, during my court case of 4 December 1979, that this letter, together with the papers that I had written in December 1978 and March 1979, were in the possession of the prosecutor.

At the invitation of Dr. Allan Boesak, I gave a speech about conscientious objection to the Theological Society of the

---

[23] See *Contours of the Kingdom* (August 1979), p. 4; Wits, Rob. Coll., A2558-9.13.

[24] Publications Control Board in July 1979, quoted in Grundy (1983:114).

[25] Wits, SAIRR Coll., ZA HPRA AD1912A-S236.9.

University of the Western Cape in August 1979.[26] I also published a lengthy article about conscientious objection in *Dunamis*, the magazine of the Belydende Kring (roughly translated, Confessing Circle), a group of ministers from the NG Kerk in Afrika and the NG Sendingkerk.

The responses of my office-mates at the Old Mutual were, I think, typical of those of white English-speaking South Africans. They disliked petty *apartheid* for its obvious discriminatory intent. Some voted for the Progressive Federal Party and one used to volunteer for the PFP at election time. However, when it came to the wars of the SADF their view was similar to that of Alan Paton, mentioned earlier: they believed that communists were attacking South Africa and Namibia and had to be repulsed in order to prevent chaos and protect religious freedom. My good friend Anthony Asher, who was a student a year ahead of me in the B.Bus.Sc. (Actuarial) at the University of Cape Town, exemplified this understanding. I used to attend meetings at his house where he arranged speakers on a variety of topics, usually with a religious element and always in opposition to *apartheid*. He did not, however, support my stand as a conscientious objector because he believed that, for all its ills, the South Africa we had was better than a 'communist take-over.'

Peter Gerhard de Beyer, another trainee actuary, told me once that the country would be a shambles if 'they' took over. Barry Coates, my line manager, tried to persuade me to do my camps because, understandably, he needed me to work on the Functional Expense Analysis; at least he did not try the tired old line about defending Christianity from communism. My only supporters were Idris Elias, Michael S. Jongwana and Margaret Ramsay. It is no coincidence that the first two were from groups

---

[26] Article in *Argus*, 31 August 1979.

subject to racial discrimination. To their credit, though, everyone at the Actuarial Valuations office signed a birthday card for me for 12 March 1980, which was sent to me with a letter by Gary Palser.

The army persisted. The Cape Flats Commando called me up for shooting practice at the Simon van der Stel Range in Bellville for the period 25 to 28 June 1979. I refused to go, by letter. I went out to the Youngsfield base by bus early in the morning of 21 September 1979 to be tried by ordinary court-martial. It was a cold, rainy day. Dot Cleminshaw was there to greet me. We talked at length and I greatly valued her support. This time there was more public interest because I and others had been active in talking and writing about conscientious objection. About 100 people attended the court-martial, much to the surprise of the military personnel present. The hall was too small. Extra chairs had to be brought in, and people were allowed to stand outside and lean in through the windows. My cousin Richard Steele attended, as did many friends including Vincent Gray, Tony Saddington and Keith Gottschalk. Several academics from the University of Cape Town, notably Dr. John de Gruchy (Religious Studies), Dr. Jim Cochrane (Religious Studies) and Dr. Kenneth Hughes (Mathematics) were present. Rev. Dr. Allan Boesak, pastor of a parish in Bellville, Western Cape, attended, as he had strongly supported my position. There were friends from the Students' Christian Association, the Young Men's Christian Association, the Anglican Society and the Catholic Society at the University of Cape Town. Again Professor Johan van Rooyen represented me.

Rev. John Dennis Wilton, the minister of my church (Claremont Baptist), appeared as a witness, mainly to say that the Baptist church recognises the right of each individual to make up his own mind about military service, whether in favour or against. He explained that he felt he understood how I had come to my decision, even though he did not agree with my precise understanding of my case. He emphasised that he respected me for the stand I had taken, and would welcome it if alternative national service under non-military direction were to become available. I pleaded not guilty, while acknowledging that I had failed to report for the shooting practice, but my counsel and I insisted that this was for good reason, namely conscientious objection.

My counsel's argument was not accepted. In line with penalties for previous no-shows for shooting practices at this unit, the officers imposed a fine of R50 and there was no prison sentence, suspended or otherwise. I had been fully prepared for immediate imprisonment and so this relatively light sentence was a relief. I returned to work at the Old Mutual.

At the invitation of Francis Wilson, I started to organise book reviews for *South African Outlook* magazine, and participated generally in the production of each issue. I was guest editor of the October 1979 issue, 'Christians and War', the centrepiece of which was a debate between myself and my friend and colleague Anthony Asher about military service. I repeated my argument in 'Debate about military service'[27] that I would not do military service because the army was defending the unjust system of *apartheid*. The wars pursued by the SADF were not the last resort—because negotiation with black leaders had never been attempted. I reasoned that the war was a civil war of white against black: it was "not the defence of South Africa against foreign aggression but the defence of the privileged group of South Africa against the rest of her citizens." Anthony contended that the basic purpose of the SADF was to maintain order, and therefore was just, because "order benefits all even though whites have obtained unfair privileges within it." His

---

[27] Wits, Rob. Coll., A2558-15.8.

example: "Our unjust system provides but one tap for every hundred people at Crossroads, but the destruction of the system will leave no water in those taps." He argued that there was no hope of negotiating for a common future of black and white. "One might as well bark at the moon … At this stage negotiation is impossible, and makes the use of force inevitable." The issue was banned by the Publications Control Board.

Together with my cousin Richard Steele, I was involved in an embryonic conscientious objector support group in 1979 that met at the premises of the Centre for Intergroup Studies of the University of Cape Town, by the kind permission of the head of the Centre, Professor H.W. van der Merwe, who was a Quaker. Young men facing call-ups, mostly students, participated, as did several women. One memorable meeting was addressed by Professor John Howard Yoder of the Mennonite Biblical Seminary in Elkhart, Indiana, USA. He was famous for advocating Christian pacifism on the basis of a 'realistic' interpretation of the Gospels, as exposited in the book *The Politics of Jesus*.

As a devout Baptist, I was wedded to the practice of Sunday School for all ages. At the beginning of 1979 I was asked by David McMinn to help with the high school students at Claremont Baptist Church. He and I jointly ran the assembly time and I accompanied chorus singing on the guitar. Then for the lesson time I took the older students in standards eight to ten while he took those in standards six and seven. My students included David's son and daughter. I invested much time in this work and tried to prepare something special for every lesson. In addition to the customary Baptist fare of biblical exposition, I explored some social-ethical subjects in a gentle way, introducing them to these vistas for the first time. These included a lesson about the theologian Dietrich Bonhoeffer. Once we examined the issue of riches and poverty using Ron

Sider's *Rich Christians in an Age of Hunger* and the excellent biblical and historical work by Julio de Santa Ana, *Good News to the Poor: The Challenge of the Poor in the History of the Church*. I also wished to give the class some thought-provoking experiences outside of the church context, and so at my own expense I took them to see Woody Allen's film *Interiors* and a contemporary South African play at the Baxter Theatre in Rosebank, followed by coffee and discussion at a nearby restaurant.

On the Saturday night after my court-martial at Youngsfield, I received a phone call from David McMinn. He said I was not to come to the Sunday School any more because my actions as a conscientious objector gave the 'wrong example.' I protested that I had never breathed a word about conscientious objection or the military or the civil war to the Sunday School teenagers. To no avail. I felt deflated. I had devoted myself to this task, critically important in the Baptist mind, and had then been fired for exercising my freedom of conscience. For Deacon and Sunday School Convener David McMinn, the Baptist principle of freedom of conscience was not good enough; only if I did my military training would I be qualified to teach. I appreciated David's anxiety about his son who would in a year or two be facing a military call-up; probably he felt that the very fact that I was a conscientious objector might have been enough to convince his son to follow suit, even if I refrained from broaching the matter in class. If this was the case, however, the solution was not to summarily dismiss a diligent teacher, in violation of the Baptist principle of freedom of conscience. Other solutions could have been found.

My friend Owen Tudor, also a deacon at Claremont Baptist, urged me to contest this ruling by approaching the diaconate. At that juncture I did not have the time for the endless meetings, letters and phone calls that such an appeal would have cost; I had my work at the Old Mutual, I was preparing for the examinations of the Institute of Actuaries (London) and for Religious Studies III (University of Cape Town), and had to prepare for the next round of the cat-and-mouse game with the SADF. I let the matter go.

The call of the churches for non-military national service

Publicity about conscientious objection was mounting. In 1979 several churches made appeals to the authorities to permit conscientious objectors to serve as non-combatants or to perform their national service under civilian direction. To judge by the timing, I suspect that this flurry of appeals was prompted by my papers of 1978 and 1979. The Baptist Union adopted a resolution about military service at its Assembly in October 1979. The resolution was proposed by Rev. John Wilton, the minister of Claremont Baptist Church of which I was a member—indicating that this resolution had been prompted by my specific case. It was seconded by Rev. Colonel Norman Wood, the Chaplain-General of the Rhodesian armed forces. The resolution was passed by a 'large majority.' The Assembly affirmed the right of individuals to object to taking up arms "on the ground of conscience or religious convictions."[28] It noted that members of so-called peace churches had legal grounds for rendering service in a non-combatant capacity, while members of other denominations did not, and it requested that legal avenues be provided for non-combatancy. Finally, it requested that for religious pacifists—"individuals who, on religious grounds, cannot conscientiously serve in any armed forces"— there be provision to serve in a civilian capacity. It is worth noting that had the Baptist request been granted in full, Richard

---

[28] All the church statements from 1979 may be consulted in: Christian Citizenship Department of the Methodist Church of Southern Africa (1980).

Steele would have benefited as he was a religious pacifist. I, however, as an objector to all *un*just wars, including that waged by the SADF, but not to *just* wars, would not have been helped by the Baptist request.

The Presbyterian Church of Southern Africa issued a similar statement in September 1979. It affirmed "its support of the right of young men to be conscientious objectors" and deplored "the practice of sentencing conscientious objectors to a period or recurring periods in prison or detention barracks," and appealed that the law be amended to provide an alternative form of national service to military service. It should be noted, however, that the Presbyterian statement made no distinction between pacifist objectors and objectors to unjust wars. Presumably, then, its reference to conscientious objectors includes both or all kinds of conscientious objectors.

The Methodist Church of Southern Africa had already recognised my kind of conscientious objection in 1974, noting that conscientious objection may be based "on purely pacifist convictions" or "through the peculiar circumstances of a specific conflict." In October 1979 it proposed that recognised conscientious objectors should be offered the option of work outside the structure of the SADF, such as teachers, firemen, ambulance workers, and welfare officers.

Similarly, the Congregational Church resolved in 1979 that conscientious objection not be limited to religious pacifism. It "expresse[d] its concern about the legislation on conscientious objection. It note[d] that this grants the right to be exempt from military service on religious grounds only to members of religious organisations with a pacifist tradition or confession. A basic tenet of Congregational tradition, however, is the liberty of individual conscience under God and his Word. Therefore ... we strongly support those who do object to military service on religious or moral grounds ... This Assembly recommends ...

alternative forms of non-military national service for all sincere conscientious objectors who refuse to serve in the SADF."

In October 1977 the Cape Town Diocesan Synod of the Church of the Province of South Africa resolved, *inter alia*, "We sympathise with those who in conscience believe that it is an act of disobedience to God to be part of the military structures of this country, because they are convinced that by doing so they would be defending what is morally indefensible." In November 1979 the Provincial Synod of the Church of the Province requested that the Department of Defence discuss specific proposals concerning "non-military forms of national service."

Thus in this series of church statements in 1979, the Baptist one stands out for the narrow scope of its call for non-military service, which was intended to be limited to religious pacifists. By contrast, the Presbyterian, Congregational, Methodist and Anglican churches called for non-military national service for all objectors, both those on religious pacifist grounds and those on moral grounds.

Further efforts by the army to avoid confrontation

The senior officers of the SADF were very concerned about the publicity arising from my two papers and various letters to the newspapers, as well as the court case in September 1979. One of the army's tactics was to get a chaplain to speak to me and try to persuade me to take a non-combatant role. Indeed I did receive another phone call from Chaplain Rev. Middlemost, seeking again to persuade me to take a different course. He assured me that if I changed my mind my past misdeeds would be erased and I could work as a non-combatant. I replied that this was cold comfort given that by that stage I had already received another call-up, had refused it in writing, and was awaiting arrest.

Another attempt by the army to steer me away from direct confrontation was an offer to me to run a survey in the townships. One afternoon while working at the Old Mutual I received a phone call from Major Beyers, Public Relations Officer at the Castle, who made the offer. The army needed, he said, to know something about black people's opinions vis-à-vis the army. He knew I was skilled in survey techniques and data analysis, and so he proposed that I undertake this. He imposed the condition that I would have to be in military uniform when conducting the survey. I explained to him that I objected to any association with the military and in any case wearing military uniform in the townships would bias the findings and needlessly endanger myself and other survey participants. He was very angry and warned me that this was my last chance.

I did not know it at the time, but the publicity caused by my articles, letters, papers and speeches was later to provide me with a measure of protection. The generals feared the possibility of ministerial inquiries if they handled me in an illegal way; the officers at the Detention Barracks knew that I would be able to use the law against them because I quoted the *Detention Barracks Regulations* (1961-1976) in my defence in the summary trials that were to follow; and due to the publicity I was given blue overalls when I entered the Voortrekkerhoogte Detention Barracks, thereby igniting the debate over whether I was to be recognised as a conscientious objector or not. Furthermore, the letters written to me were a continual reminder to the corporals that if they were to take any illegal action against me they would meet with legal charges.

I had by now read of the tragic case of Signalman Arnold Lewin,[29] who fell asleep while on switchboard duty, and was

---

[29] See the SA War Graves Project at http://www.southafricawar graves.org/search/print.php?id=31325, which reports that Lewin, born on 20

imprisoned on 17 November 1978 in the Detention Barracks in Grootfontein (Namibia). The next day, after exhausting exercise carrying webbing filled with gravel, he collapsed. He was flown to 1 Military Hospital in Voortrekkerhoogte, Pretoria, where he died on 19 November 1978. The military doctor told Lewin's parents that he had died of heat exhaustion. But the parents had seen him in hospital, barely alive, covered in bruises. The parents hired a pathologist who found that he had died from a "pulmonary haemorrhage due to blunt trauma to the chest," and that he had multiple bruises and abrasions. It later emerged that during extra obstacle course punishment, Lewin had been hit and kicked many times, had had a tyre thrown at him, fell while doing 'pole PT' for punishment, and that water had been forced down his throat while his nose was held closed. After collapsing, he was left unresponsive in his cell for three and a half hours, on the pretext that he was malingering, before receiving medical treatment. Two military policemen and five inmates were tried at the Windhoek Magistrate's Court. Five were found innocent; the other two were found guilty and were cautioned and discharged. Lewin's parents were horrified: their son was dead but the perpetrators got off scot free. There were real dangers involved with detention by the army.

November 1959 to Mr. Alex and Mrs. Jean Lewin of Cassandra, Kimberley, died on 19 November 1978. See the following articles at Wits, SAIRR Coll, ZA HPRA AD1912A-S236.6: Geoffrey Allen and Ray Smuts, 1978. 'Father probes son's Army death,' *Sunday Times*, 3 December 1978. Mike Dennehy, 1979. 'Dead boy's parents refused to accept Army finding,' *Sunday Express*, 18 January 1979. 'Lewin slept on duty—officer,' *Rand Daily Mail*, 22 June 1979. 'I hit Lewin until he fell—co-detainee,' *Rand Daily Mail*, 20 June 1979. Jeremy Gordon, 1979. 'Barracks bullying out, says general,' *Sunday Express*, 27 May 1979. 'Lewin: court hears of delay in treatment,' *The Star*, 22 May 1979. ' "Eye drops soldier kicked during drill," ' *Rand Daily Mail*, 18 May 1979.

As a result of the Lewin case, the SADF set up a committee of inquiry which recommended a long list of reforms. These included making the *Detention Barracks Regulations* available to every inmate and having a warrant officer on duty at each shift.[30] Neither of these reforms was implemented, as I was later able to observe at both the Wynberg and the Voortrekkerhoogte Detention Barracks.

I had long been thinking hard about the sacrifices conscientious objection was going to entail: scrapping a career, the time wasted, conflict with those dearest to me, even the loss of some friendships. How committed was I to striking out into the unknown? I should try to unveil my own psychology, thoughts and emotions. Orderly economic, political, moral and theological arguments are one thing. One's day-to-day ruminations are another. "The heart has reasons of which reason knows nothing" (Pascal, *Pensées*). Many of these thoughts were not pleasant. I can recollect clearly some six avenues that my inner mind took in an unoccupied moment.

I knew I was up against overwhelming force, but I had been in the army and knew the culture. I had withstood bullying by the two corporals of Alpha company of 1 Maintenance Unit where I did basics in 1974. One day after lunch they struck my chest with their knuckles scores of times, leaving my chest cage a huge single yellow, swollen bruise. I was now five years older, had seen more of the world, and was more sure of myself, so I thought I would be able to hold true.

I had a sense of the power that a single determined nay-sayer can wield in the face of hundreds of yes-men. I was reminded of the carpenter from the underdeveloped north (Galilee) who

---

[30] Willem Steenkamp, 1979. 'On Parade: A solid response on DBs,' *The Cape Times*, 24 September 1979. Wits, SAIRR Coll., ZA HPRA AD1912A-S236.9.

"steadfastly set his face to go to Jerusalem" (Luke 9:51), despite his suspicions that the eternal city harboured dark forces that were going to buy his betrayal by a disciple.

I had an acute sense of sadness and tragedy. I visualised a painting that I had admired in the Baxter Theatre in Rondebosch in 1977: a huge canvas depicting an elongated hearse vehicle, on a monochrome yellow background, with the driver in black on the extreme right looking backwards. The yellow seemed to be the sand of the Karoo where the road in front, straight as a die, disappears in a haze of floating mirages. What body did the hearse bear, that it was worth the driver's while to peer backwards? To me the painting was a parable of a backward-looking South Africa going nowhere. Conrad's *Heart of Darkness* came to mind, as I had studied the novel in English I at the University of Cape Town in 1977, with its unforgettable image of the skulls of Kurtz's victims arrayed on picks around his trading station. Not for me, to "penetrate deeper and deeper into the heart of darkness". I saw a parallel between Kurtz's civilising mission that culminated in his "exterminat[ing] the brutes", and the defence by the SADF of *apartheid*, that culminated in the murder of Steve Biko and Signalman Arnold Lewin and so many more. Not for me, to be led by the SADF "into the heart of an immense darkness," where we end up saying with Kurtz, "The horror! The horror!"

I had a sense of guilt. Though I had never experienced luxury, I had been fortunate enough to get a good education. I could not turn the clock back to 1948 or to 1652 or 1498 and let everyone in the country start over from a level of equality; but at least I could exercise some choices now to avoid being dragged into the heart of darkness, and to expose the lie that the SADF was defending Christianity. To think that the corporals wanted me to deploy my shooting skills with the R1 rifle—for which I had received the sharpshooter badge at 84 Technical Stores Depot in

1974—and use this deadly force against peop_e whom I respected and may even have met! No, that would be to extend my unchosen privilege of a good education into a chosen collaboration with a racist system.

I would not live a lie. I would not pretend that all was quiet on the north-western front, parading Paton's pretti‍fication that the military was a shield behind which *aparthe‍id* could be dismantled. All of this was just a thicket of lies. Tha‍t is not what I was brought up to be. My origins could not allow me to live a falsehood: my Baptist upbringing, my parents' ir‍sistence on total honesty even when inconvenient, the search for biblical truth during my years with the Students' Christian Association—putting all of this together, it became impossible to promote my interests or those of my family/clan/group/race by means of the lie of racism.

The images of the heroes and martyrs crowded in: Luther's "Here I stand", the miry clay into which Jeremiah was lowered for days, Latimer's appeal to Ridley, upon their martyrdom, to "light such a candle as shall never be put out", Stephen's "forgive them, for they know not what they do," Bunyan's "fear not what men say", Rev. David Russell kneeling before the front-end loaders at Modderdam with his Bible on his neck. I knew these from countless sermons, talks and books, starting from my mother's Good News Club when I was eight.

Whenever I reflected on the dreaded manila envelopes containing the army's repeated call-ups, all these thoughts popped up at once: No lies! No collaboration! Don't be dragged into the heart of darkness! Don't look backwards! Stand up for what you believe! I can do no other! These images used to flash through my mind in a second. I cannot say that I was torn this way and that. I was not seriously tempted to recant, to leave the country, or to take refuge in one of the Bant‍ustans. My upbringing, my thoughts, my reading and study—all pointed in the same direction: *a war to defend apartheid is unjust.* I was to set my face towards Voortrekkerhoogte.

Chapter 3. Court-martial at the Castle, 4 December 1979

The army continued its pursuit. I was called up for 19 November 1979, officially for two weeks, but I was verbally informed that this was to be extended to three months and to include 'border' duty. Given how long the army had been hounding me, I knew that if I refused it was likely that I would be sent to the Detention Barracks. I wrote to the Officer Commanding refusing to heed the call-up, citing the fundamental injustice of *apartheid* and the lack of a just cause for war.[31] I also gave the army my phone number at home and at work.

The statement of my reasons for objecting concluded with a reproduction of the poem *Caprivi Lament* by Alan Paton, published in 1973. This was a threnody about the death of four black policemen killed in an ambush in the Caprivi Strip by guerrillas active in south-western Zambia. Paton ends by asking whether the policemen died for a "new heaven and a new earth," or whether they had been led into ambush.

To my surprise I received a phone call at work on 22 November 1979, just three days after the date of the call-up, from a Staff-Sergeant Pool, at the Wynberg Military Police, informing me that he had bad news. He joked about it and said that I had to prepare myself for arrest. I congratulated him on his recent promotion—he had been a Sergeant when I first reported

---

[31] My letter of refusal, in the form of an open letter, 19 October 1979, summarised by Dot Cleminshaw, is reproduced in the section of original documents. I am thankful to the Alan Paton Will Trust for permission to reproduce Alan Paton's poem *Caprivi Lament* in the letter of refusal (granted on 20 June 2023).

to him to inform him of my whereabouts a few weeks earlier. I decided to go home and I would meet his men there. A colleague at the Old Mutual, John Bestbier, kindly gave me a lift back to my house at 'Lynden', Avenue Road, Mowbray, where I packed a bag of clothes and some books and went with the military police to the Detention Barracks at the Wynberg military base. It was five o'clock in the afternoon.

I was told to take off my suit and put on brown overalls and boots, and was shown to my cell, which they called a 'hok.' "Klim in jou hok, troep!" (Get in your cage, troopie!) they yelled. I was told to clean up my cell. It was not much of a shock, since I had been preparing myself psychologically for the occasion, and because I knew the military way of life from my basic training in 1974. I started cleaning my cell. Supper was brought to me later. The food at Wynberg was quite good, compared with that at Voortrekkerhoogte. There was enough and the quality was better.

The sergeant came around to inspect and considered my cell too dirty. I had to clean it up again and get all the dust out of the place. He hated dust. Later that evening I had the chance to do some reading. My brother Terence kindly obtained copies of SALDRU[32] Working Papers. Over the subsequent weeks I read Wilson and Perrot's *Outlook on a Century*, Robert Lauer's *Perspectives on Social Change*, and theological works including Roland Bainton's *Christian Attitudes to War and Peace*, Reinhold Niebuhr's *The Nature and Destiny of Man: a Christian Interpretation*, Karl Barth's *Church Dogmatics Vol. II:2*, Edward Schillebeeckx's *Jesus: an Experiment in Christology* and Karl Rahner's *The Experience and Language of Grace*. At

---

[32] Southern African Labour and Development Research Unit, at the University of Cape Town, director Professor Francis Wilson.

ten in the evening the lights were turned out and the officers inspected to make sure that everyone was silent.

For the first few days at Wynberg I was not allowed to speak to anyone. I guessed that they thought I was subversive and did not want me to influence young conscripts in the other cells, most of whom had not committed any 'real' crime except for absenting themselves without leave (AWOL). In time I made friends with the other inmates on the ground floor, all of whom were also *arrestante* (men under arrest before trial). I had little contact with the *gestrafdes* (men undergoing punishment) on the upper floor. In time, the officers also grew friendly. I became good friends with a Permanent Force Sergeant I., who happened to be so-called Coloured and who at times was the most senior officer on duty at the Detention Barracks. On the day after my trial he came to my cell late at night, speaking quietly so that no one else could hear. He explained that he understood my reasons for conscientious objection and agreed with them, but said that he was a married man with children and somehow needed to earn a living. He was not proud of being in the army but felt he had no alternative. He secretly gave me copies of newspaper articles about my case, at considerable risk to himself, for this was fraternising, explicitly prohibited by the *Detention Barracks Regulations*. I was grateful and indicated that I understood his predicament.

After a few days I was told by the Lieutenant to join in with the marching and physical training. I did so without protest, even though I saw the contradiction between such military training and my position as a conscientious objector. I grew physically fit and sunburnt. We had to run the '2.4 kilometres' (ten times around the inner perimeter of the detention barracks campus) every day, in addition to much physical training and marching. Luckily there were warm showers available, one at the end of the lower floor where the *arrestante* were housed, and one at the end of the upper floor where the *gestrafdes* were housed.

There was a pleasant spirit of camaraderie between the officers and the inmates at the Detention Barracks in Wynberg, unlike the Pretoria Detention Barracks to which I was later transferred. One Sunday evening, the sergeant kindly allowed us to stay out of our cells for a little longer than usual, and we played volleyball. All of a sudden there was a ring at the gate and we thought it must be a senior officer. We immediately formed up in a squad, so as to protect the sergeant from the officer's wrath. The sergeant went to the gate only to find a minor official inquiring after the welfare of the troops from his unit. It was great fun seeing the sergeant cooperating with us in this way. If we cleaned our cells properly, for instance, he would let us keep our cells open a little longer in the evenings, which again was kind of him.

Some of the men could not bear being locked up at night. The psychological strain was too great. They often cried. In desperation they would bang the door and yell. They could not bear being alone. I was fortunate not to be that type; I like being alone and it did not worry me to have the door closed behind me. It was irritating to the extent that it limited my freedom, but I did not find it psychologically taxing.

There were some ten Jehovah's Witnesses at the Wynberg Detention Barracks. I befriended them and was impressed at their gentleness and their clarity of thought. I asked after their views on performing military commands, because the contradiction between my conscientious objection and military training was becoming starker. I had already spoken with both the English Churches' chaplains, and with the Officer Commanding (a Colonel) about this question, but all three officers urged me not to disobey the law. The Jehovah's Witnesses said they were not willing either to identify with, or to support, or to misrepresent the army. By 'identify with' they meant the wearing of military dress; by 'support' they meant the performance of essential military tasks; and by 'misrepresent' they meant that they would have no truck with the propaganda picture of an army officer holding a little black baby from Namibia. They would not aid or abet the 'killing machine' of the army in any way. Hence they refused to wear the brown military overalls and did not obey military commands.

I discovered, from these Jehovah's Witnesses and from the many more whom I met in the Pretoria Detention Barracks, that their predecessors from 1969 to 1972 had gone through times of terrible suffering before the SADF recognised them as conscientious objectors. The Detention Barracks authorities tried to force them to become soldiers by any means, legal or not. They were beaten, placed in dark cells, deprived of food and denied visits from relatives. But the SADF eventually came to acknowledge their sincerity, ceased its policy of persecution and violence and adopted the policy that conscripts from 'peace churches', nearly all of whom were Jehovah's Witnesses, would be sentenced to three years' detention, during which they would do gardening and road repair, and in return would manage their own affairs, separate from the other inmates. The Jehovah's Witnesses had blazed the trail.

'No identification, no support and no misrepresentation.' The scales fell from my eyes. This was the clarity that I needed. I considered taking the overalls off right away and refusing to march. On the advice of the chaplains, I decided to wait for a while and see what my lawyer could do about it. It turned out, however, that the penalties for refusing military commands could be serious: I could be sentenced to an additional year in the Detention Barracks for refusing to obey commands, or I could be given solitary confinement. I waited for a more 'convenient season.'

I was fortunate to have a stream of visitors while an *arrestant* in the Wynberg Detention Barracks. My mother and my youngest sister Brenda came all the way from Umtata. While my mother had tried to dissuade me from conscientious objection up to this point, she relented once I was arrested and came out strongly in my support. She and Brenda surreptitiously slipped me a favourite delicacy, white chocolate, during their visits. They told me all the news they could. My mother, Brenda and my brother Terence kindly cleared out my rented room at Avenue Road in Mowbray. My aunt Dorothy Steele—mother of Richard Steele, who was later to join me in Voortrekkerhoogte—came all the way from Kempton Park to visit me in the Wynberg Detention Barracks.

I had a visit from Rev. Andreas 'André' Johannes Erasmus of the Orange Street Baptist Church, a family friend. He tried to persuade me to cease being a conscientious objector. He made many racist comments during the interview, asserting straight out that non-whites were not yet fit for the responsibility of voting. I objected that Dr. Allan Boesak, a highly trained theologian and author of a famous book, *Farewell to Innocence: A Socio-Ethical Study on Black Theology and Black Power* should surely have the same voting privileges as white people who had not even completed high school. He replied that Boesak was not really a Christian since he subscribed to a social gospel. It was painful to hear a respected minister of my denomination making incoherent statements without even realising that they were racist.

Dr. John de Gruchy of the Religious Studies Department at the University of Cape Town came to visit. This was one of the most satisfying visits because we were aligned theologically and ethically. Dot Cleminshaw also came to visit; I was cheerful to be reunited with a friend of long standing.

I used to look forward to the visits of my lawyer, Charles David Nupen. I had called him on the day of my arrest (22 November 1979) to ask if he would represent me, which he kindly agreed to do. His firm was Buchanan Boyes. He used to pop in from time to time to check that everything was all right. The advantage of his coming at odd times was that the visit gave me a welcome break from the square-bashing and physical training. Charles enlisted the services of a senior advocate, Mr. Ian Gordon Farlam, who interestingly had defended the right-wing agitator Brian Hack with remarkable success (see below). Charles was also in contact with Dr. James Moulder, a lecturer in philosophy at Rhodes University, who was well known for his Ph.D. thesis on conscientious objection and subsequent publications on the issue. Together with them Charles worked out a strong defence.

The National Union of South African Students (NUSAS) met at its annual Congress in Durban in November 1979. Chris Swart, the chairperson of the Durban branch of NUSAS, proposed, and the Congress adopted, Resolution 95/80, referring to my arrest and detention, condemning the government's "continued persecution of conscientious objectors", demanding my unconditional release and calling on the government to introduce alternative forms of national service.[33]

A blunder by the Old Mutual

I received a visit from my manager, Ray Murray, whose mission was to turn over to me a letter with the Old Mutual's demand that I repay the bursary totalling R5,145[34] in six-monthly instalments, starting while in the Detention Barracks. I

---

[33] NUSAS resolution—see p. 130 at https://disa.ukzn.ac.za/sites/default /files/pdf_files/min19791100.026.022.000.pdf .

[34] My Old Mutual salary, before tax, was R480/month, so this represented 11 months' salary.

knew this was coming but it was still a disappointment. Mr. Ralph Roseman, an Assistant General Manager of the Old Mutual, declared that I could return to the firm provided I agreed to obey my call-ups.[35] When challenged by the press as to why the firm meted out this punishment, on top of my 18-month sentence, the spokesperson said that the firm's policy was to forbid "high profile" political and religious activities.[36] This gauche statement converted me into a "moral cause célèbre."[37] For it was pointed out that some employees and Board members of the firm had high profiles both politically and religiously. For instance, the head of the personnel department was a well-known lay preacher, Bert Pfuhl, beloved throughout the Cape for his witty and engaging sermons; I heard him speak several times at the University of Cape Town. The chairman of the Board of the Old Mutual, Mr. Jan van der Horst, sat on the government's Economic Advisory Council. One commentator described the Old Mutual's position as "slightly revolting."[38] Prominent individuals such as Dr. Kenneth Hughes (Mathematics, University of Cape Town, and chairperson, Civil Rights League), Dr. Margaret Nash (theologian, SACC), and Mr. I.C. Aitken (General Secretary of the Presbyterian Church of Southern Africa)[39] wrote letters of protest.

Stung by this criticism, the Old Mutual revised its rationale for firing. Now it was because I had broken the contract with the

---

[35] 'Diensplig-ontduiker welkom hier as ...,' *Beeld*, 8 January 1980. Wits, SAIRR Coll., ZA HPRA AD1912A-S236.9.

[36] 'Objector Moll sacked by Old Mutual', *Cape Argus* 5 January 1980. See also 'Employers fire jailed objector,' *Cape Times* 7 January 1980.

[37] This phrase was from the *Sunday Times*, 14 February 1980.

[38] 'Policy Profile' in *Rand Daily Mail*, 11 January 1980.

[39] Wits, Rob. Coll., A2558-9.13.

firm by not turning up for work on 23 November 1979.[40] This was less crude than their first statement but was no less insincere because, as was pointed out by Rev. Douglas Bax in a letter to the *Cape Times*,[41] the firm had employees who did their one- or two-year basic training and who were retained, and the firm paid the salaries of employees when they attended three-week or three-month camps. So the firm rewarded conformity with the army, but penalised conscientious objection. To the firm's credit, it later indicated that I could return to its employ once freed from detention.

When Mr. 'Mac' Thomas, whom I had met on Christmas Day in 1977, heard about the Old Mutual's demands he mailed a cheque for R100 to the firm, with the request that this be used to reduce the debt owing. Over subsequent months, several more people did the same, even though they did not know me at all.

There was one advantage to the Old Mutual's ham-fisted management: free publicity. For weeks afterwards there were letters to the newspapers from angry policyholders complaining that the firm had shown no civic courage and had become 'His Master's Voice'. More people learned about conscientious objection without our having to lift a finger.

The trial

My trial was set for 4 December 1979. I was taken out by the corporals at eight in the morning to go to the Castle at Cape Town. I was required to wear the Detention Barracks overalls.

---

[40] 'Moll broke contract says Old Mutual', in *Sunday Times*, 14 February 1980. See also D.A. Matthews, 'Dismissal did not violate Moll's freedom of speech', *Cape Times*, 21 January 1980; and D.L. Craythorne, 'Moll and the rights of an employer', *Cape Times*, 29 February 1980.

[41] Rev. Douglas Bax, 'Why was Moll punished by his employers?', *Cape Times*, 21 January 1980. Also Rev. Douglas Bax, 'Employers' action on Moll discriminatory.' *Cape Times*, 21 February 1980.

The SADF had placed misinformation in the local press about the venue, and at the last moment changed the venue to the Castle. We suspect that this was an army trick to avoid the embarrassment of a large audience. A crowd of about 25 friends arrived anyway, wishing to enter. Among the people present were Jim and Renate Cochrane, Margaret Nash, Stephen de Gruchy, Kathy Luckett, Dot Cleminshaw, Professor Francis Wilson, Rev. Douglas Bax and Rev. John Wilton. Rev. David Russell was prevented by banning orders from attending. The Regimental Sergeant-Major at the Castle said that there was room only for the newspaper reporters and two relatives. That was an interesting number because indeed there were just two members of my immediate family present, my brother Terence and my mother; in addition, there was my cousin Heather Steele, sister of Richard. I learned later that a young female soldier had mixed in with the crowd and found out that there were two immediate family members, and had passed this fact on to the Sergeant-Major.

Dot Cleminshaw, Jim and Renate Cochrane and Francis Wilson, among others, were angered and tried to persuade the Sergeant-Major to move to a bigger venue. He refused. They tried to speak to the Officer Commanding of the Western Province Command, Brig. Louis Howell Robertson, but were told that he would not be available any time that day. Whereupon they complained to the Brigadier's secretary that they had been unfairly excluded from the hearing. Out of embarrassment she blurted out that General Magnus Malan, the Chief of the SADF, had given instructions that morning that no one was to attend besides members of my immediate family.

Years later I learned from one Norman Patterton, who was a lawyer in the Army at that time, that we could have insisted on the court's being open to all, according to law. We did not know this and so felt we had to settle. It had already become a kangaroo court. Later we managed to add a further chair for Francis Wilson in the morning, who had become an uncle, and for Adrian 'Adi' Paterson in the afternoon, now a cousin.

I began the court hearing by explaining that I refused to fight for a system which I believed was fundamentally unjust and unchristian. Thus I had moral reasons for refusing to obey the SADF call-up. I considered the war against the ANC, PAC and SWAPO unjust because non-violent alternatives for change in South Africa had not been tried, let alone exhausted; there had been no round table conference with representatives of all the country's peoples to plan a new, more just order and thereby avoid war. My lawyers put up a determined case that lasted well into the afternoon. They maintained that the law has a broader interpretation. The charge was that I had failed to attend this camp 'without good reason.' They contended that I did have good reason not to attend, namely a conscientious one. They argued that mine was not a maverick view, and that the individual's right to conscientious objection was supported by my church. Advocate Farlam added:

> [Moll] was genuinely prepared to serve for longer than a national serviceman for subsistence remuneration and in addition more arduously. He had a willingness to serve his country, but had a religious objection.[42]

He stressed that it was for reasons of conscience that the Huguenots had left France and come to the Cape. Standing on a point of conscience, he said, was not strange to us as South Africans, but was part of our heritage. Only totalitarian governments use force to prise individuals away from their

---

[42] 'Objector gets 18 months' detention,' *The Star,* 5 December 1979.

conscientious beliefs. It would be "monstrous" to try to force someone to do something against his conscience.

Rev. John Wilton, the minister of my church (Claremont Baptist), again appeared in the witness stand. He said he knew me very well and that he had had long discussions with me about my "crisis of conscience" about military service. He added that Baptists had a history of belief in religious liberty that extended back to the Reformation, and their fundamental authority was the Bible which "overrules every other authority."[43] He noted that in the Baptist church it is the individual who decides whether a particular war is just or unjust. He reminded the court that the Baptist Union of South Africa had recently adopted a resolution recognising that some members are unwilling to serve in any military capacity, and recommending that alternative service under civilian direction be provided.

The minister of the Rondebosch Congregational Church, Rev. Douglas Bax, noted that conscientious objection was a theme stressed by many theologians including the reformer John Calvin. He contended that since I, like many Baptists, hewed to the Reformed tradition, it was consistent to deploy Calvin's just war theory such that if the war was unjust I had no obligation to participate in it.

All that fell on deaf ears. It was obvious that the outcome of the court-martial had been rigged in advance, and that I had been brought to book not in order to decide on the justice of the case, but merely in order to determine the extent of the punishment that I would receive.

The President of the court-martial, Major Hermanus Willem Dempers, asked few questions. He appeared uninterested in what Advocate Farlam had to say. Finally the young prosecutor,

---

[43] See 'Jail for man who defied call-up', in the *Rand Daily Mail*, 5 December 1979.

Lieutenant Daniel Mills, who I learned had consulted with a theologian from Pretoria University, Professor Johan Heyns, lectured me for having propounded my views in open letters to newspapers and university students "with the intention of challenging and provoking the SADF," which was not "the sort of action expected from a serious Christian."[44] He called for the maximum sentence of two years as a deterrent for other conscripts.

Major Dempers pronounced a sentence of 18 months.[45] That came as a shock. I had anticipated something less than that, although I had tried to prepare myself psychologically for anything up to two years, the maximum for that offence at the time. I felt a lump rising in my throat. I was to find the same thing happening when I was put into solitary confinement later. Even though I knew what the sentence was to be, even though I knew that in their distorted sense I was technically guilty, and even though I was resigned to the fact of sitting for 14 days in solitary confinement, I felt crushed every time.

I spoke briefly with Advocate Farlam and Charles Nupen, thanking them for representing me. Mr Farlam was of course disappointed at the heavy sentence, the more so since I had indicated that I was willing to do a nonmilitary alternative. I turned to my mother to say goodbye. She said that Francis Wilson had mentioned to her that morning, "Cometh the hour, cometh the man." Those were great words to hear at that moment. My thoughts kept flitting between being the man for the hour and being the man with 18 months to serve in the Detention Barracks.

---

[44] Objector gets 18 months' detention,' *The Star*, Wednesday 5 December 1979.

[45] Another record of proceedings of the trial, typed up, is at: Wits, Rob. Coll., A2558-9.13.

I walked down to the car to be taken back by two corporals. I fought back tears as we took de Waal Drive, past Rondebosch and Constantia, arriving eventually in Wynberg. It was sad looking over that vast expanse of beautiful countryside and thinking that I was to be removed from the great city of Cape Town, and that only for holding moral and Christian views.

We arrived at the Detention Barracks at five in the afternoon and I told the other inmates that I had just been given 18 months. They were incredulous. A sentence of 18 months was unheard of. For them, who had mostly been AWOL (absent without leave), the sentences were mostly 20 to 40 days, sometimes 60 days and rarely 90.

A depressing evening followed. By the next day I was resigned to my fate and carried on with the work at the Detention Barracks, the maintenance, cleaning, marching and physical training, without demur.

I did not know it at the time, but shortly after the verdict was pronounced, a former member of my church (Claremont Baptist) wrote to the officers of the Cape Flats Commando to congratulate them on securing a stiff sentence. He was Cecil F. Hack. We knew each other and had participated in church-based discussions about social justice. Before proceeding to his letter, here are some snippets about his son, Bryan Cecil Hack, whom I likewise knew through the Claremont Baptist Church. Bryan was the President of the Conservative Student Alliance at the University of Cape Town. Late at night on 12 April 1979 three shots were fired at head height into the door of the apartment of the Leader of the Opposition, Mr. Colin Eglin. Bryan Hack, David Beelders and Arnold van der Westhuizen were charged under the Terrorism Act; Beelders was sentenced to seven years and van der Westhuizen to six years, but Bryan Hack was eventually acquitted thanks to Advocate Ian G. Farlam's expert representation.[46]

The letter from Bryan's father Cecil F. Hack was addressed to the Officer Commanding of my unit, the Cape Flats Commando, dated 7 December 1979. He applauded my imprisonment because I had "come under strong communistic influence" from the "enemies within our borders, in particular, it would seem, lecturers at universities." He lauded the "good work" of the Officer Commanding "in the interests of the defence of our beloved country." I quote this letter from among the many documents that were circulating in the Baptist community at the time, to give a flavour of the controversial atmosphere.

Dot Cleminshaw had compiled a substantial press release, quoting my letter to the Officer Commanding, giving my reasons for conscientious objection, and also quoting Alan Paton's poem 'Caprivi Lament'. She gave copies to the journalists and the case was thoroughly covered in the newspapers.

The day after the trial, 17 church leaders and others published a joint letter about my case. The signatories included Bishop Desmond Tutu, the General Secretary of the South African Council of Churches; Owen Cardinal McCann of Cape Town; the Catholic Archbishops of Pretoria and Durban; the Anglican Bishop and the Suffragan Bishop of Natal; and several Methodist, Congregational and Dutch Reformed Church ministers. They noted,

It is well known to us that there are many young men facing the same dilemma as Peter Moll, that is, whether to undertake military

---

[46] South African Institute of Race Relations, *Survey of Race Relations in South Africa,* 1979:168.

service in conflict with their conscience or whether to suffer the harsh penalty of refusal ...

We plead with the government to understand that in the present circumstances of our country, conscientious objection can be based on genuine religious and moral convictions.

We plead with the government at the earliest possible opportunity to regularise the position of conscientious objectors through the provision of alternative non-military forms of national service and in the meantime to exercise in regard to Peter Moll and all other conscientious objectors the humanity and clemency that should be characteristic of a Christian society.[47]

I discovered only in 2022, 42 years later, that this statement had been formulated, typed up and phoned through a few days in advance by the indefatigable Rev. David Russell and Dot Cleminshaw.

On 5 December 1979 Rev. Martin Holdt of the Cambridge Baptist Church in East London wrote to the Minister of Defence:

I have noted with deep disappointment the conviction of Mr. Peter Moll for his unwillingness to complete his national service under military authority. I consider his sentence to be all the more tragic in view of his willingness to do national service, albeit in a non-military [emphasis in the original] sphere.

I wish to make it clear that I do not agree with Mr. Moll's convictions. However, they are sincere ... The findings of the judge and the severe conviction will, I believe, erode the confidence many of us have placed in the military authorities. I believe that the judgment was biased and I now seriously question whether a military court is competent to deal fairly and justly with matters of this kind ...

---

[47] 'Conscientious objection: Church view,' *Cape Times*, 5 December 1979: Wits, SAIRR Coll., ZA HPRA AD1912A-S236.9.

I respect the right of the individual's freedom of conscience and therefore wish to lodge my strongest personal objection to the injustice meted out to Mr. Moll. I have reason to believe that many of the members of my congregation share my sentiments.

On 6 December 1979 Rev. Dr. Allan Boesak, pastor of a church in Bellville (Western Cape), and associated with the theology faculty at the University of the Western Cape, said, "I support Peter with all my heart. His argument is impeccable from an informed Christian point of view."[48]

---

[48] See 'Tutu slams sentence on objector,' *Post*, 6 December 1979, p. 7. Wits, SAIRR Coll., ZA HPRA AD1912A-S236.9.

Chapter 4. The Detention Barracks at Voortrekkerhoogte, Pretoria

News came of an imminent transfer to the Detention Barracks at Voortrekkerhoogte (Pretoria). This was puzzling. My unit was Cape Flats Commando—why then Pretoria? Presumably they wanted me under the eye of senior officers. On 16 December 1979 a corporal took me to the Milnerton military airport, where briefly I was able to greet my friends Tony Saddington and Gill Westcott who had somehow found out that I was to be in transit. The corporal put me on the plane alone, without an escort. I was in civilian dress, because I was not allowed to travel in the Detention Barracks uniform. I could easily have walked off at the next stop, Saldanha Bay, and absconded. When we arrived at the Waterkloof airport, I approached two corporals who were looking expectant and suggested that I might be their man. They agreed and took me to the Detention Barracks.

Description of the Detention Barracks

The Detention Barracks[49] were located five miles to the south-west of Pretoria, between Johannes Bekker Street, Jan Lombard Avenue and Stephanus Schoeman Road (coordinates -25.7961, 28.1334). The earliest satellite

---

[49] See: (1) A. de V. Marais, 1972. 'The penned-in life of the objectors,' *Rand Daily Mail*, 29 April 1972. From the website of Thomas Budge. (2) Tim O'Hagan, 1972. 'Rehabilitation is army detention centre's theme,' *Sunday Express*, 16 April 1972. From the website of Thomas Budge. (3) 'Woman tells of shock after barracks arrrest,' *Sunday Express*, 16 April 1972. From the website of Thomas Budge. (4) 'Detained for other ideas,' *Rand Daily Mail*, 18 September 1980. Wits, Rob. Coll., A2558-16. (5) Jeremy Gordin, 1979. 'Life in DB—three men tell their stories,' *Sunday Express*, 15 July 1979. Wits, SAIRR Coll., ZA HPRA AD1912A-S236.9.

photograph available is that of 2002 in Google Earth, by which time the Barracks were no longer in use as a prison. By 2004 all but two of the buildings had been razed to the ground, and by 2005 the area was turned earth, after which it reverted to bush. An artist's rendition of an aerial view of the Detention Barracks is given in the photography section.

There were four blocks of cells, named Blocks One to Four, and at the end of the administrative buildings there was the smaller Block Five. Between the main administrative building in the shape of an L, and the cell blocks, there was a courtyard of black slate. Inmates used to clean and polish it regularly, and this was the place for visits by relatives. Blocks One to Four each had 68 cells,[50] 34 on each side, with a grey cement courtyard in between, in the middle of which ran a cement gully for drainage. The courtyard within the block was mostly covered by the roof but in the middle it was open to the sky. Using measurements from Google Earth, I found that each block was 251 feet long and 35 feet wide. The walls between cells were four inches thick. By deduction the interior of the cell was seven feet square, four inches longer than a Queen-sized bed. The cells were painted yellow. The door had an open judas-hole two inches in diameter and a metal skin, painted green. Above the door there was a gap up to the ceiling; this had six vertical iron bars as well as horizontal slats of wood. Opposite the door was a window, with seven iron bars. There was no glass in the window and so hot days became very hot and cold days very cold.

Some months after my release from the Detention Barracks, a sink-hole appeared and the barracks had to be vacated for safety's sake. The next conscientious objector to turn up at the

---

[50] My recollection, and also Steele's (1983).

Voortrekkerhoogte Detention Barracks, Charles Yeats, was held in a temporary enclosure next door.

To sleep one had an old foam rubber mattress four inches thick, that lay directly on the cement floor. I had to lie in a careful way to avoid hurting my hips. One had three blankets. There were no pillows. One fabricated oneself a pillow from some garment, or used a folded blanket, or cut off a piece of a foam rubber mattress. I inherited a piece of foam from another inmate and used it for most of the year. At the beginning of 1980 each cell had a green metal cupboard but this was withdrawn a few months later to facilitate searches. There was no sink or water source in the cell. There was a 'blink bak' (shining basin) for washing clothes. There was no toilet in the cell or in the block; instead one had a chamber pot which one emptied at the ablution block when taken out of the cell. The pot had no cover but fortunately I have only a minimal sense of smell and was not bothered. About mid-year the pot was replaced with a much larger bucket with a lid, making the cell slightly less smelly.

At the time I was there, Block One was reserved for 'arrestante,' arrested inmates whose sentences had not yet been confirmed. There were some departures from this rule: Evered Poole, a Christadelphian conscientious objector, stayed in Block One, as well as a dozen or more oumanne (old men in Afrikaans, inmates serving longer sentences). Blocks Two and Three were occupied by 'gestrafdes,' inmates with confirmed sentences who were undergoing punishment. Block Four was occupied only by Jehovah's Witnesses. There was a barbed wire fence between Block Four and the other blocks.

Most of the time there was a functioning light in the cell. In early 1980 this was a naked bulb which the men used to light their cigarettes. They reached up, took the bulb out, and jabbed a piece of steel wool into the socket, short-circuiting it and heating the steel wool enough to light the cigarette. Later in the year this was replaced by a heavy-duty steel holder with a striated glass/perspex window in front, blocking access to the bulb. The light was rather dim due to the metal and thick glass/perspex, but the 60W bulb was just sufficient for reading if one had good eyesight. The light was kept on throughout the night, so that the corporals could easily check that the inmate was there. Nothing could be hooked onto the light fitting, and there was only one switch, which was controlled by the corporals outside. Some inmates managed to prise out the glass/perspex from the light fitting, damaging it irreparably and costing the army much money, to light their cigarettes.

The alternative was to organise lighters, which inmates obtained illegally from the corporals, or secure lighters from men who had just arrived in the Detention Barracks and had not yet surrendered all their possessions. The *oumanne* used to go up surreptitiously to these fellows and ask them for the stuff, and they would normally comply. It was funny to see the ingenuity and aplomb with which people smuggled. From this was derived an apt expression invented by the corporals: when an inmate was refusing to cooperate with them, they said, "Jy smokkel met my kop" (You are smuggling [with] my head.)

Many inmates could not sleep with the light on. I was one of them. At about ten in the evening I used to stand on the chair and using a pin which I carefully hid somewhere, I would pin a towel over the light to get near-darkness. I would then go to sleep. If a corporal came I had to leap up and pull the towel down, very quickly, to make sure he did not see, otherwise I would have been deprived of my precious pin and subjected to more inspections. Sometimes when I did not have a chair it was more difficult. The light was high up. I used to fold up a two-foot high pile of blankets upon which I would precariously balance, trying to press the pin in without falling. Some of the inmates did similarly, though their method was rough-and-ready: they used to chop away some of the cement from behind the light, thereby easily fitting a towel over the light fitting.

The outside wall of the Detention Barracks was corrugated iron, about twelve feet high. Above this were about four feet of barbed wire, of which the first foot went straight upwards, and the next three at a 45° angle pointing inwards. To this were added rolls of barbed wire. Despite these challenges, inmates frequently escaped, using blankets to protect themselves from the barbs. One boasted, "All you need is a blanket, ten minutes and a gap!" The Detention Barracks had only skeletal security arrangements compared with civilian prisons; the main gate was staffed 24 hours out of 24, but there were no guardhouses or guard towers or dogs, nor was there a second perimeter to permit capture of escapees.

Block Five had been engineered in various ways for solitary confinement. It had just six cells, each 6' x 6' 6", smaller than the ones in Blocks One to Four. The solitary cells lacked the grating above the door to let air through; instead they had a funnel through the ceiling, which seemed to have no effect other than to house cicadas. There was extra security in the form of a large metal box attached outside that covered the small window entirely, to prevent anything from being put through, e.g. food, literature or cigarettes. This made the cell darker. At the far end of the box was a grating through which I could see the outside corrugated iron wall of the barracks, with barbed wire above, on which a bird sometimes alit. The walls between the solitary cells were much thicker, making communication more difficult. If one stood up and spoke through the window fairly loudly, or if one put one's mouth to the judas-hole in the door and one's interlocutor put his ear to his judas, audibility was adequate. I had a chair in my cell, fortunately; sitting on the thin foam rubber mattress all day would have given me back pain.

The cells in Block Five could have been darkened completely by covering the grating on the outside of the large metal box around the window. This was not done during the time I was in the Detention Barracks. In 1972, one nineteen-year-old Jehovah's Witness was kept in a completely dark cell for a period of 18 days (Budge, 2013:78-82). The cells in Block Five were painted light green on the inside. Upon peeling away the coats of paint, one came across the bottom coat: black—on the walls, the door, everywhere—a reminder of crueller times when men were locked up in total darkness.

The ablution block had five toilets, an area for washing clothes and washing one's face and shaving, and a showering area with three showers. All the water was cold, and icy in mid-winter. The official military magazine *Paratus* carried an article in October 1979 claiming that the institution was awaiting the installation of geysers to provide hot water for shaving and bathing.[51] From my arrival in December 1979 until my departure in December 1980 there was no hot water and the geysers were not installed.

The toilets were often blocked. The men emptied their chamber pots directly into the cement-lined sewer drain between the ablution block and Block Two. About once per month the sewer drain became blocked, and faeces and urine would pour out of the ground from a hole a few yards further down, which was right next to Block Two where I was kept for a long period. The filth lay all over the ground over a radius of ten feet, covered with bluebottle flies, stinking to high heaven. One then had to do a detour, or pick one's way carefully to avoid stepping on the stools, when coming from the cellblocks to the ablution block to shower, shave, wash clothes or empty chamber pots/buckets.

---

[51] 'DB: The Facts'. *Paratus*, October 1979, pp. 18-21.

On arrival at the unit, the new inmates had to surrender all their possessions which were kept in the storeroom adjoining the parade ground. They were permitted to retain a Bible. They were given overalls, socks, boots and a hat. They were allowed to bring in polish for their boots. One inmate had his relatives open the polish tin and insert money underneath the polish, before giving him the tin during a visiting hour. A corporal sensed that something was afoot, and found the cash. Thenceforward the corporals dug into polish tins with a knife before handing them on to the inmate.

Most new inmates ate very little for the first three days, probably because they were anxious about their new environment and treatment. After that they ate healthily. As a disciplinary device, the corporals treated the new arrivals especially harshly for the first month before they let up somewhat. They would belittle the new inmates in every way they could, and the *oumanne* added their insults and violence. They were especially hard on prisoners in their first few days in the Detention Barracks, when they would have to 'polish' the cement floor of the block. The new arrivals were commandeered into emptying the chamber pots of the *oumanne*.

In addition to the military hierarchy (Officer Commanding, Citizen Force Second Lieutenant, Sergeant-Major, Staff-Sergeant, sometimes a Sergeant, always Permanent Force and Citizen Force corporals) there was a medical doctor (Lt. Louwrens), a social worker/welfare officer (Lt. Kritzinger), and a unit chaplain. The medical doctor came in from Monday to Friday for the 'Sick Parade' when men who were ill could report. The doctor's office was two doors away from Block Five. I had little contact with the social worker. The unit Chaplain was ds. Dawid Venter, a dominee (minister) of the Dutch Reformed Church. His office was in the south-west corner of Block One.

The daily and weekly routine

The routine for men undergoing punishment started with being woken by a yell from the corporals at five in the morning (six on Saturdays and Sundays).[52] The corporals yelled, "Tree an met julle pisspotte!" (Fall in line with your pisspots!) The sound of the first few minutes is unforgettable: Bzzz, Bzzz, Bzzz all over. The men had slept soundly and needed to urinate as soon as they woke. The filling chamber pots were audible throughout the block. The men were taken out to the latrine to empty their pots and use the toilets. Back inside, they had to clean and polish their cells. Then started the first needless punishment of the day, the 'polishing' of the courtyard between the two long rows of cells. The corporals, or the *oumanne*, yelled, "Tree aan met julle taxis" (Fall in line with your taxis). The taxi was a piece of blanket, about a foot square, used for polishing the cellblock courtyard. The 'polishing' is described further below. Then the men were taken out to have breakfast. Usually they lined up in the courtyard between the kitchen and Block One, and ate in the mess. (Food was served on trestle-tables in the blocks over the weekends.) As in the army, they used a 'varkpan' (pig-pan) to hold their meal: a large compartmentalised metal meal-tray, 31 cm by 42 cm, with five compartments of which two were cup holders. There were only spoons, no knives or forks. Most of the time the food was standard army fare, except that they did not serve us soup, presumably because it would have slopped out of the *varkpan*. Breakfast usually consisted of porridge or cereal, plus bread and egg or bacon. The eggs were boiled or scrambled. Often the cereal was mixed in with the milk, making a semi-solid mass that was easy to serve in one dollop from the large container

---

[52] See my letter to friends, 3 February 1980. Wits, Rob. Coll., A2558-9.13.

with a ladle. The bread had a sparing scraping of something; the inmates joked, "Vind die jêm en wen 'n Datsun" (Find the jam and win a Datsun.)

After breakfast the inmates returned to their cells for the inspection by the senior officers. At eight o'clock they were taken to the parade ground. The day sometimes started with a Bible reading and a prayer by the unit Chaplain. On Tuesday mornings there was the chaplain's period when the inmates were split up by denomination (Dutch Reformed; Free Churches; Pentecostal; and so on) and had about three-quarters of an hour with a chaplain. The Free Churches group, of which I was a member, usually met in the mess. Alternatively, the square-bashing and physical training began immediately after breakfast. On a few very hot days when the temperature rose above a predetermined level, instructions were given that the marching was to stop until the temperature fell.

At ten in the morning everyone stopped for tea, which was brought in an enormous urn. By the time the men received their tea it was long-brewed and lukewarm. There followed more square-bashing and physical training until lunch. The midday meal usually included meat or fish, and cooked vegetables such as squashes, carrots and potatoes. Marching and physical training continued in the afternoon until tea at three, then more marching until four when the men were taken back to their blocks. Sometimes the afternoon was taken up by work groups cleaning the office block, gardening, (illegal) work on staff members' houses, and other tasks.

From four o'clock in the afternoon the inmates were taken out, in sequence (viz. Block One, Block Two and Block Three) to the latrines where they could shave, shower and wash their clothes. Supper was at about five o'clock. Their cigarettes were given out. At six o'clock everyone was locked in their cells. In early 1980 the lights were turned out at ten in the evening; once the big metal light-holders were installed, they were left on the night through.

All detainees had to surrender their cigarettes upon entering the Detention Barracks. These were stored, with the inmate's name recorded, in a large metal box in the administrative offices at reception. The corporals brought the box out once or twice per day, after breakfast and/or after dinner, unlocked it and proceeded to hand out the inmates' ration of three cigarettes. Sometimes the *oumanne* organised the cigarette distribution. Cigarette trades were arranged at night as inmates yelled through their judases to one another. Some trades were for food when food supplies were low. The cigarette distributions were a disciplinary device. If an inmate's cell had not been satisfactorily cleaned, or if he had been obstreperous, or if in any way he had displeased the corporal, he could miss out on one, or two, or all three of his daily ration of cigarettes, or even miss out for a whole weekend or a week. The men found this frustrating because they developed a kind of addiction to smoking when they were in detention, because there was little else to do. One found 'stompies' (cigarette butts) lying around in the Detention Barracks, but there was never a grain of tobacco left as everything had been smoked to the finish.

Most of the men undergoing punishment (other than the Jehovah's Witnesses) did not work in the sense of doing something productive other than military training or punishment. There were too many inmates to create meaningful activities for them. Some were needed daily to clean the passageways in front of the offices, and to polish the black slate courtyard between the main administrative building and Block One. A few inmates worked full-time in the kitchen. From time to time there was renovation work to be done in the unit, such as a big job in late 1980 laying down gravel on the roadway outside the Detention Barracks. Sometimes the men were required to pick up litter inside the barracks. On occasion, work was done (illegally) on a staff member's house nearby. Previously, inmates were made to chop wood but by 1980 this had ceased.

Saturdays were devoted to such things as haircuts which were done in the unit by one of the inmates. Over the weekends the men were taken out to the ablution blocks to wash their clothes, shower and shave. Lunch over weekends was sometimes served in the cellblocks, where the cooks set up trestle-tables to carry the large deep stainless steel pans containing the food.

There was a small one-room library, between Block Five and the doctor's office. It was well supplied with books from the Pretoria City Library system. Saturday would have been the ideal time for the inmates to borrow books and read, but I do not recall a single instance when anyone but I and the Jehovah's Witnesses used the library. There were two difficulties: the first is that visits by inmates to the library would have had to be organised by the corporals, and this would have required extra manpower of a weekend. The second is that the administration would have feared that the inmates would lose or deface the books, or steal them upon their discharge from the Detention Barracks. The administration's line of least resistance was then to neglect to arrange visits to the library. It was not because the inmates did not read. I would estimate that about one in ten of the men had books or magazines. I once borrowed a German novel from one of the regular inmates. These people could have been given access to the library and would probably have valued the opportunity.

Sunday mornings were devoted to the church parade. As in the rest of the army, it was compulsory for every inmate to attend the church parade once per week. The church communities were divided into Dutch Reformed Church, Catholic, Anglican, 'Free Churches' and Pentecostal. The Free Churches refer to the

Presbyterian, Methodist, Congregational and Baptist denominations; their meeting was sometimes held in the mess. The small chapel in the Detention Barracks was never used. The chaplains for the church communities other than the Dutch Reformed Church came from the outside. They were either conscripts who had completed their theological studies before doing their military service, or Permanent Force chaplains, e.g. Chaplain (Rev.) James Michael Gray, or Chaplain (Rev.) Donald Murrell Williams of the Methodist Church.

On Sunday afternoons relatives could visit the inmates. No more than three relatives could turn up, and they were limited to one hour per month. The visits were contact visits, that is, the relatives were permitted to greet and hug, and they spoke with no glass or Perspex between them as is common in civilian prisons. Since this provided opportunities for smuggling, the inmates were subjected to a full-body search after the visit before they returned to their cells. Chairs for the visits were moved from the mess and elsewhere to the courtyard of polished black slate between the office of the Officer Commanding and Block One. The relatives were not allowed to bring presents of food or cash; they could bring only items such as cigarettes, shoe polish, clothing and books. Most inmates had short terms in the unit and were far from home, and so did not have any visitors.

Inmates were allowed to write one letter per week, of a maximum of two pages. They did not have to write letters, and many of the short-term detainees did not write at all. They were allowed to receive all letters that came.

Conversation was generally permitted, except that ordinary detainees were not allowed to speak with Jehovah's Witnesses at all, though it was difficult for the authorities to enforce this. Sometimes the inmates were told not to speak with a new entrant. On one occasion a man was brought in and placed in Block Five alone, with no other detainees in the block. He was watched over by two corporals at once when he was taken out to wash. I was told I was not allowed to speak with him at all. I never did get to discover his alleged crime.

Newspapers were forbidden and there was no radio or television. Sometimes men used to retrieve newspapers from the waste paper bins after they had been discarded by the officers. I also resorted to this practice whenever I could. On one occasion a thoughtful mother brought some issues of *National Geographic* for her son who was in detention. These magazines were widely read and exchanged. I filed a request for a subscription to *Die Transvaler*, a conservative Afrikaans newspaper, but this was turned down by Colonel Friebus. Apart from the library, which the administration allowed only me and the Jehovah's Witnesses to use, but not the regular detainees, there were no facilities for recreation. I filed a request to have a chess set, but this was rejected by Colonel Friebus. One film was shown at the Detention Barracks during my stay; I did not see it because I was in solitary confinement.

The official magazine *Paratus* stated that "Sport is also organised for the men, and every Wednesday team-work is encouraged in soccer, cricket, baseball, volleyball and trampolining."[53] This statement was false in every detail but one: the regular inmates played soccer on the parade-ground on Wednesday afternoons. Early in 1980 the Jehovah's Witnesses were permitted to play soccer on the parade ground on Wednesday and Saturday afternoons, while most of the regular detainees were kept in their cells. Later in the year the Saturday afternoon soccer for the Jehovah's Witnesses was stopped. Neither the Jehovah's Witnesses nor the regular detainees had any access to cricket, baseball, volleyball or trampolining. Furthermore, *Paratus* stated that "Reading is another avenue

---

[53] 'DB: The Facts', *Paratus* October 1979, p. 20.

that is catered for with a well-stocked library." Once again, this statement was mostly a falsehood: not once did I see any of the regular detainees use the library, and this was because the corporals never gave them the opportunity to do so.

Rape was not uncommon. During my time in the Voortrekkerhoogte Detention Barracks I met two men who told me they had been raped. One showed me the bruises on his upper leg where the inmate Tolmay had struck him to make him open his legs. One inmate was nicknamed 'Jenny' van der Merwe because it was widely known that he was homosexual. On 26 December 1979, at six in the evening after we had been locked up in our cells for the night, I heard someone passing my door, from the main door of Block One to the toilet side. It was 'Jenny.' He walked slowly, listing from one leg to the other. His left hand was placed over his anus. From his facial expression it seemed he was suffering pain in the anus. He was unaware of my watching him. He stopped and put his hands over his face, sobbing—I was able to hear the sobs distinctly—before walking on, slowly, until out of sight. The pain and sobbing may have been caused by an incident of rape.

There was a great deal of dagga (marijuana) in the Detention Barracks. It came in via *oumanne* who worked outside the Detention Barracks, via visitors who came of a Sunday afternoon, and via corporals who smoked. A certain corporal Swart, who used to smoke, was blackmailed by some inmates who caught him smuggling dagga. They made him bring them dainties and food at night. The inmates sometimes said that there was more dagga inside the Detention Barracks than there was outside.

The oumanne system

The corporals' way of running the Detention Barracks initially was to subcontract much of the work, and all of the violence that this required, to the *oumanne*. The *oumanne* were some ten percent of the 200 men who had received their sentences and were undergoing punishment. The *oumanne* acquired that status either through being in the Detention Barracks for several months, or through the recommendation of a friend who was an *ouman*, or by being visibly very strong or a karate expert, or even through adopting a certain bearing and manner that won the admiration of the inmates.

The *oumanne* did all the administrative jobs that the corporals found onerous. They unlocked the men's cells in the morning, took the men out of their blocks in the early morning to empty their pots/buckets, took them out of the blocks for a shower in the late afternoon, dealt out the cigarettes, made the men stand in squads for roll-call, locked them up in their cells at night, and so on. Above all, they applied rough discipline, hitting whomever the corporals deemed uncooperative, and administering other punishments that will be described below. In return the *oumanne* received privileges, for instance not being locked up at night, receiving smuggled dagga and cigarettes, and avoiding some of the square-bashing and physical training. Sometimes there were tasks to be done outside the Detention Barracks, such as working on renovations to Staff-Sergeant Erasmus's house nearby. These tasks were highly prized because they came with a certain degree of freedom: the *oumanne* seized these opportunities. Early in 1980 the *oumanne* in Block One had a beaten-up guitar that they used to jangle on, especially after ten o'clock at night.

Although the *oumanne* system was illegal, based on wanton violence and a corrupt non-commissioned officer corps, one can understand why it came to be. Someone who has suffered the stresses of the Detention Barracks for a year is unlikely to feel empathy for a recent arrival. The pursuit of individual self-interest by the venal corporals and the resentful *oumanne* was enough to ensure this outcome.

A key element in the punishment the Detention Barracks inflicted was the requirement to 'sak op die blok' (lower oneself on the block). This meant forming in a squad and then going down on hands and knees with a piece of blanket (a 'taxi') under each knee and in each hand. The squad worked its way round and round the cement courtyard between the cells, polishing it endlessly. These Sisyphean labours took an hour or more. The net contribution to the cleanliness of the floor was barely noticeable; this supposed polishing was an instrument of control and punishment by the corporals, and was administered by the *oumanne*. The process damaged the knees and was exhausting. Often the men were made to sing at the same time, for morale. They sang choruses popular in Pentecostal churches. Cynically, the *oumanne* manipulated religion to establish tighter control. They made the men assemble for devotions early in the morning, and had someone read the Bible and pray. Then the men were in a fit mood—that is, malleable enough—to do anything that the *oumanne* required. After some time on their hands and knees, the men were sometimes permitted to stand up and then, still in a squad, they went around in their threes, and were able to sing with gusto. With their bits of blanket beneath their feet, they slid along, further polishing the floors. It was a strange spectacle.

It was, of course, a form of punishment. Instead of forcing 50 men to 'taxi' their way over the block for an hour or more, two men with a polisher could have done the job in half that time. Charles Yeats gives a graphic account of his use of the polisher at the huge cement courtyard in the Pretoria Central Prison (Yeats, 2005:120). Hard work it was, no doubt; but it was *work*, accomplishing the objective of cleanliness quickly with a simple machine.

The Jehovah's Witnesses

As of 1980 there were some 90 Jehovah's Witnesses in the Voortrekkerhoogte Detention Barracks (and 200 regular prisoners, whose conditions have been described above.)

I learned from these young men about the cruel and demeaning treatment given to the first conscientious objectors after universal conscription was introduced in 1967. It became clear to me that the treatment Richard Steele and I were receiving was mild compared with what they had been through. We were not kept in solitary for longer than 14 days, or deprived of daylight, or beaten by corporals. In the early 1970s such punishments were common. The Jehovah's Witnesses told me of young men who were kept in complete darkness for months, punctuated by the corporals' bursting into their cells in midwinter and throwing cold water over them. One Jehovah's Witness spent the entire winter in nothing but underwear (Mureinik, 1977: 30-36). Jimmy Visser, the head Jehovah's Witness in 1980, told me that he knew of at least ten inmates who had died in the Detention Barracks, prior to the reforms that were introduced after the death of Signalman Arnold Lewin following maltreatment at the Detention Barracks in Grootfontein (Namibia) in 1978.

Thomas Budge, sent to the Detention Barracks in 1971, was sentenced repeatedly until he spent 512 days in the Detention Barracks, of which 432 days were spent in continuous solitary confinement (Budge, 2013:84). This was illegal in terms of the *Detention Barracks Regulations* (1961-1976) which specified a maximum period of solitary confinement of 14 days, after which the inmate was to be taken out for at least two days. Furthermore, according to the Regulations the periods of solitary confinement could not be imposed administratively but had to be the result of a summary court-martial by the Officer Commanding. The proceedings of the court-martial were subject to review by higher military authorites. Budge, however, did not have the benefit of supporters in civilian life who could have used the law to force the military to abide by its own rules.

Thomas Budge also lacked the active support of his church, because the Jehovah's Witness organisation considered the decision to reject military service to be an entirely personal one, thereby relieving the organisation of any responsibility. Nevertheless, if a young man went into the military he could suffer 'disassociation', or possibly 'disfellowshipping' by the church.[54] This was a serious matter because members of the church were then forbidden to speak with or associate with the disfellowshipped or disassociated person. At times even members of the person's immediate family could be forbidden from any association with the person. The Jehovah's Witness organisation could have saved its young men from untold suffering by appealing to politicians and generals, speaking to the newspapers and using the law to force the SADF to abide by its own rules, the *Detention Barracks Regulations* (1961-1976).

In 1972 the authorities yielded somewhat by providing that a Jehovah's Witness sentenced to the Detention Barracks for one year or more would not be pursued further. In 1978 the law was amended to raise the maximum period of detention to three years (Berat, 1989: 147,156). In parallel with the legal change of 1972, there were changes in the way Jehovah's Witnesses were treated in the Detention Barracks. The cruel cat-and-mouse games of the Detention Barracks staff were terminated and the Witnesses were treated with a certain degree of humanity. They wore blue overalls and worked outside the Detention Barracks in gardens, tending fruit trees, pulling out weeds, growing vegetables, doing maintenance jobs like cleaning up, moving earth, mowing

---

[54] Watch Tower Bible and Tract Society of New York (1977-1980).

lawns, mending roads, cutting fire breaks in forests, and putting up game fences in the Kruger National Park. Sometimes they were taken out into the veld in work groups on army property. They were not involved in any military exercises or parades. They were left to manage their own affairs in Block Four, with an elected leader communicating on their behalf with the Detention Barracks authorities. They took their meals in Block Four. They had visits, as did the regular prisoners, on Sunday afternoons. On Wednesday afternoons the regular inmates were relieved of marching and were allowed to stay in their cells, while the Witnesses used the parade ground for a soccer game; I observed this during my stay, and it is confirmed by a newspaper report from September 1980.[55] They were also allowed to play soccer on Saturday afternoons, but in about March of that year the Saturday soccer stopped. The Jehovah's Witnesses were allowed a set of weights for physical training, but in about March 1980 this privilege, too, was withdrawn. Several of the Jehovah's Witnesses complained bitterly to me about this.

There were four further privileges enjoyed by the Jehovah's Witnesses that were not granted to the regular detainees: weekend passes, passes for marriage, beds and personal items. Mureinik reported, on the basis of interviews with Jehovah's Witnesses who had been detained, that weekend passes were granted with increasing frequency in accordance with seniority. On occasion, as of 1979, they were given passes to get married, according to Colonel du Plessis, SSO Personnel, Northern Transvaal Command, and supervisor of the Detention Barracks.[56] While none of the regular detainees had beds, the

---

[55] 'Detained for other ideas,' *Rand Daily Mail*, 18 September 1980. Wits, Rob. Coll., A2558-16.

[56] 'DB: The facts.' *Paratus* October 1979, p. 18-21.

Jehovah's Witnesses in the Voortrekkerhoogte Detention Barracks did. They were permitted some personal items such as a photograph of their family.

Other than these aspects, the Jehovah's Witnesses were subject to the same privations as were the regular military detainees. They had cold water to wash, even during winter, and visits only once per month. Many had relatives far away, such as Cape Town, and hardly ever received visits. They could write only one letter per week. The food was sometimes grossly inadequate. They were not allowed games such as chess sets, and indeed there were no facilities for recreation except for the use of the parade ground on Wednesdays for soccer. They were not allowed newspapers or magazines of any kind. They were not accorded the privileges awarded to long-term prisoners in civilian prisons. For instance, the civilian prisons used to grant a modest allowance per month for groceries and other small items, as a reward for good behaviour by long-term prisoners, but the Detention Barracks had no such arrangement.

The Jehovah's Witnesses understood that I was a conscientious objector and many were very supportive of me. They used to help me by, for instance, smuggling out letters. One of them helped me with German pronunciation.

They were keen to proselytise. They tried continually to reason with me and persuade me to their doctrinal positions. Their technique was to get started on a point of doctrine on which they knew I would disagree. Then they would selectively quote Biblical verses off by heart in support of their particular interpretation, in the hope of emotional engagement. They were surprised to discover that I knew my Bible as well as they did, and could quote the Greek words involved. After a time both I and they realised that these discussions were fruitless and we laid off.

I thought it wrong that the Jehovah's Witnesses should be persecuted for their religious beliefs by being put in the Detention Barracks, the conditions of which were worse in many respects than those in civilian prisons. They were treated more harshly than were anti-social individuals who committed rape and other violent crimes and who did not know how to live in society. I once brought up this point when arguing with Staff-Sergeant Erasmus and Lieutenant von Brandis. I said, "You say the SADF is guarding our freedom of religion against the communists. What do you think about the Christadelphians and the Jehovah's Witnesses? Do you think they experience freedom of religion?" They were indignant at being hoist by their own petard. The Jehovah's Witnesses were being persecuted for their faith, and should have been given a non-military alternative. It is one thing to punish an AWOL conscript with 30 days' detention with these privations. It is quite another to subject a conscientious objector, Jehovah's Witness or other, to the same privations for three years.

In light of the inhumane treatment they received in the early 1970s, and the lack of support from the Jehovah's Witness organisation, the persistent refusal by hundreds[57] of young Jehovah's Witnesses to do military service was all the more heroic. Jan van Wyk, Anton Eberhard, Richard Steele and I were the proverbial dwarves standing on the shoulders of giants. By the time the SADF started its pursuit of us, conditions in the Detention Barracks had already changed for the better as the SADF had come to accept the reality of conscientious objection. The military had reason to fear bad publicity and the civil courts should the *Detention Barracks Regulations* (1961-1976) be

---

[57] To give a rough order of magnitude to the numbers: Smail (1980) estimates the number of Jehovah's Witnesses detained from 1975 to 1979 at 441 (p. 14).

infringed, and were concerned about the likely reaction of the 'English-speaking' churches should their members be detained.

My welcome

I was welcomed by one Evered Poole, a Christadelphian—a member of a 'peace church' that requires its members to be pacifists, as does the Jehovah's Witness community. Evered was the only Christadelphian in the Detention Barracks at the time. He said he was the grandson of Major-General William Henry Evered Poole, a senior SADF officer in the Second World War. Evered sported blue overalls, showing that he had been recognised as a conscientious objector, and worked as a clerk in the offices at the Detention Barracks. He felt he could reconcile doing such work with his pacifism, whereas the Jehovah's Witnesses were willing to work only outside the Detention Barracks in tasks that were not essential to the functioning of the military. Evered had read about me in the newspapers, and knew that I was a conscientious objector. He took me under his wing and persuaded the corporals to give me blue overalls. He showed me to cell number 65 in Block One, which was next to his. He also spoke to the *oumanne* of the unit and explained that I was a conscientious objector like himself.

During December 1979 I was still under arrest because my sentence had not been confirmed in the standard review process. This review was done rather late in my case, and the review reduced the sentence from 18 months to twelve, for reasons I have not been able to divine. I was told about this by my family only on 1 January 1980, and by the officers on 4 January 1980. After that I was an inmate undergoing punishment.

While under arrest the men were not supposed to do any work, although they were required to march and do physical training. Nevertheless the officers breached the regulations and made the arrested men work by way of cleaning and maintenance all over the barracks. This was illegal; if one of the men had been injured while working, the officers could have been held liable.

While I was still under arrest I was left in my cell most of the day. I read a good deal. Unfortunately all my books—about 30—were taken away by Staff-Sergeant Erasmus and Brigadier Pretorius, to be checked by officers at the army headquarters in Pretoria. So I had to borrow. I managed to get a history book and I borrowed a Bible commentary from Evered Poole. All my books were returned some weeks later but I had to leave them in storage in a shed next to the parade ground, and keep a maximum of three of them with me at once. The Major mentioned that the Commandant who checked my books complimented me on my reading material!

I fell to thinking what I would do if I were required by the officers to take off my blue overalls and directed to undergo military training and to march. I decided to be an objector straight out, just as the Christadelphians and the Jehovah's Witnesses did, as that would be the only consistent position to adopt.

I was given another welcome in Voortrekkerhoogte—from the Chaplain-General ds. Jakobus A. van Zyl who wrote a Christmas message in the December 1979 (vol. 30, no. 12, p. 3) issue of *Paratus*, the SADF magazine. Among other things he declared,

In these times, no conscientious objector or pacifist can kneel at the crib of Bethlehem with a clear conscience. How can he enjoy Christian freedom without fighting for it; how can he follow Christ without defending Him and His message?[58]

---

[58] See Christian Citizenship Department of the Methodist Church of Southern Africa, 1980. *Church and conscience: a collection of church and*

Ridiculous and blasphemous though this statement was, its ultimate impact for the movement of conscientious objection was likely positive because van Zyl gave the notions of conscientious objection and pacifism some free publicity. *Swak, Piketberg!* It was clear that our little movement was causing much discomfiture for the military brass.

I was cautiously optimistic as of the end of 1979. I wrote a letter to friends telling them about the daily regimen while I was still under arrest in Block One, and noting that I had blue overalls and was expecting after a time to be put to work as a clerk.

Violence

On the night of 24 December 1979, I was woken at two in the morning by the sound of yelling, crying, shouting and hitting. I jumped up and looked through the judas in my door to see three men being chased around by the *oumanne*. They were made to run the length of the cellblock, with weights, and were hit repeatedly and mercilessly. This continued for about an hour. I was shocked at seeing this terrible spectacle of violence. There was nothing I could do about it as I was locked up in my cell.

I called to one of the corporals, saying, "Look there, can't you see what's going on right there? Can't you see Tolmay hitting that man?" The corporal said he could not see anything. The corporals were in league with the *oumanne* who conveniently did their dirty work.

I discovered later that these men had tried to escape. They had been caught by the corporals and had been handed over to the *oumanne* for jungle justice. They were deprived of their overalls and locked up in their cells the whole day in solitary confinement, without any legal process. Informal solitary confinement without clothes was a common punishment in the Detention Barracks. Frequently the *oumanne* went into the cells, day after day, and beat the men up. I saw the *ouman* Patrick Els opening the cell door, going in and yelling at the man, telling him how bad he was, and delivering many *warm klappe* ('warm hits') in the face. A *warm klap* was administered with the open flat of the hand, striking the cheek and the neck, making a painful sting. It left no scars or bruises and the red colour subsided after five minutes. It was an effective way of reducing the victim to tears and diminishing his human worth.

I was so repulsed by what I had seen that evening and in the subsequent days that I secretly wrote several reports.[59] I gave one to Rev. James Gray, who was a Permanent Force chaplain for the Free Churches and an old friend of mine from the Students' Christian Association at the University of Cape Town. He spoke to the Officer Commanding, Lieutenant von Brandis, who was acting for the Major who was away due to illness. Von Brandis apparently indicated to James that there was not much that he could do about it. (On the contrary, by tolerating the violence of the *oumanne* system, Lt. von Brandis was violating the *Detention Barracks Regulations* (1961-1976) in four respects: he was allowing prisoners of different categories to occupy the same cellblock; he was not taking measures to "avoid harsh treatment of inmates"; he was allowing inmates (namely *oumanne*) to take a disciplinary role; and he was permitting physical punishment.)

It seemed that my protests through the official channels were not working, so I smuggled some reports out to various relatives and friends. One report of 24 December 1979, 'Certain events

---

[59] See three of these reproduced in Appendices A, C and D.

of evening of 24-12-1979 at the Detention Barracks, Voortrekkerhoogte, by Peter Moll' was transcribed and typed by my sister Jen. I smuggled the same manuscript to Adi Paterson in Cape Town, who had it meticulously transcribed by Dr. Margaret Nash and distributed by her and Adi. On putting the jigsaw puzzle together forty-two years later, it seems that Margaret and Adi's version of the report was picked up by some police or military intelligence agent either in the Black Sash or in the South African Council of Churches, and thence turned over to the SADF. I also smuggled out two further reports and made all three manuscripts available to Chaplain James Gray.[60] I heard that at least one report reached the desk of the Chaplain-General. It is likely that James's channels, possibly via the Chaplain-General, were eventually responsible for their reaching the generals' attention.

Eventually change came. During the period March to May, the officers charged the *oumanne* who were engaging in violence. Some *oumanne* were put in solitary confinement and others were discharged from the Detention Barracks and sent to civilian prisons or returned to their army units. After that there was less violence.

However, the violence continued until the time I left. More of it was done by the corporals because the *oumanne* were wary since their fingers had been burnt. Nevertheless, many *oumanne* continued their violence anyway. To me, violence seems to be endemic in that kind of system. As long as no one knows his rights and has no legal recourse, violence is the corporals' way of saving themselves trouble, and the *oumanne* will be willing to work in tandem.

---

[60] The three reports about violence are transcribed and reproduced in Appendices A, C and D in this volume.

Getting the reports out was easy. All I had to do was approach one of the men who was about to leave the Detention Barracks. As long as I was able to get stamps stuck into the books that visitors brought for me I was able to post letters. After April there was more monitoring and I smuggled very little for fear of my inmate friends being caught at the gate and being searched.

Early on I met Staff-Sergeant Erasmus, a hard and vindictive man. In addition to giving orders downwards, he had the remarkable ability to give orders upwards, to the Sergeant-Major and the Officer Commanding. The latter consistently followed Erasmus's recommendations. Erasmus had several advantages: he was diligent, he lived close to the Detention Barracks, he often spent time in the barracks after hours, and he had an overpowering personality. He was known for his loud yelling. He was nicknamed 'Volume Control' because his staff-sergeant's insignia had three stripes with a castle in between. We sniggered sometimes when he barked drill commands. He yelled so loudly that his voice would leap into falsetto as he shouted "Halt!" or "Voorwaarts mars!" (forward march), much to our amusement.

Solitary confinement

On 4 January 1980, Brigadier C.J. 'Neels' Pretorius (Director of Military Law, under whose jurisdiction the Detention Barracks fell) came to the Detention Barracks to see me. I surmise he wanted to check that appropriately harsh 'punishment' (his word) was being meted out. He had a hard personality, not unlike Staff-Sergeant Erasmus's, and was an intellectual of sorts: he boasted to my mother that he wrote the *Detention Barracks Regulations*, a copy of which I had in my cell. My father, after speaking with him in Pretoria, wrote that he was "a most unpleasant and difficult man."

On striding into the Detention Barracks, the Brigadier was shocked and angry to see me in blue overalls. Why, he yelled in a fury, had I been given blue overalls, by whose authority? He spoke to Lieutenant von Brandis, who told me to take the blue overalls off and don brown military overalls. I refused. Staff-Sergeant Erasmus said he would try to sort the matter out. He got only as far as persuading me to take off the blue overalls. I remained in my elegant light blue underpants, with no other clothes, and walked around the barracks like that for four weeks.

I had suspected that trouble was brewing. On 8 January I was charged for not wearing the brown uniform and was tried by summary court-martial while standing in my underpants, in the office of the Officer Commanding, Lieutenant von Brandis. In my defence I argued that I was being punished twice for the same thing. I had been imprisoned in the Detention Barracks for being a conscientious objector, and now they were intent on putting me in solitary confinement for being a conscientious objector. Von Brandis prudently adjourned the case and sought the opinion of Brigadier Pretorius. On reconvening, von Brandis said that I had been sentenced to the Detention Barracks for having failed to attend a camp, but I was now being sentenced to solitary confinement for refusing to obey an order within the barracks; and those were two different offences. The sentence was ten days' solitary confinement.

This sentence of solitary confinement was mild compared with what the military might have done had I not actively sought publicity over the period 1978-1979, and had there not been hundreds of supporters all over the world who wrote letters of protest to Prime Minister P.W. Botha, and letters of support to me. The publicity and the support were my protection. The corporals could easily have hinted to the *oumanne* that they needed to "get me right", leaving them to dole out the same violent treatment as was meted out to the inmates who had attempted to escape on Christmas Eve, or the third degree abuse in the Grootfontein Detention Barracks that ended the life of Signalman Arnold Lewin.

The next day I was locked up in Block Five. Inmates in solitary were supposed to be taken out of the cell twice per day, for half an hour each time, to do exercise, wash, shave and wash their clothes. Quite often the corporals forgot, especially during the first period of solitary confinement. They were unfamiliar with this form of punishment. At the beginning I took this loss of my precious half hour of sun in my stride. Over the second weekend I was not taken out from Friday until Monday morning. My chamber pot filled up completely, whereupon I used the 'blink bak' until it also filled up. I had to ask the corporal to help me lug the disgusting stuff out.

Once the corporals forgot to bring us food of a Friday lunchtime. We just went without. There was another man in the block at the time, although he was not in solitary confinement. At other times the corporals remembered about us only once the food had nearly run out, and so we ended up with very little, or else we had to shout to attract their attention. Again, I did not find myself becoming very angry at that time. It was later on that the anger and resentment built up.

Evered Poole kindly looked after me. He smuggled in some extracts from Thomas O. Lambdin's *Introduction to Biblical Hebrew* (London: Darton, 1973). I had given him this book and asked him to cut out some chapters with a blade, the easier to slip them under the door. I studied Chapters 20 to 32 in this way, for the Hebrew I course with the University of South Africa. We did likewise with a hundred pages severed from Calvin's *Institutes*. That made the days pass faster. I had a Bible, *Nestle's Interlinear Greek-English New Testament*. Luckily the authorities did not notice the mysterious Greek script, for then they would have rushed it to the censors. I smuggled in my sister

Jen's copy of the novel *Boetjer Basch* by Theodor Storm, so small it was easy to hide between the blankets. I read the Gospels of Matthew, Mark, Luke and John very carefully, trying to figure out which was the first written and which passages had been culled from which, and what was the meaning of Christ's death, etc. The officers of the Detention Barracks were not the type who read books and did not guess how important the act of reading was to me. They did not bother to read the *Detention Barracks Regulations* which clearly state that no reading or writing materials were allowed to an inmate in solitary confinement. Hence they made surprisingly little effort to take reading materials away; during this first period of solitary there was no search at all.

The first period of solitary ended on 20 January 1980. I was brought before Major A.L. Venter, who by that time had returned after a period of ill health. He told me that since I was a conscientious objector I could use blue overalls, but that I needed to do productive work and so I was to work in the garden within the barracks. I was happy to comply, so I and two other inmates planted carrots, bell peppers, pumpkins and lettuces for a halcyon three weeks.

The other two men were also objectors of a kind. Johannes B. Strydom had neglected to attend one of his camps and was sentenced to three months' detention. He told me he was a conscientious objector but was not able to articulate a rationale for his position. After one period of solitary confinement he changed his mind and agreed to do his camps. His sentence was suspended and he returned home. Chris Boshoff (see below) told me, with a laugh, that Strydom had confessed to him that actually he was not a conscientious objector and just did not care to do his camps, but that he had now changed his mind.

Chris Boshoff, the other man who worked with me in the garden, was on the political far right. A sincere Christian, he read his Bible, prayed and was forever singing songs, much to the despair of the other denizens of Block Five. He was a member of a small church whose name I did not recognise, and refused to eat in the company of others. He told me he stood to the right of the Herstigte Nasionale Party.

Chris based his belief on the story of the Tower of Babel in Genesis 11. At that time there was but one language. The people vowed to build a tower that would reach to heaven, and they would make a name for themselves. But realising that as long as they all had the same language they would be unstoppable, God confused their languages and scattered them all over the earth. This proved, Chris said, that whites and blacks, and all other races, were to be entirely separate and were not to mix at all, that whites were not to rule over blacks, and likewise blacks were not to rule over whites. Blacks were the sons of Ham, he said, and bear the curse pronounced by Noah over his son Ham and grandson Canaan, that they would be "servants of servants" (Genesis 9:25). Chris supported Verwoerdian ideas of separate development as the will of God. President P.W. Botha was disobeying the divine will by his 'Twelve Point Plan' which might enable Coloureds and Indians to rule over whites. Therefore he refused two call-ups (for camps) to the Air Force Gymnasium at Valhalla (Centurion, Pretoria). He was sentenced on 17 January 1980 to 18 months' detention, of which nine months were suspended for three years.

Chris was strong-minded. A farmer,[61] married with a child, he was entirely isolated in his stand: no support group, no publicity, and no visitors. Once in the Detention Barracks, he refused to march or wear the brown overalls, was charged and

---

[61] See my letter to friends, 3 February 1980. Wits, Rob. Coll., A2558-9.13.

found guilty on both counts, and was sentenced to fourteen days of solitary confinement.

I looked after Chris when he was in solitary, by making sure he got his food, and reminding the corporals to take him out, and he reciprocated. He had passed matric and had been to an agricultural college. He spoke English most of the time, although sometimes we chatted in Afrikaans in which I am fluent. He was one of just two men I had met in the Detention Barracks (apart from the Jehovah's Witnesses) who had completed matriculation. Nearly all the men had between standard four and standard seven, very few standard eight. (In South Africa, standard four meant six years' schooling, standard seven meant nine years' schooling, and matric meant twelve years' schooling.)

Chris and I discussed politics incessantly. I discovered that he had no conception of political or economic reality. He had philosophical notions about whites being separate from blacks, and whites being the chosen nation, but had never related these to political happenings in South Africa. For instance, he was unaware that under the Verwoerdian scheme of separate development only 13 percent of the land area would be given to blacks. He admitted that that would be unfair, but would not believe me when I told him that that indeed was the case. He had no notion of the poverty of black people. He had no idea that the system favoured whites at the expense of blacks. He lived in a world of his own.

He said that I was a 'communist' or at least was helping 'the communists.' To him a communist is someone who rapes, plunders and murders, and who tries to steal the minerals of South Africa to further Soviet imperialism. As with many white South Africans, that was as far as his understanding of communism went.

After Chris had completed three periods of solitary confinement, he was persuaded by the chaplain of the Detention Barracks, dominee Dawid Venter, to throw in the towel. Chris accepted then that the government's 'Twelve Point Plan' had become *de facto*. It was now inevitable that coloured and Indian people would be drawn into the white political scheme in some way, and that 'homelands' would be allocated to the black tribes where they would have self-rule. Chris explained that there was no longer any point in resisting, and so he might as well cease to be a conscientious objector and do his camps. He added a biblical argument for his temporary objection to bearing arms, citing Ezekiel chapter 4 where the prophet lies on his left side for 390 days (viz. not permanently), taking upon himself the iniquity of the house of Israel, and prophesying against Jerusalem. After this sign to Israel the prophet arises and proceeds to other demonstrations of God's forthcoming judgment against Jerusalem. Chris signed a statement that he was henceforward willing to do his camps. On 20 June 1980 the remainder of his sentence of nine months' detention was suspended and he went home.

Meanwhile support for me was building up inside and outside the country. Rev. Rob Robertson was one of the leading organisers. He published an appeal for support in *Non-Violence News* (February 1980).[62] The Committee on South African War Resistance (COSAWR) arranged pickets around Trafalgar House, and lobbied church groups and provided information to organisations such as Amnesty International. The latter declared me to be a prisoner of conscience and Amnesty groups in Britain started writing to me and to the military authorities. COSAWR also approached the Labour Members of Parliament Frank

---

[62] *Non-Violence News*: See Wits, Rob. Coll., A2558-1, Correspondence Series 1.

Allaun and Tony Benn,[63] both of whom wrote to me indicating their support and noting that they had written to the Prime Minister requesting my immediate release (Collins, 1995:72-73).

Most of the chaplains were of tremendous help. At first Rev. James Gray visited me fairly regularly, even when I was in solitary confinement. I always used to rejoice when the Tuesday morning chaplain's period arrived, because that would be my time, after the period was over, to have some intellectual conversation with the chaplain. During my first period of solitary confinement he came to see me. We met in a meeting room near the main entrance. He tried to persuade me to wear the overalls rather than hold out for conscientious objector status. I argued back strongly, surprised that he would adopt the army's line. After I had finished, he told me he accepted my position, and indicated that he had been asked by the Officer Commanding of the Detention Barracks, Lieutenant von Brandis, to persuade me for my own good. He did not raise the matter again. Once, during my fourth solitary period or so, James brought me a copy of that day's newspaper which contained an article about me. (Seeing a newspaper was against the rules of the barracks.)

After I had had a few periods of solitary, things became 'hot' for James. He was once asked, by his head chaplain, why it was impossible for him to 'minister' to me without 'supporting' me. He also came under suspicion because the officers thought he was helping me. Eventually he decided that things were getting so hot he had better seek another chaplain as a replacement.

---

[63] Benn's letter is reproduced in the section of original documents.

Solitary again

Amid all the bullying, there is one cherished memory that I still chuckle about forty years later. First a word about the military rank system. The inmates were at the lowest rank, Rifleman or Private. Next up was Lance-Corporal, then Corporal, Sergeant, Staff-Sergeant, Sergeant-Major, then the commissioned officers: Second Lieutenant, Lieutenant, Captain, Major, Commandant, Colonel, Brigadier, Major-General, Lieutenant-General, and finally General. A regular troop rarely encountered a Commandant, who was ten ranks his senior.

Once a Commandant to whom the Major reported came to visit. I happened to be standing outside the Major's office, as usual with my feet apart and my hands in front—a deliberately non-military but respectful way of standing. I looked the Commandant in the eye as he passed. A stride later, noticing that I had neither stood to attention nor saluted, he swung round, and said, "You're Moll, huh? And you don't salute, do you?" Did he think I would be terrified into compliance? I replied, "No, Commandant." He glared, speechless, swung around and stomped off. How are the mighty fallen! Despised inmate though I was, the Commandant was powerless.

Major Venter had not realised that he did not have authorisation from Brigadier Pretorius to give me blue overalls. Pretorius came to visit a second time in early February and discovered that I was once again wearing blue overalls, and was very angry. He gave immediate instructions that I was to take them off and to put on the brown ones and, as he bellowed at me, undergo the same 'punishment' as the other inmates. That was an interesting slip of the tongue, because in the *Detention Barracks Regulations* the inmates were not supposed to be punished. They were to be rehabilitated and to be made into 'better soldiers and citizens.' The word punishment does not appear in the Regulations. But Brigadier Pretorius, who claimed he wrote the Regulations, used the word. Pretorius added, "And I command the Major to use such force as is necessary to make you wear the brown overalls."

Again I refused to wear the military overalls. The Major did not try to use physical force to get me to don the brown overalls. This time, fortunately, I was not left in my underpants but was allowed to wear some oversize tan shorts that did not button properly at the waist, and an ancient and torn white shirt. The outfit looked ridiculous but it was not as dehumanising as was going about in my underpants. I was sentenced to another fourteen days' solitary on 11 February 1980. My father phoned the Detention Barracks to complain about the 'sword of Damocles' over my head about my apparel. He insisted that the officers be 'fair' and permit me to wear normal clothes.

I smuggled in several books in my second period of solitary, including Paul Tillich's *Systematic Theology Vol. 2*, the *Pelican History of the Church*, Alan Paton's *A South African Tragedy: The Life and Times of Jan Hofmeyr* and some German books. At one stage the Lieutenant Spriestersbach burst into my cell and caught me writing something on toilet paper. He took it. He went away to find out what was permissible and discovered that inmates in solitary were allowed only a Bible and no other reading or writing material. He searched all over my cell and found nothing, except for a second Bible. I had two Bibles at the time, an Afrikaans Bible owned by a friend of mine who was also in that block, and my Greek Interlinear New Testament. He took away the latter, leaving the Afrikaans Bible. A few days later that friend was transferred to Bloemfontein and took his Bible with him. So for a few days I had no Bible at all. I still had the Tillich and the Pelican History, carefully stashed among some clothing. The Lieutenant did not search that packet. That was fortunate, because had he found my books, he might well have ordered meticulous daily searches. Or did he find the books, but decide to turn a blind eye?

After Chaplain James Gray had moved on, Rev. David Hart, a conscript chaplain, from the Church of the Province, visited regularly. He came even when I was in solitary. On one occasion he arranged for me to have a breaking of bread service—the only one I had the entire year. He even went to the length of borrowing books from the University of South Africa and bringing them to me, which entailed a long trip out to the UNISA campus.

I was fortunate enough to enjoy a visit by Grace Townshend, whom I knew from the Students' Christian Association at the University of Cape Town where she did her B.Sc. She was then living in Lynnwood, Pretoria.

During this time Evered Poole, the Christadelphian conscientious objector, left the Detention Barracks. I was surprised as he had completed only 18 months of his 36-month sentence. I was not able to find any further news of him.

Brigadier Pretorius visited a third time in late January to angrily reprimand Lieutenant von Brandis for having permitted me, without the Brigadier's permission, to speak over the phone to my lawyer, Mr. John Brand in Johannesburg. Pretorius instructed him that thenceforward I was never to be allowed to speak to a lawyer. (I later learned that this order was illegal because the *Detention Barracks Regulations* (1961-1976) specify in Chapter III, 31. (1) that "an inmate who is a party to or a witness in any legal proceedings, shall be afforded every reasonable opportunity and facility of consulting with counsel...") I had already had a visit from the lawyer Terence P. Rex (of Buchanans Incorporated Attorneys) without Pretorius' knowledge.

The lawyers sought a further review of my sentencing on April 30, 1980, before the Review Council at the office of the

Chief Magistrate of Pretoria, Mr. M.J. Prins. The review was held in camera. Lieutenant Mills was again the prosecutor. Mr. Terence Rex defended, assisted by Rev. Rob Robertson. Mr. Rex argued that the Baptist Church has 'dual tenets' and recognises that certain of their members could not wage war. Accordingly I belonged to a religious denomination by the tenets whereof *I* may not participate in war. The Council demurred and reconfirmed the sentence of twelve months.[64] The possibility of recourse to the Supreme Court was considered (and the South African Council of Churches offered a substantial sum to facilitate this) but was eventually dropped.

Richard Steele arrives

On 25 February 1980 Richard Steele, my cousin, arrived at the barracks. He was a universal pacifist on the grounds that he did not wish to participate in any form of violence, whether physical, psychological or structural, all being antithetical to the Christ-like way of love and healing. He clarified that "central to my being a peacemaker is the pursuit of justice. I view the SADF as being a major pillar of a fundamentally unjust political, social and economic system: by co-operating with the military I would be representing and perpetuating those injustices and I am unwilling to do so."[65] Thus he was a conscientious objector to *all wars* and to the *war waged by the SADF.* He was willing to do alternative non-military service. He refused to do his initial military training of 24 months which was to commence in January 1980. He was sentenced on 25 February 1980 to 18 months' detention, of which six months were suspended for

---

[64] Rev. Rob Robertson's summary of the proceedings, dated 30 April 1980, is at Wits, Rob. Coll., A2558-9.13.

[65] Richard Steele, 'Grounds for conscientious objection.' Kempton Park: typewritten manuscript, 23 February 1980. 1 page. Wits, Rob. Coll., A2558-9.20.

three years. On arrival at Voortrekkerhoogte he was given military overalls, which he refused to wear. He nevertheless had to change out of his civilian clothes. Instead he wore shorts and a T-shirt he had brought with him.

After my release from solitary after 14 days, I was able to see Richard. It was a tremendous encouragement having him there. We talked a great deal, all against orders which were to maintain silence. We discussed everything about conscientious objection. He told me recent news about his adventures in Namibia in December 1979. He and Professor Paul Hare (Sociology, University of Cape Town, a US citizen) had gone up there in a Landrover converted into an ambulance, in the hope of starting an ambulance unit in Rundu. They had been arrested at the entrance to the military police control post into the security area, and had been escorted back to Windhoek by the security police.

We were able to strengthen each other in our resolve neither to wear the brown overalls nor to obey military commands. I had earlier written a long letter explaining why I refused military commands, and smuggled it out to him. In turn he made photocopies and distributed it to people familiar with the issue all over the country. This contributed to his determination to refuse to wear the overalls. The key principle I outlined followed the rationale given to me by the Jehovah's Witnesses: no identification with the South African military structures. I wrote, "I will not receive a salary from the military, work for the military, morally support the military or be perceived to be in support of the military."[66]

On 1 March 1980 we were both put into solitary confinement in Block Five, for ten days. This was my third period and Richard's first. We preached sermons to each other. I did one

---

[66] 'News: Moll in solitary,' University of Natal, Durban student newspaper, March 1980.

from the Gospels, he one from the Psalms. I was reminded of the famous passage where Paul and Silas were imprisoned in an inner dungeon in Philippi (today Philippoi in Greece), their feet clamped in stocks. At midnight they sang hymns and the other prisoners listened (Acts 16:16-34). My untrained voice would not have done justice to vigorous Baptist hymnody, so we stuck with preaching. Later Chris Boshoff joined us in solitary. His voice was no better than ours, but he sang enthusiastically for hours at a time, much to our dismay.

By this time my mother had sent some civilian clothes for me to wear: long trousers, shirts, jerseys and pyjamas. She posted these directly to the Detention Barracks.

I read the novel *Voss*. I do not recall having read a novel that impressed me so much. The Prussian explorer, the creation of the writer Patrick White, crosses the Australian desert amid great privations with a team of six men in 1845, only to be killed by aborigines. Voss, a "crag of a man," is humiliated by a seemingly endless flood that forces the party to take refuge in a cave. Starvation threatens. Voss gathers watercress to feed one of his men who is ill. He learns compassion. He continues, in his imagination, a fleeting relationship with a young woman whom he met before his departure. This tale of redemption amid tragedy was especially meaningful to me because I was under immense psychological pressure. I felt much stronger after reading it.

On the first day of solitary, Richard discovered a large clot of blood, ten centimetres in diameter, on the floor in his cell. It had come from an attempted suicide of some weeks previously, when I was in my second period of solitary. An inmate had feigned suicide in order to get to the hospital, whence it was easier to escape. I knew it was a feint because he made the arrangement with another inmate of Block Five by speaking into the judas, thus exposing the entire deal both to the other inmate and to me. The deal was that the other inmate would yell to the corporals upon hearing the signal that he had slashed his wrists. The ruse was successful and he managed to get to the hospital. The blood clot had not been properly cleared up. Furthermore, the walls were very dirty indeed, and the window sill was thick with dirt and dust.

Richard submitted a written complaint about the filth in the cell, and we jointly complained about the poor airing of the solitary confinement cells. Not much air could pass through, and the corporals often forgot to take us out for our breaks, and the chamber pots stank to high heaven. It was awful for people coming to my door bringing me food, because they could smell it, and sometimes drew back in shock after opening the door. I was less bothered, luckily, because my own perception of smell is limited. Richard's complaint did not fall on deaf ears. By the next time we were placed in solitary, the cells had been cleaned and painted yellow, and the blood stain had vanished.

Our friends back in civilian life were doing their best. A statement came out from 36 'Concerned Christians', protesting the repeated periods of solitary confinement, on the grounds that Richard and I were already serving long sentences for conscientious objection. Thus we were being punished repeatedly for the same thing.[67]

---

[67] 36 'Concerned Christians': See 'Protest over solitary confinement,' *Cape Times,* 11 March 1980. The signatories were Adi Paterson, Cathy Paterson, Dr. John de Gruchy, Rev. Roy Barker, Rev. Rod Botsis, Rev. Howard Eybers, Rev. John Dixon, Rev. Michael Rowe, Rev. Norman Mayall, Rev. David Profit, Rev. Jim Cochrane, Dr. Margaret Nash, Professor Francis Wilson, Professor Paul Hare, Tony Saddington, Di Scott-Saddington, Rev. Douglas Bax, Sheila Brokenshaw, Rev. Renate Cochrane, Sandy Staal, Stephen de Gruchy, Mike de Klerk, Liz Fish, Caroline Long, Rommel Roberts, Celeste Santos, J.G. Foxcroft, E.K. Mitchell, M.G. Dale, Anne Palm, D. Thornton, D.E. Bull, Virginia Zweigenthal, Hilary Rosental, Sylvia Collier and Brigid-Rose Tiernan.

When Richard and I came out of that period of solitary, Staff-Sergeant Erasmus had just arrived back from a month's holiday in Cape Town. He was full of zeal for the Holy Grail of getting us to don the brown overalls. With silly cat-and-mouse tactics he cajoled, yelled, reasoned, bickered and mocked us. We answered politely, holding our hands in front, rather than at the back, which could be confused with the military 'at ease,' or at our sides, which could be confused with the military 'attention.' We refused to be part of a squad or to march. Erasmus tried to make fools of us in front of the other men by getting us to stand in a row in front of each other (myself, Richard, and Chris) as though we were to go to the toilet. Then he said, "Look, you're standing in a row to go to the toilet. Why not just stand in the same row next to the squad? You won't be part of the squad, you'll just be next to the squad." In our opinion, we would actually be part of it. He knew that, we knew that, and everyone else did too. His tactic failed.

A few of the corporals were fairly sympathetic to Richard and me. For instance, one of the staff members of the Detention Barracks, probably a corporal, took it upon himself to call my sister Jen regularly to confirm the dates of her forthcoming visits. Corporal Gebhardt disagreed with my ideas, but had a certain respect for them, and definitely showed respect for us as persons. Corporal Gebhardt was kind to us when we were in solitary confinement. He sometimes allowed us to eat our meals outside our cells so that we could converse, which was against the regulations. We had many interesting conversations. He told me about the news that he had read in the papers. Sometimes he would even read the news specially so that he could tell Richard and me about what had been going on. Once he told us that there had been a news report about us on Capital Radio.

Most of the corporals, however, were cold and offish. Some of them were frankly opposed to me. Some were indifferent and did not really care either way. Some were irritated by me because I did not do what the other inmates were required to do. They thought I considered myself to be something different and special. They repeatedly asked, "Is jy dan beter as die ander ouens, dat jy nie 'n overall kan dra nie?" (Are you better than the other guys, so you can't wear the overalls?)

Similarly, the response from the more senior officers was mixed. One Staff-Sergeant Marais was sympathetic towards me. He recognised that I was a conscientious objector and treated me with the same kind of respect that he did the Jehovah's Witnesses, while not agreeing with me. He and I had been to the same school, Selborne College in East London. Some of the officers were friendly. A Staff-Sergeant Engelbrecht, who had been one of the officers at the Detention Barracks at Wynberg, and was later moved to Pretoria, was very decent to me. He told me that he felt sorry for the fact that I was in solitary confinement, and always made sure I got my food and was taken out regularly. He was a grand gentleman and was critical of the army for its disorganisation. He told us that he comforted himself with the prospect that he had 'min dae' (few days left) in the army. Most of the other officers preferred to ignore me and not to talk to me at all.

I received a visit in March from the Assistant Chaplain-General of the Air Force Colonel (Rev.) Andrew van den Aardweg. We met in a meeting room near the main entrance. He started by saying, in earnest tones and grave, that he was "very, very sorry" that I was in the Detention Barracks. I never did plumb the depths of this sentence. Was he sorry that I had persisted in considering the SADF's wars unjust? Or was he sorry that the SADF had pursued me? He wanted to be sure that my Bible had been restored to me, because news had reached him about how for some days in February my Bible had been taken away. I thanked him for expressing his sympathy and voicing his concern. As at our first encounter in 1977, he did not mention anything about my right as a Baptist to freedom of conscience, that is, the right to interpret the Bible and arrive at ethical and conscientious conclusions without the mediation of church or state authorities.

The Chaplain-General, Major-General ds. Jakcbus A. van Zyl, published his arguments about conscientious objection in *Paratus* in March 1980. He argued that there is only one possible Christian view of the matter by asking rhetorically, "Is the Word of God ambiguous, in other words does it lead to conscientious objection for one person, while for another it is a call to responsibility—a God-given assignment to defend his country, his nation, his church, women and children and Christian civilisation?" He also asked, "Are some churches not opening the door for young men who wish to evade their responsibilities to do so under the cloak of conscientious objection?" His reasoning was that genuine Christians are entitled to interpret the Bible, but that God did not lead some people to become conscientious objectors and other people to become responsible soldiers. The nub of his argument was:

> It is a question to be asked to those who defend the right of conscientious objection, if they are not playing into the hands of these Marxist powers by way of indirect support. They must also remember that it has been shown over and over again that those who have conscientious objections against Communism or Marxism and then express those objections in those states, end up in punishment camps or gaols. This is what our Defence Force is fighting to defend us from! (Quoted in CIIR and Pax Christi, 1982:60-61).

How ironic that in March 1980 the Chaplain-General would bemoan the imprisonment of conscientious objectors in communist countries. For right under his nose Richard Steele and I were imprisoned, in his 'Christian' state, for conscientious objection! And moreover, as shown above, the army had pursued me relentlessly without any objection at any time from the senior chaplaincy of the Army or that of the Defence Force.

In March 1980 the amount of food served at meals fell sharply. Two generals had visited the Detention Barracks in February and the news had come to me that they had decided to 'straighten things out.' They allegedly said that the barracks were becoming too slack; the conditions needed to be so rigorous that the men would never want to return. Among the innovations was the introduction of dry rations on five days in the week and wet rations on two days, Thursday and Sunday. Dry rations were those that could be taken by a soldier on a manoeuvre, e.g. bread, biscuits, rusks, dried fruit, energy bars, cheese, corned beef, or ready-to-eat meals such as pasta with peppersteak, etc. Wet rations were foods that required water for preparation. The dry ration was nutritious enough, but we could never get enough food into our stomachs. This was particularly tough for Richard who was a vegetarian, so could not eat all the food on an already meagre serving. We were always hungry. We never had the feeling that we had eaten our fill. By contrast, hunger in civilian life can be a healthy sensation, as long as one knows that one can fill up whenever one needs to do so. In the Detention Barracks it was irksome never to know when the next full meal was going to be. One way of adapting was to approach a new inmate in his first three days and see if he would give one his left-overs. (The new entrants typically had little appetite, as explained above.)

Another problem with the food when in solitary confinement was that inmates used to bring it on the corporal's instructions, from the mess. The corporal could not watch them, and these men were subject to temptation themselves because they had an exhausting routine of military training and marching five days per week. They were not above helping themselves to the food they conveyed. Three slices of bread became one. A big chop became a small one. A bit of ice cream (on Sundays) disappeared. For one breakfast I received two Vienna sausages—the normal inmates had had porridge as well. I shall never forget that feeling of hunger gnawing away all the time and causing me to fantasise about the delicious foods that I would get for myself once I left the Detention Barracks. That was one of the most frustrating things I experienced. Normally I am not like this: my attitude towards food is one of the most casual disregard. In the Detention Barracks I started thinking and imagining and could not control my mind and emotions. I resolved that once I was free I would never send anyone away from my door hungry.

A trick by Staff-Sergeant Erasmus

On Friday 14 March, Staff-Sergeant Erasmus brought two pairs of grey-pinkish overalls to Richard and me, and announced, "Here are your overalls." We had requested to be able to wear any non-military overalls, even if they were the yellow overalls of the municipal workers. And here was our solution: overalls that were clearly different from the standard military issue. We were overjoyed. We thought that Erasmus had tried to accommodate us, and we thanked him profusely. We congratulated each other on having sat through our periods of solitary confinement and having attained our objective of recognition as conscientious objectors. We yanked on those overalls with great gusto and returned to work.

An hour later we saw other inmates of the barracks wearing the same grey-pinkish overalls. And then more: all the men under arrest had been given these overalls, which distinguished them from the men undergoing punishment. We realised that we had been tricked. These overalls were just as much military overalls as were the brown ones. (In a few more months they were abandoned anyway, in favour of the standard brown.)

We stuck it out for that weekend, pondering our next move. We knew that if we took these overalls off, we could sit in solitary confinement repeatedly for the remainder of our time in jail. They could put us in for 14 days at a time and take us out for only two and then put us in for another 14, and so on. (In fact they did not. I had one break of three days between periods of solitary; most of the other breaks were seven days, and one was 14 days.) On Monday morning we took the overalls off, with the Major's knowledge, and they put us in solitary again. This was to be my fourth period, and Richard's second.

We were in such bad odour with the authorities that we feared that Erasmus might order searches of our cells, so I did not dare smuggle anything in. So this time I read the Bible and only that, in the Good News Bible translation. Again all the Gospels, as well as Isaiah, Amos and Hosea. I know those books well to this day. In the event there was no search: as before, the Detention Barracks authorities did not take the trouble to read the Regulations, or failed to surmise how important our reading was to us.

Richard was separated from me. I was left in the solitary confinement block, and he was locked up in solitary in Block Two. He organised a clever scheme with inmate Robbie Paine, who opened Richard's door at night with a piece of wire, gave him books, and then took them out of his cell in the morning, so as to avoid trouble in the event of a search.

Richard and I met Gary 'Red' Murgatroyd, who said he was from Durban. He had bright red hair and freckles. Robbie and Red used to get us food, and made sure we had literature when possible, and conveyed messages between us. Sometimes Red appeared at my cell with his pockets full of vegetables, notably carrots and bell peppers, that I wolfed down. It was good to have the support of these fellows, especially as Staff-Sergeant Erasmus was trying to alienate us from the rest of the men. Red said that he had been in court before because he had smuggled rifles out to guerrillas fighting the SADF. He said it was a scary time because if you were found guilty, you could get the 'nine to never', viz. nine years' imprisonment to life. He believed the future of South Africa was "in the hands of the black man." He said he was a member of a guerrilla opposition group, but would not name which one. He added that he had a camera in his cell and was taking photographs, intending to expose the filth and the violence of the Detention Barracks once his sentence was over. He came into the Detention Barracks again later, this time for 60 days. During this stint he told me that he had left the guerrilla group.

It did not occur to me then, but it is obvious to me now, that Red was a spy. Putting together his nickname, his egregious claims about smuggling rifles to guerrillas, his 'nine to never' lingo, and the story about the camera—it was all too smooth and too calculated to be genuine. Probably he was trying to find out if I had any connections with the ANC myself. I did not, but that did not stop the army or security apparatus from sending him in a second time. *Swak, Piketberg!* So much effort for zero return.

The inmates saw that we were successfully resisting the administration, and surviving our periods of solitary confinement. Many came out in strong support and thought that what we were doing was admirable. They used to encourage us verbally and help us in all sorts of little ways. They told us to "vasbyt!" (Hang in there), and said, "It's not so bad! Show them what you're made of! Wys hulle dat julle die punch kan vat!" (Show them that you can take the punch). It was good to have their support, even though they had little conception of what we were doing as conscientious objectors. Their friendship was invaluable. Sometimes they organised extra food for us. Another reason for their support was the Prisoners' Code. Every prisoner is afraid of coming into conflict with the administration at some time, so he supports other prisoners in the hope of gaining their support in return.

A three-day fast protesting repeated solitary confinement

Richard and I suggested that our supporters participate in a three-day fast on the days leading up to Easter, Thursday 3 April to Saturday 5 April 1980, just after my fourth and his second stint in solitary. We compiled a joint statement explaining our motivation and smuggled it out to supporters far and wide. Richard and I drank only water over the three days. Fasting was not easy as it was becoming colder and we had not had much food in the first place.

The fast received much attention in the press. Rev. Rob Robertson helped with communication with churches and support groups;[68] he in turn was able to call upon Di Scott-Saddington and Adi Paterson in Cape Town and Paddy Kearney in Durban.[69] As Corporal Gebhardt told me at the time, the fast was announced by Capital Radio, a privately owned venture transmitting from the Transkei on medium wave, and which supported the anti-*apartheid* struggle. Vigils were held at St. George's Cathedral and Rondebosch Congregational Church in Cape Town; about 200 people attended at one of these two venues. A vigil was held at St. Anthony's United Church in Mayfair, whose minister was Rev. Rob Robertson,[70] and Rev. Joe Wing called for a lunchless vigil at the Congregational

---

[68] Statement to the press about the vigil at the Cathedral and at Rondebosch Congregational Church, 2 pages. Wits, Rob. Coll., A2558-9.20.

[69] Letter from Richard Steele to Rev. Rob Robertson dated 16 March 1980. Wits, Rob. Coll., A2558-9.20.

[70] Wits, Rob. Coll., A2558-9.20.

Centre on the Saturday.[71] A statement by 70 sympathisers was published in the Cape Times; these included Professor Paul Hare, Dr. Ivan P. Toms, Dr. Margaret Nash, Dr. Mary Ellis, Rev. Ernie Ashcroft, Rev. David Cook, Rev. Roy T. Barker, Rev. Louis Bank, Rev. Douglas S. Bax, Rev. David Profit, Rev. J. Dixon, Rev. C.J. Gregorowski, Rev. N.S. Mayall, Rev. Brian J. Woods, and Rev. M. Rowe.[72] Rev. Douglas Bax, minister of the Congregational Church in Rondebosch, explained, "Peter and Richard feel they would be identifying themselves with the South African Defence Force against their will if they wore the uniform."[73] Written comments by attendees at the Rondebosch Congregational Church filled a vigil book of thirty-one pages. One ran, in Xhosa: "Bamthatha, bambeka e DB, Wasuka wakhala, wathi 'amandla'. Tula, Peter and Richard, Tula." (They have taken you and put you in DB, we wipe away our tears and say 'strength.' Hush, Peter and Richard, hush.)

The full list of people who wrote messages during the vigil includes: Tony Saddington (two days), Anonymous, Tony Harding, Adrian Paterson (three days), Cherry Squair (three days), Martin Klopper, Anonymous, Anonymous, Les Walters, Francis Wilson, Noelle Cox, Victor McGregor (two days), Douglas Bax, Stephen Granger (two days), Isobel de Gruchy, Anne Palm, David Russell, Louis Bank, Jim Cochrane, Elaine Tucker, Heleen Vreede (two days), Martin Anonymous, Peter Coxon, Kevin Wright, Anonymous, Denise Velthuis (two days), Aneene Dawber, Penny Cooper, Clive Trollip, Rob Campbell, David Mattey (or Hattey?), Jane Keen, Michelle Rundle, Sharon Wilmers, Johann Maree, Shaun Bloomer, Anne McCrindle, Cathy Paterson, Penny Dichmont, Marj Brown, Terence Moll,

---

[71] Appeal dated 1 April 1980. Wits, Rob. Coll., A2558-9.20

[72] 'Three-day fast by military objectors', in *Cape Times* Tuesday April 1, 1980.

[73] 'Vigil begins for fasting objectors,' *Cape Times*, 3 April 1980.

Matthew McNally, Caroline Anonymous, Rod Douglas, James Thomas, Margaret Nash, John Dixon, Barbara Coxon, David Holgate, Roxane Saks-Smotu, Dot Cleminshaw, Lynne Lawrence, Mike Lawrence and Bruno Aheafts.

Francis Wilson participated, and wrote a long letter from the Rondebosch Congregational Church. Mrs. Helen Suzman, the Progressive Federal Party's spokesperson on prisons, condemned the practice of imposing sentences of solitary confinement on conscientious objectors, describing it as "cruel and unnatural." Bishop Tutu supported the fast, asserting that we had the "right to be recognised as conscientious objectors."[74] Many people all over the country showed support by arranging their own fasting schedules or writing letters, cards and telegrams, and by praying for us at their churches. For instance, my friend Aneene Dawber of the Catholic Society of the University of Cape Town, together with her house community of eight others, fasted for a day and spent time meditating on our situation.

Lunch on Easter Sunday, 6 April 1980, was special. The cooks set up trestles in the cellblocks and served right there: it happened to be a favourite delicacy of mine, oxtail, which is always good but this time was even better because it was like a reward after the long fast. The same day there came a colourful greetings telegram from Francis Wilson at Hogsback near Alice, with a verse from Romans 8.38f: "I am convinced that neither death, nor life, nor angels, nor principalities, nor things present, nor things to come, nor powers, nor height, nor depth, nor any other created thing, shall be able to separate us from the love of God, which is in Christ Jesus our Lord."

---

[74] Arnold Geyer, 1980. 'Objectors in DB: now Tutu joins protest,' *Rand Daily Mail*, 8 April 1980.

Protest was building up against the army's sentences of solitary confinement. The minister of the Cambridge Baptist Church, Rev. Martin Holdt, a good friend of the family, took the matter up. I knew Rev. Holdt from Cambridge Baptist where I attended during our family's stay in East London. He had embraced Reformed theology and in 1975 introduced me to the Evangelical and Reformed Studies Conference at Skoegheim, Port Shepstone. When he learned of the repeated sentences of solitary confinement, he wrote on 20 March 1980 to General Magnus Malan, the Chief of the South African Defence Force:

> I find it hard to believe that such inhumane and sadistic treatment can be meted out to a man only because his request to wear the blue overalls worn by the Jehovah's Witnesses in the camp is bluntly turned down. Not only do I find this type of military behaviour on the part of those directly responsible cruel to say the least, but it is surely wholly unreasonable. It seems clear to me and to others who are conscious of what is happening to Mr. Moll, that the members of a sect like the Jehovah's Witnesses are accorded privilege that are denied to a man who is a member of a Protestant denomination and who has put forward a well-reasoned argument for his conscientious objection.[75]

In the absence of a satisfactory reply, and given the continued solitary confinement sentences, he wrote a fiery letter to Brigadier Pretorius, on 8 April 1980, complaining of

> blatant inconsistencies in your military legislation ... ridiculous and senseless treatment ... gestapo type oppression and persecution .... When the law closes in on a man's freedom of conscience, it is beginning to defeat its own ends, and the image that it creates of the powers that be is one of a dictatorship rather than a democracy.

---

[75] See the letter at Wits, Rob. Coll., A2558-9.13.

I protest in the strongest terms about such inconsistent and distorted laws.

On 11 April 1980 I was again locked up in solitary for 14 days, for my fifth such sentence. Richard followed on 18 April for his third.

During these periods of solitary I was in Block Five which was ordinarily used as the solitary confinement block. Between periods I was removed and put in Block Two or Three, where I remained for approximately a week, and was then moved back. The process of putting me in solitary was fairly complicated. One day someone would come to me with the overalls. It might be a staff-sergeant, a sergeant or a corporal. He would issue me with the instruction to put it on, usually jokingly, because he knew that I was a conscientious objector and that I would not. He would smile, I would smile and refuse. He would warn me that he was going to charge me. He would go away and charge me using the DD1 form.

The next day I would be brought before the Officer Commanding of the unit, without representation as explained above, and be tried. I had the chance to present my own view and to present facts in mitigation. Then sentence would be pronounced, almost always 14 days, the maximum allowed by the *Detention Barracks Regulations* (1961-1976). The Major insisted that once I had been given a sentence of 14 days it could not go any lower. Then on the following day I first had to see the doctor in the early morning, to check that I was in a fit physical state for solitary, and then I would be locked away by one of the corporals.

When I went to see the doctor, he would ask me if I was all right. I would say, "Yes, except that I don't like being in solitary confinement." Then he would say to the corporal, "OK, take him away." Once or twice, he picked up his stethoscope and listened to my heart and breathing. It was never a careful physical examination, and there was never any psychological examination.

To my mind, this was a failure on the doctor's part. He ought to have made quite certain that I was not deteriorating psychologically. Luckily I have the psychological disposition that would not send me into a panic. I can imagine that some other men in the Detention Barracks would have gone to pieces after a short period of solitary.

During my fourth period of solitary, there was a Jehovah's Witness in with us, just 19 years of age. He did not have a letter from his Jehovah's Witness Kingdom Hall, and thus he lacked proof that he was a fully-fledged member. On refusing to wear the military overalls, he was sentenced to solitary confinement for 14 days. After six days he was yelling and kicking the door in utter frustration. He could not bear being locked inside. Chris Boshoff and I tried to encourage him, saying vasbyt and stick at it, and don't let them get you down too much and try to get used to it and don't worry. Somehow he just could not pull himself together. Eventually he agreed to give up. He was taken to court where he announced that he would do his military training. In fact his intention was to go into the railway police and thereby avoid military training altogether. He received a suspended sentence of 18 months for having refused his call-up and then left the Detention Barracks.

Richard's parents, Dorothy and John Steele, came the long distance from Kempton Park to see Richard and me on Sunday afternoons whenever they were allowed, and Dorothy also paid the occasional brief visit on weekdays whenever she could manage it. She had a way with Major Marthinus C. Krige. She must have kissed the Blarney stone. She had extraordinary powers of persuasion. She was always able to talk him into letting her see me for a few moments, and to bring me books.

Once John and Dorothy Steele came to meet Staff-Sergeant Erasmus. In their long interview with him, they tried to convince him that Richard and I did not hate him and were not seeking to undermine the administration of the Detention Barracks. Far from this, our attitude was to follow the injunction, "Love your neighbour as yourself," and "Love your enemies. Do good to them that hate you." Erasmus's attitude changed dramatically. Another factor in his change of attitude was that he realised he was not achieving any success with bullying us into obeying military commands. He became polite, and I had only one or two nasty incidents with him after that.

On Sunday 27 April I enjoyed the first of many visits from Rev. Rob Robertson, the minister of St. Anthony's United Church in Mayfair, Johannesburg. I was surprised that the guards allowed him in, because officially I would have been permitted visits only by the pastor of the church of which I was a member, which was in Claremont, Cape Town. But Rob had a way of persuading, which together with his dignified appearance and bass voice must have inspired confidence. It was good to be reunited with an old friend. I had spent five years in the same class as his son Hugh Robertson at Selborne College, East London, from 1969 to 1973.

It was clear that Richard and I had caused the military much hand-wringing. A letter was sent by the Head of the SADF to the Military Secretary of the Minister of Defence, on 24 April 1980, saying

HSP notes that it appears that Steele's parents' petition is part of an organised campaign against conscription. Amongst other things there are the changes they propose to Article 126A of the Defence Act of 1957, which are the same as those proposed by Moll's parents which were sent directly to the Director of Military Law (my translation).[76]

So two letters, one from the Steeles and one from the Molls, made an "organised campaign against conscription." At the highest level in the land, where any information could have been sought, they had no idea that the two mothers were sisters and communicated daily, and that the imprisoned men were cousins. Hence of course the changes proposed by the Steeles and the Molls will be the same! *Swak, Piketberg!*

Alone again, and more solitary

On 2 May 1980, Richard was transferred to the Tempe Detention Barracks at Bloemfontein. The motives for this move are hard to discern. Perhaps the generals thought we were aiding each other in our resistance to the demand that we wear the brown overalls. Possibly they felt they might divide and conquer. I was disappointed. It was sad parting.

My parents came to visit during my fourth spell of solitary, on Monday, 24 March 1980. They had made the trip from Umtata to Pretoria to visit me and to lobby with Major-General Fourie and Brigadier Pretorius, as well as other highly placed personnel. My visit took place in the office of the Officer Commanding, Major Krige. I had not been able to shave for a week because my new razor was in the storage shed and I was denied access to it because I was in solitary. The Major was horrified on seeing me unshaven and of course blamed me, but it was obvious to all that this was a slip-up by his administration.

---

[76] Letter obtained by Judith Connors in the research for her master's degree (2007), from documents that the South African National Defence Force (SANDF) had declassified. Sent to me in August 2006 and retained by Terence Moll.

My parents were deeply worried about me, concerned especially that I might be suffering mentally. I tried to engage them in conversation and assure them that I was physically and mentally strong. My father even tried, right there, to persuade me to give in and follow military orders. I explained that putting on the overalls and doing military training would be a betrayal of all that I had stood for thus far; that I wanted no involvement with SADF operations because it was defending *apartheid*. Of course my father was not convinced, but I think this conversation and the subsequent one were nevertheless useful to my parents because they could see I was the same person they had last seen the previous year.

My parents were permitted to visit again on Saturday, 29 March, together with my sisters Brenda and Jen. It was a very happy visit and I was pleased to be let out of solitary for a couple of hours.

During April my aunt Dorothy and uncle John Steele went to Cape Town in the hope of having an interview with the Prime Minister. For five days they sat, literally, in the 'corridors of power' but Mr. P.W. Botha remained incommunicado. On the fifth day they were given an interview with Botha's chief of staff, to whom they explained that their son and their nephew were being treated unfairly by being placed in solitary confinement repeatedly for the same 'offence.'

During April 1980 the Executive of the Baptist Union, headed by the General Secretary Rev. Trevor Swart, had contact with the Prime Minister about the issue of repeated solitary spells, but were informed in May that no further contact about the matter of conscientious objection would be entertained.[77] Also during April 1980, the Executive of the Baptist Union

---

[77] Letter from Rev. Trevor Swart on 20 May 1980 to Rev. Rob Robertson. Wits, Rob. Coll., A2558-9.8.

sought to interview the top generals about my and Richard's position. I do not know whether these intended meetings took place. What did eventually materialise was a meeting with the Prime Minister in November 1980 (see below).

My sixth spell of solitary confinement started on 1 May 1980. Solitary confinement continued in June and July. At each sentence I appealed, arguing that I was being punished twice for the same offence, namely being a conscientious objector. The appeals were rejected. I gradually acquired techniques to distract myself from the loneliness and silence of the solitary cell: I shaved every day, showered (in cold water) every day, polished the cell regularly, brushed my teeth after every meal, washed a few articles of clothing every day, and did much exercise in the cell in the form of running on the spot and exercises for my back. I went into long reveries over my childhood, recalling the Residency in Alice and the primary school in Lady Frere. I found that the best solution to the problem of the inadequate food was to resolutely forbid myself to think about it at all, otherwise the desire for food became a controlling obsession.

In late May 1980 my parents visited again. Since my father was to retire on 30 May, he received an invitation to attend a gathering to be addressed by Prime Minister P.W. Botha in Pretoria. My parents piggy-backed on this to visit me and also to interview certain of the generals.

My father intensified his letter writing. Among many other communications, he wrote to Rear-Admiral H.P. Botha, Deputy Chief of Staff (Personnel) on 17 July 1980. He noted that solitary confinement had been abolished as a form of punishment in the South African courts, and expressed his shock that an "exemplary young man" was still being subjected to such "inhumane treatment" by the SADF. He wrote again on 29 July 1980 to Rear-Admiral Botha, noting that the military authorities were encountering much embarrassment owing to the treatment meted out to me. He proposed that the remainder of my sentence and the remainder of my military training should be spent as a teacher on secondment to the Department of Education of Transkei.

My mother mentioned in a letter that she was in the habit of phoning the Officer Commanding every week or ten days to ask how I was doing. She frequently wrote letters to an ever increasing number of supporters, including all the Baptist and other ministers she and my father knew—which after their decades of Christian activity was a vast company. In these she gave news about Richard and me, and appealed to them to contact their Members of Parliament.[78] I did not know at the time that all these efforts by my parents, Richard's parents, Rev. Rob Robertson, Rev. Douglas Bax, and letter writers from overseas, were having a real impact on the military authorities. Besides being forced to explain themselves over and over again, and respond to ministerial inquiries and inquiries from the press, there was clearly internal dissension as the top brass started to realise that their acting the martinet had failed in the eyes of the general public.

Another element of pressure was that a conference was held at Botha's Hill in Natal in July 1980 to discuss conscientious objection.[79] Participants included ministers and lay people from several churches, and university lecturers. The focus was on alternative non-military service for conscientious objectors whether from religious conviction or reasons of conscience. Speeches were given by the Catholic Archbishop of Durban, Denis E. Hurley, ds. Willem Saayman of the Department of Missiology at UNISA, Dr. James Moulder of Rhodes

---

[78] My parents' circular letter to supporters, dated 19 May 1980, page 3. Wits, Rob. Coll., A2558-9.13.

[79] Wits, Rob. Coll., A2558-6.

University, the Member of Parliament Graham McIntosh, Rev. Douglas Bax, Sheena Duncan of the Black Sash, and Rev. Francois Bill of the South African Council of Churches.

I valued at these times being able to speak with the chaplain Gerry O. West during the week when I was not in solitary. He was a conscript from a Pentecostal church. We often talked about pacifism, conscientious objection and other issues. He was a keen linguist. Once we were caught chatting by Staff-Sergeant Erasmus, after one chaplain's period, and Erasmus told the Major, who went higher up, until the matter reached the chief chaplain of Northern Transvaal Command. Gerry was in trouble. They alleged he was sheep-stealing, since I was from the Free Churches and he Pentecostal, but it was obvious that they feared that I was talking to him about conscientious objection. A justified fear, I agree! After that we were forbidden to speak to each other.

I had several long conversations with the resident chaplain of the unit, ds. Dawid Venter of the Dutch Reformed Church. Elated by his success in persuading Chris Boshoff to give up his conscientious objector stand, he was hoping to follow suit with me. He honestly believed that P.W. Botha was the salvation for South Africa and the war of the SADF was for a just cause, that we had to fight off the terrorists, and create a black middle class, etc. We argued incessantly about this and made no headway. I wrote to my parents after one of these conversations on 29 June 1980:

I had a 3-hour discussion with the Dominee of the DB. He's young and very personable but quite honestly we got nowhere at all. I suppose we were both too aggressive. His opening sally was to assure me that I had very little support and would soon be forgotten; he gulped a bit when I showed him last week's post, but abandoned the line altogether when I said I was standing for a principle anyway, the question of social approval being irrelevant.

He was basically a pietist—I mean in the bad sense of consigning the world to providence, basing his case largely on the 'absolute obedience' interpretation of Romans 13:1-7. We disagreed on so many things, it was discouraging: if understanding cannot be achieved in the Church, will it ever be achieved at all? I, Bishop Tutu and others like us should be jailed, he said later, and that for the sake of the Gospel! I was dumbstruck.

In the end he insisted that the classified information to which he has access would not fail to bring me round to his view, if he could reveal it to me. There the discussion ended; you can't discuss with someone who appeals, gnostic fashion, to a hidden source of information whenever he's in hot water. How easy it is for the morally insensitive to cloak their disregard for the sufferings of the poor with respectability by appealing single-mindedly to Romans 13!! If only they would study Bonhoeffer or check over the Nuremberg trials! I don't know if you find this awfully interesting, but honestly this has been plaguing me for the last few weeks. Moral sclerosis! And yet, I guess, it's in trying to solve that problem that I am here.[80]

Luckily I had a light in my cell, so I was able to read at night. When I wanted to sleep, I reached up using the chair, and used a piece of blanket to wrench out the bulb and put it back in the next morning. Reading made the solitary easier; that was one of the important factors in my survival during the whole saga with solitary confinement, which lasted until 8 August 1980. Reading the Bible is a fine thing to do, especially as I was a budding theologian. But I became bored during the fourth period of solitary when I had only the Bible to read.

I suffered constipation. It did not worry me at first, but after the fourth period of solitary, I sometimes had no bowel movement at all for four days, and then had a terrific case of diarrhoea and was awake half the night trying to get all the stuff

---

[80] Wits, Rob. Coll., A2558-9.13.

out. I asked the doctor for medications, and took the tablets he offered, but all to no avail. The problem was that I was sitting still (except when doing press-ups and sit-ups to keep warm), the food was starchy, and I had little exercise.

The lack of food continued to bother all the detainees. Once on going past the toilets—always dirty—I saw half a rusk on the ground. I leapt at it and wolfed it down. Some of the inmates looked after me and would organise me extra 'chow,' or, as they used termed it, a 'betters chow.' I valued their support.

Among the *oumanne* was Brian van Zyl, who along with three others raped a girl from Botswana in 1977 and was sentenced to two years' detention.[81] He escaped in January 1978 but was quickly recaptured,[82] and was still in the Detention Barracks in 1980. Eventually he was given a three-month prison sentence, after which he would receive an automatic discharge from the army. He was a hard-boiled character and used to bully the newcomers, but to me he was a real gentleman. One afternoon he came to my cell and unlocked it and we talked for several hours. He told me all about his problems, difficulties with a previous girlfriend, what his parents were doing, the work he had been involved in, and so on. Because he gained a sympathetic ear, he was only too willing to help me, almost like a guardian angel. This is amazing to say, because in civilian life I would actually be scared of his type! But the need for survival in the Detention Barracks makes people cooperate. Once he

---

[81] https://www.news24.com/News24/the-dros-rape-and-the-history-of-race-and-rape-in-sa-20181008. See also https://sinananewsrwanda.blogspot.com/2018/10/a-history-of-race-and-rape-in-south.html . The four men were Peter Faught, Petrus Liebenberg, Ivan Bernado and Brian Kenneth van Zyl. On 9 October 1977 they were court-martialled at Pont Drift on the Botswana side of the Limpopo River, charged with rape and assault.

[82] 'Soldate ontsnap ná Botswana-aanval,' *Rapport*, 29 January 1978. Wits, SAIRR Coll., ZA HPRA AD1912A-S236.7.

brought me a massive breakfast consisting of a large helping of porridge, six slices of bread, and a large mug of coffee. Sometimes he arranged with the corporal to open the cell for an extra while so that I could be out for longer.

When I was staying for a week in Block Three we once got, among other things, half-cooked squashes for supper. Many men did not care for this ill-made fare, but I tucked in, never minding the stringy tastelessness. Once when I was in solitary confinement people were visiting on a Sunday afternoon. Amid the confusion the remains of the lunches of several other inmates in Block Five were left in the block. I accosted a passing inmate and asked him to push some of the food through the judas. Which he did—two plates of cabbage and other vegetables. He marvelled that a 'klein ou' (small guy) like me would eat so much. Being a short-timer he did not realise the need to stock up.

A friend of mine from the Detention Barracks, Ottie Lange, had his mother write a letter to one of the generals in June. She obtained an interview with him and told him about the food situation, mentioning that the men were fighting for it at mealtimes. In mid-June[83] the food improved miraculously. It was still inadequate for men who were on a heavy programme of physical training, but for me it was more or less sufficient. Sometimes I felt a bit hungry, but at other times I was able to fill up.

Ottie Lange had an unusually long sentence, about a year. He and I came to be good friends. He helped me in all sorts of ways, in getting me light bulbs in the early part of my sentence, and securing food for me, and I helped him by acting as a willing ear, among other things.

---

[83] Letter from me to my parents, 29 June 1980. Wits, Rob. Coll., A2558-9.13.

I tried to help Ottie once when the corporal refused to bring food for him. He was wanting to charge the administration, and I too wanted to charge one of the corporals for not taking us out one morning for our half-an-hour exercise period. I asked Second Lieutenant Smith to bring the papers. He gave all sorts of excuses. He said it was a new sergeant, the corporal did not know. After more argumentation I said I had had enough of this. "Hierdie ding moet nou end kry. Ek het lank genoeg in hierdie eensame opsluiting gesit" (This business must stop. I have been in solitary confinement enough), I warned. I laid it on thick, and he said he would bring the papers. The next day he arrived for the daily inspection of the solitary confinement cells, and I asked for the papers. "No," he said, "I'll bring the papers tomorrow." We got the message. From solitary confinement it was impossible to sue.

A Staff-Sergeant Coombe was assigned to the Detention Barracks in May and June 1980. He was angered when an inmate in Block Two failed to empty his chamber-pot out. He made everyone line up and wash their hands in the urine. I half hoped that he would instruct me to do so as well, for then I would have refused and the incident would have been embarrassing for him and encouraging for the prisoners. Prudently, he left Chris Boshoff and me alone. I contemplated taking the pot and emptying it into the gully between the two rows of cells, before the line of men got to it, but decided against that because I feared victimisation. When I was in solitary Staff-Sergeant Coombe used to come to me of a morning and argue stupidly for half an hour about why I was a fool to be a conscientious objector. He repeated himself incessantly, calling me by racist and obscene names. I tried to humour him, in the end successfully, thereby avoiding persecution.

By this time, Major Venter had retired owing to ill health. Major Krige took his place as Officer Commanding. Krige was from the civilian prisons where he had been an inspector for many years in the Cape and Namibia. He was Afrikaans-speaking, with rather stilted English. He struck me as a hard and unfeeling man. He believed in treating inmates harshly. He gave instructions that men in solitary were not allowed to have their bedding in their cells during the day because they were not to sleep. So at four or five in the morning the corporals took away our blankets and mattresses, and returned them to us late in the afternoon. It was hard having only one blanket and a chair in the cell because it became very cold. The solitary confinement block was even colder because it was angled in such a way that the sun never shone onto it, so the temperature barely changed between day and night.

Major Krige went away for a month for a course and was replaced by a Major J.P.O. Fourie, from the Military Police headquarters, a grand gentleman who had been brought back from retirement. He was 63 years of age. He had considerably more influence and power over Staff-Sergeant Erasmus than did Major Krige. He kept Erasmus in his place and stopped him from shouting all the time, much to our relief. He came up to me and Chris Boshoff one day when we were in solitary, and said, "Is there anything I can do to help you men? Is there anything the matter? Do you have enough blankets? Are you getting enough food?" Then he actually told us to "vasbyt"! What a contrast to the mechanical army mind that sees only its own interests and cannot see the other person's view. The Jehovah's Witnesses gave him the nickname Popeye, because his eyes protruded slightly. He had an affectionate relationship with them, and it was sad to see him go.

From May to August 1980 it was cold, particularly in the solitary confinement block. My hands became chapped and my knuckles bled due to the cold, dry air and the near-freezing water. At one stage I was moved out of the solitary confinement block into Block Three because Sergeant-Major Els[84] said it was warmer there. That was considerate of him, but I found the noise so intolerable there that I arranged to move back to Block Five, where at least it was quiet, enabling me to think, read, and sleep in peace. Sometimes I had on three pairs of pyjamas, plus two jerseys, and then I wrapped three blankets around myself, and had a cap on my head, but my teeth still chattered. The cold was unbearable. I had never experienced anything like it.

A few officers were well-disposed to me all along. One was a Permanent Force Lance-Corporal H.[85] who never forgot about my half-hour break in the morning and afternoon, and who called me by my first name. One cold night in June, he noticed that I was the only person in solitary confinement in Block Five. Very kindly he went to the kitchen and brought me a *bakkie* of hot coffee. I was very grateful.

One of the Jehovah's Witnesses located my solitary confinement cell and somehow clambered up on the big metal box that covered the barred window, getting close enough to be able to talk. It was no surprise that he was keen to proselytise. It was enjoyable having a bit of conversation with him from time to time, even if we were unable to find any real common ground on religious or political matters. Through him I learned more about the terrible persecution that the young Jehovah's Witness conscripts had been through in the early 1970s. This included repeated imprisonment in the Detention Barracks, sometimes amounting to years behind bars; being locked up in dark cells, viz. the cells I was in with the metal box covered to exclude light; and being physically beaten by the corporals.

---

[84] My letter to Rev. Rob Robertson dated 14 October 1981. Wits, Rob. Coll., A2557-1\ITEM A Correspondence Series 1.

[85] My letter to my parents of 10 August 1980. Wits, Rob. Coll., A2558-9.13.

A Second Lieutenant Smith was assigned to the Detention Barracks from June 1980. He was doing his national service and had to act as the prosecutor in summary courts-martial for my refusal to wear the uniform. He had completed a B.Juris. at the University of Potchefstroom. We sometimes talked for hours about all sorts of things, especially philosophy and Afrikaans literature[86] and he was—clearly, but quietly—sympathetic to my political ideas. He once told me that mine was a 'noble cause.'

I read assiduously, diligently studying Greek and Hebrew, memorising vocabulary lists, declensions and conjugations. A set work for Hebrew was Sabatino Moscati's *The Face of the Ancient Orient: A Panorama of Near Eastern Civilisations in Pre-Classical Times*, which I found an entertaining distraction from the desiccated conjugations. I studied German, helped by two hurried conversations with a Jehovah's Witness who helped me with pronunciation, and read the gripping classic *Schimmelreiter* by Theodor Storm, the wayward, if well-constructed, novel *Wir Sind Utopia* by Stefan Andres, *Wilhelm Tell* by Schiller, and *Ansichten Eines Clowns* by Heinrich Böll, a present from Renate Cochrane. I beavered away at an elementary French grammar. My motive for studying German and French was that many theological seminaries required a reading knowledge of these languages as a prerequisite for doctoral work. I worked at an elementary Spanish grammar, which was to stand me in good stead when I visited Nicaragua the next year.

Philosophy proved to be highly accessible: the history of political philosophy—Hobbes, Locke, Montesquieu, Mill—fostered my thinking about *apartheid* and conscientious

---

[86] My letter to my parents of 10 August 1980. Wits, Rob. Coll., A2558-9.13.

objection. My aunt Dorothy fetched, from the library of the University of South Africa, the textbooks *Ideology and Utopia* by Karl Mannheim, *Religion and the Rise of Capitalism* by R.H. Tawney, *The Open Society and its Enemies* by Karl Popper, *Contemporary Missiology* by Johannes Verkuyl, and *A History of Israel* by John Bright. Once she had handed them in at the Detention Barracks, they were sent for inspection at the military headquarters, with a turnaround time of at least six days. My mother sent me books from time to time by post, including *The Imitation of Christ* by Thomas à Kempis.

My sister Jen Beck brought me novels and non-fiction, e.g. Joyce Cary's *Mister Johnson*, Nadine Gordimer's *No Place Like: Selected Stories*, Anna M. Louw's *Kroniek van Perdepoort*, Lionel Trilling's *The Middle of the Journey*, Patrick White's *The Vivisector* and his *The Aunt's Story*, Olive Schreiner's *Story of an African Farm*, Carson McCullers' *The Heart is a Lonely Hunter* and her *The Member of the Wedding*, Pauline Smith's *The Beadle*, Pieter Geyl's *Debates with Historians*, Johannes Meintjes' *Olive Schreiner: Portrait of a South African Woman*, Saul Bellow's *The Adventures of Augie March*, and a collection of Aldous Huxley's short stories. I was allowed three visitors—as were the other inmates—once per month for an hour, during the time that I was not in solitary confinement. It was then that Jen and her husband Andrew Beck would bring me books, and I handed back to them the materials I had finished with.

From the unit's library I borrowed Augustine's *Confessions*, a book on prison reform in the USA, Lawrence of Arabia's *Seven Pillars of Wisdom*, Graham Greene's *Our Man in Havana*, and Pasternak's *Doctor Zhivago* in Spanish translation. The latter had been bequeathed by a captured Cuban soldier who had been kept in the Detention Barracks for a time. Once one of the friendlier corporals noticed I was studying Spanish, and so he brought along a former Cuban soldier to meet me. This soldier had been captured by the SADF in Angola and brought back as a prisoner of war. He then decided to join the SADF. There he was at my cell door, the first Cuban I had ever met! He was fluent in English. Right away I peppered him with questions about pronunciation, especially the Spanish double r ('rr'). Language work was suitable for solitary confinement because the books were compact and I could spend two weeks studying one grammar book without running out of material. They were easy to stash if a corporal came past, as long as I stuck them under the blankets very quickly.

I recalled that Martin Luther, when in protective custody in the Wartburg which he called his 'Patmos,' studied Greek and Hebrew, wrote many theological works and sermons, and translated the whole New Testament into German. The solitary cell in Block Five became my Patmos, rendering me unusually industrious. I was able to put myself onto a massive study programme. I pretended that I was putting myself into a smaller cell than the army had placed me in, and so it did not matter that my door was locked, because I was voluntarily limiting my freedom so that I would be able to study more. That was a useful psychological mechanism to overcome the feeling of frustration and claustrophobia that floods one inside the solitary confinement cell. I divided morning, afternoon and evening into three periods of an hour each. I started with grammar and syntax of one of the languages, switching to set-work novels or philosophy, then back to grammar, until the evening when I would allow myself as a reward an hour or two with an English-language novel. By compelling myself to study and read nearly all the time, I was able to avoid excessive depression. Sometimes depression came nevertheless. It was fairly deep, especially in June, July, and August 1980, even after I gained recognition as a conscientious objector. Luckily the depression did not usually last for very long. It would be just for a morning, or an evening, and I was able to beat it. I spent much time thinking about my childhood, finding that to be a good therapy. I would think about all the people I knew and try to make plans for what I would do once released from the Detention Barracks.

I spent a good deal of time exercising inside the cell to keep my morale up. This included much running on the spot: I could run for long periods, even 20 minutes, without discomfort. This was followed by press-ups, sit-ups, and back exercises. I found, especially when I had no chair and sat on my mattress on the floor leaning my back on the wall, that my back became very painful. When I did sit-ups I would hear a loud crack as I rose. That disappeared soon after I was able to get a chair.

There were times of anger, frustration and resentment. But there were also times of great satisfaction. My thoughts went to the Beatitude: "Blessed are those who are persecuted because of justice. Blessed are you, when people insult you and persecute you. Rejoice, and be exceeding glad: for in the same way they persecuted the prophets" (Mt. 5:10-12). And then to the book of Revelation, where John declares himself "your companion in suffering" and gives a hint why: he "was on the island of Patmos because of the word of God" (Rev. 1:9). At some times I identified with Paul of Tarsus's exhortation to the Romans, to "rejoice in hope, be patient in tribulation ... bless them who persecute you, bless, and curse not" (Rom. 12:12f). I prayed, and found that this had a calming influence. I had a real sense of God's presence even in these depressing circumstances. I felt that I was doing the right thing, and that I was doing something that, besides being a point of conscience, was also effective in persuading people that it was time to stop defending the morally indefensible. At no stage was I tempted to escape from the barracks or, worse still, to succumb to the army's bullying as had Johannes B. Strydom and Chris Boshoff. My mother's impression of me when she visited in late July 1980 was that I was "bright and shining, calm, resolved, warm and loving and just fine ..."[87]

Suspicion and spying

The Major regularly called in men whom he had seen speaking to me, and asked them all sorts of questions about me. Where do you know Moll from? Do you like him? If so, why? What do you talk about? What kind of things does he tell you? What are the addresses that he has been giving you? What names has he given you? Wie is Moll se *kokkedoor*? (Who is Moll's bigwig?, i.e. who is giving him his orders?) He tried in vain to pin a South African Communist Party, African National Congress or Pan-Africanist Congress connection on me. This may have been because articles on conscientious objection appeared in *Sechaba* (the mouthpiece of the African National Congress) and other magazines, exciting the suspicion of the security police.

On two occasions security personnel—whether the security police or military intelligence, I do not know—came to find out what they could. On 31 January 1980 they interviewed Chris Boshoff for two hours[88] and asked him about me and tried to extract what information he had. Chris promptly told me about their inquiries—against orders of course. The security personnel, regrettably, did not give me the courtesy of an interview. Again in mid-year certain security personnel came in and interviewed at length a friend called Johan (described below) and two others. They had them write out statements and sign a promise to inform on me. Luckily these men were

---

[87] Letter from Dorothy and John Steele to supporters, 30 July 1980. Wits, Rob. Coll., A2558-9.20.

[88] My (smuggled!) letter to friends, 3 February 1980. Wits, Rob. Coll., A2558-9.13.

sympathetic and loyal towards me. Immediately afterwards they came to me and told me everything that had happened, even though they had been told by the Major that they should not breathe a word. Of course I would not have been such a fool as to give them any valuable information even if I had any. They said they would try to cover for me anyway.

It was funny when one day I was talking to the inmate Bam. We had just finished drinking our tea and were still in the mess. The other men were on the parade-ground. The Major happened to walk in together with a Commandant who was inspecting the unit. The Major asked us indignantly what we were doing there. We said we were finishing our tea. Angrily he told us, "Get out of here and don't let me see you separate from the other men again!" We had not committed any crime, but he had to say something because the Commandant was there. I told Bam, "Watch! Later today you will be called in by the Major, and he'll ask you ..." and I named the questions, reeling off the best answers for him to give, for good measure. Sure enough, Bam was called in by the Major, and he gave the right answers.

The same thing happened with one Tony Wells. This was in July or August 1980 when he was discharged. He was in the Detention Barracks twice during the time I was there. The second time he was discharged I had a short chat with him outside the Detention Barracks where I was directed to pick up cigarette butts. Staff-Sergeant Erasmus came past. I said to Tony, "Watch, Staff-Sergeant Erasmus is going to call you in just now, and ask you all sorts of questions." Tony was sceptical, having no idea that the suspicion of me was so great. But sure enough, Erasmus called him and asked him the usual things. Tony came to me later and told me the story, amazed at the extent of their suspicion.

I was told by these inmates that the Major "hated my guts." He apparently told the inmates that I was Robben Island material, that I was wicked, that I would turn on them and shoot them in the back, and asked them, "What do you feel for Moll anyway?" They also said—but I cannot verify this—that he offered them parole if they would split on me.

* * *

In July 1980, at the request of my mother, I was required to go to the psychologist. I did not know at the time that this was at her request, so I was suspicious—what did the army want of me now? Her motive was simply that I have someone to talk to in case of need. In fact, I felt quite all right mentally. I hated the Detention Barracks but I knew I was not suffering any psychological damage. In the event the psychologist was a kind person. He was an Afrikaner but told me that he knew another conscript who really did not want to serve in the army, and had helped him skip the country. He was surprised and pleased at my use of the word 'gingerly.' He put me through an IQ test, a general knowledge test, Rorschach ink blot tests, and others. I underwent a test with the EEG machine. He concluded that: (i) I had not suffered any damage; (ii) I tended to be aggressive, because there was a part of my brain which had not yet matured; (iii) I was nevertheless able to control my aggression acceptably; and (iv) I had problems submitting to authority.[89]

Because I was in solitary for so long, I met other men who had been put in solitary for various crimes such as hitting or insulting officers or refusing to obey military commands. One such was a little fellow called Billy, who had three stints in detention during my year there. He had been AWOL repeatedly and would not subject himself to discipline. He was tiny, with

[89] My letter to my parents, 21 September 1980. Wits, Rob. Coll., A2558-9.13.

bright red hair, and was lacking his two front teeth, thereby earning the nickname 'Viper.' Once when we were in solitary together, he was accused by Lance-Corporal Opperman of having smoked, which was against the rules while in solitary. Billy contested this vehemently—whether rightly or not, I shall never know—and the corporal grabbed him by the collar, lifting him off his feet, and yelled, "Jy het! Jy het! Jy het!" (You did!) Billy again denied it. So the corporal lifted him off his feet once more. Billy still denied it. The corporal grabbed him by the collar again and made threatening noises, and then pushed him aside. Billy, in sheer frustration, smashed the mirror at the washbasins. At this the lance-corporal chortled. To him this was funny. Maybe it was exactly what he wanted. He said Billy would get more time in detention, or would be put into solitary confinement again.

I approached the lance-corporal and said, "I don't think it was right that you treated Billy in that way." I gave him to understand that I would be Billy's witness if he tried to charge him for having broken the mirror. Amazingly enough, the lance-corporal never did charge him. He was personable to both me and Billy after that. He even smuggled cigarettes to Billy when he was in solitary!

That was one instance, of so many, when violence was used by the corporals against hapless inmates. It was only because Lance-Corporal Opperman knew that I knew the law, and could have used it against him if I had wanted to, that he desisted from trying to charge Billy. I felt sorry for the other inmates. With their poor education, they could not defend themselves either in speech, or in writing, or through legal processes. They had no choice but to submit.

Another inmate I met while in the solitary confinement block was Johan. He was well educated and had done some legal studies. He and another inmate shaved each other's heads as smooth as eggshells. This was just to insult an officer who had told them to cut their hair more carefully the next Saturday. For this they were photographed and charged for having damaged state property and were put into solitary confinement for 14 days. Both of them had previously been through a good deal of solitary confinement. We became good friends and spent much time talking. They had a feeling of tremendous resentment against the army. They felt the army had done them down and wanted to get revenge in any way they could. I suspect they believed the officers' stories about my being a communist and a terrorist, and I am sure they would have been enthusiastic if I had had any leads to give them.

Another of my mates in Block Five, one Rademeyer, had been AWOL repeatedly over the past three years and had come in and out of detention. He and two others eventually escaped, towards the end of 1980, apparently headed for Namibia. Johan told me he had gone because he wanted to "join the Communists." Is it possible that they were all spies, sent by the security police or by military intelligence? If so, why would they expend so much effort on small fry like myself? More likely is that Rademeyer was just another youth who found military discipline uncongenial. He was subsequently caught and sentenced to civilian jail, and presumably was then given an automatic discharge from the military.

Five black Permanent Force soldiers came into the Detention Barracks at different times when I was there. They were all very young and spoke good English. I was able to talk a little with two of them who were in Block Five. Unsurprisingly, it was for social and personal problems that they had gone AWOL. These black soldiers were treated shamefully by some of the white inmates, who addressed them with racist epithets and obscenities. I witnessed several instances of white inmates handling them violently.

Chapter 5. Recognition as a conscientious objector

I did a second fast from Wednesday to Friday, 16 to 18 July 1980. Again Rev. Rob Robertson's support proved invaluable. He had come to visit in June when we did some planning. He wrote about it in an issue of the South African Council of Churches' *Non-Violence News*.[90] He clarified that this was not a protest against the original sentence of detention, but a protest against the repeated sentences of solitary confinement which amounted to a double penalty. For three days and nights I drank only water: it was a struggle but I stuck to the regimen.[91] Several church communities participated in various ways, e.g. a service was held on the Thursday evening at St. Mary's Cathedral (Anglican) in Johannesburg.[92] The fast was widely reported in the press.[93] Many people joined in, e.g. a group of Quakers around Fred Moorhouse of Yatton (in Avon, UK) who fasted on Friday, 18 July 1980, wrote to the South African Ambassador in the UK, informed the media and sent me a telegram of support.[94]

Meanwhile my parents, Richard's parents and other individuals took up the matter with the military authorities, appealing for an end to the repeated spells in solitary. Between March and August 1980, barrages of letters were written to the

[90] Wits, Rob. Coll., A2558-9.13.

[91] See *Non-Violence News*, 29 June 1980.

[92] 'Moll ends 3-day fast,' *Cape Times*, 19 July 1980. Wits, Rob. Coll., A2558-16.

[93] For example, 'Fast planned over "double penalty,"' *The Star*, 7 July 1980.

[94] Fred Moorhouse's letter to Rev. Rob Robertson of 15 July 1980. Wits, Rob. Coll., A2558-9.13.

Prime Minister and Minister of Defence, various generals, various politicians and Brigadier Pretorius, and were deemed significant enough that the military authorities felt obliged to reply: Rev. Martin Holdt (four letters and replies), Rev. Errol Hulse of *Reformation Today* (one), Mrs. Beryl Moll, my mother (one), Mr. Theodor Moll, my father (ten), Rev. Rob Robertson (three), and Chris Swart (one).

My father's letters cited several legal points. For instance, he pointed out that the Jehovah's Witnesses were recognised as conscientious objectors on the grounds that their organisation had 'tenets' that required their members to be pacifists. He noted that these grounds were questionable: the Jehovah's Witness organisation had no such tenets. (Instead it frequently, though apparently not always, followed a *practice* of 'disassociating' members who entered the military, hence its reputation as a 'peace church.') Thus, he argued, the Jehovah's Witnesses' organisation and the Baptist Church were no different in respect of their tenets; and so it was unfair not to recognise me as a conscientious objector. Some of my father's letters included stinging accusations, e.g. on 10 June 1980 he wrote to Rear-Admiral H.P. Botha stating that I was being given "worse treatment than a caged animal." The flood of letters must have been exasperating for the military authorities as each letter had to go through a commenting process and then each reply had to go through a long clearance process including translation from Afrikaans to English, culminating in a sign-off by a Lieutenant-General or by the Prime Minister P.W. Botha himself. Many more letters were written to the authorities by friends and Amnesty International supporters whose practice was often to write simultaneously to me, Richard, and the Minister of Defence or the Prime Minister. The letters to Richard and me frequently mentioned that the authors had also written to the authorities, but in many cases we lack a paper record of the latter writings.

The senior military staff were also bothered by the attention in the South African press. For instance, a 'Reader—Mother' from Newlands in Cape Town wrote to the *Rand Daily Mail* in early April reasoning that the punishment of being in the Detention Barracks was sufficient, and that it made no sense to put such a conscientious objector in solitary confinement repeatedly. On 30 June Brigadier Pretorius wrote to the newspaper asserting that "there is nothing special or unusual about the treatment in detention of Messrs. Moll and Steele."

Other people and organisations also wrote to the Prime Minister, the Minister of Defence or the various generals. For example, on 21 July 1980 the Rondebosch Congregational Church, represented by Dr. John de Gruchy, wrote to the Minister of Defence, pointing out that the repeated periods of solitary were a "cruel punishment … unbecoming in a land that claims to be Christian," and noting that in civil prisons, solitary confinement is used only in the most extreme cases.[95]

In March 1980, my parents travelled from Umtata to Pretoria to meet with the Chief of Staff (Personnel) Lieutenant-General G.J.J. Boshoff; Major-General Fourie;[96] the Deputy Chief of Staff (Personnel), Rear-Admiral H.P. Botha; Brigadier C.J. Pretorius; and other high-ranking military officials. To a man the military brass insisted that my parents should use their influence to persuade me to do military training and wear military overalls. Disappointed by the unflinching generals, my parents took the decision to go public. My father would draft the bulk of the letters while my mother would sign letters to

---

[95] Wits, Rob. Coll, A2558-9.8.

[96] My parents' circular letter to supporters, 19 May 1980. Wits, Rob. Coll., A2558-9.13.

newspapers and take interviews. My mother signed an impassioned letter entitled 'Vicious sentence on objector' in *The Star* of 5 August 1980.[97] She argued that the repeated solitary confinement, totalling then 118 days, "amounts to nothing less than the persecution of a Christian, on account of his Christian principles, in a so-called Christian land, and it is time that the Christian public called a halt to this vicious and inhumane treatment." She noted—and here my father's legal training as a magistrate came in useful—that solitary confinement had been abolished in the civilian court system in 1977. She concluded that the SADF "should stop immediately the harmful persecution of a courageous young man whom I am honoured to call my own son."

Rev. Rob Robertson approached his Member of Parliament, Mr. Roelof Petrus Meyer. He presented questions about conscientious objection in Parliament for answer by the Minister of Defence, as did Member of Parliament Alex Boraine. My parents also approached Ray Swart, Chairperson of the Progressive Federal Party and Member of Parliament, who arranged for a meeting with the Head of the Defence Force, General Magnus Malan, for Monday, 11 August 1980. This *terminus ad quem* was to prove critical.

In June, Brigadier M.J. du Plessis, Officer Commanding of the Orange Free State Command, made an offer to Richard: if he were to wear the brown overalls,[98] he could work during the day as a chaplain's clerk, and spend his nights at the Detention Barracks for the remainder of his sentence, without any requirement for military training or military procedure. Richard politely turned down the offer on the grounds that he did not

---

[97] Wits, SAIRR, ZA HPRA AD1912A-S236.5.

[98] From Rev. Rob Robertson's notes of a visit to Richard Steele on 9 July 1980: Wits, Rob. Coll., A2558-9.20.

wish to be involved in the military line of command in any way, or in any work whatsoever that served the SADF organisation and its function.

Then on 23 July 1980[99] Rear-Admiral Botha came to the Detention Barracks at Voortrekkerhoogte. He and I sat on cushioned chairs in the Major's office, I in civilian clothes, with the Major at his desk and the other officers including the social worker standing. Botha proposed that if I wore the *blue* overalls—thus making a concession beyond that made to Richard—and "behaved well," I could work in a military hospital or assist a military chaplain and spend my nights in the Detention Barracks. His code language was obvious: "behave well" meant 'stop the criticism of the SADF in the press.' I explained that I objected in conscience to any contribution to the war effort, including medical or religious contributions. The Admiral was visibly disappointed and said so. He left.

Days later, Botha wrote to my father explaining to him that he had come to see me and offered me blue overalls on condition I worked in the military hospital, but I had turned the offer down. He had done all he could; Richard and I were simply being intransigent; he had stretched as far as he could go. Now, he wrote, all my father could do was to use his influence over his son to try to persuade him to comply with the regulations. Our rejection of Rear-Admiral Botha's offer became public thanks to my mother's speaking with the newspapers.[100]

Clearly pressures were building up. On 29 July 1980, after my ninth period of solitary, I was working outside the unit cleaning the fish pond when Major Krige walked over to me to tell me, rather apologetically, that he had to put me in solitary

---

[99] From my mother's summary of events. Wits, Rob. Coll., A2558-9.13.

[100] 'Moll turns down plan to ease his life in DB,' *Sunday Express*, 3 August 1980. Wits, SAIRR, ZA HPRA AD1912A-S236.9.

again for seven days. He added, to my amazement, "Ek wil nie by vervolging betrokke wees nie." (I do not want to be involved in persecution.) Then he returned to his office. A few days later I was placed in solitary confinement for seven days. The following table contains the dates of my solitary spells.

Period	Start	End
1	10/1/80	20/1/80
2	11/2/80	25/2/80
3	1/3/80	10/3/80
4	20/3/80	2/4/80
5	11/4/80	24/4/80
6	1/5/80	14/5/80
7	22/5/80	5/6/80
8	11/6/80	25/6/80
9	3/7/80	16/7/80
10	23/7/80	6/8/80

Note that the last period, from 23 July 1980 to 6 August 1980, was implemented late, such that I sat only the last seven days of the 14 days. These dates are corroborated by a list that appears in *Hansard*.[101]

After I had sat this tenth period of solitary, making 125 days in total, I was called in by the Major, on Friday, 8 August 1980, and told that I should go up to the store and collect two pairs of blue overalls.[102] I immediately knew what that meant: that I was no longer to be regarded as a military defaulter but rather as a conscientious objector. I was in the seventh heaven. It took me some time to think out the implications of this enormous change.

---

[101] *Hansard* dated 6 June 1980, p. 850f: Wits, Rob. Coll., A2558-9.8.

[102] 'A mother prays …'. *Sunday Times*, 10 August 1980, and Editorial, *Argus*, 17 July 1980. Wits, Rob. Coll., A2558-9.13.

In a way it was an anti-climax, because there was so much publicity in the papers, and I had prepared myself psychologically to sit in solitary until the end of my sentence. On the other hand it was a great relief. I was at last able to get the food I needed. I would be able to move around. I was getting tired of being forgotten about when I was in my cell, and missing meals and exercise. Towards the end of my periods of solitary I used to become aggressive when I was not looked after. I would want to hit the corporal and yell. Luckily I was able to control this aggression at the last moment.

Sergeant-Major Els told me, "Jy is al klaar so bleek in die gesig, Moll" (Your face is already so pale), and gave instructions that I was not to be locked in my cell over the weekends as the other inmates were. I commented in a letter to my parents, "It's like getting a promotion, a raise, a new car and the jackpot all at once!"[103]

Later I learned that my parents heard of the concession by the army in a phone call from Rear-Admiral Botha to my father in Umtata.[104] My father said to my mother, "I have the best news you could ever receive right now." She immediately guessed, and my father burst into tears. I think they were under more tension than I was.

A SADF spokesperson stated,

Peter Moll is not a member of any of these churches [by the tenets whereof members are forbidden to do military service]. He claimed, however, that he was a conscientious objector as opposed to a radical politically inspired service dodger.

---

[103] My letter to my parents of 10 August 1980. Wits, Rob. Coll., A2558-9.13.

[104] Barry Levy, 1980. 'Lone army rebel with a cause wins his victory: conscientious objector status for Peter Moll,' *Sunday Express*, 10 August 1980. Wits, SAIRR Coll., ZA HPRA AD1912A-S236.5.

This could not easily be verified by the defence authorities and he was therefore treated the same as any member who refused to do military service or who contravened the Detention Barracks Regulations.

After months of careful investigation and observation, it was decided to give him the benefit of the doubt and he will therefore be treated as a conscientious objector for the rest of his term in detention, provided that he fulfils all obligations and actions required from a bona fide conscientious objector.[105]

Why did the army blink? There were four options facing the army at that point: (a) to keep going with solitary confinement in the hope that I would break; (b) to recognise Richard Steele as a conscientious objector, but try me again and send me to civilian jail for a further year, as they subsequently did with Charles Yeats and Neil Mitchell; (c) to try both Richard and me again, and send us to civilian jail for a year; or (d) to recognise both of us as conscientious objectors.

Option (a), more solitary confinement, was no longer sustainable due to the endless correspondence that the SADF had to deal with, the adverse publicity in the press, the repeated statements by church bodies and prominent church leaders, and the *terminus ad quem* given by Ray Swart's planned meeting with the Chief of the Defence Force, General Magnus Malan, the following Monday.

I speculate that option (b), recognising Richard and sending me to civilian jail, would have been quite attractive. The army believed that I was more dangerous than Richard because I was older, I had obtained much publicity through distributing my papers and delivering speeches, and especially because my

---

[105] Gherard Pieterse, 1980. 'A mother prays … and now pacifist son will be freed from solitary confinement.' *Sunday Times*, 15 August. Wits, Rob. Coll., A2558-9.13.

rationale for objection was more explicitly political. The army took a harder line with me than with Richard after separating us on 2 May 1980, by subjecting me to a further 63 days' solitary, while Richard did a further twelve. Yet the option of discriminating between Richard and me would have had no legal basis and would likely have provoked an outcry from civil society and particularly the churches.

I speculate that the military brass pondered long and hard about option (c), retrying us both and sending us to civilian jail. Yet resorting to the civilian courts and relying on jail was not favoured by the military. It would have amounted to an acknowledgement of failure. The military preferred to solve its problems internally. Sending a conscript to civilian jail involved a dishonourable discharge from the army and the loss of a potential soldier. Nevertheless this is exactly what the military did from the next conscientious objector (Charles Yeats) on. I puzzle over why the military did not give Richard and me this treatment. Was it that our stand was a complete surprise to the generals and so the easiest stop-gap was to recognise us as conscientious objectors? Or was this the effect of the sympathetic Rear-Admiral H.P. Botha?

There were advantages to option (d), recognising both of us as conscientious objectors. Many of the churches were pushing for such recognition, and also for alternative non-military service. The military had agreed to review the entire matter of conscientious objection and this option may have 'bought the peace' while the review was under way. This approach would also immediately end all the negative publicity and the embarrassment that our parents' visitations were inflicting on the generals. The military brass also had to act quickly because the meeting of Ray Swart with the head of the SADF was looming.

The latter meeting took place as planned on 11 August 1980. Ray Swart asked that the whole matter of solitary confinement and conscientious objection be reviewed by the military.[106] He reported later to the press that General Malan had agreed to such a review.[107] I was fortunate enough to be able to meet Ray Swart at the wedding of his son Chris to Phoebe Russell in 1983, and again in 2018 at Chris and Phoebe's house in Hout Bay, Cape Town, and thanked him both times for his intervention.

My parents continued to ply the SADF with letters[108] requesting that I be paroled and permitted to work as a mathematics teacher at the Cicira Training College in Umtata, but to no avail.

It was a little thing to be granted an administrative concession and be treated like conscientious objectors. It did not amount to legal recognition: in law we were still military defaulters. But it was remarkable, considering the ham-fisted approach of the SADF to the attempts by Professor Paul Hare and others to start a non-military alternative, and considering the *kragdadigheid* (appearance of power) with which many Afrikaner politicians believed they ought to govern. We imagined that in future the military would be forced to rethink its approach to conscientious objectors. Our joint stand had brought conscientious objection to the attention of the generals of the army in a way that quieter approaches could never have done. If we had complied with their demands and then made requests, nothing would have been achieved.

---

[106] John Murray, 1980. 'No further "solitary" for jailed objectors,' *The Star*, 11 August 1980. Wits, SAIRR, ZA HPRA AD1912A-S236.5.

[107] 'Defence Force to rethink on conscientious objection,' *The Star*, 12 August 1980. Wits, SAIRR Coll., ZA HPRA AD1912A-S236.5.

[108] My father to Rear-Admiral H.P. Botha, 26 August 1980 and 8 September 1980. Wits, Rob. Coll., A2558-9.13.

It was remarkable to observe the change in the attitude of the Detention Barracks officers after our recognition as conscientious objectors. Overnight many of them became friendly. The stand-offish and insulting manner that many of them affected disappeared. They no longer saw me as the enemy but simply as another prisoner, albeit with ideas they found incomprehensible, much like their view of the Jehovah's Witnesses.

After 8 August 1980, I worked with the Jehovah's Witnesses outside the Detention Barracks. I attended zealously to the fishpond, and cleared up litter, picking up beer bottles and cigarette butts from people smoking in their cars outside, and from corporals' parties the night before. I picked fruit for the officers sometimes and also picked some for myself. The plums and the peaches, and especially the mulberries, were quite superb, indeed divine, after eating only starchy foods for eight months. The work was boring. It was in the open air, though, which was pleasant, and I was not closely supervised. I was not continuously surrounded by cement, barbed wire and corrugated iron and I was a little further away from the yelling of the corporals. I often took a book with me and slipped off behind a tree or some safe place and did some revision of the study I had done the night before. I took notes when studying at night, storing the notes in my pocket, which was valuable for revision of Greek vocabulary.

There followed a bungled attempt at muzzling. In late July 1980 the Major had called me to his office. He and Staff-Sergeant Erasmus had both told me that I was henceforward not allowed to speak to anyone at all—not to the regular inmates, not to the Jehovah's Witnesses, not even to the corporals, only to Staff-Sergeant Erasmus and to the Major. I asked the Major why, and he said he did not know. Evidently he had been given instructions from higher up. On Sunday, 10 August 1980, my sister Jen and her husband Andrew came to visit; surely the happiest visit of all the visits I had. I mentioned the Major's muzzling order. Jen was horrified at how "unjust and inhuman" this was, and Andrew, who was a lawyer, contended that the authorities would not be allowed in law to enforce such an order. Jen complained to my mother, who complained to Rear-Admiral Botha, who complained to the Major. Who—luckless fellow— then received a phone call from my mother. Just to make sure nothing was lost in translation, on Tuesday a telegram from my mother arrived: "PHONED MAJOR SAID YOU MAY TALK TO ANYONE LOVE."

The surprising thing was that when my mother phoned the Major, he did not immediately acknowledge to her that he had received instructions to bind me to silence. He told her that he had never given any such instruction. She replied that her son never tells lies. Then he "remembered" that "a long time ago" he had "told Moll something about not speaking to people outside the Detention Barracks." He was obviously trying to hedge. When he next spoke to me he was very angry. He asked me, "When was it that I told you you were not allowed to speak to anyone?" I replied, "Just the other day, Major." Suddenly he feigned remembering, and said, "Oh, but that does not apply any more. You have been given blue overalls now, don't you know that it's different now?" He had not included that in the original instruction! This illustrates again how he would prefer to blame somebody below or above him, but not take responsibility himself.

I was disappointed on Sunday, 17 August 1980, to observe the performance of a Permanent Force chaplain, Rev. Donald Williams of the Methodist Church. An inmate called Mortimer Lee, who was doing the three-year Permanent Force option instead of the regular call-up, attended the church parade. After the service he remonstrated with Chaplain Williams about his insistence that all the men join the church parade. Lee challenged Chaplain Williams to explain why a man of God should resort to the use of force to make inmates listen to his sermon. Chaplain Williams' excuse was that it was part of his job to see to it that the message reached the people for whom he was responsible. Lee questioned whether Chaplain Williams was allowing his responsibility to God to play second fiddle to his responsibility to the SADF.

Whereupon Chaplain Williams, who was dressed in full military uniform, threatened to charge him with insubordination. He raised his voice, in front of the other inmates present, and could be heard throughout the courtyard. He took Lee off to the Major's office and was on the point of charging him, but eventually let him off with a reprimand. Ironically, Lee had in the first place been detained for refusing to go to a church parade! I asked Lee to write an account of his treatment by Chaplain Williams.[109] I was glad to have written proof of this incident as it showed, to my mind, the folly of allowing ministers to become full-time Permanent Force chaplains, with rank and uniform, for the chaplain is then tempted, or forced, to act more like a military officer who commands obedience than like a church minister who performs services for his or her members.

A vigil of thanks for our recognition as conscientious objectors was held at the Rondebosch Congregational Church on Friday, 22 August 1980. The vigil book ran to 24 pages, with every hour of the night covered.[110] Rob Goldman, a friend from UCT, had a penetrating comment quoting Dietrich Bonhoeffer on 23 January 1944 from his prison cell: "The idea that we could have avoided many of life's difficulties if we had taken things

---

[109] I can make Mortimer Lee's account available upon request.
[110] The call for the 2nd fast: Wits, Rob. Coll., A2558-9.8.

more quietly is one that cannot be taken seriously for a moment." Stephen de Gruchy wrote down the poem he had composed the previous December, "Peace man."[11] In addition there were thoughtful comments from Ax (code for security[112]), Dot Cleminshaw, Jim Cochrane, Aneene Dawber, Isobel de Gruchy, Sally Didcott, Liz Fish, F.J.G. (code for security), Larry Kaufmann, Lynne Lawrence, Mike Lawrence, Margaret Malherbe, Bruce Meier, M.K. (code for security), Terence Moll, Adi Paterson, Cathy Paterson, Pir (code for security), R. (code for security), Rev. David Russell, Cherry Squair and Ivan Toms.

On 12 October 1980 the Synod of the Anglican diocese of Cape Town commended the military authorities for having recognised me and Richard as conscientious objectors and praised them for this "change of heart." At the same time it reiterated its call that provision be made for alternative non-military national service for conscientious objectors [113]

After my recognition as a conscientious objector, I had more frequent contact with the Jehovah's Witnesses. Officially I was not allowed to talk to them, but the corporals often tolerated our conversing and in any case were not always able to monitor every corner of the unit. The Jehovah's Witnesses used to cut my hair once a week on Wednesdays.

Min dae[114]

I was moved to Block Two in October, where I stayed until the end of my time in the Detention Barracks (2 December

---

[111] 'Peace man' is reproduced in the section of original documents, with permission from Steve's widow Marian Loveday.

[112] Some individuals feared that the police might harass them if they revealed their full names, so signed with a brief code.

[113] ' "Change of heart" on objectors', *Cape Times,* 13 October 1980.

[114] Literally 'few days' in Afrikaans, the slogan used by men in the army when counting the days to freedom.

1980). That was a difficult period owing to the noise at night. We were locked up at about half past five in the evening. The lights were turned out at about ten. Most of the inmates had nothing to do during those four and a half hours. They were never given access to the library. Their way of entertaining themselves was by talking to one another. Sometimes there would be conversations from one end of the block to the other, which could be accomplished only by shouting. I found this frustrating. I dislike noise in civilian life, but under the constraints of detention it was awful. I could not move away to find quiet, as I could in civilian life. Yelling at the person(s) making the noise would have been ineffective and would have encouraged the worst in them. At times it was worse than solitary confinement in that I could force myself to accept the loneliness of the latter, but I had no coping mechanism for the noise problem. I went to the psychologist about it, asking for tranquillisers, which he would not give. I tried to get moved back to Block Five—even though it would be trying over weekends, when I would be locked up all the time—but that was not allowed.

The noise did not worry the other inmates too much, partly because they themselves were doing the talking, and partly because they were mostly short-timers. I do recall, though, that Richard found the noise unbearable too when he was in the Voortrekkerhoogte Detention Barracks.

I was taken to the nearby military hospital at the psychologist's instance to have hearing tests, just in case the problem was occasioned by excessively acute hearing. I was placed in an anechoic chamber to test my keenness of hearing. It turned out that my hearing was far from acute; my problem was nervous or mental, not acuteness of hearing. In the end nothing was done. I used earplugs but these were painful if used for many hours at a stretch, and I could hear through them anyway. Luckily nothing serious happened and relief came when I was discharged from detention.

In the last months of my sentence I received two visits from Dutch Reformed Church theologians. The first visited on the afternoon of Friday, 22 August 1980, introducing himself as Chris Marais, a final-year 'tokkelok' (theology student) at the University of Pretoria (the word is onomatopoeic for the Afrikaans 'teoloog' and the English 'talk-a-lot'). He said he was writing a paper on 'dienspligontduiking' (draft dodging), and thought it a good idea to speak to a conscientious objector directly. I explained to him at length how I came to be a conscientious objector, as I have done in the earlier chapters of this book: my start as a Baptist, my involvement in the Students' Christian Association, the shock of the Soweto uprisings and the brutal police response, my Damascus Road experience at the SCA Conference at Pietermaritzburg in 1976, the murder of Steve Biko, the theological investigations, the study of just war theory. Since the theology student had said he had had a full theological training, I described in detail the broadening of Just War doctrine from precedent to precedent: Augustine, Aquinas, Calvin, de Victoria, and the Baptist Confession of 1689.

Finally, I explained that I believed that South African society was fundamentally unjust because it was based on a racial ordering of society. I stressed that black people had been deprived of all opportunity to express their political views: they had no vote, their presence in 'white' South Africa was intended to be temporary only, they were subject to curfews at night, and any attempt to form unions or political movements was likely to be met with imprisonment, torture and even death. Small wonder that in the face of this, the primary violence exercised by the state, young black men left the country to seek out some means of fighting 'the system.' This gave rise to the second violence, namely guerrilla action at the borders or in urban areas, typically focused on key infrastructure. I said it was obvious to me that the wars the SADF was fighting were civil wars, wars of brother against brother. What was needed was a national convention at which all the parties would set up a government of national unity and let the ballot box determine the country's future. In the meanwhile, I considered the role of the SADF to fall well short of the standard set by the 1689 Baptist Confession for a Christian to participate, namely that the war be 'just and necessary'.

The theology student appeared receptive and convinced. I was glad of the opportunity to talk, at last, with an Afrikaner who understood me. After nine months' intellectual starvation in detention and the monachal silence of solitary confinement, I valued this intelligent conversation. I discovered 33 years later that this tokkelok was much more than a theology student—see the next chapter.

The second theologian to visit unexpectedly was a young chaplain in the SADF, who introduced himself as Jan Nieder-Hartmann. He told me he had been to the South African Christian Leadership Assembly in 1979 and that his views had changed radically there and he had emerged a convinced liberal. He came to see me one afternoon in my cell in Block Three. He was apparently unaware that staff were not supposed to go into inmates' cells, and that meetings were held in the meeting room near the main entrance. Needless to say, I did not consider it my job to tell him of the rules of the Detention Barracks! For I believed that if the Major had got to know about this, both of us would have been in trouble. Nieder-Hartmann expressed sympathy for my views. We chatted at length about my stance as a conscientious objector. I vowed that I would try to contact him once I had left the Detention Barracks. I was out of luck, however. I could find no such person. It was puzzling that a well-spoken, well-educated young dominee could disappear into thin air. Was he genuine, or was he perhaps another spy?

Meanwhile the Baptist church, in its typical low-key manner, continued to seek ways of accommodating conscientious objectors. In October 1980, Rev. Trevor Swart of the Baptist Union Executive submitted a six-page memorandum to the Prime Minister. (Rev. Swart had in turn relied on assistance from Rev. Rob Robertson for information about alternative service options.) It followed up on the Baptist Union Assembly resolution of 1979 in favour of non-military alternative national service for conscientious objectors. It proposed that individuals who "on religious grounds, cannot serve in any armed forces"— thus religious pacifists—be permitted to do alternative service in rural development and other areas of need.[115] Rev. Swart and Rev. Theo Pass met with the Prime Minister P.W. Botha and the Chaplain-General on 6 November 1980 to discuss the resolution and the memorandum. The Baptist delegation also included Professor Johan van Rooyen and Colonel (Rev.) van den Aardweg. During the 35-minute interview, conducted mostly in Afrikaans, the delegation referred to the Assembly's statement of 1979, calling for legislation to provide for genuine conscientious objectors, and asking for alternative national service.[116] The Assembly's minutes do not record the response from the Prime Minister. In the interim the SADF had set up a committee to investigate the matter, whose report was due in November.

I was able to write my examinations. My brother Terence, my sister Jen and our aunt Dorothy had kindly helped me enter for

---

[115] The memorandum of the Baptist Union Executive: Wits, Rob. Coll., A2558-1.

[116] *Minutes of Officers' Meeting* at King William's Town and East London, 21 and 22 November 1980, page 4, item 6. The volume is held at the Baptist Union Archive at the Baptist Theological College, Johannesburg.

Philosophy III, Hebrew I, German I and Hellenistic Greek II
with the University of South Africa. I wrote the Hebrew I and
Philosophy III exams in October in the little library, invigilated
by Lieutenant Smith. My sister Jen and our aunt Dorothy
persuaded the UNISA officials to allow me to write the German
I and Hellenistic Greek II examinations in February 1981 as
supplementary examinations, thereby giving me more time to
study. The examinations went well because I had worked hard.
I had had little else to do, especially over weekends: we were
locked up at six in the afternoon on Friday, and we were kept
locked up almost the whole weekend barring mealtimes.[117]

In November I received a letter from Joel Gwabeni, a school
teacher in Herschel in the north-western part of the Transkei. He
had been a student at the Cicira Training College, Umtata, where
my mother taught English. My mother had told him that I was
in solitary confinement, and that she was worried for my mental
health. He was able to comfort her on account of his own
remarkable story.

Joel Gwabeni and Caswell Mbelebele were sentenced at
Queenstown on 18 November 1964 to seven and a half and five
years' imprisonment respectively, for sabotage, following the
burning of a dairy by alleged members of the Pan-Africanist
Congress.[118] Joel was imprisoned at Robben Island but he and
Sedick Isaacs and others had the courage to find ways of
teaching literacy skills, mathematics, physics, philosophy and
economics to their fellow prisoners over the weekends.[119] Upon
his release, Joel was served with a banning order restricting him

---

[117] I attained 93% in Hebrew I, 75% in Philosophy III, 69% in German I
and 75% in Hellenistic Greek II.

[118] *Contact for united non-racial action*, Volume 7, No. 13, 27 November
1964, available at https://disa.ukzn.ac.za/sites/default/files/pdf_files/Ctv7n
1364.pdf .

[119] Isaacs (2010).

to the town of Herschel in the Transkei. The order expired on 31 December 1978.[120] It was after his release from banning that he was able to attend the Cicira Training College.

Joel told my mother of his long time in jail on Robben Island, of which two years had been in solitary confinement. He said he had been able to survive and had not suffered psychological damage. He emphasised that what is important is the prisoner's belief in his cause. People who have 'no hope—no goal' become 'nervous wrecks'; people who have the will and believe in their cause survive unscathed. He was detained again for a time by the Transkei government, which accused him of involvement in the school boycotts of 1980. He was released, however, and soon after that was able to write to me. His letter repeated the message he had kindly passed on to my mother and I found it highly encouraging. I met up with him in 1981 at my parents' house in Umtata. He was a tall, slightly built gentleman, quiet-spoken and gentle. I was glad to be able to thank him personally for his support.

In September 1980 Stephen Granger very thoughtfully found a poster which he attached to cardboard and cut up into 20 'jigsaw' cards which he distributed to friends who could send me a card each. I eventually received 16 of the original 20. The deficiency of four was probably not ascribable to censorship; more likely to ineffective army bureaucracy. These 16 were written by Doug Bax (one), Ron Begbie (one), Liz Fish (one), Owen Franklin (one), Rob Goldman and Sally Didcott (one), Marj Graham (two), Stephen Granger (two), Bev Haddad (one),

---

[120] *Political prisoners and banned persons in apartheid South Africa.* United Nations Centre against Apartheid, no. 39/78. 58 pages. Available at http://psimg.jstor.org/fsi/img/pdf/t0/10.5555/al.sff.document.nuun1978_ 38_final.pdf. Banning: 'List of people banned under Apartheid', in *South African history on-line: towards a people's history.* Available at https:// www.sahistory.org.za/article/list-people-banned-under-apartheid .

Jane Keen (one), Tony Saddington (one), Di Scott (one), Cherry Squair (one), Meg Tourien (one), and Mary [no surname stated] (one). What an imaginative and thoughtful gesture.

People continued to show interest in my case and Richard's. On Sunday, 12 October 1980, the Catholic Society at the University of Cape Town held a mass at Kolbe House in which the focus was my stand as a conscientious objector.

Inmate Patrick 'Pat' Els bequeathed us one of the funniest incidents. Short of stature, and English-speaking, he used to call me 'larney'[121] owing to my Cape Town English accent. He was among the *oumanne* who had done much violence to the new arrestees in December 1979. Later he became a good friend. We would talk about all sorts of things. He told me about the problems he was having at home, with his girlfriend, with the Detention Barracks, etc. He and three others made a bold escape at seven o'clock one morning by bending back a piece of the corrugated iron fence. They walked along the road on the way to the N1 highway, where they planned to hitch-hike. They were seen by a Lieutenant and the Chaplain, ds. Dawid Venter, who stopped immediately, climbed out of the car and gave chase. The dominee, with amazing presence of mind, took his pipe (being an inveterate smoker) and held it as though it were a pistol. He yelled, "Stop or I'll fire!" The silly boys stopped! They were brought back to the barracks, much to the other inmates' merriment. On account of the now diminished status of the *oumanne,* Pat was not subjected to the violence that he himself had used against escapees in the past. He was sentenced to six months in civilian prison owing to his repeated escapes, and was dishonourably discharged from the army.

---

[121] Johannesburg slang meaning expensive or fancy.

Family

My family's support during the whole year was of the greatest importance. Although my parents tried their best to dissuade me from becoming a conscientious objector, once I was imprisoned my mother came out strongly in my support and travelled with my sister Brenda from Umtata to Cape Town to visit me and attend the trial. My mother made two trips to Voortrekkerhoogte to see me, one with my father in April and the other in July.

My father's support was of a different kind. He disagreed with my reasoning about the moral probity of the wars of the SADF but, knowing that there was trouble ahead, he wrote to the military authorities in 1979 without my knowledge and tried to persuade them to drop the call-up. The SADF was thereby given an honourable way out. If they had cleverly reassigned me to an inactive unit, there would not have been the masses of unfavourable publicity that the SADF was subsequently to suffer. In their ideological closedness they ground ahead with issuing call-ups and summonses. When the repeated sentences of solitary confinement began, my father's position shifted altogether. Now he became a ferocious opponent of the generals' decisions and wrote in his personal capacity to the SADF, and had my mother sign letters to the press. When I was finally recognised as a conscientious objector, he wrote on 13 August 1980 to congratulate me on my "stickability and determination." His last work day as Regional Magistrate of the Transkei was 30 April 1980. He submitted his notice of retirement (three months) at the beginning of February. The timing was providential in that he was then able to devote his time to making appeals on my behalf. My mother told me he had retired because the job demanded too much long-distance travel. My father did not ever mention to me why he retired at that juncture, but he did tell me some years later that he regretted having done so because shortly after that the entire civil service received a substantial pay raise which would have improved his pension.

My eldest sister, Lorraine Burger, also opposed my ideas but not to the extent of being unsympathetic: when she and her husband Carl Burger came to Pretoria on holiday, they made a point of visiting for an hour, having arranged this through the Baptist Chaplain (Rev.) Lucas Johannes Potgieter. She also wrote letters to me. My elder brother Douglas was ambivalent about my ideas, but was sympathetic enough to come to see me at the Voortrekkerhoogte Detention Barracks in January 1980. My younger brother Terence was strongly supportive and wrote regular letters. He came to visit me—in the Major's office—and related to me his activities with student politics. (He tried to persuade the guards that our friend who drove him there, Alan Ralphs, should join him because he was an uncle, but they were not so gullible.)

My middle sister Jen and her husband Andrew Beck came and visited me many times and saw to my needs as far as books and toiletries went. Andrew gave me a denim hat that was the envy of the other inmates. It was as much as I could do to prevent its being 'scored' (stolen) and resist the bartering offers made in variable amounts of food and cigarettes. Jen and Andrew were very kind in serving as a conduit for friends and supporters to call, whose messages they would then pass on to me. I was also able to channel one of my reports on violence in the Detention Barracks through Jen, who kindly transcribed and distributed it.

My youngest sister Brenda, who was a boarder in standard seven (the equivalent of grade nine) at the Kaffrarian High School in King William's Town, came with my mother to see me in the Detention Barracks in Wynberg at the time of my trial, and wrote many entertaining letters, always full of good cheer. She proudly told me of her school results, which were mostly from 70% to 90%, but said she could not share the results for Afrikaans and English, because she "nearly pegged" when she saw them!

My cousin and co-conscientious objector Richard Steele came to see me in February 1980 just before his own trial. It was useful for him to see the layout of the Detention Barracks and to get some sense of the 'vibe,' in preparation for his own incarceration there a few days later. My cousin Martin Henry Pohlmann, a probationer Baptist minister at Edenvale Baptist Church, came to visit me after making the arrangement through the chaplaincy system. My aunt Dorothy came all the way from Kempton Park to Cape Town in December 1979 to visit me. I had regular visits from her and my uncle John Steele while I was at Voortrekkerhoogte. How Dorothy fitted in these visits despite her heavy work schedule as the editor of the *South African Pharmaceutical Journal* I do not know. She helped with obtaining clothes in December 1979 after I had lost my suitcase at the Waterkloof military airport, and helped with registration at UNISA, with finding books and with arranging UNISA examination dates. She and her daughter Heather came to fetch me from the Barracks upon my release on 2 December 1980.

During the year I received about 60 letters from my family. They had written some 60 more—which were either mislaid by the army or censored. My family was highly supportive and this was one of the important factors in my survival. I am eternally grateful to them for that.

Visits

Technically I was allowed visits only from family, but the Officer Commanding also had considerable leeway in this respect. Beside the family visits mentioned above, I also enjoyed visits from Rev. Rob Robertson on many occasions; from Grace Townshend, whom I knew from the Students' Christian

Association at the University of Cape Town; and from Professor Johan van Rooyen (University of South Africa), who had been my lawyer at my first two trials.

Several more people made the long trek from Johannesburg out to Voortrekkerhoogte in the hope of visiting but were turned away: Anthony Asher, whom I knew from the University of Cape Town and the Old Mutual; Rev. Douglas Bax of the Rondebosch Congregational Church; Peter Moodie, a high school science teacher whom I had met in Umtata; Alan Ralphs, whom I knew from the Catholic Society at the University of Cape Town; Di Scott-Saddington, whom I knew from the Rondebosch Congregational Church; Victor McGregor, who was working at the New Johannesburg Hospital; and Brian and Tilla Schultz, whom I had met at an SCA Discipleship Camp in 1977.

Letters

There arose through various avenues an international letter writing campaign on behalf of Richard Steele and myself. I received about 540 letters, telegrams and cards during the year, and have listed the authors' names in an appendix. I replied to all who supplied addresses after my release. Many were from Amnesty International supporters in England. As far as I know, Amnesty International obtained information about Richard and me from the Committee on South African War Resistance (COSAWR) in London. The Amnesty supporters often wrote to me saying they had just written to the Prime Minister and the Minister of Defence demanding that I be released. An example of an Amnesty group is given by the letters from Norah McClelland, whose Amnesty group was associated with the local churches in Stockport near Manchester. Many of the Amnesty writers were Baptists whose churches had 'adopted' me.

There emerged a roll-call of an international brigade of conscientious objectors. A heart-warming example is given by Raymond Matchett, writing from Norfolk, UK.[122] His father had been imprisoned in 1917 for conscientious objection, and died of tuberculosis as a result of the privations in prison. Even though there were only a few hundred objectors in the UK in the First World War, Mr. Matchett noted that their impact was such that the laws were changed to provide for conscientious objection, and prison conditions were reformed. Another letter writer, Rev. Ralph L. Ackroyd, had three uncles who were imprisoned for conscientious objection in the First World War. The letter writers Harry Lees, E.S. Spencer and Derrick Knowlton had themselves been conscientious objectors in the UK in the Second World War, and were able to do alternative non-military service. Another writer, Dean Meyer, had been a conscientious objector in the Second World War in the USA; he was sentenced to work in a mental hospital. The father of another writer, Billie Werenich, had been a conscientious objector in Poland. Another writer, Rev. Franz Hildebrandt, a former pastor of the Confessional Church in Germany, related that he was a life-long pacifist and was imprisoned briefly by the Hitler regime.

An unusual letter arrived from Alison Christie-Murray, a professional actress in the UK. She was at the time performing the role of a girl who had been in prison for three years. She said she had to search with her imagination and with the help of the author for the reality of the situation. What struck her most was the "heaviness of time passing—the state of limbo." There was something that I could identify with.

The newsletter *Non-Violence News* run by Rev. Rob Robertson on behalf of the South African Council of Churches

---

[122] Matchett's letter is reproduced in the section with original documents.

proved to be an important supplier of information about Richard and myself for people overseas. For instance, the International Fellowship of Reconciliation, headquartered in Alkmaar, the Netherlands, republished some of the *Non-Violence News* advertisements requesting prayers, letters and telegrams. Several writers learned of Richard and me through the IFOR's *Reconciliation Quarterly*, e.g. Dorothy I. Green, of Nottingham in the UK, and Leonard Webb of Kingsway, London.

A second large group of letters came from Mennonite Christian people in the USA. This was prompted by the fact that Richard and his parents had had Mennonite connections. The official magazine of the church, *Gospel Herald*, published an appeal for letter writing to Richard and myself.[123] Some of the Mennonites wrote repeatedly—once per month or once per fortnight. Many of them were newsy and interesting letters. They knew that what we really wanted was not so much sympathy and identification with our positions but just news— news about any little thing that was going on, anything interesting. For instance, Anna Juhnke, a professor in English at Bethel College in Kansas wrote that two of her fellow faculty members at Bethel College had been imprisoned as conscientious objectors in the 1940s.

Letters came to me and Richard from Tomás and Disa Rutschman of the Comunidad Cristiana in Barcelona, Spain. Their prime task was pastoring a church on behalf of the Mennonite Mission Network, but the community was also creating employment by making wooden children's toys and puzzles. The Dutch workers Maarten and Margreet van der Werf wrote many letters and cards from Gabarone, Botswana,

---

[123] 'South Africa COs held in solitary confinement,' *Gospel Herald*, 6 May 1980.

where they were busy on Mennonite Central Committee projects.

Some Americans obtained my and Richard's particulars from *The Other Side,* a magazine which was evangelical and had a strong concern for the poor. I received, for example, several letters from Bill and Brenda Lane via *The Other Side.* He was a professor of religious studies at Western Kentucky University in Bowling Green, Kentucky, and was also a Presbyterian minister at a racially mixed church.[124] She was a missionary with the Methodist church, and later an office coordinator for the Religion Department of Western Kentucky University.[125] Knowing that Richard and I were theology students, they told us about Bill's well-known commentaries on the Gospel of Mark and on the book of Hebrews.

COSAWR staff in London alerted the Labour Members of Parliament Tony Benn[126] and Frank Allaun to my situation, resulting in their writing letters to me and simultaneously to the Prime Minister. In September 1980 I received a card from Bruce Kent, General Secretary of the Campaign for Nuclear Disarmament. I think he came to hear of me through Amnesty International or COSAWR. Some people, like the German theology student Rolf Bielefeld, read of me in the magazine of Pax Christi, *JUSTPEACE.*

I received many cards and letters from the Women of the UCCSA (United Congregational Church of Southern Africa) in Zimbabwe, headed by Jean Campbell.

I received several letters from Richard Knottenbelt, then based in Botswana. Originally British, he spent some years teaching mathematics and science at the Chikwingwizha Minor

---

[124] Lane's Wikipedia entry is https://en.wikipedia.org/wiki/William_L._Lane.

[125] See her obituary at https://www.goadfh.com/obituary/Brenda-Lane.

[126] Benn's letter is reproduced in the section of original documents.

Seminary in Rhodesia, and acting as the secretary for the International Fellowship of Reconciliation.[127] In terms of Rhodesia's strict conscription laws, he was called up in 1977. He refused as he was a Quaker and a universal pacifist. The Exemption Board refused his application, interpreting it to be "political rather than religious." Despite being married and having two small children, he was sentenced to five months' jail which he spent at the Khami Medium Security Prison before being released in January 1978. It was encouraging to hear of his determined stand for peace. He subsequently lived in Botswana, the UK and the USA.

A card came from two French people in the Pyrénées, Barbara Guthiez and Alain Dejelley. Several cards and letters came from the writer and playwright Marie Aspioti, M.B.E., from Corfu (Greece), who was linked with Amnesty International. Other countries from which people wrote included Canada, Germany, the Netherlands and Saudi Arabia.

A Dutch volunteer Teresa in Guinea Bissau wrote an unusual card. She had learned of Richard and me from the HAPOTOC Collective (Help A Prisoner, Outlaw Torture Collective), based in Amsterdam, whose aim was to improve conditions in prisons worldwide. I had a good laugh when I saw the picture side of the card: it showed five visibly armed PAIGC fighters crossing a river! The PAIGC was the African Party for the Independence of Guinea and Cape Verde, which turned to guerrilla warfare in the 1960s. Somehow this card made it through the censors … maybe they could not recognise a rifle slung over a shoulder? *Swak, Piketberg!*

Most numerous were letters from people in South Africa. Bishop Desmond Tutu, then head of the South African Council

---

[127] https://www.friendsjournal.org/wp-content/uploads/emember/down loads/1978/HC12-50646.pdf .

of Churches, wrote to me once per month.[128] Other well-known individuals wrote, including Dr. Margaret Nash, Stephen Mulholland (editor, Financial Mail, Johannesburg) and Bishop Philip Russell (Anglican, Natal). I received many letters from students at the University of Cape Town because the Christian magazine *Comment*, associated with the Students' Christian Association, ran a column with my and Richard's particulars.[129] I looked forward eagerly to letters from Gary Palser, Stephen Granger and Margaret Ramsay, all of whom I knew from the Students' Christian Association. They filled me in on much national and international news, which compensated for the lack of access to newspapers. One especially touching note came from Michael G. Smith of Tamboerskloof, Cape Town, who enclosed an envelope and a stamp to enable me to reply, suggesting I tell him of anything I needed which he might send in a parcel.

Mismatch of sentencing and the Detention Barracks setup

The physical design and the administration of the Detention Barracks was aimed at the short-term offender. It was ill adapted for long-term prisoners. According to the *Detention Barracks Regulations*, the institution was to be managed "so that a person serving a sentence shall be treated and trained in such a manner that, on his release, he may be better equipped to adjust himself in employment and in the community."[130] This objective may

---

[128] A representative letter from Bishop Tutu is reproduced in the section of selected letters.

[129] 'A matter of conscience: Peter Moll and Richard Steele,' *Comment* (Christian student newspaper at the University of Cape Town), March 1980, p. 15-16. Also Adrian Paterson, 1980. 'Recognition: conscientious objectors recognised,' *Comment*, September 1980.

[130] *Detention Barracks Regulations* (1961-1976), Chapter II. 2.(1).

have been realised to some extent for the short-term detainees, but was unachievable for the long-term ones.

The Detention Barracks had been set up initially as a deterrent to minor offences such as AWOL (absence without leave), disrespect to an officer, or minor physical damage. It delivered an intensified type of basic military training in the form of marching and physical training, administered by army officers who were deliberately rough with their language and who frequently used violence as enforcement. The 'short sharp shock' was effective for some of the minor offenders, particularly those gone AWOL, who after serving their sentence returned to complete their military training.

The physical design of the Detention Barracks was similar to any military unit of the time except that instead of large dormitories there were individual cells. The construction of the Detention Barracks was not that of a prison with high security. The outside fence could be scaled by a determined inmate. Although the *Detention Barracks Regulations* forbade contact between arrested persons and other inmates,[131] this was honoured more in the breach than in the observance. There were no facilities for separating inmates by the seriousness or nature of their crimes, except for the Jehovah's Witnesses who were self-governed and were instructed to keep to themselves in Block Four. There were no high-security cells. There were no facilities for rehabilitation in the form of opportunities for productive work or acquiring skills in woodworking, metal-working and other trades. The Detention Barracks also lacked the staffing that would have been needed for such rehabilitation; apart from Major Krige, the doctor and the social worker, the staff were ordinary military officers with no specific skills in

---

[131] *Ibid*, Chapter II.2.(2)(b).

penitentiary management, and their stint in the Detention Barracks was just one brief assignment of many.

Thus the physical design and the methods of administration of the Detention Barracks were such as to deter AWOL and minor offences, thereby enforcing conscription among the white male population. The Detention Barracks was not equipped to deal with regular military offenders who had committed more serious crimes such as rape, with men who had suffered rape, with the men who habitually went AWOL, with drug addicts, or with conscientious objectors such as Jehovah's Witnesses, Christadelphians or Richard and me. In some ways the Detention Barracks imposed harsher conditions than did civilian prisons, especially for long-term inmates and conscientious objectors: stinking chamber pots, blocked sewage drains with overflowing faeces, freezing cold water in winter, no beds, no pillows, no recreational facilities, no magazines, no productive work, and so on. There was a library but only I and the Jehovah's Witnesses were given access; the other long-term prisoners were kept out—even though the *Detention Barracks Regulations* specify that "a library containing literature of a constructive and educational nature may be placed at the disposal of inmates."[132]

Once Major Krige, in a moment of frankness, told me that he believed that 80 percent of the inmates had gone AWOL for a specific reason. I think he was right: only a minority of conscripts were pure chancers in the sense that they went AWOL in the hope that the army would not catch them out. That specific reason for absenting themselves often became apparent in a brief conversation with the inmate. Most had little schooling (between standard four and standard seven, as explained earlier) and came from families that were poor or psychologically disturbed through drink or drugs or violence. The men would go

---

[132] *Ibid*, Chapter II.2.(2)(d).

AWOL to try to sort out personal problems, having achieved little success in resolving them through the army welfare system. For men with serious personal problems the Detention Barracks were a hindrance, not a help, to their recovery.

Some conscripts aimed at securing a discharge. They would go AWOL repeatedly and escape repeatedly, to force the army's hand. That took much patience. Some tried this stratagem for years without success. One man, Jakes, for instance, came in five times while I was in the Detention Barracks, and we became friends. Jakes eventually left by escaping. I met another inmate who told me he had been in the Detention Barracks 16 times in total. He said that he would be caught, be escorted by an 18-year-old corporal to the Detention Barracks, and on the way in the train he would tell the corporal, "Look, you know me, you know that I have been in the Detention Barracks 16 times and that I've escaped 16 times. You know that I am bigger and older and stronger than you. I think it will be better if we just separate. You go your way and I'll go mine. Then there won't be any trouble." The hapless corporal would instantly concur and unlock the handcuffs. Clearly the effort spent by the army trying to corral recalcitrants like the two just described was not worth the expense, and the Detention Barracks was not equipped to manage them, still less to make better soldiers of them, as the *Detention Barracks Regulations* (1961-1976) bravely envisaged.

A similar assessment of the inability of the Detention Barracks to rehabilitate its inmates was given in 1984 by Anthony Waddell:

A system such as DB obviously takes a terrible toll on its inmates and there are people who cannot or will not adjust to the essential barbarity of being labelled a social misfit and a criminal. The attempts at 'rehabilitation' through negative reinforcement and the manipulation of structural violence literally kills some of those people who don't have the mental tools to adapt. (Louw, 1984)

Drug addiction was another problem area that the Detention Barracks could not manage. I do not know whether dagga is addictive in general. I did, however, meet some inmates who acknowledged that they were addicted and could not shake it off. I spent a long afternoon talking in my cell with an inmate Bam who was deeply disturbed by his situation. He had a wife with a baby and a girlfriend who was pregnant, to name but the start of his problems. He confessed he was addicted to dagga. As long as he did not smell it, all was well, but as soon as he caught the scent he would go crazy with an irrepressible urge to get it. I felt sorry for him. We agreed that the next time he sensed the danger approaching, he would come to my cell and we would try to talk it over.

The dysfunction of the Detention Barracks was exacerbated by the military's manipulation of the media. Reports appeared from time to time in the newspapers about the Detention Barracks, giving the institution far more credit than it deserved. The reporters had little choice and they were, frankly, naive. When they were shown around the barracks, all the inmates were locked away in their cells. The reporters were not allowed to speak to anyone privately. They were shown over the most attractive parts of the Detention Barracks, such as the administrative offices, the kitchen and the mess. They were not taken to the back where the ablution blocks were, which were often filthy as described earlier. They were not given interviews with, say, Richard or me or the Jehovah's Witnesses, out of earshot of the officers. Furthermore, the reporters did not state in their final pieces that they had been denied interviews with inmates outside of earshot of the officers, or had been forbidden to inspect the ablution blocks, or had been prevented from conversing with the conscientious objectors out of earshot of the officers. In short, the journalists were hoodwinked.

Chapter 6. Free at last! Legal changes and resistance to conscription

I was released on 2 December 1980 amid thorough reporting by the press.[133] My aunt Dorothy and her daughter Heather came to fetch me by car from the Detention Barracks in Voortrekkerhoogte. The first thing I did upon arrival at their home in Kempton Park was to take a shower—with warm water! I must have spent half an hour enjoying this exquisite pleasure. Then Heather took me to visit some friends who happened to have an eight-month-old baby, whom I had the chance of holding on my lap, another memorable experience after twelve months of mixing only with adult males. I went then to stay with my brother Douglas and his wife Cas (Carol) in Johannesburg for a few days. Then I took a lift with my brother-in-law Andrew, via Aliwal North, to Umtata, to be with my parents. The family spent a fortnight at Hluleka national park, staying in rondavels. That was the best holiday of my life, with hours and hours of intelligent conversation without the stress of having to cram everything into brief hour-long visiting periods. Meanwhile I was busily studying German I and Hellenistic Greek II for the delayed examinations in February 1981.

Upon my release I received a telegram from Rev. David Russell saying, "Your endurance has inspired many ... Onward Christian Soldier. Love, David Russell." I wrote a letter to all the people from whom I had received a communication, thanking them for their "unstinting support, [their] prayers, and [their] letters, which made life much more bearable in DB."

---

[133] For example, Marja Tuit, 1980. 'Peter Moll released from DB,' *Rand Daily Mail*, 5 December 1980.

One of the important consequences of the objection stands by Richard and me was that the issues of militarisation, of civil war, and of conscientious objection were brought out into the open where they could more easily be discussed. For instance, the National Union of South African Students (NUSAS) had for some time been studying the military issue and had created a committee 'Milcom,' but this was done quietly for fear of the serious consequences of being charged with incitation. As conscientious objectors were imprisoned amid much criticism from church bodies, it became easier to discuss military matters openly. The increased openness was to have important consequences later as people started to question the very notion of conscription; this will be treated below.

On the day after my release, the Congress of the National Union of South African Students passed a unanimous motion congratulating me on my "courageous and consistent stand." The motion, which was seconded by my brother Terence, also called upon the state to amend the laws governing military service, providing a non-military option for genuine conscientious objectors.[134]

The Presbyterian Church of South Africa passed a resolution at its 1980 Assembly:

The Assembly pays tribute to Peter Moll and Richard Steele as courageous confessors of the faith who, as conscientious objectors in detention barracks and solitary confinement, have shown their supreme loyalty to Christ as Lord and their faithfulness to what they understand His will to be, and so have served as witnesses to

---

[134] The minutes of this NUSAS Congress are available at: the National Union of South African Students. *Summary of Congress Reports and Recommendations for 1981*. Digital Innovation South Africa, JSTOR, https://jstor.org/stable/al.sff.document.rep19801100.026.022.000.

Him who endured the cross, despising the shame, for the joy that was set before him.[135]

An impact was registered in the Students' Christian Association. My stand and Richard's were like a wake-up call to the organisation in which we had been involved throughout our four years at the University of Cape Town. This rethinking encouraged a drawing together of the SCA with its sister organisation, the Students' Christian Movement, which encompassed coloured and black students. The SCA and the SCM held a joint conference in July 1980 at Cyara, where conscientious objection was one of the key issues discussed. (They were eventually reunited as the Students' Christian Organisation in 1997.)[136]

Great consternation was expressed in military circles. One R.A. Holtzhausen, from the Chief of Staff Personnel at Defence Headquarters, wrote on 12 December 1980 to the General in charge:

1. See the attached photocopy of a newspaper article in 'The Chronicle' which is published in Zimbabwe.
2. The fact that Moll now apparently recognises that he is not a pacifist indicates that we erred by considering him and recognising him as a conscientious objector (my translation).[137]

---

[135] Contained in a letter to me from Rev. I.C. Aitken, General Secretary, 23 December 1980.

[136] See *BC 1473: The Students' Christian Organisation Archive.* Deposited with UCT Libraries by Mr. Barry Haschik: A list compiled by André Landman, 2011. The reunification is cited on page 9. Source: https://atom.lib.uct.ac.za/pdfs/BC1473.pdf.

[137] Letter obtained by Judith Connors in the research for her master's degree (2007), from documents that the SANDF had declassified. Sent to me in August 2006 and retained by Terence Moll.

And yet my papers had made it abundantly clear that I was not a pacifist; and the army had newspaper articles where I explained that my objection was to this particular war, not all wars, and I had gone to great pains to explain this also in my court case on 4 December 1979. One marvels that a senior official 'wakes up' to this fact over a year later. *Swak, Piketberg!*

* * *

An early consequence of the conscientious objection stands taken by Richard and me was the formation of several Conscientious Objector Support Groups. One such group was formally constituted at a Durban conference in July 1980 (Connors, 2007:72). A group had already arisen in Cape Town. Other groups arose in Johannesburg and other cities. In February 1981 I visited my brother Terence in Cape Town and attended a meeting of the informal conscientious objector support group at the meeting place of the UCT Students' Christian Association at 6 Christow Road, Mowbray. I was given a hero's welcome. Several of the men present were considering becoming objectors themselves and there were friends and family members present who sought to be their supporters.

Another consequence of our objection stands was that more objectors began to appear. The wide publicity engendered by Richard's and my trials emboldened other young men faced with the call-up to think again. Charles Yeats had left the country for the UK in 1979 in order to avoid the call-up but after reading of the detention and solitary confinement of Richard and me, returned to South Africa in March 1980 to 'face the music' (Yeats, 2005). He was sentenced on 13 May 1981 to twelve months in the Detention Barracks. After refusing to wear military overalls, he was again sentenced, this time to twelve months in civilian prison; he did an effective term of 21 months in the two institutions. More men refused service openly, and most were tried and sentenced: Graham Philpott, Michael Viveiros, Neil Mitchell, Billy Paddock, Etienne Essery, Adrian Paterson, Peter Hathorn, Stephen Granger, Paul Dobson and Brett Myrdal.[138]

A table of all conscientious objectors of interest whom I have been able to trace is presented in Appendix H. I have omitted the numerous Jehovah's Witnesses, other 'peace church' members, and conscientious objectors recognised by the Board for Religious Objection, because I am unable to find their names. Similarly, I have omitted the exiles and evaders, whose name is legion but unavailable to even the most determined researcher. Thus I have focused on the non-peace-church men who refused service openly from 1977 to 1993. There were 56 in all. The first was not Anton Eberhard, as noted above, but Johan van Wyk, an Afrikaner poet who refused service for political reasons.

Another effect of our stand was the custom of writing a detailed statement explaining one's stand, done with publication in mind. My two statements were eleven and eight pages in length. Many of the subsequent conscientious objectors followed suit. For example, Billy Paddock brought out a closely argued paper of 16 pages.[139]

A further impact was the 'duality in unity' of our motivation. We were united in our opposition to *apartheid*, and agreed that we wanted nothing to do with the army. Our positions diverged in that I argued that *this particular war waged by the SADF* was unjust and so I would not participate. Richard believed that *this*

---

[138] Additional lists of objectors: Connors, 2007, pp. 68-79 and 97-103; Jones (2013); and Wits, Rob. Coll., and Wits, ECC Coll.

[139] Billy Paddock, 1982b. 'Why I say 'No!' to collaboration with the S.A.D.F.,' typewritten manuscript, September 1982. 16 pages. Wits, Rob. Coll., A2558-9.16.

war and all other wars were wrong. Some subsequent objectors came out with strongly pacifist positions like Richard's, e.g. Neil Mitchell; others with non-pacifist anti-*apartheid* positions like mine, e.g. Peter Hathorn and David Bruce. This duality persisted until the end of conscription in 1993. Some combined the two arguments, e.g. Charles Yeats, Michael Viveiros and Ivan Toms reasoned that owing to their abhorrence of violence, they would not be prepared to be a combatant in any war; at most they would serve in non-combatant roles. In South Africa, however, where the war to which they were called up was unjust, they would not serve at all.

One impact that was short-lived was my attempt to turn the traditional 'just war' doctrine of the church on its head to show that the war waged by the SADF did not satisfy the criteria laid down by Aquinas, Calvin and others. Billy Paddock took up the challenge and produced a cogent and thorough argument, using 'just war' theory, that the war was unjust. Most objectors, however, used general reasoning without reference to the millennium-old theories, e.g. Charles Yeats, Michael Viveiros and Ivan Toms, as noted, said the war was unjust because it was not the last resort since no effort had been made to resolve the conflict by negotiation.

Another pattern set by Richard's stand and mine was the strive for publicity. I had three trials (December 1977, September 1979, December 1979), garnering increasing publicity each time. I invited Rev. Douglas Bax as an expert witness and was fortunate enough to have a legal A-team in the persons of Charles Nupen and Advocate Ian Farlam. Douglas Bax was a thorn in the military's side, as he was the author of the famous Hammanskraal statement by the South African Council of Churches in 1974, urging the churches to consider conscientious objection. Many subsequent conscientious objectors similarly used the dock to propagate their views and persuade the general public. Charles Yeats had the Anglican Archbishop-elect Philip Russell and the Catholic Archbishop Denis E. Hurley of Durban witness at his trial. Philip Wilkinson also called Bishop Hurley as a witness.[140] David Bruce had Dr. Nthato Motlana, businessman and member of the Soweto Civic Association, provide evidence in mitigation. Fourteen of the country's business heavyweights called for alternative non-military service for Saul Batzofin, an employee of the insurer Liberty Life. The press was highly responsive and remained attentive to conscientious objectors throughout the 1980s. As can be seen in the diagram, the most visible were, in order, Moll, Bruce, Toms, Steele, Bester, Wilkinson, Torr, Batzofin and Yeats.[141]

The 56 conscientious objectors identified amounted to a tiny proportion of the total number of men called up: about 0.0048 percent, or fewer than one in twenty thousands.[142]

---

[140] Michael Desmidt, 1987. 'Hurley praises courage of conscientious objector,' *Evening Post*, 14 May 1987. Wits, ECC, ZA-HPRA AG1977-I3-I4.

[141] The complete list of citations of the 56 objectors, which encompasses 185 pages, is available from the author. Sources: the author's archives, the archives of the Steele family, several collections at the University of the Witwatersrand (R.J.D. Robertson Collection, ECC, SACC, newspapers, SAIRR) and at the University of Cape Town (SCA/SCO, Nathan Collection), at the National Library of South Africa (Cape Town and Pretoria campuses), and at the Baptist Theological College in Johannesburg. Sources unavailable from the University of Cape Town included the collections of the ECC, of Dot Cleminshaw, of the Conscription Advice Service, and of COSAWR, owing to the fire of 2021.

[142] The size of the call-up was 63,104 men in 1976, according to the Minister of Defence, Mr. P.W. Botha ('Servicemen will double', *The Star*, 3 June 1977—Wits, SAIRR Coll., AD1912A-S236.5). Then, using population figures from Wikipedia, I calculate population growth of 1.036 percent annually until the end of conscription in 1993.

Yet a further effect was to inspire our successors to refuse to wear the military uniform—which in turn led to conscientious objectors ending up in civilian jails rather than the Detention Barracks.

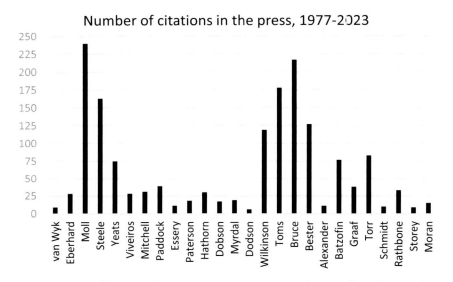

Number of citations in the press, 1977-2023

Richard and I insisted on being recognised as conscientious objectors while in the Detention Barracks, which meant wearing the blue overalls that were given to the 'peace church' objectors. Our refusal of the military browns was met by summary courts-martial and solitary confinement. After Anton Eberhard's 14 days' solitary, my 125 days (of which the first 10 in underpants only) and Richard's 52 (the last of which was with bread and water only), Charles Yeats refused the uniform and spent some 70 days in solitary, in the bitter cold, the first few days of these dressed only in underpants (Yeats, 2005). Neil Mitchell spent 23 days in solitary. Whereupon the generals reluctantly decided to leave the matter of conscientious objection up to the civilian courts and civilian jails, where the issue of the military uniform and training would not arise.

211

I continued my activities in talking and writing about conscientious objection. In March 1981 the University of Cape Town student newspaper *Varsity* published an interview, 'Peter Moll after one year in D.B.'[143] Also in March 1981 I wrote a report about conditions in the Detention Barracks and went to Pretoria where I handed it to Colonel M.A. van den Berg with the request that the violence be stopped and that conditions be improved (Moll, 1981c). I spoke at churches, student organisations and civic groups, in Cape Town, Johannesburg, Pretoria and Durban. While attending a War Resisters' International conference at the Abbey of Saint-Michel de Cuxà in Prades, France, in April 1981, I was interviewed and an article appeared in the WRI newsletter.[144] Further articles appeared in newspapers, magazines and books. For instance, in 1986 I wrote an article, 'Conscientious objectors under renewed attack' in *South African Outlook* (October 1986),[145] and gave a talk about militarisation and conscientious objection to the SAAK association at the University of Stellenbosch on 4 September 1986. A commemorative book by Trevor Webster about the 150th anniversary of Selborne College in East London carried an article about my experience as a conscientious objector (Webster, 2014: 125).

Meanwhile the military had been working on legislative changes to adapt to the new situation. The ds. Christiaan Petrus Naudé, now promoted to Chaplain-General, led the investigative part, having enlisted the services of Professor Johan Heyns of the University of Pretoria. This resulted in the new Act of 1983, by which religious pacifists were permitted to do non-military alternative service. Such is the 'received wisdom' about how the

---

[143] Wits, Rob. Coll., A2558-9.13.
[144] *WRI Newsletter* No. 183, July 1981, pp. 1-4. Wits, Rob. Coll., A2558-1.
[145] Wits, Rob. Coll., A2558-12.3.

precedent of conscientious objection broadened out into the military's legislative response. The truth, as always, is more complex. I was contacted, 33 years after my imprisonment, by a former operative of Military Intelligence who mentioned to me that he had paid me a visit in the Detention Barracks in 1980. He had been despatched to discover my 'handler.' I immediately remembered that I had had a visit from someone who claimed to be a theology student in August 1980—Chris Marais by name. (See my account of this visit in the previous chapter.)

In our phone call in 2013 he explained that he was unable to identify any 'handler' or indeed any political linkage, because it became apparent that I had thought out my conscientious objection position from scratch and independently. He had had access to letters written by myself, Richard Steele and Charles Yeats, and to telephone calls made by Richard and Charles. He was struck by my "absolute honesty and openness," he said, and when I reached the conclusion that we were fighting our own people, "the penny dropped." A technical slip-up was to give him wider leeway. He was of course bugged and his colleagues were sitting outside the Detention Barracks in a car trying to listen in. They had forgotten, however, that the exterior of the Detention Barracks was made of corrugated iron. The bugging device barely delivered them anything comprehensible. *Swak, Piketberg!* The 'theology student' was therefore entitled to interpret my statements for what they were, without admixture of ideological constructions from his colleagues. He then gave a debriefing to his superiors: there is no "big enemy" behind Moll, he contended, he is doing it for what he believes; the natural force behind him is people who naturally feel like him; and he argued that the state should recognise conscientious objectors. Then he wrote up his report, recommending that conscientious objection be recognised.

In a spectacular bureaucratic misunderstanding, this position paper was taken by the Chaplain-General to be the approved position of Military Intelligence and hence constituted a mandate. A slip-up, but a happy one because the Chaplain-General formulated legislation accordingly. This resulted in the recognition of religious pacifism in the 1983 legislation.

I hate to imagine what sort of legislation would have turned up in 1983 if instead of my being visited by this young and open-minded representative of Military Intelligence, I had instead been visited by closed-minded ideologues such as Brigadier Pretorius, Director of Military Law, or Lieutenant Daniel Mills, the prosecutor at my trial in 1979. The military failed in its attempt to get me to 'turn'; but unwittingly I had managed to get one of its operators to 'turn', because the 'theology student,' now convinced that the SADF was involved in a war of brother against brother, left Military Intelligence to devote himself to other causes.

Back to the new 1983 law. The length of alternative nonmilitary service, for religious pacifist conscripts who had done no training, was to be one and a half times the total duration of military service. Now the latter consisted of basic training of two years, plus a number of camps which together amounted to two years, giving a total of four years. Therefore alternative service was to last for six years. If, however, conscripts refused military service for other reasons, e.g. if they were not pacifists or not religious, then they would be sentenced to prison for six years. Thus some conscientious objectors were advantaged while others were much more seriously penalised. The Conscientious Objector Support Group expressed its deep disappointment in this divisive legislation (Connors, 2007:82). Nevertheless there ensued an enormous response by religious pacifists who sought this welcome accommodation. From February 1984 to September 1989, a total of 1890 conscripts submitted applications to the Board for Religious Objection, of which 124 were withdrawn by the applicants themselves before consideration by the Board and 44 were refused (Connors, 2007:82). Presumably the remaining 1722 applicants were successful. They worked in a large variety of government departments. Jehovah's Witnesses formed the bulk of these. For them the new regime represented a major improvement in quality, since they were no longer in detention but living independently as civilians, and doing more productive work, but it had also become less attractive in quantity, in that they had to do six years' work instead of enduring three years' Detention Barracks.

Initially the much stiffer penalty for non-religious or non-pacifist conscientious objectors discouraged further outright refusal of military call-ups. Nevertheless, from 1984 to 1993, another 39 men refused service openly despite the risk of extreme hardship. Up to 1991, most of these were tried in court, the most prominent being Philip Wilkinson, Ivan Toms, David Bruce, Charles Bester, Saul Batzofin and Douglas Torr. The longest sentences were handed down to the bravest of all, David Bruce and Charles Bester in 1988: six years' imprisonment. They were freed in 1990 on appeal to the Supreme Court on the grounds that the six-year sentence was not mandatory but a maximum.

Interest in the subject of alternative non-military service continued in the 1990s. My contribution to this discussion was to seek to broaden the basis for alternative service from the initial rubric of *religious pacifism* to the wider rubric *pacifism, whether religious or non-religious* (Moll, 1990). I considered this broadening the first step in the process. Recognising non-religious pacifism would involve no challenge to the authority of the state and would thus be a realistic short-term goal. In the longer term one could seek to move towards recognising objection to military service on general moral or political grounds, as several European countries had done. The requisite broadening eventually came about in 1992 when the Board for Religious Objection became the Board for Conscientious Objection, and the criteria could now include non-religious pacifism (see below).

A new phenomenon appeared: the joint—indeed, mass—defiance of military service (Connors, 2007:91-92). In 1987, 23 young white South African men issued an announcement that they would not serve in the SADF. On 3 August 1988, 143 men, of whom I was one,[146] signed a joint statement of objection to military service. On 21 September 1989 a total of 771 men including myself declared, at the launch of a national register of conscientious objectors, that they would object to service in the SADF.

* * *

I pointed out above that one of the results of the stands by Richard and me was the creation of the first Conscientious Objector Support Groups. In turn the activities of the COSGs, and a resolution by the Black Sash at its 1983 National Conference, led to the creation of local End Conscription Campaign chapters during 1983 (Connors, 2007:86). A 'Declaration to End Conscription' was published in the COSG newsletter in August 1984.[147] In 1985, a widely publicised three-week fast was held by Ivan Toms in Cape Town, Harold Winkler in Johannesburg, Richard Steele in Durban, David

---

[146] See p. 7 of 'Patriotic revolt: Press clippings of the 143', typewritten manuscript including press clippings. 34 pages. Wits, Rob. Coll., A2558-16.

[147]

https://www.saha.org.za/ecc25/towards_a_just_peace_in_our_land_a_declaration_to_end_conscription.htm .

Hartmann in Grahamstown, and others (Jones, 2013:75). At the end of this enormous challenge the ECC in Cape Town held a rally entitled 'Troops out of the Townships' at the City Hall. Toms spoke. I was present and can confirm that the applause was rapturous. He said that troops were being used in the townships to quell unrest, and declared that he would never again don the military uniform. The organisation had remarkable success in mobilising a wide array of support among different religious groups, civic associations and students. Other campaigns organised were the 'Working for a Just Peace' campaign, the 'Know Your Rights' campaign and the 'Alternative Service Campaign.' ECC members were frequently detained or subjected to harassment. The organisation was banned in August 1988 under emergency regulations but unbanned in February 1990.

In 1989, the call-up for initial military training was reduced from two years to one year. But conscription did not just turn over and die. The role of the ECC and the COSGs continued to be important as they supported conscientious objectors all the way through to 1993 and raised awareness about the lack of need for conscription. Following the dropping of charges against Rev. Alan Storey in June 1991, the chairperson of the ECC in Johannesburg, Chris de Villiers, declared that the system of conscription had become unenforceable (Jones 2013: 135).

The Defence Amendment Act of 1992 broadened the scope for legal conscientious objection. It provided for a Board for Conscientious Objection, allowing people with moral, ethical or religious objections to serving in the SADF to apply for a hearing.[148] In December 1992 General Andreas 'Kat'

---

[148] SAPA and Carol Hills, 1992. 'Call-ups: Roster of legal men to aid objectors,' *The Citizen*, September 1992. Wits, ECC Coll.. ZA-HPRA AG1977-E1 (1.34).

Liebenberg stated that the July intake of 1993 would be the last whites-only call-up (Jones 2013: 137). The last time conscripts were charged, to my knowledge, was in July 1993, when eight men appeared in the Johannesburg and Pretoria magistrates' courts on charges of failing to report for the January 1993 call-up. Most of them paid admission of guilt fines of R300.[149] On 24 August 1993 the Minister of Defence, Gene Louw, announced the end of conscription (Jones 2013: 138).

One of the results of the continual stream of conscientious objectors in the 1980s was that overseas organisations such as the Committee on South African War Resistance (COSAWR) in the UK and the Netherlands, and South African Military Refugee Aid Fund (SAMRAF) in the USA, had plenty of grist for the mill: they were able to organise campaigns, do research and provide information through magazines, e.g. COSAWR's *The Resister* and SAMRAF's *News & Notes* and *Omkeer*. COSAWR organised various campaigns on my behalf. On 12 January 1980 some 70 people picketed the South African embassy in London, with placards reading 'Support all SA war resisters' and 'Free Peter Moll.'[150] As a result of COSAWR's activities, Amnesty International took up my case, and letters were written by Members of Parliament Tony Benn and Frank Allaun to the Prime Minister pleading for my release. When travelling with the International Fellowship of Reconciliation in 1981, I met with members of COSAWR in the Netherlands, among them Gerald Kraak, and took the opportunity to thank COSAWR for its support. I also contacted Andy Smail, a lawyer who had written about the legal situation of conscientious objectors in South Africa (Smail, 1980). A conscientious

---

[149] 'Update on S.A. militarism and resistance,' *The Objector* (September 1993), p. 8. Wits, ECC Coll., AG1977-H9.4.

[150] International action on war resistance,' *Peace Action News* no. 5, March 1980, p. 5.

objector himself, he had opted for exile rather than imprisonment.[151]

In the USA in 1981 I met with Don Morton, the staff coordinator, and several other members of SAMRAF in Brooklyn, New York. The organisation distributed information encouraging resistance to service in the SADF, and helped draft resisters who fled from South Africa. Don had worked as a Methodist minister for six years but after disclosing evidence of police torture, had to leave the country to avoid arrest by the security police.[152] He and others founded SAMRAF in 1978. The organisation took up my case: on 12 January 1980 there were demonstrations outside the South African consulates in New York, San Francisco and Chicago, demanding an end to the repression of conscientious objectors in South Africa.[153] SAMRAF also mounted a campaign of support for Charles Yeats and other conscientious objectors.[154] I was glad of these opportunities to thank the SAMRAF members for their support for us conscientious objectors.

There were many Baptist church members in the UK who were also involved with Amnesty International. A campaign of letter writing was organised by Rev. Don Black at the Baptist Church House in London.

An ironic consequence of my detention was that conscientious objectors who opted to leave the country and seek

---

[151] Melanie Gosling, 1980. 'Conscientious objector seeks asylum,' *Natal Mercury*, 15 August 1980. Wits, SAIRR Coll., ZA HPRA AD1912A-S236.5.

[152] SAMRAF North American Tour, October 14—December 14, 1978'. (Available at https://projects.kora.matrix.msu.edu/files/210-808-6386/ samrafnatour.pdf .)

[153] International action on war resistance,' *Peace Action News* no. 5, March 1980, p. 5.

[154] *SAMRAF News & Notes*, August/September 1981, no. 3. Page 2 has the appeal for letters to Charles Yeats. Available at https://projects.kora. matrix.msu.edu/files/210-808-10975/GMHSAMRAFAugSept81.pdf .

asylum frequently referred to my case to strengthen their applications. Some foreign governments required that any asylum seeker present evidence of a justified fear of persecution. The repeated bouts of solitary confinement provided such evidence.[155]

With the activities of COSAWR, SAMRAF and other organisations, there was more awareness in the international press about the issues of conscientious objection and resistance to the South African military. For instance, a full-length article about my detention experience appeared in the American magazine *The Christian Century* in November 1981 (Lehmann, 1981).

* * *

A correction of nomenclature is called for. Some have labelled the first objectors who ended up in jail as 'religious' or 'pacifist', contrasting these with the later ones such as Billy Paddock and Peter Hathorn who were named the first 'overtly political' objectors.[156] Similarly it has been alleged that Billy Paddock was "the first objector to refuse to do military service on overtly political grounds."[157] The religious-political distinction is false; almost all the conscientious objectors who openly refused service, from 1977 onwards, incorporated social, economic and political arguments in their statements. For instance, Johan van Wyk stated, "I also cannot be part of a

---

[155] Letter from Andrew Smail to the author, dated 1 December 1980.

[156] See https://www.sahistory.org.za/article/end-conscription-campaign-ecc, etc.

[157] See 'Billy Paddock freed,' *Objector: Newsletter of the Western Cape Conscientious Objector Support Group*, no. 3 (September [sic] 1983), p. 4. Wits, ECC Coll., AG1977-H9.4.

system which enforces apartheid by violence."[158] Anton Eberhard told the magistrate's court in Port Elizabeth that he was a "committed Christian" and "attend[ed] church regularly", and that his refusal to attend a camp in 1977 was based on scripture;[159] in his letter of refusal he declared that the country's system of government was totally unjust and that Black people looked upon the army as sustaining the oppression they suffered, and so he was unable to participate in the army at all. His stand was accordingly no less political than were Billy Paddock's or Peter Hathorn's.

Similarly I was religious, being an active churchgoer and having invoked the Baptist church's 'just war' doctrine, arguing that the wars of the SADF were neither *just* nor *necessary*. But in order to assert that the wars were unjust and unnecessary I had to set these ethical principles against the South African reality, whether social, political or economic. I pointed to institutionalised racism and segregation of education services and residential areas; to unfair land distribution; to the absence of meaningful political expression for all other than white people; to the violent repression of demonstrations by schoolchildren; to assassinations such as that of Steve Biko; to detention without trial and bannings; to extreme income inequality; to the lack of effective bargaining structures for black workers; to the evil canker of the migrant labour system; to excessive military spending; and to the fact that the war was a civil war, not a war of defence against an external aggressor; and so on. Again, while religiously based, my arguments were no less political than those of Billy Paddock and Peter Hathorn.

---

[158] 'Pacifist poet tells why he won't serve', *Express* (September 1977), available at https://johanvanwyk.oblogs.co.za/).

[159] 'Christian won't go into army', *Rand Daily Mail* (14 December 1977). The article was reproduced in full in: *South African Outlook* vol. 108, no. 1287 (September 1978), p. 142. Wits, Rob. Coll., A2558-15.8.

Similarly, Richard Steele, while a religious pacifist, wrote "… as far as I can see, the military is one of the central features of *apartheid* and what is maintaining its power, and so I see my stand as non-cooperation with the *apartheid* structure" (Kearney, 1980:13). At the 25th anniversary of the End Conscription Campaign, Richard noted that the early objectors were perceived as being religious rather than political objectors. He stressed that these objectors' moral orientation had originated in religious commitments. He commented, "The fact is we were using religious language to help us understand what our values and principles were. We were clear that we were making a political decision with political intent and consequences" (Jones, 2013:37). Similarly, Charles Yeats, while a religious pacifist, argued in his court case that *apartheid* was indefensible and that the SADF was illegally occupying Namibia (Yeats, 2005:74-76). These were the very arguments deployed by Peter Hathorn and Billy Paddock. One might then take these social, economic, anti-*apartheid*/pro-*apartheid* and political arguments together and summarise them as 'political' in an expansive sense, and then label Johan van Wyk as the first political objector to be tried in court, Anton Eberhard as the second, me as the third, Edric Gorfinkel the fourth, Chris Boshoff the fifth, Richard Steele the sixth and Charles Yeats as the seventh, and so on.

* * *

Another result of the stream of conscientious objectors was a renewed focus on the role of the military chaplains. In my experience the different chaplaincy types had had very different roles. The citizen force chaplains, viz. conscripted chaplains such as Gerry West and David Hart, were highly supportive of my stand as a conscientious objector. The role of the permanent force chaplains was a mix of positive and negative. On the positive side, Chaplain (Rev.) James Gray held effective and communicative pastoral sessions with the inmates in the Detention Barracks, and was very supportive of me as a person without necessarily agreeing with my argument that the SADF was helping maintain *apartheid* which his own church condemned as unchristian. Some individuals were able to visit me by means of arrangements made through permanent force chaplains. Additionally, via the 'back channel' of Chaplain James Gray and his superiors in the chaplaincy, my descriptions of violence by *oumanne* in the Detention Barracks were forwarded to the generals, forcing them at last to take action to prevent physical violence.

On the negative side, Colonel (Rev.) Andrew van den Aardweg tried to persuade Richard and me not to be conscientious objectors—when as a Baptist minister and a follower of the doctrines of freedom of conscience and of the priesthood of all believers, he ought to have recognised our positions as conscientious objectors as sincere in the way that Rev. Dennis Wilton, Rev. Aubrey Phipson, Rev. Martin Holdt and other Baptist ministers did. Chaplain (Rev.) Sydney Middlemost wrote to me, visited me in Mowbray, Cape Town, and phoned me, taking much trouble with the attempt to convince me that the SADF was fighting a just war in Namibia. Chaplain (Rev.) Donald Williams used military powers to force men to attend a religious service. Chaplain (ds.) Dawid Venter of the Detention Barracks persuaded Chris Boshoff to abandon his conscientious objection stand and return to doing his camps.

In 1983 I decided to study the structure of the military chaplaincy to arrive at recommendations to the 'English-speaking' churches for a chaplaincy system that was more consistent with the churches' positions about *apartheid*, about the war and about conscientious objection. After a few months' interviewing, the Chaplain-General, ds. C.P. Naudé, forbade the chaplains to speak to or correspond with me. Nevertheless I was able to complete a master's thesis on the subject (Moll, 1984b), as well as an article in the *Journal of Theology for South Africa* (Moll, 1985b), and various other papers (Moll, 1984c; Moll, 1986b; and Moll, 1987b).

My key recommendation was that more emphasis be placed on having civilian ministers undertake chaplaincy work, so as to avoid military tasks and obligations. I proposed also that chaplains take neither military uniforms nor rank, for these convey the message to the troops that God is on the side of the military. The terms of chaplains sent to remote locations should be six years at most, as they were in the Federal Republic of Germany, after which the chaplain would revert to being a civilian pastor of a church. All payment of chaplains' salaries and benefits should be done by the church, thereby giving the minister financial security and releasing him/her from the potential threat that a senior military officer might fire him/her if, for instance, s/he refused to participate in morale-building exercises.

These works generated some interest and several more theses and papers followed in the next two decades. The Anglican (CPSA) church, at its Provincial Synod in 1985, determined that the Anglican chaplains' dress should avoid identification with the military, they should be paid by the church rather than the military, and should be directly responsible to the Bishops of the Diocese.[160] Similarly the Presbyterian Church of Southern Africa, at its general Assembly in Harare in 1986, adopted a

---

[160] See *The Searchlight* (newsletter of the Diocese of Port Elizabeth), vol. 7, no. 7 (August 1985), p. 4.

report that Presbyterian chaplains should not wear uniforms or bear arms, and should be paid by the church.[161]

* * *

On the personal level: on 15 October 1980 I received a letter from a subscriber to *The Other Side* magazine, an evangelical Christian monthly issued in Philadelphia, with a special interest in working for justice. Somehow *The Other Side* had obtained information about Richard and me, and asked for readers to write letters to us as part of their prison ministry campaign. In addition the magazine listed the names of regular U.S. prisoners. The subscriber was one Masami Kojima, a Japanese Ph.D. student in chemical engineering at the University of Stanford. She wrote letters on a regular basis to four of the people listed: me, Richard, and two U.S. prisoners. Later in 1981 she also wrote letters to Charles Yeats. Her missives were packed with news about Amnesty International in which she was involved, her teaching duties, her church activities, and her concern about hunger, poverty and inequality. I was struck by how very kind this person was and determined to make contact with her later. When I came out I corresponded with her regularly—from the Netherlands, the USA, Nicaragua and Brazil in 198_, and from South Africa thereafter.

The chance to meet came when she graduated. I approached Professor Geoffrey Hansford of the Chemical Engineering Department at the University of Cape Town to see if he might wish to hire Masami. He indicated strong interest. (Imagine: faraway UCT attracting a Junior Phi Beta Kappa from Harvard and Ph.D. from Stanford. What's not to like?) Two posts had

---

[161] See 'Presbyterians to make chaplaincy offer to ANC,' *Sunday Times*, 26 September 1986. Wits, SAIRR Coll., ZA HPRA AD1912A-S236.17.

recently been advertised, the closing date for which was later that week. I submitted a *pro forma* application on Masami's behalf, in the hope that she would follow up and send her transcripts. Luckily she did. She started the new job in Cape Town in May 1983. The next year we were married by Rev. David Russell.

With the end of *apartheid* in 1994 came a gradual rehabilitation of the movement of conscientious objection. The South African National Museum of Military History contains a display 'Rebels and Objectors' which makes reference to Anton Eberhard, Peter Moll, Neil Mitchell, Paul Dobson, Philip Wilkinson, Ivan Toms, Rev. Douglas Torr, Saul Batzofin, Michael Graaf, David Bruce and Charles Bester.[162]

Remarkably, the army did not give up on me. Although the army was legally entitled to keep calling me up until the age of 65, I had heard through Richard that our names had been "taken off the roll", and that the army might even decide that I, in particular, had been "trained to [their] satisfaction."[163] (Richard's mother Dorothy had been informed by Rear-Admiral H.P. Botha, with whom she had regular contact in respect of our cases.) But the right hand does not know what the left is doing. As of my release on 2 December 1980 the institution had all the information about me it could possibly have needed. It promptly lost track. In June 1981 while I was in Brazil, Lion's Head Commando called me up for a four-day shoot. At intervals of two years, the army tried all the old addresses for me, but my family and friends had grown wise to the army's game and ignored the requests for updated whereabouts. In January 1988 a Sergeant le Roux wrote from the Eastern Province Command at Walmer, sniffing for information about me. Finally the East

---

[162] See http://militarymuseum.co.za/main.htm.
[163] Wits, Rob. Coll., A2558-9.20.

Park Commando tried to contact me in October 1990, when they finally realised that I was living in Chicago, USA. *Swak, Piketberg!*

i

Photographs, letters, original documents

1. Peter Moll, 1979 passport photograph

2. Peter Moll, during a break at the court-martial of 21 September 1979. I have my left hand in my pocket, and am talking with Dot Cleminshaw. Rev. Dr. John de Gruchy (with the ample beard) is on the left of the photo. Rev. Dr. Jim Cochrane in a plaid jacket is facing the camera. On the right, with glasses, facing the camera, is Dr. Ken Hughes. Many thanks to the Cape Times for taking the photo and depositing it with the National Library; and thanks to the National Library for permission to use it.

3. Peter Moll, during a break at the court-martial of 21 September 1979. I am talking with Rev. Dr. Allan Boesak. In the doorway, on the left, facing the camera, is Mike Evans. Between me and Dr. Boesak, facing the camera, with a moustache and beard, is Edric Gorfinkel. Many thanks to the Cape Times for taking the photo and depositing it with the National Library; and thanks to the National Library for permission to use it.

4. Richard Steele (right) and Peter Moll (left), in March 1981, at the South African Council of Churches building in Johannesburg. Photo by Rev. Rob Robertson.

5. Peter Moll in 1983 at his parents' house in Umtata.
Photographer Masami Kojima.

6. My family in 1982 at the Hluleka Reserve on the Transkei coast, South Africa. From left to right: Jen Beck, Peter Moll, Brenda Moll, Lorraine Burger, Beryl Moll, Douglas Moll, Ted Moll, Terence Moll.

7. Masami Kojima and Peter Moll at Kommetjie, Western Cape, 1984.

8. Rev. Robert 'Rob' J.D. Robertson, minister of St. Anthony's United Church in Mayfair, Johannesburg, as of 1980. Photo taken in 1999. Photo from Pam Robertson.

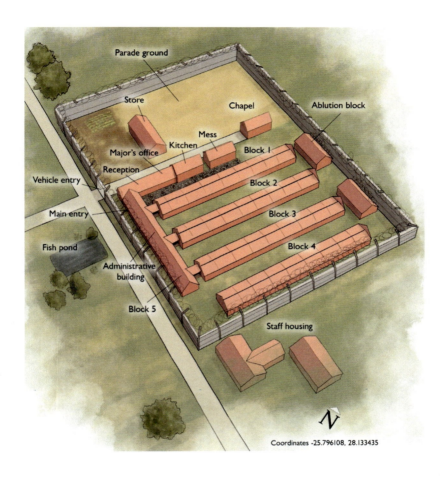

Parade ground

Store

Chapel

Ablution block

Mess

Kitchen

Major's office

Block 1

Reception

Block 2

Vehicle entry

Main entry

Block 3

Fish pond

Administrative
building

Block 4

Block 5

Staff housing

N

Coordinates -25.796108, 28.133435

9. An artist's rendition of an aerial view of the Detention
Barracks, Voortrekkerhoogte, Pretoria
The artist: Mr. Penn Tomassetti

10. An artist's rendition of the exterior view of the Detention Barracks, Voortrekkerhoogte.
The artist: Mr. Rodney Hazard

11. An artist's rendition of the interior of the cellblocks of the
Detention Barracks, Voortrekkerhoogte.
The artist: Mr. Rodney Hazard

From: Tony Benn, MP

HOUSE OF COMMONS
LONDON SW1A OAA

17th March 1980

Avon Polw

    I have heard from the Committee on
South African War Resistance formed in London
of your detention and this is just to let you
know that there are a lot of people in Britain
who are supporting those fighting apartheid.

    The recent events in Zimbabwe must be
a great source of encouragement to you.

    Best wishes,

Tony Benn

Mr. Peter Moll,
Detention Barracks,
Voortrakkerhoogte,
Pretoria,
South Africa.

12. Letter from Tony Benn, M.P., 17 March 1980.
The famous Labour Member of Parliament (and cabinet
minister in the 1960s and 1970s) was informed of my
imprisonment by COSAWR (Committee on South African
War Resistance) in London.

THE SOUTH AFRICAN COUNCIL OF CHURCHES

DIE SUID-AFRIKAANSE RAAD VAN KERKE

Mr. Peter Moll,   13th May, 1980.
Detention Barracks,
<u>VOORTREKKERHOOGTE</u>,
0143.

Dear Peter,

I have been instructed by the National Conference of the South African
Council of Churches meeting in Hammanskraal from the 5th — 9th May to
send you the following Resolution:

> That this National Conference of the South African Council
> of Churches assures Mr. Peter Moll and Mr. Richard Steele
> of its prayers in their costly Christian witness against
> compulsory military service.

God bless you richly.
Yours sincerely,

<u>Bishop Desmond Tutu</u>
General Secretary

/ems

DIAKONIA HOUSE · 80 JORISSEN ST. · JOHANNESBURG 2001
DIAKONIA HUIS · JORISSENSTR. 80 · JOHANNESBURG 2001
P.O. BOX/POSBUS 31190 · BRAAMFONTEIN 2017 · TRANSVAAL
TEL. 39-5955
TELEX No. 8-6575 TEL. ADD. 'EcuNews'

13. Letter from Bishop Tutu, 13 May 1980. The good bishop
wrote to me once per month for the whole year of 1980.

34, Morton Road
Aylsham,
Norfolk NRW 6BM
England

April 29th 1981

Dear Friend,

It was a great pleasure to get your
letter and learn that mine and so many others
had helped to sustain you during your ordeal
in prison. You ask if it was worth while and
answer yes. I can assure you in that belief.

My father was imprisoned 64 years ago
here in Britain for making a similar stand.
He died of T B a result of the privations he
had to endure in prison but of millions
conscripted at that time only a few hundred made a
similar stand and about sixty died possibly as
a result of their ordeal.

When the strong feelings aroused by the war had
died down the impact of that witness upon public
opinion was immense and led not only to C.O's
right recognition of C.O's right to stand by their
beliefs but to prison reform in other directions
as well

Just now, as you try to get used once more
to freedom you may find it hard to forgive
those who persecuted you Do not blame
yourself, nor feel that you never can. I recall
speaking in my youth with men who went to

14. Letter from Raymond Matchett, from Norfolk in the UK.
His father had been imprisoned in 1917 for conscientious
objection, and died of tuberculosis as a result of the privations
in detention. After the war the laws were changed to provide
for conscientious objection, and prison conditions were
reformed.

prison with my father and fourteen years
after the event they were able to recall
with something close to amusement and
sympathy the bewilderment of warders who
could not understand what gave them
strength to endure.

Many people were forced to realise
there is a Power which enables us to stand
and of which they have never really thought.

You have in our time made a similar
witness in S. Africa. God bless you and guide
you and your family as you carry that
witness forward in new ways and guard you
against the pitfalls that will come your way.

Please thank your parents for me
for their letter.

Yours sincerely
Raymond Matchett

15. Letter from Raymond Matchett (concluded)

UNITED CONGREGATIONAL CHURCH OF SOUTHERN AFRICA

RONDEBOSCH
CONGREGATIONAL
CHURCH BELMONT ROAD

TELEPHONES 65-4793
69-9814

Minister
Rev. Geoffrey C. Dunstan
The Manse
Weltevreden Avenue
Rondebosch, Cape Town
Telephone 6-6311
Minister Emeritus
Rev. W. N. H. Tarrant

14.5.80

My dear Peter

Forgive me that I have not written again sooner. I have let you down in delaying so much. I can hardly believe it that your letter to me was written so long ago.

I appreciated hearing from you very much. It was a relief to me that you had (finally!) had word from me.

We are all most concerned that they have no put you into solitary for the sixth time. This cannot be doing you any good, and the longer it goes on the more potentially harmful it would be for the ordinary person. Now they have taken Richard away and broken that tie for you as well. We support you in our prayers. We pray for you and Richard nearly every Sunday in at least one of our church services. I am sure you have heard about the vigil from several people as well. A few friends will, I am sure, be thinking how we can try to protest about this still-continuing persecution you endure.

I suppose you know that Richard's parents came down for a week to try and see the PM. They sat in the House (literally in "the corridors of power" I suppose some would call it!) trying to get an interview, and this each day for five days. Eventually they were allowed to see PW's secretary, I understand. They are, everyone agrees, a most impressive couple in terms of their Christian commitment and their spirit of love and gentleness. I did not realize that you and Richard were related - that your mother and his are (is it?) sisters.

I have tried to write a few letters to the press. The Cape Times finally stymied one particular series, but I plan to try something else soon.

I wonder if you read the Chaplain General's column in the Dec. and March issues of Paratus. I am sure they would let you have copies if you have not seen these issues. You would find them...well, at least interesting.

I was delighted to hear about your letter from 42 UK Baptists. That was great news. As for your future denominational allegiance: well, that is perhaps something a non-Baptist should not try to counsel you about too directly!

16. Letter from Rev. Douglas Bax to Peter Moll, 14 May 1980

As far as our Presbyterian Committee is concerned we are really battling. Time is now beginning to run out and in spite of seemingly endless work we seem to have produced very little. Revision of reports has taken a lot of work and time, and we have also been involved in a lot of correspondence with various Ministers and others (e.g. the farming Elders of Stutterheim!) who have reacted to sections of our 1979 report that were sent to them for consideration. The part of the report you worked on eventually involved a correspondence with the person concerned that included one typed letter of about 12 pages...but to no avail. We miss you on the Committee!

Peter, may God be with you. I send you this special text as one that at one time meant a great deal to me:

Grace and peace to you from God our Father and the Lord Jesus Christ.
Praise be to the God and Father of our Lord Jesus Christ, the Father of compassion and the God of all comfort, who comforts us in all our troubles, so that we can comfort those in any trouble with the comfort we ourselves have received from God. For just as the sufferings of Christ flow over into our lives, so also through Christ our comfort overflows.
(II Cor.1:2-5 NIV)

God is with you!

Shalom.

Douglas.

P.S. Sydney Carter, the modern-hymn writer, saw something you had written and commented in my hearing that you should take up writing for a career, as he thought you wrote so well.

Do you know whether anyone has taken over reviewing my booklet for the Outlook? It got a good review (the first one and 5 pages!) in the latest NGTT.

17. Letter from Rev. Douglas Bax (continued)

DB, Pretoria
20 July 1980

Dear Mom and Dad

I've just had a visit this afternoon from Jim, Andrew and Ian McLeod, for at least an hour and a half -- a great deal better than the official 15 minutes because there are always fewer visitors on the 3rd Sunday of the month. We always talk "aanhoudend", not a moment's intermission, there's so much to hear.

The fast last week wasn't at all easy. I was in solitary for the 8th time, and the fast occupied the last 3 days of it. Usually I gave my food away to the guy who brought it, telling the corporal who has to accompany him (to unlock the door) to take note that I haven't eaten. The fact was then recorded in the "V.E.", the daily events book. Once or twice the corporal insisted that I keep the food in the cell — so as soon as anyone came past, I yelled to him to come and take my food which I would scrape into a cup + hand to him thro' the grating above the door. Otherwise the temptation would have been far too much!! The main hurdle is that a mealtime forms a definite break in the tedium of the day, which you notice more strongly when there are so few distractions as in
   solitary. This is quite apart from feeling plain old hungry; tho' I must say my hunger peaks on the 2nd day in the morning and then all but disappears — so in fact once you're past the 2-day barrier, 3 days would probably not differ much from 5, or 7, except that I'm no Loyola. During mealtimes I prayed + read the gospel of John, which I've been really intrigued with all year. John, the mystic, eminently the theologian, enamoured with otherworldly concepts like light, grace, truth, glory... but also FOOD, man: Jesus' body as the sacrament to eat and drink, becomes all the more meaningful in these surroundings. But not even these elevated thoughts can stop you from fantasizing endlessly about the scrumptious dishes you're going to concoct on getting out of the place, and the hotel menus you're going to go thro', and the cafes and the steakhouses and, and, and!! I doubt if I'll ever be able to discipline my mind not

18. Letter from me to my parents, 20 July 1980, describing the second protest fast.

to rush off in these flights? But as soon as I was eating normally again, they disappeared altogether. It was exhilarating, though, when on the third day I refused my last meal and I knew that I'd won. It seems such a small thing to me now, but at the time it was a colossal victory which made me feel immense, invincible – I had overcome! What a relief.

Last week I was moved out of block 5, where I have been most of the year, into block 3 because its warmer there. I think the welfare officer Lieut. Kritzinger, had something to do with it. Its a much more humane existence in the big block with ±80 other guys – you can have conversations, they can remind the corporals to get your food + take you out, etc. Also the simple fact of hearing voices and sounds of life etc. But I found the noise in the evening unbearable. Most of the guys have nothing to do. There are very few books (paperbacks, if found, get torn up) and few guys have any inclination to read. Result: yelling, screaming, singing (all the current hits are well known to me now!) and eternal swearing. Is it the guys themselves or their environment that makes them so obscene? Three hours of this bedlam and I'm done for, nervously exhausted. I've now moved back to block 5 where I at least have plenty of blankets, scarves, pyjamas etc as a defence against the main assailant, the cold. What an indescribable lift it was coming back. Peace, perfect peace ... like the old hymn.

I've done nearly 2/3 of my sentence now. Time is flying – I really mean it. How the guys (mostly short-timers of 2 months or less) marvel when I say I've been around for 8 months already. Without escaping, many add, shaking their heads. "I'd move" (with a glance at the zinc-and-barbed-wire perimeter) "in my first exercise period if they shoved me in that hole." And they would too, and do, often with consummate skill. Anyway, not long now. Just a bit more vasbyt and I'll be back with you on Port St John's beaches, or is it Hluleka?
With lots of love
Peter –

19. Letter from me to my parents, 20 July 1980 (concluded)

D.B., Voortrekkerhoogte, 10/8/80

Dear Mom and Dad

What a day of rejoicing it was when on Friday I was issued with a blue overall again! Praise the Lord!! When I received a telegram from Aunty Dorothy and Uncle John I inferred that the same applies to Richard. This is a tremendous relief for everyone, I think, and will make my last 3½ months here much easier to bear. I'll be working in the garden just outside the DB, and what's more without supervision. At last.

I got letters from Peter Dewberry (Goodwood Bap), Bill McKenzie Phillips (Portsmouth, England), Rob Hill (Bulawayo), Victor McGregor, Rev. Mike McCoy, Marge Browne, Rob Campbell, Anne & Frank Müller, Rt Rev P Wh Russell (Natal), Roger Palmer (no, I don't want money for the books), Rob Goldman, Ron Mathias (Swaziland), Rev. Robert Smith, a telegram from Robin Horsell, Jean Campbell (Zimb) Neil Brick (Teddington, England), Orlando Redekopp + Joan Gerig, Harold + Christine Wenger, the Tudor family, John Howard Yoder (U.SA), Rob Robertson, a telegram from Rose in Mbabane regarding the last fast, and two letters from you.

I saw Jen and Andrew again this afternoon, and our hour-and-a-half together was quite extraordinarily gleeful. 'Express' were quite right in labelling it my greatest victory. The next question is: what happens to other CO's? Will they also be required to spend time in solitary, and if so how long? Just what procedure will be used to determine a CO's right to the "accommodation" which I've been given? If the last few months have been exciting, I think the next few will be even more so. There's a rumour, incidentally, that Richard might be moved back here, which would be lovely. Especially as I have been told very strictly by the O.C. that I am not allowed to ~~talk~~ talk to anyone here – not the inmates, not the J.W.'s, not even the corporals. He didn't know the reason why when I asked him, so evidently this instruction must come from higher

20. Letter from me to my parents, 10 August 1980, exulting on being relieved of solitary confinement

up. It's no fun, I can tell you, being required to be my own policeman! But luckily there is a lieutenant here who did his B. Juris at Potch, and we've spent many hours together talking about all sorts of things, especially philosophy and Afrikaans literature.

My last period of solitary, just for the record, was only 7 days. The actual sentence was 14 as usual, but was not applied for the first 7 because the offer of a job at the military hospital was being made at the time. Which brings my total time in "Noordkoppies" (don't you think that's an appropriate name?) to 125 days.

It's very interesting to see how the attitude of certain officers has already changed now that I am no longer in a position of disobedience. The blue colour is almost like a passport. Fortunately there were some, like L/Cpl H., who were well-disposed all along — he brought me coffee one cold night, and called me by my Christian name, and never forgot about my ½-hour out in the morning and afternoon.

Another nice thing — the sergeant-major told me, "Jy is al klaar so bleek in die gesig, Mal", and gave instructions that I am not to be locked in my cell over weekends as the other guys are. It's like getting a promotion, a raise, a new car and a jackpot all at once!

Thank you for the "Imitation of Christ", Mom. I'll start reading it soon. I remember noting that Bonhoeffer read it in Latin during his stay in prison — so I guess it'll be a lot better than Augustine's "Confessions", which I read some months ago and found rather difficult and foreign.

With lots of love from
Peter.

21. Letter from me to my parents, 10 August 1980 (concluded)

-1-

65 Delville Road

UMTATA

Transkei

21 November 1977

The Officer Commanding

Cape Flats Commando

Rosebank

CAPE TOWN

Dear sir

(1) I hereby make formal application to have my draft by Cape
Flats Commando for 1 December 1977 replaced by a period of
service of national interest under civilian direction of any
length up to one year. I refer to such activities as
teaching in schools or work in a hospital or a municipality.
I have completed my fourth year of academic study (chiefly
in Business Science) and I feel that this training would be
well utilized in the above-mentioned activities. I feel
further that the alternatives provided by Western countries
(e.g. West Germany, Denmark) in place of military service
are an adequate precedent for this application.

(2) Please note that the request in (1) is a repetition of a
verbal request I put to the acting Officer Commanding of
Cape Flats Commando on the evening of 3 October 1977.

(3) If, however, this request cannot be granted, I refuse to obey
my call-up instruction on 1 December 1977. My reasons for

22. My letter of refusal, 21 November 1977. A scan from my
own archive, of the carbon copy of the original.

doing so will be found in the appendix. Please note that this statement of the subject supersedes all others, verbal or written.

(4) My place of residence from 26 November to 10 December 1977 will be

> Room C11
>
> University House
>
> Rhodes Drive,
>
> MOWBRAY
>
> 7700

'Phone numbers for this address are: 699975, 699940 or 699931.

Yours faithfully

P G Moll (Rfn.)
72476690KT
B Company, Cape Flats Commando

23. My letter of refusal, 21 November 1977 (continued)

-1-

APPENDIX: WHY I AM A SELECTIVE CONSCIENTIOUS OBJECTOR

By way of definition

A selective conscientious objector is one who for reasons of conscience refuses to participate in a war but whose objection does not extend to all war.

Norms and Standards

By what norms does one evaluate society?

The social message of the Old Testament is that God requires justice of his subjects.   All human conceptions of justice must be founded upon Him who only is just.   Justice in society ought to be a reflection of the divine justice.   In the theocratic state of Israel the rich had to show compassion to the poor; all men were equal before the law; there was to be no exploitation by corrupt business practice such as the weighting of scales or usury; legal checks were built in to ensure that the structure of society did not develop into one in which the demands of divine justice could not be fulfilled - for instance, the strongly redistributive nature of the Jubilee.   God has required nothing of man but "to do justly, to love mercy, and

24. My letter of refusal, 21 November 1977 (continued)

to walk humbly with (his) God". While there is scanty evidence
for egalitarianism, stress is laid on the virtue of fairness
and compassion.

In the New Testament, the sayings of Jesus and the apostles
expand and intensify the above. In the Sermon on the Mount
we read of going the second mile, giving the cloak and and
the coat as well, and the evil of hypocrisy; Peter was reprimanded
for taking up a sword in self-defence; Paul insists in Romans
chapter 13 that a good government, being under God's authority,
will punish the evildoer; pure religion, for James, is caring
for orphans and widows.

A just war?

In the popular mind, several requirements for the definition
of a just war have been developed, for instance:

   (i) the war must be in defence of a just society
  (ii) the war must not be unduly prolonged
 (iii) the warring side must be assured of victory
  (iv) there must be reason to expect that a successful war
      will leave matters better than they were before the war.
   (v) all possible methods of resolving the conflict by peaceful
      means must be exhausted.

These conditions challenge South Africa's conflict on at least
two points.

25. My letter of refusal, 21 November 1977 (continued)

-3-

I

The definition of a just war excludes war in defence of a
basically unjust and discriminatory society. South African
society, I believe, is basically unjust and discriminatory.
The founding motive of apartheid policy is that racial groups
be separated, be allowed to develop along their own lines and
be permitted, eventually, to achieve self-determination.
This fine ideal is found to be hollow when we realize that,
when all the partitioning has been completed, the White community's
share of South Africa's land and riches will be out of all proportion to its population size.

To achieve this ideal, radical methods have been applied. For
instance, there have been vast forced movements of population.
By far the larger proportion of the people affected have been
black. There are sever restrictions on the private movements
of blacks, particularly in the urban areas. The economic
superiority of the White community is assured by, among others,
laws prohibiting the operation of trade unions among blacks.
Blacks who have been living and working in urban areas, sometimes for three generations, are denied meaningful political
rights there, under the superficial gloss that they may exercise
their rights in their respective homelands.

II

Several pointed questions will lead us further into the argument.
Whom and what are we defending? Against whom and against what
are we fighting? Are we fighting an external aggressor?

26. My letter of refusal, 21 November 1977 (continued)

The first question is partly answered in (I).   In my view,
we are defending the interests of the ruling group.   We are
not acting in the best interests of all the peoples of South
Africa.   The almost unabated civil unrest in black townships
around large South African cities affords abundant proof that
there is a significant body of black opinion that considers
the wider policies of the present government to be directed
mainly in the interests of the White race.

This brings us to the second question.   The high incidence
of black youths fighting amongst the guerillas whose homes are
inside South Africa, places doubt on the celebrated formula
"Communist imperialists".   Certainly there is a Communist
presence among the insurgents, but that is not the end of the
matter.   There is also a large element of legitimate outrage
which finds its expression (whether legitimately or not, I
cannot tell) in armed revolution.   It would be hypocritical
in the extreme to condemn terrorism without first condemning
the forces which have provoked it; likewise it would be hypocritical to combat terrorism militarily without simultaneously
seeking to eliminate the causes that lie behind it.

Pursuing this line of argument further, it emerges that the
border conflict is rapidly assuming the proportions of a
civil war.

Another salient point in this connection is the sheer size of
the military budget, the extent to which the large increases
in recent years have been prompted by burgeoning internal unrest,

27. My letter of refusal, 21 November 1977 (continued)

-5-

and the probability that military might will be the ultimate
sanction in the case of serious unrest.

Conclusion

My essentially moral, as opposed to pragmatic, view of South
African society springs ultimately from my commitment to God as
a Christian.   Where the laws of men depart from the law of
God, there can be no obligation to obey those laws.

P G Moll (nfn)

72476490KT

21 November 1977

28. My letter of refusal, 21 November 1977 (concluded)

GRENSDIENS: MAN GESTRAF

„EK glo daar is 'n hoër gesag as die wet van die land en as die twee in konflik is, moet die Wet van God die voorkeur kry," het Peter Graham Moll (21) gister in die Wynbergse landdroshof gesê. Moll is skuldig bevind op aanklag dat hy versuim het om hom op 1 Desember aan te meld. Hy is tot drie maande gevangenisstraf, opgeskort vir vyf jaar, gevonnis.

Moll, 'n lidmaat van die Baptiste-kerk in Claremont en voorsitter van die Students' Christian Association van die Universiteit van Kaapstad, het getuig dat hy uit 'n Christelike oogpunt geruime tyd oor militêre diensplig bedenkinge het.

Nadat hy vroeër vanjaar opgeroep was, het hy aangebied om burgerlike diens te doen en 'n brief aan die Weermag geskryf waarin hy sy redes vir diensligweiering uiteengesit het, het Moll gesê.

Landdros H. van Wyk het in sy uitspraak gesê uit Moll se brief aan die Weermag wil dit vir hom lyk of daar ook politieke redes vir die weiering was.

Moll het in 1973 aan die Selbourne College, Oos-Londen, gematrikuleer en was onder die twintig beste kandidate in Kaapland. Tans is hy 'n derdejaarstudent in bedryfswetenskap aan die Universiteit van Kaapstad.

Ná Matriek het Moll 'n jaar militêre diensplig gedoen en later weer 'n kamp van drie weke bygewoon.

Mej. E. Rall het vir die staat verskyn.

29. Report of the trial of 27 December 1977, in *Die Burger* (29 December 1977)

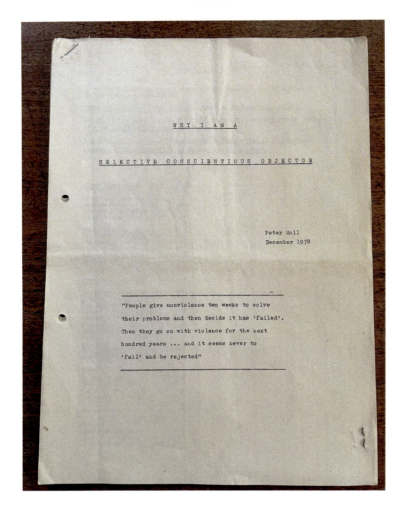

30. 'Why I am a selective conscientious objector' (December 1978). I printed 300 copies of the paper on the Gestetner machine at the SA Institute of Race Relations in Mowbray, with the help of students from the Catholic Society at the University of Cape Town, and distributed it to ministers, priests, students and newspapers all over the country. The prosecutor at my trial on 4 December 1979 had a copy. From Wits, Rob. Coll, A2558-9.13. Scanning by Hannah Cuaterno and Caleb Manikam.

Dear Reader

Much thought and research have gone into the preparation of my document "Why I am a conscientious objector". Believing it to be an important issue facing the Church of Christ in contemporary South Africa, I would like theological debate on the subject to continue. Hence I invite your critical comment: any suggestions/additions/corrections/criticisms are welcome. My address is "Lynden", Avenue Rd, Mowbray 7700.

Yours in Christ's service

P. Moll.

Peter Moll

31. 'Why I am a selective conscientious objector' (Dec. 1978) (continued)

-1-

My motivation for selective conscientious objection can be summarized in three basic propositions.

First Proposition: South African society is fundamentally unjust.

Second Proposition: The definition of a just war excludes war in defence of a basically unjust society.

Third Proposition: Selective conscientious objection is a Christian response to the injunctions of Romans chapter thirteen.

.oOo.

FIRST PROPOSITION: SOUTH AFRICAN SOCIETY IS FUNDAMENTALLY UNJUST.

I believe that there are sufficient non-religious grounds for selective conscientious objection (meaning the refusal to participate in a particular war while making no assertion about war in general). The addition of Christian morality makes my own duty to objection more binding.

Every country has built into its operations a measure of injustice. This much is inescapable on account of the fallen nature of man. While one should certainly strive to eliminate the remaining vestiges of injustice, these do not of themselves constitute sufficient grounds for selective conscientious objection. Only when the society is shot through with injustice does one have sufficient grounds for such objection.

Justice in the Bible: Old Testament

In the Old Testament Israelite theocracy, God demanded justice of his people. Their justice was to be a reflection of the divine righteousness. "Be holy as I am holy" was a command that extended beyond men's private lives to their societal relationships as well. There was to be equality before the courts; there was to be compassion by the rich and strong for the poor and weak; merchants were not to weight their scales to their own advantage; all debts were considered scrapped each Jubilee year. Not least among the sins Israel committed when she was unfaithful was that of depriving the poor of their means of income, the land, thus bringing about an unequal distribution of income where justice could not possibly prevail.

"Hate what is evil, love what is right, and see that justice prevails in the courts", Amos urges upon his hearers. Prophetically, Amos said "You people that hate anyone who challenges injustice and speaks the whole truth in court, have oppressed the poor and robbed them of their grain". Obviously there are no simplistic conclusions to be drawn. These men's ideas are not a model for our society. Yet they can serve as the raw material for each subsequent generation to process in order to come to a better understanding of the weaknesses of the society of the time. Nowhere does the Old Testament speak of egalitarianism, but there is a strong emphasis on fairness and equity, i.e. while the Bible does not teach a primitive socialism where equality is the norm, it does insist on fair dealing, a principle which must be applied in every society.

32. 'Why I am a selective conscientious objector' (Dec. 1978) (continued)

Justice in the Bible: New Testament

In the New Testament, Jesus spoke of going the second mile and giving the coat as well as the cloak. To James, true and undefiled religion is to visit the fatherless and the widow. Jesus spoke at great length about the evils of hypocrisy, calling the Pharisees 'whited sepulchres'. John Howard Yoder has advanced convincing arguments for a literal understanding of the words that Jesus quoted from Isaiah:

"The Spirit of the Lord is upon me,
because he has chosen me to bring good news to the poor.
He has sent me to proclaim liberty to the captives and
recovery of sight to the blind,
to set free the oppressed and announce that the time has come
when the Lord will save his people" (Luke 4:18f).

Paul insists that government is ordained of God and that a good government will reward the good man and punish the evildoer. He urges that prayers be made for all in authority, so that we will be able to live peaceable and quiet lives. The vineyard owner in Jesus' parable pays his labourers one denarius for their work (equivalent to a fair day's wage) whether they have worked for one hour or the whole day — clearly their financial need is the criterion by which payment should be made: given the situation of unemployment in Israel at that time, the needs of their families would all have been the same (Matthew 20). There is a sense in which we can say that love in the New Testament is the same as justice in the Old Testament.

The Christian norm of law has never been embodied in any historical system of law. Nevertheless, it is the Christian's concern that the overall direction which his society is taking should not, at least, be away from the Kingdom of God.

Justice in South Africa

The motive of separate development is the political and social, though not necessarily the economic, separation of distinct nations, followed by self-rule or self-determination for each. There is no biblical teaching against this fine ideal, in principle; indeed there are many who find theological justification for it; but careful examination of the South African reality reveals its moral barrenness. When the partitioning is complete, the white race will have a share of the land area and the country's natural wealth which is out of all proportion to its population size. The total homeland area will be 13% of South Africa's land area; the homelands have low labour retention abilities, which show little sign of improvement. Therefore there will always be approximately nine million Africans or more working in so-called White South Africa, unable to take an effective part in decisions which affect them, except in their own homelands — their connection with which, admittedly, is becoming increasingly tenuous.

Separate development politics makes lofty ethnical appeals to "spiritual" values like language and culture, but whites still dominate the economy and the society is rife with racism. Separate development may be the ideal, but white racial domination is the reality. The proposed new constitution does not alter the position materially. By its own confession, the African is left out of its reckoning, and it will fit in with the separate development scheme, hence it will not embody power-sharing.

33. 'Why I am a selective conscientious objector' (Dec. 1978)
(continued)

-3-

Incipient totalitarianism?

To achieve the separate development ideal, radical methods have been applied.
The word 'radical' may be taken to mean that which reaches down to the
existential roots of a man's being.   To assume, as the National Party
has done, that the most precious thing to a man is his sense of national
pride and national security, is radical .   Nic Diederichs wrote: "Without
the uplifting, ennobling and enriching influence of this highest inclusive
(ethnic) unity which we call a nation, mankind cannot reach the fullest
heights of his human existence ... Only in a nation as the most total,
most inclusive human community can man realize himself to the full.   The
nation is the fulfilment of the individual life". (Nasionalisme as lewens-
beskouing)

Criticism of the state totalitarianism to which this belief in the nation
leads was the gist of the South African Council of Churches' publication
"A Message to the Peoples of South Africa".   State totalitarianism
occurs when the state seeks to absorb non-political spheres of society
into the structure of the state in such a way that the state obtains
determining control over areas which are non-political.   Paradoxically,
this is exactly the official criticism of leftism and of socialism: that
these doctrines are too idealistic, utopian, and omnivorous; therefore
it is in the name of conservatism, a "limited style of politics", that
I experience difficulties with the official preoccupation with ethnicity.

One example of a radical method is the application of the Immorality Act
and the Mixed Marriages Act, with the insistence that ethnicity, as opposed
to the Christian formulation of the 'equal yoke' (common belief) must
determine who one may and who one may not marry.   Another is the pass
law system, restricting the movements of blacks and doing little to encourage
interracial contact and hence promote goodwill.

Laws concerning trade unions are discriminatory.   Whites can have trade
unions, Africans cannot.   The Government's objections to granting trade
union rights to Blacks are that Blacks would wield their new-found power
to overthrow the government; but that is precisely the point: the overarching
aim of any government should be to create a society free from tensions like
that which require the repression of worker grievances.

Education funds are distributed unequally.   While more than R500 is spent
each year on a white child, less than R50, on average, is spent on each
black.   And thwarted ambition is made more galling by the social snub of
what has become known as 'petty apartheid'.

The practice of prolonged detention without trial, without subsequent
judicial examination, is without justification, as is the unbridled power
currently granted to the Security Branch.   Small wonder, then, that
Lucas Mangope, and more so Gatsha Buthelezi, have indicated their dissatisfaction with the white government -- to say nothing of the unrecognized
leaders, who distressingly often are incarcerated.   Urban blacks have
registered their non-compliance with the system by showing little interest
in the Community Council elections -- the total Soweto vote was 6%, but
erstwhile minister Mulder made the brilliant observation that in some of
the Soweto wards it was a higher percentage.   Which shows how lamentably
far the government is from the opinions of the average black.

34. 'Why I am a selective conscientious objector' (Dec. 1978) (continued)

-4-

What about the Communist threat?

During the 1950's, the A.N.C. tried non-violent means (e.g. the pass-book burnings) to achieve change. The Government responded with arrests, bannings, detention and the time-honoured method of shooting. Can we be surprized, then, that blacks are leaving the country and are working for change by armed insurgence? Like all decent people, we deplore the use of violence. Yet when the African realizes that he has precious little means of bringing about change by constitutional processes, and then turns to unlawful means, we are the first to respond with the threat of armed force.

The doctrine of populism, in China, consists of the elimination of the isolated 'foreign capitalist devil'. The South African variant consists of the elimination of the isolated communist 'agitator'. The intellectual content may differ, but the essential idea is eternally the same: the populist sees the people as a body of virtuous toilers constructively working, but confronted by a handful of infiltrators, and if these uitlanders — whose ghostly presence has haunted every populist since Robespierre first denounced them as corrupters of the Revolution and enemies of the General Will — could be purged, all would be well.

However, things are never so simple. The application of pressure may stop a wound from bleeding outwardly, but then it bleeds inwardly. Far better is a sincere search for the causes of discontent. Quite possibly many of the so-called agitators would disappear if the legitimate causes of dissatisfaction were removed. It has been argued that present government policy is creating the conditions under which the Soviet brand of communism, with its blandishments and false promises, becomes attractive to a disillusioned African intelligentsia. Those who make pacific revolution impossible make violent revolution inevitable.

SECOND PROPOSITION: THE DEFINITION OF A JUST WAR EXCLUDES WAR IN DEFENCE OF A BASICALLY UNJUST SOCIETY

Minimum conditions for a just war

Centuries of church history have yielded seven criteria by which to judge whether a war is just.

i The cause fought for must be just
ii The purpose of the warring power must remain just while hostilities go on
iii The war must be truly the last resort, all peaceful means having been exhausted
iv The methods employed during the war to vanquish the foe must be just
v The benefits the war can reasonably be expected to bring for humanity must be greater than the evils provoked by the war itself
vi Victory must be assured
vii The peace concluded at the end of the war must be just and of such nature as to prevent a new war

Karl Barth insisted that the only criterion should be 'ultima ratio' —

35. 'Why I am a selective conscientious objector' (Dec. 1978)
(continued)

-5-

whether the war is truly the last resort. Now, without asserting the universal validity of the just war argument (modern theologians, e.g. Moulder, Ellul, question both the traditional and the Barthian formulations) we can assert that the above conditions are the minimum which must be satisfied if a war is to be declared just. And even these conditions are not met by the South African guerilla war. The SADF part of it is not a last resort -- peaceful means like gradual enfranchisement, removal of objectionable laws, and consultation with popular black leaders have rarely been tried, let alone exhausted. If proposition one above is correct, then we cannot even start thinking of a just war, i.e. condition i above is not met.

Who is the enemy?

Then there is the further question of the identity of the enemy. The life situation of Whites leads them to perceive the guerilla as a foreign aggressor; as a Soviet catspaw. However, the life situation of the Black leads him to think in naked terms of civil war. The longstanding injustice of apartheid is the cause; terrorism (he would say, self-defence) is merely the result. When the South African Council of Churches turned its thoughts to conscientious objection at Hammanskraal in 1974, the majority of the delegates present were black. The Roman Catholic Church conference of bishops, whose constituency is 80% black, has indicated its firm support for selective conscientious objectors.

Jacques Ellul refers in his book "Violence" to the "sameness of violence". Whether the violence is military, economic, or psychological, by a recognized government or by the guerilla movement, it remains violence. Violence has been defined as "the destructive imposition of power". Helder Camara, a Latin American bishop, develops this theme. The state engages in "violence no. 1", the primary violence of suppression of freedoms, corruption in high places and exploitation of the weak. The people react with "violence no. 2", the provoked violence of guerilla warfare and urban terrorism, whereupon the state replies with "violence no. 3", repressionary violence of police crackdowns and yet further suppression of freedoms. This argument cannot be applied in South Africa without qualification. Like all liberation theologies and theories, it tends to idolize the particular group one stands for. Nevertheless it does form part of a cumulative case for objection in a turbid situation where it is difficult to tell which side is more wrong.

Ultimately South Africa's problems do not admit of a military solution. The long-term solution must be a political-economic one. It would appear that the authorities are not sufficiently aware of this. The idea of "winning the war" is playing a disastrous part in the popular mind, but, in my opinion, it has no place in South African reality. The inculcation of a war psychosis through the aggressive marketing of Defence Bonds, the enormous increases in the military budget in recent years, the use of civilian troops to suppress riots in 1976, the fact that the Defence force comprises almost exclusively white troops, and statements of threatened apocalypticism by South Africa's top soldiers, reveal, as far as I can see, the myopia of their vision.

36. 'Why I am a selective conscientious objector' (Dec. 1978) (continued)

-6-

The 1977 end-of-year message of the Minister of Defence, Mr PW Botha, included the following:

> "We will, in increasing measure, be subjected to coercion, persuasion and even seduction, to submit to the will of the aggressor. This cannot, and shall not happen, in South Africa. We shall not waiver and we shall not succumb".

General Magnus Malan, the Chief of the Defence Force, said

> "Hand in hand, white, brown and black citizens of South Africa warded off the enemy, once again showing the world that we are a nation united against all foreign ideologies".

Are they tilting at imaginary windmills? Significantly, I think, the "enemy" and the "aggressor" remain anonymous. Perhaps closer definition of the enemy would reveal him to be a Soweto civilian — which could be embarrassing. Human kind cannot bear very much reality. Their intemperate fulminating against the nameless "enemy" seems to me like the rage of Caliban seeing his own face in a glass.

THIRD PROPOSITION: SELECTIVE CONSCIENTIOUS OBJECTION IS A CHRISTIAN RESPONSE TO THE INJUNCTIONS OF ROMANS CHAPTER THIRTEEN

The theory of civil disobedience

Civil disobedience is the non-violent violation of a public norm, generally regarded as legally binding, as a means of social or political protest. For instance, an action of civil disobedience occurred in 1957 in South African religious life when the proposed Native Law Amendment Bill would have required the organisers of multiracial services to apply for permits, had it been passed. The heads of most of the denominations informed the government that this would amount to a denial of their hard-won freedom of worship, and the bill was dropped soon afterwards. The three necessary motifs

    i strict nonviolence
    ii ready acceptance of all penalties
    iii persuasion of the majority

were included.

To qualify for civil disobedience, one must first have rendered a willing and respectful obedience to the State laws. Only then does the right accrue to one of the civil disobedience of certain laws in well-defined circumstances. It is intended as a limited, non-revolutionary form of protest. It is intended to encourage a deeper realization of the values which law must embody in a democracy if it is to maintain a durable legitimacy in the minds of the large majority of its citizens. Ultimately the act of civil disobedience may lead to a greater respect for law by bringing law and justice together. There is little evidence that civil disobedience has encouraged widespread disrespect for law. Of course the action is not generalizable, i.e. the civil disobedient recognizes that it would be chaotic if everyone copied him; but the important fact is that

37. 'Why I am a selective conscientious objector' (Dec. 1978) (continued)

-7-

civil disobedience is permissible under only certain carefully defined conditions, i.e. it is intended to be limited and to uphold public security.

This method was often used, and with reasonable success, during the Civil Rights movement of the 1960's in the United States. Henry David Thoreau was imprisoned in 1848 for refusing to pay his Massachusetts poll tax as a protest against slavery and the federal government's imperialist war against Mexico. In his widely read statement of the subject, entitled "Civil Disobedience", he wrote:

> "No man must ever allow himself to be an agent of injustice to another .. he must never lend his support to a wrong which his conscience condemns".

Law and Order versus Freedom

I think that traditional Christians sometimes equate law and order with Christianity too readily. In so doing, they are seeking to attain a false security and so to avoid the anxiety and complexity of moral choice. Order should not be regarded as the presupposition and condition of freedom; rather freedom is the presupposition and condition of order. Once it is acknowledged that freedom is necessary for good order, and that justice is the proper foundation and criterion of law, then it is possible to perceive that law and order may have to be opposed in the interests of freedom and justice. Order qua order is nothing — the question is whether it is or is not just, whether it does or does not allow freedom, and whether, if it favours both injustice and oppression, it can be changed without an increase in either.

All this is not to say that law and order are not valuable; it is to point out that they cannot be regarded as the supreme value before which all other moral considerations have to give way. Man is ultimately accountable to God and not to man-made institutions. The Koinonia Declaration of 1977 has the right balance when it says

> "We as Christians are convinced that we must continue to practise love towards those people in authority ... we declare our complete willingness to submit to the order of the civil establishment as such, to be obedient to those in authority, provided that their exercise of authority is in accordance with the precepts of God's Word, and to show love toward them ... It is our conviction that the maintenance of justice rather than the maintenance of law and order and state security is the prime God-given task of the government and the governed, and if they strive with all earnestness for justice, then law and order will be added as a blessing."

This does not mean that it is possible to frame a universally valid statement which would indicate exactly when a person may legitimately disobey the laws of a state. We simply have to recognize that there are occasions when the Christian may have to act illegally if God is to be obeyed rather than men. Dietrich Bonhoeffer, known for his resistance to the Nazi government, said

> "In the course of historical life there comes a point where the exact

38. 'Why I am a selective conscientious objector' (Dec. 1978) (continued)

-8-

observance of the formal law of the state, of a commercial undertaking, of a family, or for that matter of a scientific discovery, suddenly finds itself in violent conflict with the ineluctable necessities of the lives of men; at this point responsible and pertinent action leaves behind it the domain of the normal and regular, and is confronted by the extra-ordinary situation of ultimate necessities, a situation which no law can control".

Biblical examples of disobedience to authority

So much for the theory of civil disobedience. But aren't there verses in the New Testament which expressly forbid such action for Christians? Passages like I Timothy 2:1-3, I Peter 2:13f and especially the classic statement of the duty of the Christian to the state in Romans 13:1-7 have often been taken by Christians to require passive submission to the state. Certainly they do demand obedience; but they do not demand unquestioning obedience independent of social ethics taught elsewhere in the Bible. Paul must have known that not all of God's people have always adopted an attitude of unconditional submission. Jesus once referred to King Herod as "that fox". In Acts 5 we read of Peter breaking out of prison. Moses defied Pharaoh and led Israel out of Egypt, Samuel rebuked King Saul, Daniel and his friends opposed King Nebuchadnezzar, Jeremiah and other prophets exposed the injustice of the civil authorities. Jonathan was saved from Saul's wrath by his countrymen. Doeg's compliance with an unjust sentence made him a murderer (I Samuel 22:17-23). Elisha told Jehu to kill Ahab (2 Kings 9:1-10). Elijah remonstrated with Ahab and Jezebel for their killing of Naboth. Jehoida the priest ordered the killing of Queen Athaliah (2 Kings 11:1-16). Hebrews 11 numbers Rahab among the faithful for the allegiance to Israel and treason to Jericho which she showed.

Paul's teaching could not have been at variance with their example. Nor could it have been at variance with his own example — James Moulder (Journal of Theology for Southern Africa no. 21) points out that Paul disobeyed his prison warders, refusing to leave the prison; he insisted that the magistrates had to acknowledge their unjust treatment of Paul. This act of disobedience is important because it shows that violation of the right to worship is not the only instance when Christians are called upon to disobey the authorities.

Many South African Christians who incline to the 'passive submission' view would have no serious objection to the critical stance the Anglican bishops of Uganda adopted to their President in 1977, or to the letter two Russian Orthodox priests addressed to the 1975 WCC assembly, accusing their government of the denial of religious freedom. Christian Missions International encourages the smuggling of bibles into communist lands — a form of civil disobedience which exceeds the bounds normally accorded it, in that it does not seek to persuade the majority and it does not willingly submit to the punishment consequent upon the action. The influential Underground Evangelism performs a similar task. Apparently conservative churchmen do distinguish between what they consider to be good governments and bad governments, even if they pretend to accept that Romans 13 teaches submission to all governments.

39. 'Why I am a selective conscientious objector' (Dec. 1978)
(continued)

What does Romans 13 teach?

Paul's observations follow from the previous remarks in chapter twelve. There he had declared that the Christian must not return evil for evil; the state, on the other hand, does the opposite; it does take vengeance on those who do wrong. What then are we to think of those civil authorities whose function it is to control and repress evil actions? In so far as they execute vengeance, says Paul, they do so as the "servant of God"; their function is not therefore outside God's providential will. So Christians should adopt an attitude of obedience as long as the authorities observe the claim implicit in their role. The logical corollary of this, although it is not explicit but implied, is that if they cease to serve the good, Christians would no longer have the same reason to accept their authority. It is important to remember that Paul was not concerned to provide a theological interpretation of the state's essence and meaning. Indeed his concern is not with civil government per se, but with the Christian and his conduct.

The state is God's servant "for your own good" (vs. 4). The state is, therefore, not only God's servant, but also man's. It can lay claim to respect and obedience only insofar as it stands under God's authority and insofar as it serves its subjects. If, therefore, it acts contrary to the welfare of its citizens, it is not God's servant "for your own good".

We are reminded here of Thielicke's concept of 'derived authority'. The state derives its authority from God, but if it practises wickedness it ceases to derive that authority.

We must juxtapose our understanding of Romans 13 with that of Revelation 13. The first was written in the period of transition from Claudius to Nero, under a reasonably just government, in a time of relative political calm. The latter was written in the period when Emperor Domitian oppressed his subjects, persecuted Christians, and usurped for himself divine characteristics. The state in Romans 13 is regarded as God's servant for the good of its citizens; in Revelation 13 it is portrayed as the beast that has to be resisted. The conscience which submits to the state when the well-being of the people is promoted, is the same as the conscience which opposes the state when it acts contrary to the good of the people.

Oscar Cullman sums up his survey of the state in the New Testament with the words:

> "according as the State remains within its limits or transgresses these, the Christian will describe it as the servant of God or the instrument of the Devil". (The State in the New Testament. SCM Press, 1957, p86).

We should guard against identifying the orthodox state morality with Christian morality. This is often done, and it is done in order to avoid the anxiety and complexity of moral choice. When you obey traffic regulations, for instance, you are really pursuing your own interests. It can be argued that the state morality expresses our self-interest. Whereas Christian morality is love, altruism; it is not self-interest; therefore it must be carefully distinguished from the state morality.

40. 'Why I am a selective conscientious objector' (Dec. 1978)
(continued)

Since Constantine united Church and State in the fourth century, the church has lost sight of the moral cynicism of the apostle John who wrote "The world lies under the dominance of the wicked one" (I John 5:19) and "Do not be surprized if the world hates you" (i.e. for the very love which you espouse). The almost universal pacifist stance of the church in its first two centuries of existence has been forgotten. It is heartening to see contemporary theologians reexamining the role of the Anabaptists in the Reformation. They held no brief for the moral grandeurs of the temporal powers, and, for their trouble, were massacred in their thousands — at Luther's behest. Add to these the Dissenters and Nonconformists, the Bonhoeffers and Niemollers of wartime Germany, the civil rights movement of Martin Luther King and the persecuted church of Uganda and the USSR and we see that civil disobedience is in the finest church tradition.

All this is not to deny that the state has the right to self-defence. To deny, on ethical grounds, the elementary right of the State to defend itself is to deny the existence of the State. Whoever affirms the State as a necessity must also affirm war as a contingent necessity; the force which each state possesses alone protects it against the force exercised by other states.

Selective conscientious objection: a special case of civil disobedience

Selective conscientious objection is in fact civil disobedience of a military command. I contend that it ought to be civil disobedience of the direct, and not of the indirect, type. Mahatma Gandhi supported both kinds of disobedience. The former is disobedience of a law which is itself regarded as morally wanting; the latter is deliberate disobedience of a law unrelated to the evil being protested. It is rather a symbolic action — obstruction of traffic while bearing placards, etc. Because selective conscientious objection is more directly related to the issue of public security, it is desirable that the military itself be involved in the perceived wrong, and that symbolic protest, if contemplated at all, be limited to 'safe' and non-military areas. An ethical right to selective conscientious objection which can be expressed in general terms does not exist, but the issue does arise of making a responsible choice in a specific situation.

The United States, Canada, Australia, Sweden, Norway, Belgium, Italy, Holland, France and West Germany provide conscientious objectors with alternatives outside the military framework. Usually the period of civilian service is longer than the original military call-up, to compensate for the rigours of military life. The number of objectors in West Germany has now risen to 22 000. This in fact constitutes only 1,5% of the total number liable for military service. Objectors registered in Britain under the National Service Act of 1941 during the war years represented 0,77% of the total number of men registered. It would appear c t that a relaxation of the laws in South Africa would not result in a dangerous number of men turning to conscientious objection.

It must be borne in mind that the selective conscientious objector does not act paradigmatically, as an example. He does not confer a universal value upon his action. He does not do it in the hope that all other conscripts will do the same. South Africa's solution is obviously not

41. 'Why I am a selective conscientious objector' (Dec. 1978) (continued)

-11-

the retraction of troops from our borders. Nor is it the refusal to engage
in civil defence, where the latter is taken to mean suppression of township
riots. Retraction and refusal cannot reasonably be expected of any government. I am under no illusions about the supposed rightness of the
revolutionaries' cause. How many betrayed revolutions have we not
already seen in Africa? But that is not the end of the matter. I
think that without a simultaneous confrontation with the real roots of
the problem, such fighting is certainly wrong   for me personally
and I am constrained to disobey.

"Total war" is no solution

A recent open letter by a number of missionaries in South Korea illustrates
my point. They write, inter alia:

> "Many say that while freedom, justice and civil liberties are not
> important, these must take second place to defence against the
> expansion of communism in Asia, and that therefore, those who are
> actively working for those issues must postpone their efforts in
> light of the more important priority of defence and security".

Referring to what had happened in South Vietnam and which, they believed,
was busy happening in South Korea as well, they argue that the people,
because of the actions of their government, were too little motivated to
combat communism. They proceed:

> "By destroying freedom and justice, by trampling on human rights,
> by outlawing all voices of opposition or differing opinions, the
> Park regime is destroying the only hope of unity and common commit-
> ment to its goals, even to one as important as national security.
> The goals of national security are actually dependent upon an at-
> mosphere of democratic freedom and justice, but these are the very
> things which present government practices tend to smother. This
> in itself, is, in our opinion, the real threat to national security".

Jeremiah's word was that faith and justice were Israel's sure defence.
He urged the people not to trust in those deceptive words, "The temple
of the Lord" -- for they had assumed that their temple worship would
save them from God's wrath despite the injustice they were practising.
Likewise, faith and justice are South Africa's sure defence. There is
no moral imperative that South Africa should survive. But there is
a moral imperative that South Africa should live justly.

XXXXXXXXXXXXXXXXXXXXXXXXXXXXXXXXXXXXXXXXXXXXXXXXXXXXXXXXXXXXXXXXXXXXXXXX

42. 'Why I am a selective conscientious objector' (Dec. 1978)
(continued)

-12-
..7

A D D E N D U M

WHY I REQUEST A NONMILITARY ALTERNATIVE

If it is the Christian's duty to discern and pursue the truth, it is also his duty to be a <u>witness</u> to the truth. For instance, the apostle Peter, at great risk to himself, stated that he could not but speak about the things he had seen and heard. One of the best known examples from church history is that of Martin Luther, who nailed his 95 Theses to the church door of the Wittenburg castle. A less known one is that of Franz Jägerstätter the German martyr. It would surely not have 'hurt' him to take the military oath of loyalty to Hitler in 1943, and to return to his family, but he refused both army service and the oath. He was jailed and executed and is remembered today for his humble witness.

It is for the witness value of the action that I am a selective conscientious objector and demand a nonmilitary alternative, as opposed to accepting a noncombatant position. Hopefully the outcome would be a serious examination of the war in terms of the Christian principles outlined above.

.oOo.

Peter Moll

December 1978

43. 'Why I am a selective conscientious objector' (Dec. 1978) (concluded)

EXCERPTS FROM AN OPEN LETTER, DATED 19TH OCTOBER 1979, BY PETER MOLL
(IN WHICH HE AGAIN REFUSES TO ATTEND MILITARY CAMP) ADDRESSED TO THE
OFFICER COMMANDING, CAPE FLATS COMMANDO.

(Distributed by friends of Peter Moll, 23 year old selective
conscientious objector, committed Baptist, and past chairman
of the Students Christian Association at University of Cape
Town.   Peter has already been tried twice, first in a civil
court in 1977, when he was sentenced to 3 months' imprisonment suspended for 5 years;   and on 21st September 1979 when
a military court fined him R50.   He has now been ordered to
attend a training camp from 19th November.)

Dear Sir,
CONSCIENTIOUS OBJECTION TO CONTINUOUS TRAINING CAMP

I note that I am required to attend a training camp from 19 November to
7 December 1979.   After much serious consideration and study, and after
consulting my church leaders about the matter, I have come to the conclusion that to obey would be a grave moral compromise of my faith.
I therefore refuse to do so.   My explanation is as follows.
(For purposes of this leaflet, Peter Moll's first two points have
been summarised as follows: -
1. Pacifism: ... The Christian Church has traditionally been concerned about involvement with the military which means the
taking of men's lives.

2. Civil Disobedience: ... Christians obey the government, but
reserve the right to disobey if obedience does not conform to
their religious and moral convictions.)

3. Selective conscientious objection

Selective conscientious objection is the refusal to engage in a particular war, while making no necessary statement about war in general.   I
have decided to be a selective conscientious objector because

(a) in terms of Christian moral standards, South African society is
fundamentally unjust;
(b) the insurgents are generally not foreigners but South African
citizens -- ie the situation is one of civil war;   and
(c) this makes one question very seriously just what one is required to
fight for, and what one is required to die for.   I shall devote one
paragraph to each of these three points.

In the Pentateuch we are commanded to protect the widow, the orphan,
the slave and the foreigner.   The prophets castigated Israel for her
oppression of the poor, for her unfair trading methods, and for the way
the rich were favoured in the law and the courts.   In the Gospels we
find Jesus urging us to break with Mammon (i.e. riches) once and for all
Paul urges us to do good to all men, and James rails at rich landowners
who exploit their labourers.   In South Africa we seem to find precisely
the conditions which the biblical writers condemned so forcefully.   Our
land is one of vast inequalities -- in wealth, in power and in education.
White hegemony is guaranteed because they have taken to themselves 87%
of the country's land area, leaving a meagre 13% for the larger part of
the population.   What is more, the so-called "white homeland" has the
lion's share of the country's mineral wealth.   Migratory labour, which
has been condemned by all the churches in the country, reinforces this
skewed pattern of development, whereby some get rich at the expense of
others.   To keep it all intact there is that most hated aspect of a
hated system, the pass laws, under which more than 1 000 people are
being imprisoned daily.   This is a situation of fundamental injustice.
Until it is the government's express intention to remove it, I will be
unable in conscience to defend it.

/For decades ...

44. My letter of refusal, 19 October 1979, excerpted by Dot
Cleminshaw.

2.

For decades blacks have tried to change matters by constitutional and peaceful means. Their attempts have been fruitless, because of the violent reprisals by the government of the day. Bannings, detentions without trial and shootings have removed all hope of peaceful change. Dare we be surprised if blacks turn to violent means? This is exactly what many have done. Those who go up to fight for the SADF on the border should remember that they are fighting against their own deeply disaffected fellow-citizens. They are taking part in a highly partisan civil war. It is as Lyndon Johnson said: Those who make pacific revolution impossible make violent revolution inevitable.

Young men are being required increasingly to risk their lives under arms. Many, like myself, are already asking: Just what are we fighting for? Just what are we being required to die for? Are we going to die for a better society, for a more just society, perhaps even for a more loving society? Are we really defending the last bastion of Christianity, as we are so often told? Is this that we are defending really to be termed "civilisation", as against its alternative "barbarism", as again we are told by those who are left cold by the extraordinarily barbaric death of Steve Biko? There is a mockery in all of this. We fail to see that it is our own vices that are thrown back in our face by the revolutionary movements.

4. Churches support selective conscientious objection

There is a cloud of witnesses to support my understanding of the situation. Archbishop Denis Hurley (Ecunews, 11.9.74) said that "the unjust situation in South Africa makes it justifiable for young South Africans to refuse to fight on the borders. It is our duty to discourage people from getting involved in this military conflict because of the realities of the South African situation -- a situation of oppression". Archbishop Bill Burnett said in 1975 that "we need to grasp the significance of the fact that some Black South Africans, many of whom are Christians, are outside our country seeking to change our power structure by force". In March 1979 he said even more explicitly: "Unless things change significantly I would be unable in conscience to defend a system of government which, in spite of many good features, has a basis which is indefensible and produces fruit which is unjust and cruel".

The Catholic Bishops declare that "we defend the right of every individual to follow his own conscience, the right therefore to conscientious objection both on the grounds of universal pacifism and on the grounds that he seriously believes the war to be unjust." The Anglican Synod of Cape Town (1977) upheld the archbishop's statement that "the society we have created for ourselves is morally indefensible. This is very serious at a time when we are being asked to defend it". It went on: "We sympathise with those who in conscience believe that it is an act of disobedience to God to be part of the military structures of this country, because they are convinced that by doing so they would be defending what is morally indefensible. We accept that we, as a Church, have a positive duty to make all people aware of what is involved in being used to defend the morally indefensible and to challenge each other in the cost of discipleship, putting first the claims of Christ over all our being and doing".

In October 1979 the Baptist Union Assembly requested that the authorities provide a non-military alternative to military service for conscientious objectors. In September 1979 the Presbyterian Church affirmed solidarity of fellowship to any member of the church penalized following refusal to do military service. It insisted that Christians had to reject as blasphemous a view that they should not venture into debate on bearing arms, the defence of the country or conscientious objection because of the risk of prosecution.

45. My letter of refusal, 19 October 1979 (excerpted, continued)

3.

5. Rejection of non-combatant medical service in the unit.

It is against this background that my refusal to attend the camp must be seen. I understand that I am required to be a medical officer in the unit from now on. In 1977, when I was a consciertious objector for the first time, I did not request non-combatant status but instead a "period cf service of national interest under civilian direction". The latter phrase is crucial. Being a medic does in no way absolve one from the serious moral compromise which I have explained above. A medic is a necessary part of the war machine; he too makes a direct contribution to the strength of the fighting force.

Therefore I find it impossible even to be a medical officer.

In the 1976 Parliamentary debate on the Defence Budget, J.J. Vilonel said "It would be ridiculous to argue about which division of the Defence Force is really the most important. The fact is that they are all important and that they are all essential. One important and essential division of the Defence Force is the Medical Corps. Not only does this corps play a vital role with regard to the health and physical preparedness of our men, but also with regard to the services it provides to the dependants, its welfare work and its role in regard to the wounded in wartime (Hansard, 1976: cols 6243 and 6245). He has argued my case very well. If it is morally repugnant to be a fighting member of the SADF, then to be a medical officer is likewise problematic.

6. (Peter Moll then quotes a poem by Alan Paton: CAPRIVI LAMENT - see overleaf).

Yours faithfully,

(Signed) Peter Moll

(Some quotations from the first part of the letter: -

"Martin Luther held to the above principle when he declared to the authorities, 'Here I stand, I can do no other'.
Calvin wrote in his Institutes, Book Four, Chapter XX, 32:
'We are subject to the men who rule over us, but subject only in the Lord. If they command anything against Him let us not pay the least regard to it'.
The Baptist Confession of 1646 stated 'It is the magistrate's duty to tender the liberty of men's consciences, without which all other liberties would not be worth the naming. Neither can we forbear the doing of that, which our understandings and consciences bind us to do. And if the magistrates should require us to do otherwise, we are to yield our persons in a passive way to their power. But if any man shall impose on us anything that we see not to be commanded by our Lord Jesus Christ, we should rather die a thousand deaths, than to do anything against the light of our own consciences'.

"The conservative Nederduitse Gereformeerde Kerk has also made a case for civil disobedience in the past. Early this century it declared, 'No-one may revolt against lawful authority other than for carefully considered and well-grounded reasons based on the word of God and a conscience enlightened by the Word of God' (see de Gruchy, The Church struggle in South Africa, p.225)."

46. My letter of refusal, 19 October 1979 (excerpted, continued)

A poem by Alan Paton

CAPRIVI LAMENT

Makwela, Ikgopoleng, and you two Sihekos,
what were you fighting for?
Makwela, was it for your house in Springs
and your security of tenure?
Or did you fight for me and my possessions
and this big room where I write to you,
a room as big as many houses?

Sibeko of Standerton, what did you die for?
Was it for the schooling of your children?
Were you so hungry for their learning
or were you fighting for the rich grand schools
of my own children?

Sibeko of Bloemfontein, was it for those green pastures
of your own Free State country
that you poured out your young man's blood?
Was it for the sanctity of family life
and the infinitude of documents?
Or were you fighting to protect me
and my accustomed way of life?

Ikgopoleng of Lichtenburg,
was it South Africa you fought for?
Which of our nations did you die for?
Or did you die for my parliament
and its thousand immutable laws?
Did you forgive us all our trespasses
in that moment of dying?

I was not at your gravesides, brothers,
I was afraid to go there.
But I read the threnodial speeches
how you in life so unremembered
in death became immortal.

Away with your threnodial speeches, says the Lord.
Away with your solemn assemblies.
When you lift up your hands in prayer
I will hide my eyes from you.
Cease to do evil and learn to do right,
pursue justice and champion the oppressed.

I saw a new heaven and a new earth
for the first heaven and earth had passed away
and there was an end to death
and to mourning and crying and pain
for the old order had passed away.

Is that what you died for, my brothers?

Or is it true what they say
that you were led into ambush?

- - - - - - - - -

(The poem relates to the reported death in ambush in the Caprivi
Strip of 4 black soldiers of the SADF.)

47. My letter of refusal, 19 October 1979 (excerpted, concluded). *Caprivi Lament* is reproduced with permission from the Alan Paton Will Trust, granted on 20 June 2023.

——— ✕ ———

PEACE MAN

He was created at Creation and ~~~~~~~~~~~ he's walked the earth since then
He's lived throughout history - he'll be there at the end
He's opposed to violence of every type, for violence is what hatred breeds
And though there're many who believe the same,
 he puts his beliefs into deeds

He was a slave in Pharo's egypt, Moses lead him to the promised land
God spoke to them, gave them the Law "thou shall not kill" was his command
And he walked the earth with Jesus Christ, a friend of the last and least
And he heard him bless the Peacemakers,
The ones who work for peace

'Cause he's a peace man - don't carry a gun,
Yet when the going gets tough he'll be the last to run,
He don't see courage as a gun in the hand
 but - not bowing down
  yes not turning around
   in his love for every man

48. Lyrics of the song 'Peace Man' by Stephen de Gruchy
Composed on the occasion of my sentence of 4 December
1979. Words written by Steve in the vigil book at the
Rondebosch Congregational Church, 23 August 1980. By
permission of Steve's widow, Marian Loveday.

And he did not don his armour - he saw right thru the crusades
As a sanctification of violence, an exchange of the cross for a blade
And he faced the inquisition, for the change he wished to make,
And he asked that God forgive them,
As he burnt upon the stake.

conquistidors
Yes he saw the ~~whiteman~~ coming - to convert them to the faith
with sword + shot + plundering hand - he saw the ungodly waste
And he saw the white man coming - the Peace-Pipe for to smoke
And they took his land and buffalo ~~too~~.
And left him there to choke

He's a Peace-man, don't carry a gun
Yet when the going gets tough, he'll be the last to run,
He don't see courage as a gun in the hand,
    But not bowing down
      yes not turning round
        to in his love for every man

And he walked the streets of Chicago with Martin Luther King
He spent the night in prison for the change that it would bring
He dodged the draft in '69 - not to fight the people of the east
And he's making a stand against Nuclear war
he's making a stand for peace

And he lived with Mohatma Ghandi for peace thru-out our land
And he tried to follow the way of Christ, for his loving he was banned
And he died with Steffen Biko, after facing pain + sorrow,
And he died because he believed,
that together we could face tomorow.

49. Lyrics of the song 'Peace Man' by Stephen de Gruchy
(continued)

'Cause he's a peace man　dont carry a gun
Yet when the going gets tough he'll be the last to run
　He don't see courage as a gun in the hand
　but not bowing down,
　　yes not turning round
　　　in his love for every man

He asks "how can you fight for a God that forbids you to kill?"
"how can you kill another man, when to love him is your God's will?"
"You talk of Patriotism as dying for your land - not taking another's life
- Can't you see that your actions
　Are a slap in the face of Christ?"

And he wishes for more people to stop + count the cost,
for with violence - none can win, all have already lost
Now he stops + gasps for air as hate tightens the rope
But still he has not given up,
for where there's love there's hope.

He's a peace man, don't carry a gun,
Yet when the going gets tough he'll be the last to run,
　He don't see courage as a gun in the hand,
　but not bowing down
　　yes not turning round
　　　in his love for every man.

　　　　　Steve de Gruchy
　　on Peter Moll's sentence　Dec 1979.

50. Lyrics of the song 'Peace Man' by Stephen de Gruchy
(concluded)

Appendix A. Certain events of evening of 24-12-1979 at the Detention Barracks, Voortrekkerhoogte, by Peter Moll[164]

Place: The Detention Barracks, Voortrekkerhoogte, Block 1 (composed chiefly of arrested persons).
Date: 24-12-1979.
Time: About 5.30 pm, immediately after the evening meal.

My version of what happened. We were finishing eating supper. Tolmay[165] said, "After I've counted 100 everyone must be finished, then 'tree aan' here" (in the block). Much movement. Tolmay: "Hurry!" There were a few laggards. He went up to one, hit him at least three times, hard shots, with his right hand across his face. Hits another, a very hard shot, across the face. The second (person) was passing just in front of me, just 3 feet away. When everyone was standing in the squad they were counted. Tolmay: "When I've counted to 10, everyone must be in their cells. One! Two! ..." etc. I go into my cell, standing in doorway, Tolmay into a cell opposite: "... Seven! Eight! Nine! Ten!" Hits the man repeatedly. I can hear the shots quite clearly. Many cries from the victim (footnote: van der Berg), in great distress. Tolmay yells repeatedly. More hitting. Victim cries. I call the lance-corporal into my cell—plumpish fellow, one-stripe. I ask him to please stop Tolmay. "Why?" he

---

[164] I smuggled my manuscript of my report 'Certain events of evening of 24-12-1979 at the Detention Barracks, Voortrekkerhoogte, by Peter Moll' to Adi Paterson in Cape Town. It was kindly transcribed by Dr. Margaret Nash and distributed by her and Adi.

[165] One of the *oumanne*.

says. "Because he's hitting people," I say. "Hitting people?" He looks confused. I say: "Yes, listen." And I point to the cell. He says he's not on duty. He calls Pte. du Preez, red haired man, no rank. I repeat what I said to the L/Cpl. "Hitting people?" Confused. "Yes," I say, pointing; "Can't you hear, stop him so he doesn't do any more; he's hit quite a few people tonight." Du Preez (who is on duty) goes to the room. After some few seconds (NB not immediately) the hitting stops. Tolmay goes away. Du Preez comes back to me. "Tolmay is a violent man, he must be taken out of here, otherwise he's going to hurt more people," I say. du Preez replies: "Everyone knows about it, even the major (Officer Commanding of the DB); he hits in the right places so there are no marks, everyone is afraid of him, you won't persuade any of these guys to be witnesses." L/Cpl: "There is a background to this; he's been here for 36 months. While here, that fellow" (referring to the victim—van der Berg) "went around with his wife."

Du Preez: "When a guy just doesn't want to co-operate, the corporals tell Tolmay to 'fix him up'; after a few 'klaps' he's fine."

Both leave me. All the cell doors, including mine, are closed and locked. Tolmay is still out, he says he will "sommer doodmaak" (just kill) that guy (the victim). He is obviously very angry still. Someone urges him to cool down. I start writing my report, about 20 minutes after the start of the incident. Tolmay continues threatening the victim: "He is the one that fooled around with my wife, should I feel nothing for that?"

Background: (1) While I was studying, locked up in my cell this afternoon 24-12-79, Tolmay and someone else were talking about Tolmay's problems. One of the things mentioned was his marital problem. Tolmay, if I am to judge by the tone of his voice, was badly upset.

(2) I arrived at this DB, having come from Wynberg on 16-12-79. 4 men in Block 1, where I was, attempted to escape after lights-out (very soon afterwards—between the 15th and the 20th.) They were caught at the fence and brought back to Block 1. They were 'disciplined' by <u>at least 2</u> of the 'oumanne' of the DB. They were made to run from one end of the block to the other and back many times. They were hit repeatedly. I heard many shots. They were hit more the next morning. P.I. Els is one of those who hit one or more of the escapees that morning, always in their cells. Again there was crying. The rest of the men in Block 1 were 'disciplined' that morning as well. They were made to run, by Tolmay, the length of the block at least 10 times, just before we were let out to empty our bedchambers. Tolmay did this in the presence of the man on duty, who, if my memory serves me well, was a private (i.e. no rank).

(3) On many other occasions I have seen oumanne hitting 'arrestante' (people awaiting trial).

(4) My personal <u>interpretation</u> of the situation is that there is still much violence in the DB. It is no longer done by the DB staff. It is done by the oumanne in the block—with the connivance of the staff. I am quite sure all the corporals, at least, are aware of what is going on. They see it happening, they hear hitting and shouting, then crying. The troops are scared of victimisation so they don't ever complain or charge the perpetrators, which they are legally permitted to do. The corporals don't stop it because it simplifies their work.

<u>Suggested action</u>: (1) I intend to speak to Evered Poole (a Christadelphian conscientious objector, who has served 18 months of a 36 month sentence) to get more background and suggestions.

(2) Then to the Major, to ask him to remove Tolmay from the DB altogether. Otherwise more people will get hurt.

(3) If this does not succeed, I shall speak to the Chaplains and make the request as in (2).

(4) If this does not work I shall take further action.

(signed)

P.G. Moll.

P.S. At about 11 pm on night of 24-12-79 there was a fight (fisticuffs) between Tolmay and Blackie—after much <u>drinking</u> and noise.

Prepared from a photocopy of the original on request by A.W. Paterson.

Appendix B. Extracts from the *Detention Barracks Regulations*[166]

Chapter IV. Discipline.

Inmates shall not be employed in Disciplinary Capacities.

5. No inmate shall exercise discipline over another but an inmate specially selected by the superintendent may be placed in a position of responsibility and leadership within such limits as the superintendent may determine.

Corporal Punishment.

8. Notwithstanding anything to the contrary contained in any other law no inmate shall in respect of any offence be sentenced to any form of corporal punishment.

Use of Force and Arming of Staff Members.

10(1) No force shall be applied by a staff member against an inmate except in self-defence or if the inmate behaves in a rebellious or violent manner, or passively resists discipline, ... and then only so much and such force may be used as may be necessary under the circumstances to restrain and calm the inmate ...

10(4) Any staff member who in the execution of his duty uses force against any inmate in terms of this regulation, shall at the first opportunity report the fact to the superintendent or senior staff member on duty ...

Chapter II. Organisation and Control.

Organisation of Detention Barracks.

---

[166] These extracts were part of the report 'Certain events of evening of 24-12-1979 at the Detention Barracks, Voortrekkerhoogte, by Peter Moll' which had been kindly transcribed by Dr. Margaret Nash and distributed by her and Adi Paterson.

2(1) Subject to the provisions of sub-regulation (2), every detention barracks shall, insofar as the available facilities and staff permit, be organised, controlled and managed so that a person serving a sentence shall be treated and trained in such a manner that, on his release he may be better equipped to adjust himself in employment and the community.

2(2)(b) Mutual contact between arrested persons and other inmates shall as far as possible be avoided.

Appendix C. Violence in the Detention Barracks, 26 December 1979 onwards

Incident One. Immediately after roll-call taken by Cpl Venter in Block 1 at about 7 am (I don't have a watch!) on 26/12/79. Arrestante (footnote: people awaiting trial) were still standing in squad formation, and were about to continue cleaning the block. I don't know what prompted the incident. I saw Tolmay (a prisoner *ouman*) go through the squad and hit X one or more times through the face. Then he hit Y through the face once— hard—with the words "Moenie terugpraat nie" (Don't talk back), whereupon Tolmay walked away. X is tall, blond haired, with a very light face (footnote: His name, I find out on 31 Dec '79, is Johan van den Heever, in a cell opposite me still). Y is a little shorter, with darker hair and was standing on X's left. I went to my cell immediately and wrote my report.

Incident Two. 26th Dec 1979. I am standing at my cell door, resting for a moment from my studies. I hear someone walking slowly past the door, from the main door of Block 1 towards the toilet side. It is about 6 pm. The doors of the arrestante have been locked. The person is 'Jenny' van der Merwe (I think that's his name). He's known by most of the men in the block as a homosexual. He walks slowly, lifting from one leg to the other. His left hand is placed over his anus. He is wearing nutria.[167] From his facial expression it appears he is feeling pain in his anus. He does not notice me looking thru' the hole in my door. He stops; puts his hands over his face, sobs—I can hear him sobbing quite distinctly. He walks on—slowly. I sit down to write this report.

---

[167] Nutria refers to the nutria-coloured (brown) military uniform.

Incident Three. 29ᵗʰ Dec '79. About 6.30 in the morning, we have just emptied our bedchambers outside. Corporal Christie is on duty but has left the block shortly. We have just had roll-call + are standing in a squad. Tolmay has come back. He shouts, "Ek tel tien en dan moet almal aangetree wees met hul 'taxies'! Een! Twee! … Tien!" Three men are still running to the squad. As each one passes him, he hits each two or more times through the face. X is the victim Y of Incident One, 26/12/79, Y is (I think) the new guy (footnote: the new guy's name is Akers (spelling uncertain) (Of English origin, from a Vehicle unit nearby in Pretoria—31/12/79) who came in last night—taller than X. Z is shorter than X or Y—I can't make out who he is. I go back to my cell (I have been standing in the doorway) and write my report.

Incident Four. 31 Dec '79, about 3.30 pm.

I. We have just finished showering outside. About 10 metres away I see 'Toppie' Boschoff, an ouman, and one Visser, an 'arrestant' who has just recently come in. He has dark hair. They are standing where the bedchambers are emptied. Boschoff hits Visser two or more times, on the body (chest + arm). Visser's body is thrown back—obviously the blows are hard. I go to empty my bedchamber. An 'arrestant' tells me Visser's name, and says that Boschoff hit him because he was slow in running. [About 15 minutes earlier the arrestante had been having their usual smoke break, and either shortly before or shortly after that were made to run the length of the Block several times.] I go to collect my shampoo, soap and towel where they are lying on the grass.

II. Meanwhile Lance-corporal de Beer (who is on duty today) has moved from the place where the bedchambers are emptied (he saw the whole of I) to the back door of Block 1 where he sits down. Five feet from me stands a tall, well-built fellow who has come in during the last week. He has bright red shorts on.

Tolmay comes up to him and accuses him several times of stealing cigarettes and making the other guys run (cf **I**). He hits his right cheek with his left hand; then his left cheek with his right hand. The victim offers no physical resistance, but protests verbally. I go and stand in line to go back into the block. Note that Cpl de Beer is sitting about 7 metres away, on the steps of Block One. By now most of the guys are standing in line, and are able to see the next incident. Note that the unit's Medic, is I think closer to Block 2.

III. Tolmay goes up to Soon (Afrikaans-speaking; I think that's the spelling; he came in today; after incident **III** I asked him his name myself) and hits him exactly 3 times across the face. There were one or more threats from Tolmay too. He reels, evidently the shots are very hard, and falls to his knees, clutching his mouth with one hand. He does not cry out or offer resistance, either verbal or physical. I assume this is also to do with the cigarette conspiracy. As he stands up, his hand moves momentarily away from his mouth. I see two spots of red (blood), one on his lower lip, the other higher up on his left cheek. Boschoff tells him "Spoel jou mond uit" (wash out your mouth). He goes to wash his mouth out. The corporal is still sitting on the steps about 6 metres away from Soon. The medic comes walking up from Block 2 way, saying, "Waar is daardie ou wat Boschoff gemoer het?" (Where is that guy that Boschoff hit?) goes up to Visser, asks him if he is going to charge Boschoff, gets a negative answer. Boschoff addresses all the guys: "Julle mense het niks gesien nie, nê?" (You men haven't seen anything, right?) Some of them answer in chorus, "Nee" (No). In particular the victim of **II** says (in Afrikaans) that he won't charge anyone, because he can take it like a man. We all walk into Block 1. Tony Wells says to me, "Doesn't it make you sick?" I ask Soon for his name. I ask v d Heever for his name (see Incident One). I go to my cell and write this report.

Incidents **I**, **II** and **III** must be seen against the backdrop of the events of last week. S-Sgt Erasmus gave instructions that nearly all the Block 1 oumanne, incl. Bothma, Els, Blackie, Tolmay and Boschoff, move out to Blocks 2, 3 and 5. He threatened them with severe punishment if he saw them with the 'arrestante' or in Block 1 again. Today, while we showered, Bothma, Tolmay and Boschoff were with us.

[My interpretation of this incident: The corporals use the rougher of the oumanne to enforce discipline. They are obviously aware of what goes on. From talking to them it seems that they <u>request</u> guys to enforce discipline like this. So they are not only collaborators; they are also instigators. Corporal punishment is illegal in the D.B. One inmate may also <u>not</u> be set above another, unless this is done by the 'special' instruction of the Superintendent—D.B. Regulations.]

<u>Incident Five.</u> Sunday evening, 9/1/80, about 8 p.m. I am now in Block 5 because I refused to wear the brown overalls and do normal military training. The only other inmate of Block 5 (the small solitary confinement block) is Robert Paine. After supper we sat in my cell, the door of which was open, reading. At about 8 p.m. (it was dark by then) Private Harmse and Tolmay came in. At no stage of the proceedings did Harmse say anything. Tolmay (to Paine): "Get into your cell!" Paine rises, protests the he and Blackie did not get locked up, but nevertheless goes to his cell which is immediately adjacent to mine. Tolmay + he argue further. I remain silent. Harmse stands just outside my door, about 5 ft away from me. Tolmay accuses Paine of "answering back". He hits him exactly 3 times. I can hear the shots clearly. Paine does not cry out; Tolmay and Harmse leave him after Tolmay has locked his door; Tolmay closes and locks my door, and they leave Block 5.

Appendix D. Violence in the Detention Barracks, 10 Feb. 1980

Incident One: It is Sunday morning 10/2/80. I recall what I was told by 'Jackie' on Tuesday evening 5/2/80 regarding an incident which occurred on 3/2/80.

[Background: I am in Block 5 which has only 6 cells and which is normally used for solitary confinement. I am here because I am a conscientious objector and they want to keep me separate. Jackie is here because he is a homosexual and that is the reason Sgt.-Maj. Peterson gave him for putting him here. He is obviously a 'fem': strapless shoes, lipstick, eye shadow, a feminine accent, says he is legally married to a man (divorcee) of 25. Has been in DB 4 times for AWOL. Has been homosexual since age of 11—his family have accepted it. Wears women's clothes at home; has taken some hormonal pills for a sex change; fully intends continuing with the sex change when he leaves army. A few times I have seen him stroking the chests of 1 or 2 guys here. He is a member of a gay club in Jhb.]

To return: On Tuesday evening 5/2/80 Jackie told me that D. Tolmay had attempted to rape him. He had shorts on and showed me two matchbox-sized bruises: one on his right thigh, the other on his left shin. He told me that was where Tolmay hit him when he had him (Jackie) on the ground and he (Jackie) wouldn't open his legs for him. Jackie told me this had occurred on Sunday night—the bruises were 2 days old. After the scuffle, Tolmay appears to have left him.

Interpretation and comment: Jackie is a woman who has unfortunately acquired a man's body. The above is thus more than a common indecent assault. IT IS RAPE. This is not the first time—he was raped once previously, he told me. Jenny (van der Merwe) [who has now been discharged] has also allegedly had several such experiences. Previously (so I hear) there was another homosexual here—Juanita. The fame of Jenny and Juanita spread to Wynberg DB where I first heard about them. Another friend of mine told me he had heard of them in Windhoek. I think homosexuals should be discharged immediately. When they come here (i) they are used and exploited (ii) other guys learn the techniques [of rape].

(signed)

P.G. Moll 10/2/80.

Incident Two: On Sunday 10/2/80 I was sitting in the mess having breakfast. At the opposite corner of the mess were two of the duty privates, one of whom was du Preez. They were sitting on the wall + so could see everyone. About 2m from me sat Tolmay and his friends. Tolmay called to Johan Rademeyer as he came in; made him sit in front of him; accused him of being cheeky to an MP the previous day; hit him at least 5 times in the face. I saw all of this happening. I could hear the shots clearly. Rademeyer continued to eat, + every so often Tolmay would lean down to him + hit him again. When he tried to move away T. would hit him. I left and saw his face was bright red from the hitting. The two MP's could easily have heard and seen this going on. (Tolmay shouted very loudly and the shots were also very distinct.) They did + said nothing. After lunch I went up to Rademeyer + asked him his name (I didn't know it previously.) He told me. I asked him if he was the guy who was hit by Tolmay that morning. He nodded and said yes. I came to my cell and started writing.

Comment: Again connivance and bullying. Oumanne keep their form of 'discipline' at lunch-time by hitting people. Sometimes a corporal is there—but over weekends usually not. Meanwhile those very oumanne laugh + yell raucously and throw food about. No one ever stops them from 'disciplining.' However when the sgt-maj. is around they stop it. Order ought to be kept by a staff member. There ought to be a staff member in the mess as well.

(signed)

P.G. Moll 10/2/80.

Appendix E. People who wrote letters, cards or telegrams to me or about me, or visited, or signed statements, during 1980[168]

If you, the reader, wrote, visited, or signed statements during 1980, and do not appear in this list, please contact me so that I can recognise you in the next edition.

Annette and Helen S. Signed cards from the Alternative Service meeting at Quaker House in Mowbray, Cape Town.

Anonymous. Sent postcard with a picture of floral beauty of Melkbosstrand.

Anonymous. Sent postcard with a large cycad with red flowers.

Anonymous. Sent photocopy of II Tim. 2:9, "Remember Jesus Christ, risen from the dead ... for which I suffer hardship even to imprisonment as a criminal; but the word of God is not imprisoned."

Ax. Signed the 2nd vigil book.

Caroline. Signed cards from the Alternative Service meeting at Quaker House in Mowbray, Cape Town. From Aneene Dawber's Oak Street community. Signed the 1st (Easter) and the 2nd (August 1980) vigil books.

DORG. Umtata, Transkei.

Elliott. From Addo. Sent a telegram on 3 April 1980. First name not stated.

F.J.G. Signed the 2nd vigil book (August 1980).

Gaby. Signed cards from the Alternative Service meeting at Quaker House in Mowbray, Cape Town. From Aneene

---

[168] Their locations and occupations as of 1980s are also stated, when available.

Dawber's Oak Street community. Signed the 2nd vigil book (August 1980).

Hazel. From Meredale, Johannesburg South. Sent a telegram on 31 May 1980.

James. From Aneene Dawber's Oak Street community. Signed the 2nd vigil book (August 1980).

Jenny A. and Mark. Signed cards from the Alternative Service meeting at Quaker House in Mowbray, Cape Town.

Joan. Burgess Hill, Sussex. Among the letters collated by Rev. Don Black, Baptist Church House, London.

John. Cape Town.

Kevin and Sheila. Cape Town. Members of the Students' Christian Association of the University of Cape Town.

Laurine. Cape Town.

Mary. Wrote a card for the poster with Stephen Granger.

Mary. Met in Germiston.

M.K. Signed the 2nd vigil book (August 1980).

Paul. Durban.

Pir. Signed the 2nd vigil book (August 1980).

R. Signed the 2nd vigil book (August 1980).

Sharon. Signed a card from the Alternative Service meeting at Quaker House in Mowbray, Cape Town.

Teresa [surname not stated]. Bissau, Guinea-Bissau. Volunteer at HAPOTOC (Help A Prisoner, Outlaw Torture Organising Collective).

Yak. London, UK. College student.

Ackroyd, Rev. Phyllis and Rev. Ralph L. Pastors, Halifax, West Yorkshire, UK. Members of Amnesty International.

Aheafts, Bruno. Signed the 1st vigil book (Easter 1980).

Aitken, I. Christopher. General Secretary of the Presbyterian Church of Southern Africa, Johannesburg.

Allaun, Frank. London. Member of Parliament. House of Commons, London SW1 0AA, UK.

Anderson, Rev. Peter D. Minister, Moffat Memorial Congregational Church, Kensington, Johannesburg.

Andrews, Di. Cape Town. Member of the Black Sash. Signed a card from the Alternative Service meeting at Quaker House, Mowbray, Cape Town.

Angsoc (Anglican Society), University of Natal, Durban. The Chairperson.

Ashcroft, Rev. Ernie. Priest at Christ Church, Kenilworth. Among the 70 signatories to a statement on 1 April 1980.

Asher, Anthony. Mupine, Pinelands. Senior Actuarial Assistant, The Old Mutual, Pinelands, Cape Town. Signed my birthday card from the Actuarial Valuations office, 12 March 1980. Came to visit at the Detention Barracks in Voortrekkerhoogte in January 1980 but was not admitted.

Aspioti, Marie, M.B.E. Writer, Villa Rossa, Corfu, Greece. Member of the Order of the British Empire. Member of Amnesty International. Among the letters and cards collated by Rev. Don Black, Baptist Church House, London.

Bachmann, M. Kings Langley, Herts., UK. A German conscientious objector. Learnt of me through Amnesty International in the UK. Among the letters collated by Rev. Don Black, Baptist Church House, London.

Bango, M. UCCSA Women's Committee, Zimbabwe

Bank, Rev. Louis. Priest, St. Paul's (CPSA), Rondebosch, Cape Town. Donated to reduce the debt. Among the 70 signatories to a statement on 1 April 1980. Signed the 1st vigil book (Easter 1980).

Barker, Rev. Roy T. Sub-Dean at St. George's Cathedral (CPSA), Cape Town. Signed '36 Concerned Christians' of 11 March 1980. Among the 70 signatories to a statement on 1 April 1980.

Bax, Rev. Douglas. Minister, Rondebosch Congregational Church, Rondebosch, Cape Town. Signed the statement by religious leaders of 5 December 1979. Signed '36 Concerned Christians' of 11 March 1980. Among the 70 signatories to a statement on 1 April 1980. Signed the 1st vigil book (Easter 1980).

Beck, Andrew. Johannesburg. Johannesburg. Completed B.Bus.Sc. at University of Cape Town, then became an articled clerk in Johannesburg, while studying law. My brother-in-law.

Beck, Jennifer 'Jen', née Moll. Johannesburg. Library Assistant at the City Library, Johannesburg. Student of History Honours at the University of South Africa. My sister.

Begbie, Ron. Cape Town. MA student in community health at UCT, consultant to Urban Problems Research Unit.

Benn, Tony. London. Member of Parliament, House of Commons, London, UK.

Bestbier, John. The Old Mutual, Pinelands, Cape Town. Actuarial assistant. Gave me a lift home on the day of my arrest, 22 November 1979. Signed my birthday card from the Actuarial Valuations office, 12 March 1980.

Bielefeld, Rolf. Dortmund, Germany; and United Free Church, Sydenham, London. Theology student and deacon. Read of me in the journal of Pax Christi, *JustPeace.*

Biggins, Moira. Loughborough, Leicestershire, UK. Learnt of me through Amnesty International. Among the letters collated by Rev. Don Black, Baptist Church House, London.

Billingham United Reformed Church, Cleveland, England, UK.

Black Sash (Wynberg branch). Wynberg, Cape Town.

Blom, Hermann. Strijensas, The Netherlands. Employee of the African-Indian Shipping Company, Rotterdam.

Bloomer, Shaun. Signed the 1st vigil book (Easter 1980).

Boesak, Rev. Dr. Allan, NGK Sendingkerk Chaplain, University of the Western Cape. Signed the statement by religious leaders of 5 December 1979.

Bolland, Marguerite. Kenilworth, Cape Town. Member of Black Sash.

Bosch, Professor David J. Pretoria. Professor of Theology at the University of South Africa, and editor of *Missionalia*.

Botha, Rear-Admiral H.P. Pretoria. Deputy Chief of Staff (Personnel) of the SADF. Came to see me in the Detention Barracks, 23 July 1980.

Botsis, Rev. Rod J. Bellville, Cape Town. Minister of the Bellville Presbyterian Church; once a chaplain while doing National Service. Signed '36 Concerned Christians' of 11 March 1980.

Boyd, Mrs. Pat. East Blatchington, Seaford, Sussex, UK. Member of Amnesty International.

Brennan, Rose. Mbabane, Swaziland. Theology student, USA. Teacher at a boarding high school in Swaziland, via the Mennonite Central Committee.

Brettaton, Christopher and family. Marlborough, Wilts., UK. Members of the Catholic church. Among the letters collated by Rev. Don Black, Baptist Church House, London.

Brokenshaw, Sheila. Observatory, Cape Town. Nurse. Signed '36 Concerned Christians' of 11 March 1980.

Browe, Gree. Durban.

Brown, Anne and Peter. Blucher, Newcastle upon Tyne, Northumberland, UK. Read of me in the magazine *JustPeace* of Pax Christi.

Brown, Chris and family. Bonaero Park, Transvaal.

Brown, Joe Talton. London. Member of Amnesty International.

Brown, Marjorie. School teacher, Montshiwa, Bophuthatswana, South Africa. Signed the 1st vigil book (Easter 1980).

Browne, Gill and Martin. Overport, Durban. Once worked at a hospital near Engcobo, Transkei.

Buchler, Rev. Frederick Johannes. Strand, Western Cape. Baptist minister.

Buick, Neil. New Borns, Teddington, Worcestershire, UK.

Bull, D.E. Signed '36 Concerned Christians' of 11 March 1980.

Burger, Carl. Electrician and businessman, Amalinda, East London. My brother-in-law.

Burger, Lorraine. Primary school teacher, Amalinda, East London. My sister.

Burrough, Connie. Kingston upon Thames, South-West London, UK.

Calder, Graeme G. East London.

Cameron, Michael J. Mowbray, Cape Town. Mathematics teacher. Attended the first protest fast over Easter 1980. His wife: Bridget Cameron née Coppin.

Campbell, Jean. Women's Committee of the United Congregational Church of Southern Africa (UCCSA), Bulawayo, Zimbabwe. Also a youth worker of the UCCSA.

Campbell, Rob. Cape Town. Engineering student, resident at the YMCA at the University of Cape Town; member of Claremont Baptist Church. Signed the 1st vigil book (Easter 1980).

Carmichael, Rev. Canon M.J.D. Braamfontein, Johannesburg.

Catter, Myra Boyet. Dundee, Scotland, UK. Among the letters collated by Rev. Don Black, Baptist Church House, London.

Chadwick, Rt. Rev. Graham. (Anglican) Bishop of Kimberley and Kuruman.

Christian Fellowship Group, Johannesburg.

Christie-Murray, Alison. Harrow-on-the-Hill, Middx., UK. Professional actress. Member of Amnesty International. Among the letters collated by Rev. Don Black, Baptist Church House, London.

Claasen, Andries. Signed cards from the Alternative Service meeting at Quaker House in Mowbray, Cape Town. From Aneene Dawber's Oak Street community. Signed the 2nd vigil book (August 1980).

Claremont Baptist Church newsletter. Claremont, Cape Town.

Clarke, John. University student, intending to become a conscientious objector.

Cleminshaw, Dorothy 'Dot' née Mullany. Activist and organiser, member of the Civil Rights League, Claremont, Cape Town, and assistant to Rev. David Russell. Signed the 1st (Easter 1980) and the 2nd (August 1980) vigil books.

Clynch, A. Manchester, UK. Wrote together with Ann Kelly.

Cobe, Jany. Plumstead, Cape Town.

Cochrane, Rev. Dr. James 'Jim'. Lecturer, Department of Religious Studies, University of Cape Town. Signed '36 Concerned Christians' of 11 March 1980. Signed the 1st (Easter 1980) and the 2nd (August 1980) vigil books.

Cochrane, Rev. Renate, née Hofmann. Theologian of the Lutheran Church and Junior Lecturer, Religious Studies Department, University of Cape Town. Signed '36 Concerned Christians' of 11 March 1980, and the 1st vigil book (Easter 1980).

Cohen, Bev. Employee of The Old Mutual, Pinelands, Cape Town. Signed my birthday card from the Actuarial Valuations office, March 12, 1980.

Cohen, Jeff. Student of Business Science, University of Cape Town.

Coke, J. Plumstead, Cape Town.

Collier, Sylvia. Signed '36 Concerned Christians' of 11 March 1980.

Comité Libertat Objectors. Barcelona, Catalunya, Spain.

Congregational College, Manchester, England, UK.

Connolly, Cherry. Chessington, Surrey, UK.

Cook, Rev. David, minister, Christchurch, Kenilworth, Cape Town (CPSA). Among the 70 signatories to a statement on 1 April 1980.

Cook, J.T. From Bellevue Central. Wrote a letter to *The Star*, 25 January 1980.

Cooksey, Karen. Cotham, Bristol. Member of Amnesty International. Student of politics at Bristol University. Among the letters collated by Rev. Don Black, Baptist Church House, London.

Cooper, Penny. Travelling Secretary for the Students' Christian Association in the Western Cape. Signed the 1st vigil book (Easter 1980).

Copley, Mike. Cape Town.

Cox, Noelle. Signed the 1st vigil book (Easter 1980).

Coxon, Barbara. Newlands, Cape Town. Signed the 1st vigil book (Easter 1980).

Coxon, Peter. Newlands, Cape Town. UCT student. Signed the 1st vigil book (Easter 1980).

Curtis, Jack. Norwood, Johannesburg. Wrote a letter to *Rand Daily Mail*, 11 January 1980.

Dale, M.G. Signed '36 Concerned Christians' of 11 March 1980.

Daniel, The Most Reverend George Francis, [Catholic] Archbishop of Pretoria. Signed the statement by religious leaders of 5 December 1979.

Dawber, Aneene. Student, University of Cape Town, and Chairperson, Catholic Society of UCT. Signed the 1st (Easter 1980) and the 2nd (August 1980) vigil books. Wrote and fasted, together with others in her community at 8 Oak Street, Observatory: Rod Douglas, Matthew McNally, Caroline, James, Andries Claasen and Gaby.

de Beyer, Peter. Actuarial assistant, The Old Mutual. Signed my birthday card from the Actuarial Valuations office, 12 March 1980. Opponent of my stand as a conscientious objector.

de Gruchy, Isobel. Rosebank, Cape Town. Signed the 1st (Easter 1980) and the 2nd (August 1980) vigil books.

de Gruchy, John. Senior Lecturer, Department of Religious Studies, University of Cape Town. Elected Chairperson of the Assembly of the Congregational Church in Southern Africa in 1980.

de Gruchy, Stephen. Student, University of Cape Town. Signed '36 Concerned Christians' of 11 March 1980, and the 2nd vigil book (August 1980).

de Hoog, Ria. Almelo, Netherlands.

de Klerk, Mike. Senior Lecturer, Economics Department, University of Cape Town. Signed '36 Concerned Christians' of 11 March 1980.

Dejelley, Alain. French friend writing from the Pyrénées.

Dichmont, Penny. School teacher. Signed the 1st vigil book (Easter 1980).

Dewberry, Rev. Peter. Goodwood Baptist Church, Cape Town.

Didcott, Sally. Baxter Hall, Rosebank, Cape Town. Student at the University of Cape Town. Signed the 2nd vigil book (August 1980).

Dike, Ethel M. West Nyack, New York, USA.

Dinsdale, Alan. Hampton, Middlesex, UK. Catholic. Among the letters collated by Rev. Don Black, Baptist Church House, London.

Dixon, Rev. John. Heideveld, Cape Town. Minister of the Heideveld-Manenberg Presbyterian Church. Signed '36 Concerned Christians' of 11 March 1980. Among the 70 signatories to a statement on 1 April 1980. Signed the 1st vigil book (Easter 1980).

Doherty, Bede. Wrote and fasted, together with Aneene Dawber's Oak Street community. Signed the 2nd vigil book (August 1980).

Donaldson, Rev. Robert B. Minister, Trinity Presbyterian Church, Grahamstown. Donated to reduce the debt.

Douglas, Rod. Signed a card from the Alternative Service meeting at Quaker House in Mowbray, Cape Town. Wrote and fasted, together with Aneene Dawber's Oak Street community. Signed the 1st vigil book (Easter 1980).

Dransfield, P. Slaithwaite, Huddersfield, England, UK.

Driver, John and Bonny. Barcelona. Members of the Comunidad Cristiana in Barcelona, Spain.

Dube, S. UCCSA Women's Committee, Zimbabwe

Duff, Clare and Eleanor. Derry, Northern Ireland. Members of Amnesty International.

Duncan, Sheena. Parkhurst, Johannesburg. Vice-President of the Black Sash in 1980.

Dunn, Andrew P. Student at the University of Cape Town, active in the Students' Christian Association; later Voortrekkerhoogte, Pretoria. Private, Medical Training Command, candidate officer.

Eayres, Rev. Trevor Hugh. Welkom Baptist Church, Bedelia, Welkom, South Africa.

Elder, Miss C. Mary. Donated to reduce the debt.

Elias, Idris. Cape Town. Actuarial assistant, The Old Mutual, Pinelands, Cape Town. Signed my birthday card from the Actuarial Valuations office, 12 March 1980.

Ellis, J. London. S/he had read my papers. Beautifully calligraphed letter.

Ellis, Dr. Mary. Cape Town. Among the 70 signatories to a statement on 1 April 1980. Of the Quaker denomination, she signed a statement protesting the Defence Amendment Bill in March 1983.

Elster, Ellen. Oslo, Norway.

Emery, Margaret. Philadelphia, Pennsylvania, USA. Worker for the Indian Rights Association, via the Mennonite Central Committee.

Enright, Clare. Longstanton, Cambs., UK. Member of Amnesty International. Among the letters collated by Rev. Don Black, Baptist Church House, London.

Erasmus, Rev. Andreas 'André' Johannes. Minister of the Orange Street Baptist Church, Cape Town. Came to visit in the Wynberg Detention Barracks.

Evans, Mike. Along with John Frame, Clare Verbeek and others, signed cards from the Alternative Service meeting at Quaker House in Mowbray, Cape Town.

Eybers, Rev. Howard, Presbyterian minister, Retreat Presbyterian Church, Cape Town. Signed '36 Concerned Christians' of 11 March 1980.

Fawcett, John G. Swaythling, Southampton, Hampshire, UK. Member of Amnesty International. Among the letters collated by Rev. Don Black, Baptist Church House, London.

Felix, Marianne. Hillbrow, Johannesburg.

Field, Malcolm. Hinchley Wood, Surrey, England, UK. Among the letters collated by Rev. Don Black, Baptist Church House, London.

Fish, Liz. Student (B.A.), University of Cape Town. Signed '36 Concerned Christians' of 11 March 1980. Signed the 2nd vigil book (August 1980).

Fitzsimmons, Deirdre. Monreith, Newton Stewart, Scotland, UK.

Forrest, Edith. Kirkhill (later Abbey Meadows), Morpeth, Northumberland, UK.

Fox, Rev. Peter. Presbyterian minister, Chairperson of the Eastern Cape Council of Churches, resident in Port Elizabeth. Donated to reduce the debt.

Foxcroft, J.G. Signed '36 Concerned Christians' of 11 March 1980.

Frame, John. Along with Mike Evans, Clare Verbeek and others, signed cards from the Alternative Service meeting at Quaker House in Mowbray, Cape Town.

Franklin, Owen. The Centre, St. George's Cathedral, Cape Town.

Fulson, Dorothy. Colorado, USA. With Gene Stoltzfer.

Gabler, Anna. Kensington, Johannesburg. Dutch immigrant; Christian Scientist; musician (pianist) with LTCL, B.Mus. and LRSM.

Gammon, Cheryl. Cape Town. High school teacher (mathematics).

Garcia, Kevin. Travelling Secretary, Students' Christian Association.

Gardner, Helen. Johannesburg, South Africa. Member of the Society of Friends.

Garnett, Ray. Village of Happiness, South Coast, Natal, SA. Quaker and Baptist.

Geeves, Colin J. London. Senior Lecturer in Philosophy at the Newcastle Polytechnic, and chemist; works with the Portia Trust, London. Member of the Finchley branch of the Anti-Apartheid Movement.

Gentry, Mavis. Kingston upon Thames, Surrey, UK. Member of Amnesty International. Among the letters collated by Rev. Don Black, Baptist Church House, London.

Gerig, Joan. Worker with refugees in Gaborone, Botswana, and subsequently in South Africa, via the Mennonite Central Committee. Wife of Orlando Redekop. Together signed as JORG. Writing from deputation work in Kansas, Manitoba and elsewhere.

Gerig, Milburn and Doris. Wayland, Iowa, USA. Farmers. Parents of Joan Gerig.

Gerig, Pam. Wayland, Iowa, USA.

Gibson, Olive. Johannesburg. Quaker. Member of a Conscientious Objector Support Group.

Gibson, Robin. Maseru, Lesotho. Worker via Mennonite Central Committee.

Goemans, Louise. Durban, South Africa.

Goldman, Robert. Cape Town; Voortrekkerhoogte; Youngsfield; Glencairn. Student, University of Cape Town; then Private, Services School, Voortrekkerhoogte; then clerk at the Youngsfield base, Cape Town. Served as a noncombatant. Signed the 2nd vigil book (August 1980).

Gourley, Esther. Galveston, Texas, USA. Quaker, and a member of the Fellowship of Reconciliation.

Graber, Randy and Shirlyn, Crawfordsville, Indiana, USA. Read of me and Richard in the *Gospel Herald* (Mennonite). Farmers, elementary school teachers, and church youth workers.

Graham, Marj. Wrote two cards, part of Stephen Granger's poster.

Granger, Stephen. Master's student in Environmental Studies, and co-editor of the Students' Christian Association magazine *Comment*, University of Cape Town. Athlete (marathons, Two Oceans, Comrades). Signed the 1st vigil book (Easter 1980). Proposer of a resolution of support for my stand by the Student Union for Christian Action, 30 January to 4 February 1981.

Grant, Joan. Edinburgh, Scotland, UK.

Gray, Vincent Myles. Molecular Biologist, University of Cape Town; then Lance-Corporal, Katima Mulilo; then Lecturer, Botany Department, University of the Witwatersrand, Johannesburg. Member of The Loft, Germiston.

Green, Dorothy I. Beeston, Nottingham, UK. Member of the Fellowship of Reconciliation. Among the letters collated by Rev. Don Black, Baptist Church House, London.

Greenwood, Karin. Hanlow, Essex, UK.

Greenwood, Peter. Durban. M.Sc. student, and Students' Christian Association member, University of Natal, Durban; then employee of the Atomic Energy Board. Married Marit Rodseth in 1980.

Gregorowski, Rev. Christopher J. St. Thomas's Church (CPSA) in Rondebosch. Among the 70 signatories to a statement on 1 April 1980.

Gregson, Sr. Anne. New Maldon, Surrey, UK. Member of Missionary Sisters of Africa. Member of Amnesty International.

Grimmond, Karin. Harlow, Essex, UK.

Guthiez, Barbara. 'French friend' writing from the Pyrénées.

Gwabeni, Joel. Herschel, Transkei, South Africa. Prisoner on Robben Island for seven and a half years. Student, Cicira Training College, Umtata, Transkei; subsequently high school teacher.

Gweba, C. UCCSA Women's Committee, Zimbabwe

Haddad, Beverley. Travelling Secretary, Students' Christian Association, Cape Town.

Hallowes, The Right Reverend Kenneth, Suffragan Bishop of Natal (CPSA). Signed the statement by religious leaders of 5 December 1979.

Hambridge, Mrs. S. Lydden, Dover, Kent, UK.

Hamling, Mrs. Elizabeth. Mowbray, Cape Town.

Hanekom, Karel 'Kallie.' Cape Town. Travelling secretary for YCS (Young Christian Students) of the Catholic Church.

Harding, Tony. Rondebosch, Cape Town. Student at the University of Cape Town; doing military service in 1980. Signed the 1st vigil book (Easter 1980).

Hare, Professor Paul. Professor of Sociology, University of Cape Town. Signed '36 Concerned Christians' of 11 March 1980.

Hart, Yvonne. Dalbridge, Durban, South Africa.

Heisey, Nancy. Lancaster, Pennsylvania, USA. Worker of the Mennonite Central Committee.

Hewson, Glyn. Observatory, Cape Town. Deputy Editor, *South African Outlook* magazine.

Hildebrandt, Franz. Edinburgh. Former pastor of the Confessing Church of Germany; was jailed by the Hitler regime. Pacifist.

Hill, Rob. Hillside, Bulawayo, Zimbabwe. Member of Operation Esther. Determined to be a conscientious objector but the war ended before he could be called up.

Holdt, Rev. Martin. Minister, Cambridge Baptist Church, East London.

Holgate, David. Signed the 1st vigil book (Easter 1980).

Hoogerhuys, van 't. Donated to reduce the debt.

Horsell, Robin. Horison, Roodepoort, Johannesburg.

Houston, Bill. Cape Town, subsequently Johannesburg. Travelling Secretary, Students' Christian Association.

Hughes, Anne. South African Council of Churches, Johannesburg.

Hughes, Dr. Kenneth R., Senior Lecturer, Mathematics Department, University of Cape Town, and chairperson of the Civil Rights League.

Hughes, Marjorie J. Newport, Gwent, Wales, UK. Member of Amnesty International.

Humphreys, Madge. Methodist Church, Kingsway, London.

Hurley, The Most Reverend Denis Eugene, OMI, Archbishop of Durban. Signed the statement by religious leaders of 5 December 1979.

Inglis, Joan. Umtata, Transkei, South Africa. Employee of the Umtata Public Library.

Ingram, Rev. Graham. Plumstead, Cape Town. Minister of the Wynberg Baptist Church.

International Fellowship of Reconciliation. Alkmaar, the Netherlands.

Inuin, Hilary. Littlemore, Oxford, UK. Among the letters collated by Rev. Don Black, Baptist Church House, London.

Jackson, Derek. London, UK.

Jakobsen, Wilma Terry. Newlands, Cape Town. Student at the University of Cape Town (Higher Diploma of Education). National Secretary for the Students' Christian Association, and worker with the SCA at the Natal Training College and the University of Natal at Pietermaritzburg.

Jones, Alan. London.

Jones, Elizabeth. Victoria Park, Manchester, UK. Christian Organisations. Member of Amnesty International.

Jones, Evelyn, Raewyn, Peter and Leslie. Bath, UK. Among the letters collated by Rev. Don Black, Baptist Church House, London.

Jones, Peter D. Bath, Avon., UK. Quaker.

Jongwana, Michael S. Gugulethu, Cape Town. Cleaning staff at the Old Mutual. Wrote to me while I was in the Detention Barracks.

Judge, Andrew. Travelling secretary for the Students' Christian Association, Durban. Lay minister.

Juhnke, Anna, née Kreider. Professor of English at Bethel College in Kansas, USA. She served on the Board of the Mennonite Central Committee.

Kackson, Derek. London, UK.

Kampoutopoulos, Alexandra. Ashwicken, King's Lynn, Norfolk, UK.

Kasten, Maria. Cape Town. Wrote 5 October 1980 when attending the Alternative Service at the Quaker Centre in Mowbray.

Kaufmann, Larry. Catholic Church, Grassy Park, Cape Town. Signed the 2nd vigil book (August 1980).

Kauffmann-Kennel, Mary. Theology student, Elkhart, IN, USA.

Kearney, Paddy. Diakonia, Durban, South Africa.

Keen, Jane. Child Welfare employee at Philippi, Cape Town. Signed the 1st vigil book (Easter 1980).

Keeney, Bill. Kent, Ohio, USA. Professor at the Center for Peaceful Change, Kent State University. Keynote speaker for the Peacemakers' Seminar, Mbabane, in December 1981 (organised by Mennonite Central Committee staff).

Kelly, Anne. Manchester, UK. Member of Amnesty International and of Pax Christi.

Kent, Bruce. London. General Secretary of the Campaign for Nuclear Disarmament.

Kerchhoff, Peter. Pietermaritzburg, South Africa. Leader of the Pietermaritzburg Agency for Christian Social Awareness (PACSA).

Khupe, R. UCCSA Women's Committee, Zimbabwe.

Kistner, Rev. Dr. Wolfram. Minister, United Evangelical Lutheran Church; and Director of the Division of Justice and Reconciliation of the SACC. Signed the statement by religious leaders of 5 December 1979.

Klopper, Martin. UCT student. Signed the 1st vigil book (Easter 1980).

Knottenbelt, Richard. Gaborone, Botswana. He was a Quaker and a pacifist. He was called up by the Rhodesian army but refused service and was imprisoned for five months.

Knowlton, Derrick. Eastleigh, Southampton, Hampshire, UK. Member of Amnesty International. Among the letters collated by Rev. Don Black, Baptist Church House, London.

Kojima, Masami. Student, chemical engineering Ph.D., Stanford. Subscriber, *The Other Side*. Member, Amnesty International chapter at Stanford.

Kolbe House, Rondebosch, Cape Town. Catholic students at the University of Cape Town.

Krabill, Maurice E. and Verdella, Crawfordsville, Iowa, USA. Farmer. Learnt of Richard and me through Joan Gerig's father.

Kromberg, Rev. Johan P. Minister, Cambridge Presbyterian Church, East London. Donated to reduce the debt.

Lampen, John. Harmer Hill, Shrewsbury, UK.

Lane, Professor William 'Bill' L. Bowling Green, Kentucky, USA. Professor of Religious Studies at Western Kentucky University, and pastor of a racially mixed Presbyterian church. Learnt of Richard and me through *The Other Side* magazine.

Lane, Brenda née Whitaker. Office coordinator for the Religion Department of Western Kentucky University. Learnt of Richard and me through *The Other Side* magazine.

Law Parish Church. Law, Lanarkshire, UK.

Lawrence, Lynne. Kenilworth, Cape Town. M.Sc. student, University of Cape Town. Signed the 1st (Easter 1980) and the 2nd (August 1980) vigil books.

Lawrence, Mike. Kenilworth, Cape Town. Ph.D. student in physics, University of Cape Town. Signed the 1st (Easter 1980) and the 2nd (August 1980) vigil books.

Le Feuvre, Rev. Philip and Charmian. Philip: Director of Studies, St. Paul's College, Grahamstown.

Le Sève, Kathesy. Kingston upon Thames, Surrey; and 'The Grail,' Pinner, Middx, UK. Among the letters collated by Rev. Don Black, Baptist Church House, London.

Lear, Jean and Rex. Norwich, UK. Members of Amnesty International.

Lederle, ds. Dr. Henry I., Department of Systematic Theology, University of South Africa. Signed the statement by religious leaders of 5 December 1979.

Lees, Harry. Bebington, Wirral, Merseyside, UK. Among the letters collated by Rev. Don Black, Baptist Church House, London. Conscientious objector in the Second World War.

Leslie, Helen. Leigh-on-Sea, Essex, UK. Member of Amnesty International.

Liemann, Jeff. Colorado, USA.

Lind, Suzanne and Timothy, Mennonite Central Committee workers, Umtata, Transkei, South Africa.

Long, Caroline. Signed '36 Concerned Christians' of 11 March 1980.

Luckett, Rev. Sid, and Kathy. He: an economist and an Anglican (CPSA) priest. She: student of education and sociology.

Mabhena, R. UCCSA Women's Committee, Zimbabwe

McCann, Owen Cardinal, [Catholic] Archbishop of Cape Town. Signed the statement by religious leaders, 5 December 1979.

McClelland, Norah. Marple, Stockport, UK. Member of an Amnesty International group.

McCoy, Rev. Mike. King William's Town, South Africa.

McCrindle, Anne. Signed a card from the Alternative Service meeting at Quaker House in Mowbray, Cape Town. Signed the 1st vigil book (Easter 1980).

McEwan, Jenny. Higher Diploma of Education (HDE) student, University of Natal, Pietermaritzburg; then teacher, Westerford High School, Rondebosch, Cape Town.

McGee, Charles and Betty. Maseru, Lesotho. He: a trainer of tractor mechanics for the Government of Lesotho. She: a volunteer in Lithabaneng. Both: via the Mennonite Central Committee.

McGregor, Victor. Cumberwood, Pietermaritzburg. Sion Community of Reconciliation. Johannesburg Hospital, Parktown. Catholic. Signed the 1st vigil book (Easter 1980).

McIntosh, Rev. Neville. Woodlands, Durban. Baptist minister.

McKenzie Phillips, Bill. Southsea, Hants, UK. Government employee; Catholic. Learned of me through a Catholic newsletter.

McKindley, Steve. Elkhart, Indiana, USA. Student of Theology, and student of Peace Studies (M.A.) at the Associated Mennonite Biblical Seminary.

McLeod, Ian. Visited in July 1980.

McNally, Matthew. Wrote and fasted, together with Aneene Dawber's Oak Street community. Signed the 1st vigil book (Easter 1980).

Madden, Dorothea. Formerly Sister Benigna, a nun of the Catholic Dominican order, working in the informal settlement of Crossroads; Claremont, Cape Town. Married Rev. David Russell in 1980.

Magagula, S. UCCSA Women's Committee, Zimbabwe

Malan, John and Sandie. Students' Christian Association members, University of Stellenbosch. John studied for a B.Com. and then the Higher Education Diploma. Sandie was a school teacher in Somerset West by 1980.

Malherbe, Margaret. Catholic church worker, nun, Rondebosch, Cape Town. Signed the 2nd vigil book (August 1980).

Manassie, Mary E. Liverpool, Merseyside, UK. Among the letters collated by Rev. Don Black, Baptist Church House, London.

Marais, Chris. Operative of Military Intelligence who introduced himself as a theology student at the University of Pretoria; now involved in altruistic causes and a good friend.

Marchand, Ann. Elkhart, Indiana, USA. Theology student at the Associated Mennonite Biblical Seminary. Mennonite.

Maree, Dr. Johann. Labour economist, and lecturer, Sociology Department, University of Cape Town. Signed the 1st vigil book (Easter 1980).

Marr, Mr. M. North Shields, Tyne and Wear, UK.

Martin, Rev. Elsie. Warwick, UK.

Martin, Phil. Bonaero Park, Kempton Park, Transvaal.

Massey, Lyn and James. Steel Street community, Eshowe, Natal.

Matchett, Raymond. Aylsham, Norfolk, UK. Among the letters collated by Rev. Don Black, Baptist Church House, London.

Mathe, S. UCCSA Women's Committee, Zimbabwe

Mathema, L. UCCSA Women's Committee, Zimbabwe

Mathies, Ron. Mbabane. Coordinator of the Mennonite Central Committee workers in Swaziland.

Mattey (or Hattey?), David. Signed the 1st vigil book (Easter 1980).

Matthews, Ruth and John. Baptist ministers. Swindon, Wilts., UK; then Grove Hill, Hemel Hempstead, Herts., UK. He: author of a book about the ecumenical movement for the British Council of Churches. She: minister on the estate. Among the letters collated by Rev. Don Black, Baptist Church House, London.

Mayall, Rev. Norman S. Signed '36 Concerned Christians' of 11 March 1980. Among the 70 signatories to a statement on 1 April 1980.

Meier, Bruce. Student, University of Cape Town. Signed the 2nd vigil book (August 1980).

Meny-Gibert, Rosemary. Claremont, Cape Town. Secretary of the Wynberg branch of the Black Sash.

Mercer, Pat. Sheffield, UK. Among the letters collated by Rev. Don Black, Baptist Church House, London.

Meyer, Dean and Doris. Wayland, Illinois, USA. Farmer. Dean was a conscientious objector in the Second World War; he was sentenced to work in a mental hospital.

Mguni, E. UCCSA Women's Committee, Zimbabwe

Mhlanga, A. UCCSA Women's Committee, Zimbabwe

Milne, Elizabeth. Ashgate, Chesterfield, Derbyshire, UK. Amnesty International member. Among the letters collated by Rev. Don Black, Baptist Church House, London.

Minnington, Alan and Lydia. Bickley, Kent, UK. Among the letters collated by Rev. Don Black, Baptist Church House, London.

Mitchell, E.K. Signed '36 Concerned Christians' of 11 March 1980.

Mnkandla, R. UCCSA Women's Committee, Zimbabwe

Moll, Beryl Maureen. English teacher, Cicira Training College, Umtata, Transkei. My mother.

Moll, Brenda. Scholar in standard seven, Kaffrarian High School, King William's Town. My youngest sister.

Moll, Douglas. Accountant, Singer Sewing Machines; later accountant, S.A. Breweries, Johannesburg. My elder brother.

Moll, Terence. Student, Bachelor of Arts, University of Cape Town. Signed the 1st (Easter 1980) and the 2nd (August 1980) vigil books. My younger brother.

Moll, Theodor Arthur. Regional Magistrate, Umtata, Transkei. My father.

Moodie, Peter. Langlaagte Deep, Crown Mines, Johannesburg. Christian youth worker; travelling for an Urban Foundation science education project in Soweto.

Moorhouse, Fred. Yatton, Avon, UK. He and other members of the Society of Friends fasted with me on Friday, 18 July 1980, and sent a telegram of support.

Moyo, B. UCCSA Women's Committee, Zimbabwe

Moyo, E. UCCSA Women's Committee, Zimbabwe

Moyo, R. UCCSA Women's Committee, Zimbabwe

Mtulu, Thoko. Crossroads, Cape Town. Member of the CPSA. Daughter of Mrs. Sylvia Mtulu at whose house in Crossroads I spent the Easter weekend in 1979.

Mulholland, Stephen. Johannesburg. Editor, *Financial Mail.*

Müller, Frank. Kloof, Natal, SA. Theology student and member of the Students' Christian Association, University of Natal, Pietermaritzburg; training to be a Lutheran minister. Married Anne Smillie. Studied at Columbus, Ohio.

Müller, Anne, née Smillie. Pietermaritzburg. School teacher.

Munson, Julia H. and Kurt. Lake Oswego, Portland, Oregon, USA. She: teacher of deaf and hard-of-hearing children. Learnt of Richard and me through *The Other Side* magazine. He: custom woodworker, owner of Oregon Fine Joinery.

Murray, Duncan. Donated to reduce the debt.

Murray, Ray. Manager in the Actuarial Valuations Department at the Old Mutual. Left for Australia in 1981.

Murray, Trish. Married Derek Hanekom in 1980.

Nash, Margaret. Theologian, researcher, and human rights activist, Kenilworth, Cape Town; Ecumenical Education Officer for the South African Council of Churches, Cape Town. Signed '36 Concerned Christians' of 11 March 1980. Signed the 1st vigil book (Easter 1980).

Ndlovu, D. UCCSA Women's Committee, Zimbabwe

Ndlovu, J. UCCSA Women's Committee, Zimbabwe

Ndlovu, M. UCCSA Women's Committee, Zimbabwe

Ndlovu, R. UCCSA Women's Committee, Zimbabwe

Nel, James. London, UK.

Neufeld, Tom. Elkhart, Indiana, USA.

Newell, Christopher. London, UK. Member of Amnesty International. Among the letters collated by Rev. Don Black, Baptist Church House, London.

Ngulube, S. UCCSA Women's Committee, Zimbabwe

Ngwenya, C. UCCSA Women's Committee, Zimbabwe

Ngwenya, R. UCCSA Women's Committee, Zimbabwe

Nieder-Hartmann, ds. Johan. Citizen Force chaplain. Introduced himself as a dominee in the Dutch Reformed Church when he visited in November 1980.

Nkomo, R.S. UCCSA Women's Committee, Zimbabwe

Nyadza, D. UCCSA Women's Committee, Zimbabwe

Oliver, Barry. Polperro, Cornwall, UK. Member of Amnesty International. Among the letters collated by Rev. Don Black, Baptist Church House, London.

Orr, Bob. Donated to reduce the debt.

Osmond, Philip. Southview, Basingstoke, Hants., UK. Member of British Amnesty. Letter came via Rev. Don Black at Baptist Church House.

Owen, Sheila. The Old Rectory, Stowting, Ashford, Kent, UK. Among the letters collated by Rev. Don Black, Baptist Church House, London.

Palm, Anne. Signed '36 Concerned Christians' of 11 March 1980, and the 1st vigil book (Easter 1980).

Palmer, Roger and Les. Resident minister, Young Men's Christian Association, University of Cape Town, Rondebosch, Cape Town.

Palser, Gary. Actuarial Assistant, the Old Mutual, Pinelands, Cape Town.

Park, Audrey. Saskatoon, Saskatchewan, Canada. Responded to *Flash Point Newspaper* which sought to connect prisoners with civilian volunteers.

Paterson, Adrian 'Adi'. Master's student, Applied Science in Materials Engineering, University of Cape Town. Signed the 1st (Easter 1980) and the 2nd (August 1980) vigil books.

Paterson, Cathy. Physiotherapist, Victoria Hospital and Red Cross Children's Hospital, Cape Town. Signed the 1st (Easter 1980) and the 2nd (August 1980) vigil books.

Pearson, Peter-John. Cape Town. Faculty of Law, University of Cape Town.

Phifer, Rebecca. Houston, Texas, USA.

Phillip, Rev. Rubin. Priest of the Church of the Province, J&R, Natal. In 2000 Phillip became the first person of Indian heritage in South Africa to hold the position of Bishop of Natal.

Phillips, Bill. Southsea, Hants., UK.

Phillips, David. Shepherd's Bush, UK.

Phillips, Emays H. St. Albans, Hertfordshire, UK.

Phillpotts, Anne. Keele, Staffordshire, UK, and Bristol, UK. Student at Keele University. Member of Amnesty International. Among the letters collated by Rev. Don Black, Baptist Church House, London.

Pohlmann, Rev. Martin Henry. Probationer minister at the Edenvale Baptist Church. My cousin; visited me in the Detention Barracks.

Pombal, Lucy. Employee of the Old Mutual, Pinelands, Cape Town. Signed my birthday card from the Actuarial Valuations office, 12 March 1980.

Popper, Matilda. Uplands, Swansea, South Wales, UK. Quaker.

Price, Carolyn J. Swaythling, Southampton; later Earls Colne, Colchester, Essex, UK. Student of European languages at the University of Southampton. Baptist. Member of the movement for nuclear disarmament. Member of Amnesty International. Among the letters collated by Rev. Don Black, Baptist Church House, London.

Pritchard, Judith. Malvern, Worcs., UK.

Profit, Rev. David. Signed '36 Concerned Christians' of 11 March 1980. Among the 70 signatories to a statement on 1 April 1980.

Putchard, Judith. Malvern, Worcestershire, UK. Member of the United Reformed Church. Fine calligrapher.

Rall, Martin. Camberwell, London. South African citizen living in the UK.

Ralphs, Alan and Mary Ralphs née Ryan. Leribe, Lesotho. He: Catholic youth worker in Cape Town, then teacher of development studies and bookkeeping. She: teacher of English.

Ramsay, Margaret. B.Sc. student, University of Cape Town and then actuarial assistant, the Old Mutual, Pinelands, Cape Town. Signed my birthday card from the Actuarial Valuations office, 12 March 1980.

Rayne, Robert. Oxford, UK. Member of Amnesty International. Among the letters collated by Rev. Don Black, Baptist Church House, London.

Raynham, Sarah-Anne. Rondebosch, Cape Town. Staff member, *South African Outlook* (editor, Francis Wilson)

Read, Rev. John. Anglican chaplain, University of Cape Town. Signed the statement by religious leaders of 5 December 1979.

Read, Martyn. Sheffield, UK. Among the letters collated by Rev. Don Black, Baptist Church House, London.

Redekop, Orlando. Worker with refugees in Gaborone, Botswana, and subsequently in Umtata, Transkei, via the Mennonite Central Committee. Husband of Joan Gerig (see above).

Reiss, Michael. Trinity College, Cambridge, UK. Wrote via Rev. Don Black, Baptist Church House, London, UK.

Rius, Noel Dew. Falmouth, Cornwall, UK.

Roberts, Rommel. Theologian and human rights activist, Cape Town. Signed '36 Concerned Christians' of 11 March 1980.

Robertson, Rev. Robert J.D. Minister, St. Anthony's United Church, Mayfair, Johannesburg. Also editor, *Non-Violence News* (South African Council of Churches).

Rodband, Trevor. Sheffield, UK. Among the letters collated by Rev. Don Black, Baptist Church House, London.

Rorfu, Wayne. Elkhart, Indiana, USA. Linked with the Mennonite Central Committee.

Rosental, Hilary. Signed '36 Concerned Christians' of 11 March 1980.

Roth, Max and Berniece. Wayland, Iowa, USA.

Rowe, Rev. Michael. Minister of St. Andrew's Presbyterian Church, Cape Town. Signed '36 Concerned Christians' of 11 March 1980. Among the 70 signatories to a statement on 1 April 1980.

Royer, Wayne and Kathy. Mennonite Central Committee workers, Lesotho; and Elkhart, Indiana, USA.

Rundle, Michelle. Student at UCT. Signed the 1st vigil book (Easter 1980).

Rushmere, G.M. Donated to reduce the debt.

Russell, Rev. David Patrick Hamilton. Anglican (CPSA) priest for the Crossroads informal settlement, Cape Town. Signed the 1st (Easter 1980) and the 2nd (August 1980) vigil books.

Russell, Martha J. Bowling Green, Kentucky, USA. Employee of the State Vocational School of Kentucky. Learnt of me via *The Other Side* magazine.

Russell, Molly. Claremont, Cape Town. Mother of Rev. David Russell.

Russell, The Right Reverend Philip W.R. Morningside, Durban. Bishop of Natal, Archbishop elect of Cape Town (CPSA). Signed the statement by religious leaders of 5 December 1979, wrote to me.

Russell, Phoebe. Newlands, Cape Town. Higher Education Diploma student, subsequently Master's student and tutor, Religious Studies Department, University of Cape Town.

Russell, Tony. Toronto, Ontario, Canada. Student at Institute for Christian Studies, and subsequently a journalist. Formerly coordinator of The Loft, Germiston.

Rutschman, Tomás and Disa. Barcelona, Spain. Comunidad Cristiana in Barcelona. Pastoring a church on behalf of the Mennonite Mission Network.

Saayman, ds. Dr. Willem. DRC minister, and Professor of Missiology, UNISA. Signed the statement by religious leaders of 5 December 1979.

Saddington, Tony. Director, Centre for Extra-Mural Studies, University of Cape Town. Signed '36 Concerned Christians' of 11 March 1980, signed the 1st vigil book (Easter 1980).

Sainsbury, K.L. Stanway Green, Colchester, UK. Among the letters collated by Rev. Don Black, Baptist Church House, London.

St. Peter's Church, Morden, Surrey, UK.

Saks-Smotu, Roxane. Signed the 1st vigil book (Easter 1980).

Santos, Celeste. Community Development Officer with the Quaker Peace Centre, and Fieldworker, Catholic Church, Gugulethu. Signed '36 Concerned Christians'.

Sargeant, John and Diana Strauss. Wedmore Vale, Bedminster, Bristol, UK. Society of Friends.

Scan, Mandy. Sheffield, UK. Learnt of me through the Amnesty International newsletter. Among the letters collated by Rev. Don Black, Baptist Church House, London.

Schaerer, Norah. Joubert Park, Johannesburg. Anglican.

Schmarzentucher, Mary Mae. Kitchener, Ontario, Canada. Associated with the Stirling Mennonite Church.

Schoch, Ms. Ruth. Durban, South Africa.

Schoeman, ds. Dr. Piet, Department of Systematic Theology, University of South Africa. Signed the statement by religious leaders of 5 December 1979.

Schultz, Brian and Tilla. Port Elizabeth. I met Brian at a Leadership Camp of the Students' Christian Association in January 1977.

Scott, Cindy E. Cincinnati, USA.

Scott-Saddington, Di. Newlands, Cape Town. Secretary, Rondebosch Congregational Church, Cape Town; and organiser of the UCCSA Youth Consultation in Port

Elizabeth. Signed '36 Concerned Christians' of 11 March 1980. Signed the 1st vigil book (Easter 1980).

Semple, Fiona. Student at the University of Cape Town. Later a member of St. Anthony's Presbyterian Church in Vrededorp, conveyed her good wishes via a pamphlet for a 'Service of Hope' for Charles Bester in 1989.

Senda, E. UCCSA Women's Committee, Zimbabwe

Sharples, Peter. College House, University of Cape Town, Rosebank, Cape Town; and Kolbe House, Rondebosch, Cape Town; and Hillside, Zimbabwe. Student of economics. Member of the Catholic church. Zimbabwean.

Shepherd, Audrey. Knaresborough, North Yorkshire, UK. Member of Amnesty International. Among the letters collated by Rev. Don Black, Baptist Church House, London.

Sher, Stan and Alison. Crown Mines, Johannesburg.

Sherk, Dale. USA. Was a conscientious objector in the Second World War.

Shott, Jenny. Holloway, London, UK.

Sibacla, G. UCCSA (United Congregational Church of Southern Africa) Women's Committee, Zimbabwe

Sibanda, A. UCCSA Women's Committee, Zimbabwe

Sibanda, S. UCCSA Women's Committee, Zimbabwe

Sibindi, M. UCCSA Women's Committee, Zimbabwe

Simpkin, Barbara. Elgin, Moray, Scotland, UK. Catholic. Among the letters collated by Rev. Don Black, Baptist Church House, London.

Sirerol, Miguel and Anna. Barcelona. Members of the Comunidad Cristiana in Barcelona, Spain.

Slagel, Warren and Vernelda. Wayland, Iowa, USA. He: employee of a feed mill. She: employee of a grocery store.

Smail, Andy. Durban. Student, Department of Law, University of Cape Town. Member of the Catholic Society at the University of Cape Town. Convenor of 'MILCOM', the

Military Committee of the National Union of South African Students. Called up in July 1980, but emigrated to the Netherlands.

Smith, Michael G. Tamboerskloof, Cape Town. Member of the Catholic church.

Smith, Rev. Robert. Newlands, Cape Town, subsequently Windhoek, Namibia. Minister of the Church of England (viz. not the Church of the Province of South Africa); frequently spoke at the Students' Christian Association of the University of Cape Town.

Society of Friends (Transvaal branch).

Spanish Conscientious Objectors.

Spencer, E.S. Uckfield, Sussex, UK. Conscientious objector in the Second World War.

Spiegel, Andrew David 'Mugsy.' Cape Town. Department of Anthropology, University of Cape Town.

Spiller, Gay. Katatura Community, Scottsville, Pietermaritzburg.

Spong, Rev. Bernard. Past Chairman of the United Congregational Church of Southern Africa. Signed the statement by religious leaders of 5 December 1979.

Squair, Cherry. Student, University of Cape Town. Signed the 1st (Easter 1980) and the 2nd (August 1980) vigil books.

Staal, Sandy née Cochrane. Claremont, Cape Town. Teacher at Maurice's Secretarial College in Wynberg. Later a Master's degree student in Psychology at the University of Cape Town. Signed '36 Concerned Christians' of 11 March 1980.

Staley, Alan. Euston Road, London. Quaker Peace and Service, Friends House.

Steele, Dorothy. Kempton Park, South Africa. My aunt, mother of Richard Steele. Editor, the *South African Pharmaceutical Journal*, Johannesburg.

Steele, Heather. Rosebank, Cape Town. My cousin, sister of Richard Steele. B.A. student at the University of Cape Town. Came to my third trial, was turned away.

Steele, John. Kempton Park, South Africa. My uncle, father of Richard Steele. Editor, *Foundry, Welding and Production Engineering*, Johannesburg.

Steele, Richard. Kempton Park. My cousin. Conscientious objector, held at the Voortrekkerhoogte Detention Barracks and then at the Tempe Detention Barracks (Bloemfontein), for a total of twelve months.

Steinke, Sr. Mary Mildred, OP (Ordo Praedicatorum = Dominican). Kansas.

Stevens, Alun 'Tiger.' The Old Mutual, Pinelands, Cape Town. Actuarial assistant. Signed my birthday card from the Actuarial Valuations office, 12 March 1980. Left for Australia in 1980.

Steward, Debbie. Wrote and fasted, together with Aneene Dawber's Oak Street community. Signed the 2nd vigil book (August 1980).

Stewart, Paul and Glenda. Northcliff, Johannesburg; later Sociology Department, Rhodes University.

Stoltzfer, Gene. Colorado, USA. With Dorothy Fulson.

Stumbles, Brian. Donated to reduce the debt.

Suárez, José Luis and Gabriela. Barcelona. Members of the Comunidad Cristiana in Barcelona, Spain.

Swart, Chris. Westville, Natal. President of the Students' Representative Council at the University of Durban; studying law. Son of Ray Swart, Member of Parliament. Seconder of a resolution of support for my stand by the Student Union for Christian Action, 30 January to 4 February 1981.

Swart, Rev. Trevor Malcolm. Roodepoort, South Africa. General Secretary, Baptist Union of South Africa.

Tabera, José Fernández. Barcelona. Member of the Comunidad Cristiana in Barcelona, Spain.

Taylor, J.B. Riyadh, Saudi Arabia. Employee of the British Aircraft Corporation Ltd. Among the letters collated by Rev. Don Black, Baptist Church House, London.

Teichert, Lucille. Kanye Pitseng, Botswana. USA citizen, with Mennonite Central Committee.

The Hill Presbyterian Church, Port Elizabeth/Gqeberha. Donated to reduce the debt.

Thienann, Jeff.

Thiessen, Bill and Marianne. Calgary, Alberta, Canada. Bill: Provincial Director of the Mennonite Central Committee in Alberta.

Thomas, James. Student at the University of Cape Town. Signed the 1st vigil book (Easter 1980).

Thomas, Peter. Ashtead, Surrey, UK. Member of Amnesty International.

Thornton, D. Signed '36 Concerned Christians' of 11 March 1980.

Tickle, Tony. Mowbray, Cape Town. Architecture student at the University of Cape Town. Zimbabwean.

Tiernan, Brigid-Rose. Sister at Sisters of Notre Dame de Namur, and education specialist. Signed '36 Concerned Christians' of 11 March 1980.

Toms, Ivan. Medical doctor, Empilisweni SACLA Clinic, Crossroads informal settlement, Cape Town. Signed the 2nd vigil book (August 1980).

Tourien, Meg. Greyville, Durban.

Townshend, Grace. Lynnwood, Pretoria.

Trollip, Clive. Signed the 1st vigil book (Easter 1980).

Tshiminya, A.S. UCCSA Women's Committee, Zimbabwe.

Tucker, Elaine. Signed the 1st vigil book (Easter 1980).

Tudor, Owen and Dora, and their sons David, John and Mark. Rondebosch, Cape Town. Owen: a lawyer with the Cape Town City Council. Members of the Claremont Baptist Church. Wrote letters.

Tutu, The Right Reverend Bishop Desmond. Bishop, Church of the Province, and General Secretary, South African Council of Churches. Signed the statement by religious leaders of 5 December 1979 and wrote to me monthly.

Twomey, Kathy. Rosebank, Cape Town. Teacher in a coloured school.

UCCSA Women's Training Course in Bulawayo, Zimbabwe.

Unsworth, Sharon. Millhouse Green, Penistone, South Yorkshire, UK. Among the letters collated by Rev. Don Black, Baptist Church House, London.

Urquhart, Connie. Hove, Sussex, UK. Retired Medical Secretary doing social work among the elderly. Member of Amnesty International. Among the letters collated by Rev. Don Black, Baptist Church House, London.

van den Aardweg, Chaplain (Col.) Rev. Andrew William. Baptist minister and Assistant Chaplain-General of the Air Force. Came to visit me in the Detention Barracks in March 1980.

van der Werf, Maarten and Margreet. Hulshorst, Netherlands; and Serowe, Botswana. Mennonite Central Committee aid workers in Botswana.

van Leenhof, Willem. Montreal, Québec, Canada.

van Rooyen, Professor Jan Hendrik. Lynnwood Glen, Pretoria. Formerly advocate and professor of law at the University of Cape Town, subsequently at the University of South Africa. My lawyer for my first two trials.

Velthuis, Denise. Rondebosch, Cape Town. Signed the 1st vigil book (Easter 1980).

Verbeek, Clare. Along with Mike Evans, John Frame and others, signed cards from the Alternative Service meeting at Quaker House in Mowbray, Cape Town.

Vreede, Heleen. Signed the 1st vigil book (Easter 1980).

Vudla, E. UCCSA Women's Committee, Zimbabwe

Walters, Les. UCT student. Signed the 1st vigil book (Easter 1980).

Wanless, Rev. David. Presbyterian minister, at the Bryanston United Church. Donated to reduce the debt.

War Resisters' International. Oslo.

Ward, Jeanette, SND (Sister of Notre Dame). Member of Sisters of Notre Dame, Notre Dame Provincial House, Liverpool, UK; and active in Amnesty International.

Watson, James. Wishaw, Lanarkshire, Scotland, UK. A relative.

Weaver, Erma. Manheim, Pennsylvania, USA.

Webb, Leonard. Kingsway, London, UK. Kingsway Hall Methodist Church. Among the letters collated by Rev. Don Black, Baptist Church House, London. Learned of me through the International Fellowship of Reconciliation's *Reconciliation Quarterly*.

Webb, R. Houghton, Johannesburg.

Wells, Ann. Houghton le Spring, Tyne and Wear, UK. Among the letters collated by Rev. Don Black, Baptist Church House, London.

Wenger, Harold. Manzini, Swaziland. Mennonite missionary, working for the Council of Swaziland Churches. Wife Christine.

Werenich, Billie. Summer Beaver, Ontario, Canada. Heard of Richard Steele and me via *The Other Side* magazine. Teacher on an Indian reservation.

Westcott, Gill. Leeds. Economist, Umtata (Transkei), then University of Cape Town, then Leeds. Lecturer in Health Planning, University of Leeds. Came to see me at the military airport, together with Tony Saddington, as I was being taken to Pretoria.

Williams, Anne. Brighton, Sussex, UK. Member of Amnesty International. Via Rev. Don Black, Baptist Church House.

Williams, Rev. Ernie. Kempton Park.

Williams, Linda and Stephen. Southsea, Hants., UK.

Williamson, Mr. R. Forest Gate, London. Member of Amnesty International.

Wilmers, Sharon. Signed the 1st vigil book (Easter 1980).

Wilson, Francis and Lindy. He: Professor, Economics, University of Cape Town. Also editor, *South African Outlook*. Signed '36 Concerned Christians' of 11 March 1980. Signed the 1st vigil book (Easter 1980). She: a documentary film-maker, and Director of the South African Committee for Higher Education (SACHED).

Wilton, Rev. John Dennis, his wife Rhodabelle, and youngest son Murray. Rev. Wilton was minister of the Baptist Church in Claremont, of which I was a member. He was a witness in my trials at Youngsfield in September 1979 and at the Castle, Cape Town, in December 1979, and the family wrote letters.

Winter, Kevin. Pinelands, Cape Town.

Wolfaardt, ds. Dr. Johan A., Department of Systematic Theology, University of South Africa. Signed the statement by religious leaders of 5 December 1979.

Wood, Georgina. Seascale, Cumbria, UK. Member of Amnesty International.

Woods, Rev. Brian M. Moderator, General Assembly, Presbyterian Church of Southern Africa. Among the 70 signatories to a statement on 1 April 1980.

Wright, Kevin. Signed the 1st vigil book (Easter 1980).

Yarr, Angela. Manchester, UK. Wrote together with Ann Kelly.

Yeats, Charles. Durban. When called to trial, was serving as the Diocesan Treasurer and Secretary of the Anglican Diocese of

Namibia; sentenced to a year at the Voortrekkerhoogte Detention Barracks in 1981 for conscientious cbjection (of which he served nine months), then a further twelve months in Pretoria Central Prison for refusing to wear military uniform in the Detention Barracks.

Yoder, Professor John Howard. Elkhart, USA, and Strasbourg, France. Theologian. Author of *The Politics of Jesus.* Professor at the Mennonite Biblical Seminary.

Young, N.D. Donated to reduce the debt.

Zweigenthal, Virginia. Student, University of Cape Town. Signed '36 Concerned Christians' of 11 March 1980.

Appendix F. Publications and reports by Peter Moll about conscientious objection and related matters

Moll, Peter G., 1976. 'Black theology and the theology of liberation,' *The Christian Student* (national newspaper of the Students' Christian Association), 1976, p. 7.[169]

Moll, Peter G., 1977. 'Application for service of national interest under civilian direction,' letter to the Officer Commanding of Cape Flats Commando, 21 November 1977. Reproduced in this volume in the section of original documents.

Moll, Peter G., 1978a. 'Reapplication for service of national interest under civilian direction,' letter to the Officer Commanding of Cape Flats Commando, 25 October 1978.

Moll, Peter G., 1978b. 'Why I am a selective conscientious objector,' typewritten and duplicated 300X by Gestetner, December 1978. 11 pages.[170] Reproduced in this volume in the section of original documents.

Moll, Peter G., 1978b. 'Why I am a selective conscientious objector,' December 1978. Reprinted in: *Conscientious objection: a counsellor's resource manual.* Johannesburg: South African Council of Churches, mimeographed A4 pages; compiled by, i.a., Rev. R.J.D. Robertson, August 1985. 177 pages. Moll (1978b) appears as Appendix C.3., pages 91-98.

[169] UCT, SCA/SCO Coll., BC1473 B5.1.6.
[170] Wits, Rob. Coll., A2558-9.13.

Moll, Peter G., 1979a. 'The non-combatancy option and the dis-obedience option,' Mowbray: typewritten and duplicated 300 times by Gestetner, 2 March 1979. 6 pages.[171]

Moll, Peter G., 1979b. 'My country right or wrong?' *Comment* (Christian student newspaper, University of Cape Town), 18 April 1979. Typewritten draft covers 8 pages.

Moll, Peter G., 1979c. 'The Christian response to military service,' *Varsity* (student newspaper of the University of Cape Town), May 1979.[172]

Moll, Peter G., 1979d. 'Request for alternative service,' letter to the Officer Commanding, Western Province Command, on 2 June 1979. 2 pages, plus appendices.

Moll, Peter G., 1979e. 'Application for service under the Civic Action Programme,' letter to the Officer Commanding of Cape Flats Commando, 6 June 1979. 2 pages plus appendices.

Moll, Peter G., 1979f. 'To be a soldier or not to,' *Contours of the Kingdom* (May-June 1979). Magazine of The Loft (Germiston). Pages 12-14.[173]

Moll, Peter G., 1979g. 'Thinking No,' *National Student* (newspaper of the National Union of South African Students), June 1979, p. 15.

Moll, Peter G., 1979h. 'Is SA worth fighting for?' letter to the editor of *The Star,* 24 July 1979.[174]

Moll, Peter G., 1979i. 'Is SA morally defensible?' letter to the editor of *The Cape Times*, 26 July 1979.

Moll, Peter G., 1979j. 'Open letter: Conscientious objection to continuous training camp,' letter to the Officer Commanding, Cape Flats Commando, 19 October 1979. 6 pages.

[171] Wits, Rob. Coll., A2558-9.13.
[172] Wits, SAIRR, ZA HPRA AD1912A-S236.9.
[173] Wits, Rob. Coll., A2558-9.13.
[174] Wits, SAIRR Coll., ZA HPRA AD1912A-S236.9.

Moll, Peter G., 1979k. 'Excerpts from an open letter, dated 19th October 1979, by Peter Moll (in which he again refuses to attend military camp) addressed to the Officer Commanding, Cape Flats Commando.' Original excerpted by Dot Cleminshaw. 4 pages. Reproduced in the section of original documents.[175]

Moll, Peter G., 1979l. 'Debate about military service,' *South African Outlook*, vol. 111, no. 1300 (October 1979), p. 153-154.[176]

Moll, Peter G., 1979m. 'Excerpts from letter Moll wrote OC of his commando,' *Cape Times*, 5 December 1979. Original excerpted by the *Cape Times*.[177]

Moll, Peter G., 1979n. 'Certain events of evening of 24-12-1979 at the Detention Barracks, Voortrekkerhoogte, by Peter Moll.' Reproduced in this volume in Appendix A. 2 pages.[178]

Moll, Peter G., 1979o. 'Violence in the Detention Barracks, 26 December 1979 onwards.' Originally a handwritten manuscript. Reproduced in this volume in Appendix C. 2 pages.

Moll, Peter G., 1980. 'Violence in the Detention Barracks, 10 February 1980,' originally a handwritten manuscript. Reproduced in this volume in Appendix D. 2 pages.

Moll, Peter G. and Richard Steele, 1980a. 'Joint statement on conscientious objection,' *Comment* (Christian student newspaper at the University of Cape Town), March 1980, p. 15.

---

[175] UCT, Nathan Coll., BC912 A32 (2).

[176] Wits, Rob. Coll., A2558-15.8.

[177] Wits, Rob. Coll., A2558-16.

[178] I smuggled the manuscript of my report 'Certain events of evening of 24-12-1979 at the Detention Barracks, Voortrekkerhoogte, by Peter Moll' to Adi Paterson in Cape Town. It was kindly transcribed by Dr. Margaret Nash and distributed by her and Adi.

Moll, Peter G. and Richard Steele, 1980b. 'Public statement by Peter Moll and Richard Steele concerning their Protest Fast to be held on 3, 4 and 5 April 1980 to protest the refusal of the military authorities to regard them and treat them as Conscientious Objectors, and their repeated incarceration in solitary confinement for refusing to wear brown military overalls,' handwritten manuscript, 1 April 1980, 8 pages.

Moll, Peter G., 1981a. 'Special interview: Peter Moll after one year in D.B.' *Varsity*, March 1981, pp. 10-11. University of Cape Town.[179]

Moll, Peter G., 1981b. 'Peter Moll interview,' *War Resisters' International Newsletter* (London), no. 183, July 1981.[180]

Moll, Peter, 1981c. 'Conditions in the Detention Barracks: A short report, for attention Maj.-Gen. Fourie.' Johannesburg: carbon copy, 16 March 1981. Wits, Rob. Coll., A2558-9.13.

Moll, Peter G., 1982a. 'The South African Defence Force Corps of Chaplains: a muzzled ministry,' paper for the Church History course in the B.A. Honours (Religious Studies), October 1982. 44 pages.

Moll, Peter G., 1982b. '*Apartheid* the cause,' letter to the Editor of *The South African Baptist*, December 1982.[181]

Moll, Peter G., 1983a. 'Outlook on the month: New laws for objectors,' *South African Outlook*, vol. 113, no. 1340 (February 1983), p. 18.

Moll, Peter G., 1983b. 'Life in DB,' *South African Outlook*, vol. 113, no. 1340 (February 1983), pp. 27-28. Reprint of a letter to the *Cape Times*, 22 September 1982.

Moll, Peter G., 1984a. 'Description of the Detention Barracks,' in: Louw, Ronald (1984). See References.

---

[179] Wits, Rob. Coll., A2558-9.13.

[180] Wits, Rob. Coll., A2558-1\Item A Correspondence Series 1.

[181] Baptist Theological College, Johannesburg.

Moll, Peter G., 1984b. *A theological critique of the military chaplaincy of the English-speaking churches*. M.A. thesis, Department of Religious Studies, University of Cape Town.[182]

Moll, Peter G., 1984c. 'Controversy: chaplains in the army,' *Objector* (the newsletter of the Conscientious Objector Support Group (W. Cape)), Volume 2, no. 4 (July 1984).[183]

Moll, Peter G., 1985a. 'Anglicans' break with the military,' letter to the Editor of the *Cape Times*, 23 July 1985.[184]

Moll, Peter G., 1985b. 'Military chaplaincy and unjust wars.' *Journal of Theology for Southern Africa*, vol. 53 (December): 13-21.

Moll, Peter G., 1986a. 'Conscientious objectors under renewed attack,' *South African Outlook*, October 1986, pp. 113-115.[185]

Moll, Peter G., 1986b. 'A proposal for a civilianised chaplaincy', 1986. 10 pages, printed on the Sperry-UNIVAC computer at the University of Cape Town.[186]

Moll, Peter G., 1987a. 'The "Brazil option"', *Non-Violence News* (produced by Rev. R.J.D. Robertson, Division of Justice and Reconciliation of the SACC), Second Quarter 1987, p. 2.[187]

Moll, Peter G., 1987b. 'Ministry in conflict situations,' Durban: typewritten manuscript, August 1987. 14 pages.[188]

---

[182] https://open.uct.ac.za/bitstream/item/16895/thesis_hum_1984_moll_peter_graham.pdf.

[183] Wits, ECC Coll., AG1977-B8-8.4.5.

[184] Wits, ECC Coll., AG1977-I3-I4.

[185] See http://historicalpapers-atom.wits.ac.za/conscientious-objectors-under-renewed-attack-article-by-peter-moll-in-south-african-outlook-2 .

[186] Wits, Rob. Coll., A2558-9.13.

[187] Wits, Rob. Coll., A2558-3.

[188] Wits, ECC Coll., AG1977-24.10.1.14.

Moll, Peter G., 1987c. 'Only religious pacifists can use options for CO's,' letter to the editor of the *Cape Times*, 15 September 1987.[189]

Moll, Peter G., 1989a. 'Public statement of conscience,' submitted to the End Conscription Campaign for inclusion in the 771-strong register of conscientious objectors in 1989, dated 14 June 1989. Filled-in form of 1 page.

Moll, Peter G., 1989b. 'Why I am a conscientious objector,' *Baptists Today* (published by the Baptist Union of South Africa), October 1989.[190]

Moll, Peter G., 1990. 'Legislative change for alternative national service: past and future', in: Centre for Intergroup Studies, 1990. *Alternative National Service. Occasional Paper No. 14.* Rondebosch: Cape Town. Pages 227-234.

Moll, Peter G., 1997. *My experience with conscription: Submission to the Truth and Reconciliation Commission.* Washington, D.C., mimeo, 29 June 1997. 62 pages.

---

[189] Wits, ECC Coll., ZA HPRA AD1912AE-E93.

[190] Baptist Theological College, Johannesburg.

Appendix G. Published materials on Peter Moll's case (by date)

Moll, Peter G., 1977. 'Application for service of national interest under civilian direction,' letter to the Officer Commanding of Cape Flats Commando, 21 November 1977. Reproduced in this volume in the section of original documents.

'Grensdiens: man gestraf,' *Die Burger*, 29 December 1977. Reproduced in the section of original documents.

Moll, Peter G., 1978a. 'Reapplication for service of national interest under civilian direction,' letter to the Officer Commanding of Cape Flats Commando, 25 October 1978.

Moll, Peter G., 1978b. 'Why I am a selective conscientious objector,' typewritten and duplicated 300X by Gestetner. 12 pages.[191] Reproduced in this volume in the section of original documents.

Moll, Peter G., 1979a. 'The non-combatancy option and the disobedience option,' typewritten and duplicated 300X by Gestetner, February 1979. 6 pages.[192]

Moll, Peter G., 1979b. 'My country right or wrong?' *Comment* (Christian student newspaper, University of Cape Town), 18 April 1979. Typewritten draft covers 8 pages.

Moll, Peter G., 1979c. 'The Christian response to military service,' *Varsity* (student newspaper of the University of Cape Town), May 1979.[193]

---

[191] Wits, Rob. Coll., A2558-9.13.
[192] Wits, Rob. Coll., A2558-9.13.
[193] Wits, SAIRR Coll., ZA HPRA AD1912A-S236.9.

Moll, Peter G., 1979d. 'Request for alternative service,' letter to the Officer Commanding, Western Province Command, on 2 June 1979. 2 pages, plus appendices.

Moll, Peter G., 1979e. 'Application for service under the Civic Action Programme,' letter to the Officer Commanding of Cape Flats Commando, 6 June 1979. 2 pages plus appendices.

Moll, Peter G., 1979f. 'To be a soldier or not to,' *Contours of the Kingdom* (May-June 1979). Magazine of The Loft (Germiston). Pages 12-14.[194]

Moll, Peter G., 1979g. 'Thinking No,' *National Student* (newspaper of the National Union of South African Students), June 1979, p. 15.

Moll, Peter G., 1979h. 'Is SA worth fighting for?' letter to the editor of *The Star,* 24 July 1979.[195]

Moll, Peter G., 1979i. 'Is SA morally defensible?' letter to the editor of *The Cape Times*, 26 July 1979.

'UCT man "selective objector,"' *The Argus*, 31 August 1979.[196]

S.F. du Toit, Director of Publications, 1979. 'Publications Act, 1974: Publication: *Contours of the Kingdom*, May, June 1979,' letter to the Editor of *Contours of the Kingdom* (August 1979), p. 4. Explaining why the previous issue with Peter Moll (1979f) was banned.

Paddi Clay, 1979. ' "Unique" case for hearing,' *Sunday Express*, 9 September 1979.[197]

'Volunteer corps for pacifists,' *Sunday Tribune*, 16 September 1979.[198]

---

[194] Wits, Rob. Coll., A2558-9.13.
[195] Wits, SAIRR, ZA HPRA AD1912A-S236.9.
[196] Wits, SAIRR, ZA HPRA AD1912A-S236.9.
[197] Wits, SAIRR, ZA HPRA AD1912A-S236.9.
[198] Wits, Rob. Coll., A2558-9.16.

'I prefer punishment—objector,' *The Argus*, 21 September 1979.[199]

'Court martial fines objector R50,' *The Argus*, 21 September 1979.[200]

'Student failed to report to army,' *Rand Daily Mail*, 22 September 1979.[201]

Willem Steenkamp, 1979. 'Objector obeyed "higher laws"', *Cape Times*, 22 September 1979.[202]

Liz McGregor, 1979. 'Fined objector expected prison,' *Sunday Times*, 23 September 1979.[203]

John Murray, 1979. 'Conscientious objectors get together,' *The Star*, 6 October 1979. Mentions Peter Moll.[204]

Moll, Peter G., 1979j. 'Open letter: Conscientious objection to continuous training camp,' letter to the Officer Commanding, Cape Flats Commando, 19 October 1979. 6 pages.

Moll, Peter G., 1979k. 'Excerpts from an open letter, dated 19th October 1979, by Peter Moll (in which he again refuses to attend military camp) addressed to the Officer Commanding, Cape Flats Commando.' Original excerpted by Dot Cleminshaw. 4 pages. Reproduced in the section of original documents.[205]

'Moll fined for missing four-day camp,' *Wits Student*, 19 October 1979.[206]

'Student called up,' *Daily Dispatch*, 25 October 1979.[207]

---

[199] UCT, Nathan Coll., BC912 A32 (2).

[200] UCT, Nathan Coll., BC912 A32 (2).

[201] Wits, SAIRR, ZA HPRA AD1912A-S236.9.

[202] UCT, Nathan Coll., BC912 A32 (2).

[203] Wits, SAIRR, ZA HPRA AD1912A-S236.9.

[204] Wits, ECC Coll., AG1977-I3-I4.

[205] UCT, Nathan Coll., BC912 A32 (2).

[206] Wits, SAIRR, ZA HPRA AD1912A-S236.9.

[207] Wits, SAIRR, AD1912A-S236.9.

'Defiant objector forecasts clash over his call-up,' *Rand Daily Mail*, 29 October 1979.

'Objector says call up could lead to clash,' *Unknown Newspaper* (possibly the *Daily Dispatch*), n.d. (but from the contents, 28 October 1979).

Stephen Wrottesley, 1979. 'Objector expects court-martial,' *Cape Times*, 29 October 1979.

Moll, Peter G., 1979l. 'Debate about military service,' *South African Outlook*, vol. 111, no. 1300 (October 1979), p. 153-154.[208]

Tony Spencer-Smith, 1979. ' "I won't do army training..."' *Sunday Tribune*, 18 November 1979.

'Man refuses military training yet again,' *Daily News*, 20 November 1979.[209]

'Objector arrested,' *Unknown newspaper*, n.d. (but from the contents, 23 November 1979).

'Alternative national service', in *Non-violence news* (Justice and Reconciliation Division of the SACC, Braamfontein, produced by Rev. Rob Robertson), November 1979.[210]

'Objector to face tribunal,' *The Star*, 3 December 1979.

'Military objector jailed,' *Unknown newspaper* (possibly the *Daily Dispatch*), n.d. (but from the contents, 5 December 1979).

'An agonising problem,' editorial in *The Argus*, 5 December 1979.

'Army jails conscientious objector Peter Graham Moll for 18 months,' *Cape Times*, 5 December 1979.[211]

---

[208] Wits, Rob. Coll., A2558-15.8.
[209] Wits, SAIRR, ZA HPRA AD1912A-S236.9.
[210] Wits, Rob. Coll., A2558-1.
[211] Wits, Rob. Coll., A2558-9.16.

Moll, Peter G., 1979m. 'Excerpts from letter Moll wrote OC of his commando,' *Cape Times*, 5 December 1979. Original excerpted by the Cape Times.[212]

'Conscientious objection: Church view,' *Cape Times*, 5 December 1979.[213]

'Anti-terror battle unjust—accused,' *The Citizen*, 5 December 1979.[214]

'Army jails Moll,' *Daily Dispatch*, n.d. [but from the contents, 5 December 1979].

'SWA war is unjust objector tells court,' *Daily Dispatch*, n.d. [but from the contents, 5 December 1979].

'Military service: Churches plead for objector,' *Daily News*, 5 December 1979.[215]

'Military court jails objector,' *E.P. Herald*, 5 December 1979.[216]

'Objector says war in SWA is unjust,' *Natal Mercury*, 5 December 1979.

'SWA war unjust—army objector,' *Rand Daily Mail*, 5 December 1979.[217]

'Jail for man who defied callup,' *Rand Daily Mail*, 5 December 1979.

'Objector gets 18 months' detention,' *The Star*, 5 December 1979.[218]

'Tutu slams sentence on objector,' *Post*, 6 December 1979, p. 7.[219]

---

[212] Wits, Rob. Coll., A2558-9.16
[213] Wits, SAIRR, ZA HPRA AD1912A-S236.9.
[214] Wits, SAIRR, ZA HPRA AD1912A-S236.9.
[215] Wits, SAIRR, ZA HPRA AD1912A-S236.9
[216] Wits, SAIRR, ZA HPRA AD1912A-S236.9.
[217] Wits, SAIRR, ZA HPRA AD1912A-S236.9.
[218] Wits, SAIRR, ZA HPRA AD1912A-S236.9.
[219] Wits, SAIRR, ZA HPRA AD1912A-S236.9.

'Problems of duty and conscience,' editorial in *Rand Daily Mail*, 6 December 1979.[220]

'Provide for objectors to service—paper,' *Cape Times*, 20 December 1979.[221]

'Church says military laws must change,' *Daily Dispatch*, 20 December 1979.[222]

'Catholics call for altered Defence Act,' *Rand Daily Mail*, 20 December 1979.[223]

Moll, Peter G., 1979n. 'Certain events of evening of 24-12-1979 at the Detention Barracks, Voortrekkerhoogte, by Peter Moll.' 2 pages.[224]

Moll, Peter G., 1979o. 'Violence in the Detention Barracks, 26 December 1979 onwards.' Originally a handwritten manuscript. 2 pages.[225]

'Objector Moll sacked by Old Mutual,' *The Argus*, 5 January 1980.

'Army objector dismissed by his firm,' *The Star*, 5 January 1980.[226]

'Employers fire jailed objector,' *The Cape Times*, 7 January 1980.[227]

'Sentence reduced,' *Cape Times*, 8 January 1980.[228]

'Moll's sentence cut by a third,' *Cape Times*, 8 January 1980.

'Diensplig-ontduiker welkom hier as ...,' *Beeld*, 8 January 1980.[229]

---

[220] Wits, SAIRR, ZA HPRA AD1912A-S236.9.

[221] UCT, Nathan Coll., BC912 A32.

[222] Wits, SAIRR, ZA HPRA AD1912A-S236.9.

[223] Wits, SAIRR, ZA HPRA AD1912A-S236.9.

[224] Reproduced in full in an appendix of this book.

[225] Reproduced in full in an appendix of this book.

[226] Wits, SAIRR, ZA HPRA AD1912A-S236.9.

[227] Wits, SAIRR, ZA HPRA AD1912A-S236.9.

[228] Wits, Rob. Coll., A2558-16.

[229] Wits, SAIRR, ZA HPRA AD1912A-S236.9.

Jack Curtis, 1980. 'Policy profile,' letter to the editor of *Rand Daily Mail*, 11 January 1980.

Rev. Douglas Bax, 1980. 'Why was Moll punished by his employers?' letter to the editor, *Cape Times*, 21 January 1980.

Matthews, Mr. D.A., 1980. 'Dismissal did not violate Moll's freedom of speech,' letter to the editor, *Cape Times*, 21 January 1980.

J.T. Cook, 1980. 'Jail waste of time for this objector,' letter to the editor of *The Star*, 25 January 1980.

Margaret Nash, 1980. 'Moll's employers' negative profile,' *Cape Times*, 29 January 1980.

'Landsbelang bo persvryheid,' *Beeld,* 30 January 1980.

'Coverage of Moll hearing questioned,' *Cape Times*, 30 January 1980.

'Outlook on the Month: Peter Moll,' *South African Outlook*, January 1980.[230]

Moll, Peter G., 1980. 'Violence in the Detention Barracks, 10 February 1980,' originally a handwritten manuscript. 2 pages.[231]

'Moll broke contract says Old Mutual,' *Sunday Times*, 17 February 1980.

Rev. Douglas Bax, 1980. 'Employers' action on Moll discriminatory,' letter to the editor, *Cape Times*, 21 February 1980.

Mr. D.L. Craythorne, 1980. 'Moll and the rights of an employer,' letter to the editor, *Cape Times*, 29 February 1980.

'Richard Steele,' in *Non-violence news* (Justice and Reconciliation Division of the SACC, Braamfontein,

---

[230] Wits, SAIRR, ZA HPRA AD1912A-S236.9.

[231] This report is reproduced in full in this volume in Appendix D.

produced by Rev. Rob Robertson), February 1980. Refers to Richard Steele and Peter Moll.[232]

'News: Moll in solitary,' *Unknown newspaper* (but clearly from the University of Natal, Durban campus), n.d. (but from the contents, February 1980).

'A matter of conscience,' *Comment* (Christian student newspaper at the University of Cape Town), February 1980. Refers to Richard Steele and Peter Moll.[233]

'Protest over solitary confinement,' *Cape Times*, 11 March 1980. Refers to Peter Moll and Richard Steele.[234]

' "Release these men from solitary confinement," ' *The Argus*, 11 March 1980. Refers to Peter Moll and Richard Steele.[235]

R.C. Lloyd, 1980. 'Employers' attitude to Moll neutral and fair,' letter to the editor of *The Cape Times*, 24 March 1980.[236]

'Moll in solitary again,' pamphlet issued by MILCOM on the University of Cape Town campus, n.d. (but from the contents, 26 March 1980). 1 page.[237]

'Christ at Voortrekkerhoogte,' *Ecunews Bulletin*, 31 March 1980. Refers to Peter Moll and Richard Steele.[238]

'Another Christian objects to military service,' *Campus*, vol. 1, no. 6, 1980 (no month cited but from the contents, March). Refers to Richard Steele and Peter Moll.[239]

---

[232] Wits, Rob. Coll., A2558-1.

[233] *Comment* reference is listed in Richard Steele (1997), Appendix 2. See References.

[234] Wits, Rob. Coll., A2558-16.

[235] *The Argus:* reference is in Richard Steele (1997), Appendix 2. See References.

[236] Wits, SAIRR, ZA HPRA AD1912A-S236.9.

[237] Wits, SAIRR, ZA HPRA AD1912A-S236.9.

[238] *Ecunews:* reference is in Richard Steele (1997), Appendix 2. See References.

[239] *Campus:* reference is in Richard Steele (1997), Appendix 2. See References.

Peter Moll and Richard Steele, 1980. 'Joint statement on conscientious objection,' *Comment* (Christian student newspaper at the University of Cape Town), March 1980, p. 15.

'A matter of conscience: Peter Moll and Richard Steele,' *Comment* (Christian student newspaper at the University of Cape Town), March 1980, p. 15-16.

'International action on war resistance,' *Peace Action News* no. 5, March 1980, p. 5; in turn reprinted from *Resister*. Refers to Peter Moll and Richard Steele.[240]

Peter Moll and Richard Steele, 1980. 'Public statement by Peter Moll and Richard Steele concerning their Protest Fast to be held on 3, 4 and 5 April 1980 to protest the refusal of the military authorities to regard them and treat them as Conscientious Objectors, and their repeated incarceration in solitary confinement for refusing to wear brown military overalls,' handwritten manuscript, 1 April 1980, 8 pages.

'Vigil for two fasting objectors,' *The Argus*, 1 April 1980. Refers to Peter Moll and Richard Steele.

'Three-day fast by military objectors,' *Cape Times*, 1 April 1980. Refers to Peter Moll, Richard Steele and Dr. Ivan Toms.

'3-day fast for Moll and Steele,' *Evening Post*, 1 April 1980.

'Imprisoned military objectors plan to fast,' *The Star*, 1 April 1980. Refers to Peter Moll and Richard Steele.

'A case for tolerance,' editorial in *The Argus*, 2 April 1980. Refers to Peter Moll and Richard Steele.

'Prayer vigil for two objectors,' *The Argus*, 3 April 1980. Refers to Peter Moll and Richard Steele.

'Vigil begins for fasting objectors,' *Cape Times*, 3 April 1980. Refers to Peter Moll and Richard Steele.

[240] Wits, SAIRR, ZA HPRA AD1912A-S236.9.

'Tutu supports protest vigils for objectors,' *EP Herald*, 3 April 1980. Refers to Peter Moll and Richard Steele.[241]

Arnold Geyer, 1980. 'Objectors in DB: now Tutu joins protest,' *Rand Daily Mail,* 3 April 1980. Refers to Peter Moll and Richard Steele.[242]

'Vigil book, Richard Steele and Peter Moll, Easter 1980, Wednesday 2 April to Saturday 5 April 1980,' with entries by Tony Saddington and others, on the occasion of a fast of protest against double punishment in the form of solitary confinement. 31 pages.

Charles Yeats, 1980. 'Why I am a conscientious objector to war,' typewritten document widely distributed, Easter 1980 [6 April].[243] Refers to Peter Moll and Richard Steele.

'Church vigils for hunger-strikers end,' *The Cape Times*, 7 April 1980. Refers to Peter Moll and Richard Steele.[244]

'Vigils for 'solitary' pair end,' *Rand Daily Mail,* 7 April 1980. Refers to Peter Moll and Richard Steele.

'Matter of fact,' *Rand Daily Mail*, 8 April 1980, p. 2. Refers to Peter Moll and Richard Steele.

'Vigil: Thoughts from the vigil of fasting objectors,' *Comment* (Christian student newspaper at the University of Cape Town), April 1980, p. 9.

The Minister of Defence, 'Servicemen: solitary confinement,' *Hansard (April 1980)*, vol. 12, column 698. In answer to a question by Mr. P.A. Myburgh. Refers (not by name, but by sequence of solitary periods) to Peter Moll, Chris Boshoff and Richard Steele.[245]

---

[241] Wits, SAIRR, ZA HPRA AD1912A-S236.9.
[242] Wits, SAIRR, ZA HPRA AD1912A-S236.9.
[243] Wits, Rob. Coll., A2558-9.25.1.
[244] Wits, SAIRR, ZA HPRA AD1912A-S236.9.
[245] Wits, SAIRR, ZA HPRA AD1912A-S236.9.

'South Africa imprisons C.O.'s,' *IFOR Report* (magazine of the International Fellowship of Reconciliation), April 1980. Refers to Richard Steele, Anton Eberhard and Peter Moll.

'South Africa COs held in solitary confinement,' *Gospel Herald* (Newspaper of the Mennonite Central Committee, USA), 6 May 1980.

'Objector Moll in solitary for sixth time,' *Argus*, 8 May 1980.[246]

'Army objector in solitary confinement,' *The Star*, 9 May 1980.[247]

'Conscientious objection,' in *Non-violence news* (Justice and Reconciliation Division of the SACC, Braamfontein, produced by Rev. Rob Robertson), May 1980.[248]

The Minister of Defence, 'Servicemen: solitary confinement,' *Hansard (May 1980)*, vol. 16, column 850. In answer to a question by Mr. R.A.F. Swart. Refers (not by name, but by sequence of solitary periods) to Peter Moll, Chris Boshoff and Richard Steele.[249]

'Jailed objector to fast—SACC man,' *Argus*, 7 July 1980. [250]

'Fast planned over 'double penalty'', *The Star*, 7 July 1980.

'Moll to stage another fast,' *Diamond Fields Advertiser* (Kimberley), 8 July 1980.[251]

'Moll must repay his bursary,' *The Star*, 8 July 1980.

Arnold Geyer, 'SACC plans protest supporting objector,' *Rand Daily Mail*, 10 July 1980.[252]

Denis E. Hurley, OMI, 1980. 'Opening address,' at the Conference for the Initiation of and Organisation for

---

[246] Wits, Rob. Coll., A2558-16.
[247] Wits, SAIRR, ZA HPRA AD1912A-S236.9.
[248] Wits, Rob. Coll., A2558-1.
[249] Wits, SAIRR, ZA HPRA AD1912A-S236.9.
[250] Wits, Rob. Coll., A2558-16.
[251] Wits, SAIRR, ZA HPRA AD1912A-S236.5.
[252] Wits, SAIRR, ZA HPRA AD1912A-S236.9.

Conscientious Objectors, including a Workshop on Conscientious Objection, at Botha's Hill, Natal, 10-14 July 1980. Refers to Peter Moll and Richard Steele.[253]

'Vigils to support army objector,' *The Star*, 16 July 1980.

Editorial, *The Argus*, 17 July 1980.[254]

'Moll ends 3-day fast,' *Cape Times*, 19 July 1980. [255]

Peter Brown, 1980. 'A case of conscientious objection.' *Original journal unknown*, n.d. (but from the contents, July 1980). 2 pages.[256]

' "Make army service voluntary" call,' *Unknown newspaper*, n.d. (but from the contents, about July 1980).

'Moll turns down plan to ease his life in DB,' *Sunday Express*, 3 August 1980.[257]

'MP seeing general over army solitary confinement,' *The Star*, 4 August 1980.

Mrs. T.A. (or B.M.) Moll, 1980. 'Vicious sentence on objector,' letter to the editor of *The Star*, 5 August 1980.[258]

'Objector Moll to be freed from DB,' *Argus*, 9 August 1980.[259]

'Army relents on objector,' *The Star*, 9 August 1980.

Barry Levy, 1980a. 'Lone army rebel with a cause wins his victory: conscientious objector status for Peter Moll,' *Sunday Express*, 10 August 1980.[260]

---

[253] Wits, Rob. Coll., A2558-6.

[254] Wits, Rob. Coll., A2558-9.13.

[255] Wits, Rob. Coll., A2558-16.

[256] Brown: available at https://disa.ukzn.ac.za/sites/default/files/pdf_files/rejan80.7.pdf .

[257] Wits, SAIRR, ZA HPRA AD1912A-S236.9.

[258] Wits, SAIRR, ZA HPRA AD1912A-S236.5.

[259] Wits, Rob. Coll., A2558-16.

[260] Wits, SAIRR, ZA HPRA AD1912A-S236.5.

295

Barry Levy, 1980b. 'Army rebel wins biggest battle: conscientious objector status for Peter Moll,' *Sunday Express*, 10 August 1980.

Gherard Pieterse, 1980. 'A mother prays ... and now pacifist son will be freed from solitary confinement,' *Sunday Times*, 10 August 1980.[261]

Daryl Balfour, 1980. 'Moll wins the right not to fight: Army relents over conscientious objector... ,' *Sunday Tribune*, 10 August 1980. Refers to Peter Moll and Richard Steele. [262]

'Moll, Steele get new status,' *Daily Dispatch*, 11 August 1980.[263]

John Murray, 1980. 'No further 'solitary' for jailed objectors,' *The Star*, 11 August 1980. Refers to Peter Moll and Richard Steele.[264]

'SADF: Moll given the benefit of the doubt,' *Daily Dispatch*, n.d. [but from the contents, 12 August 1980]. Refers to Peter Moll and Richard Steele.

'Moll won't have sentence reduced,' *Daily Dispatch*, n.d. [but from the contents, 12 August 1980]. Refers to Peter Moll and Richard Steele.

'Two in bid to have "sadistic" solitary abolished by army,' *Daily News*, n.d. (but from the contents, 12 August 1980). Refers to Peter Moll and Richard Steele.

'Sentences will stay for two objectors,' *Rand Daily Mail,* 12 August 1980. Refers to Peter Moll and Richard Steele.

'Defence Force to rethink on conscientious objection,' *The Star*, 12 August 1980. Refers to Peter Moll and Richard Steele.[265]

'Objectionable,' 3rd leader in *The Star*, 12 August 1980.

---

[261] Wits, Rob. Coll., A2558-9.13.
[262] Wits, Rob. Coll., A2558-16.
[263] Wits, SAIRR, ZA HPRA AD1912A-S236.5.
[264] Wits, SAIRR, ZA HPRA AD1912A-S236.5.
[265] Wits, SAIRR, ZA HPRA AD1912A-S236.5.

Melanie Gosling, 1980. 'Conscientious objector seeks asylum,' *Natal Mercury*, 15 August 1980. Refers to Peter Moll and Richard Steele.[266]

'Moll decision a strict exception, warns the SADF,' *Sunday Express*, 17 August 1980.[267]

'Vigil book: for recording thoughts: Vigil of thanksgiving: Friday 22nd to Sat. 23rd August,' Handwritten manuscript at the Rondebosch Congregational Church, Cape Town; on the occasion of the recognition by the SADF of Richard Steele and Peter Moll as conscientious objectors. 24 pages.

'South Africans Steele and Moll granted C.O. status,' *MCC (Mennonite Central Committee) News Service* (Akron, Pennsylvania, USA), 29 August 1980.

'Conscientious objection,' in *Non-violence news* (Justice and Reconciliation Division of the SACC, Braamfontein, produced by Rev. Rob Robertson), August 1980.[268]

'Over 400 held in DB,' *Resister: Bulletin of the Committee on South African War Resistance*, no. 9 (July/August 1980). Page 2. Refers to Peter Moll among others.[269]

'Solidarity: Exiles support war resisters in SA,' *Resister: Bulletin of the Committee on South African War Resistance*, no. 9 (July/August 1980). Page 4.[270]

'Moll fights on,' *Resister: Bulletin of the Committee on South African War Resistance*, no. 9 (July/August 1980). Page 5.[271]

---

[266] Gosling article reproduced on p. 60 in: Barry Streek, ed. *South African Pressclips: The SADF and conscientious objection*. Tamboerskloof, Cape Town: photocopied and stapled document, July 1982. 80 pages. Wits, Rob. Coll., A2558-16.

[267] Wits, SAIRR, ZA HPRA AD1912A-S236.5.

[268] Wits, Rob. Coll., A2558-1.

[269] Wits, Rob. Coll., A2558-7.

[270] Wits, Rob. Coll., A2558-7.

[271] Wits, Rob. Coll., A2558-7.

'War Resistance: Broadcast from Radio Freedom,' transcript, pages 17 to 23, dated August 1980, based upon articles in *Resister* by COSAWR. Refers to Peter Moll and Richard Steele.[272]

Gary Thatcher, 1980. 'South Africa's conscientious objectors: A long fight by a nation's pacifists,' *Christian Science Monitor*, 4 September 1980. Refers to Peter Moll and Richard Steele.[273]

Chris Marais, 1980. 'Detained for other ideas,' *Rand Daily Mail*, 18 September 1980.[274]

Adrian Paterson, 1980. 'Recognition: conscientious objectors recognised,' *Comment* (Christian student newspaper at the University of Cape Town), September 1980. Refers to Peter Moll and Richard Steele.

' "We owe much to young men"—Rob Robertson,' *Kairos*, September 1980, p. 2.

Paddy Kearney, 1980. 'Conscientious objection: a Christian perspective: a lecture delivered at the University of Natal, Pietermaritzburg.' *Reality: A journal of liberal and radical opinion* (Pietermaritzburg), September 1980, pages 9-14.

'Mothers of South African C.O.s send message to Mennonite women,' *WMSC Voice* (newspaper of the Women's Missionary and Service Commission of the Mennonite Church of the USA), September 1980. Refers to Richard Steele and Peter Moll.[275]

---

[272] Radio Freedom: available at https://www.sahistory.org.za/sites/default/files/archive-files/Dav4n780.1681.5785.004.007.July1980.8.pdf .

[273] Christian Science Monitor: available at https://www.csmonitor.com/1980/0904/090469.html .

[274] Wits, Rob. Coll., A2558-16.

[275] *WMSC Voice:* reference is in Richard Steele (1997), Appendix 2. See References.

‘ "Change of heart" on objectors,' *Cape Times*, 13 October 1980. Refers to Peter Moll and Richard Steele.

'Church salutes army objectors,' *Daily Dispatch*, 25 October 1980. Refers to Peter Moll and Richard Steele.

Gary Thatcher, 1980. 'Dilemma of S.A.'s reluctant soldiers,' *The Chronicle* (possibly a US newspaper), 26 November 1980.

'Conscientious objection,' in *Non-violence news* (Justice and Reconciliation Division of the SACC, Braamfontein, produced by Rev. Rob Robertson), November 1980.[276]

'[NUSAS] Congress applauds stand by objector,' *The Star*, 3 December 1980.[277]

Marja Tuit, 1980. 'Peter Moll released from DB,' *Rand Daily Mail*, 5 December 1980.

'Moll released,' *Rand Daily Mail*, 5 December 1980.

Caroline Moorhead, 1980. 'Prisoners of conscience: South Africa: Richard Steele,' *The Times* (London), 8 December 1980. Mainly about Richard Steele, also refers to Peter Moll.

Damian de Lange, 1980. 'Suffering was worth it, says anti-war boy Peter: "I will not be part of the SADF,"' *Sunday Express*, 14 December 1980.[278]

'Tribute to Peter Moll and Richard Steele,' resolution by the Assembly of the Presbyterian Church of Southern Africa. Contained in a letter to me from Rev. I.C. Aitken, General Secretary, 23 December 1980.

Smail, Andrew (1980). See References. Refers to Peter Moll and Richard Steele.

---

[276] Wits, Rob. Coll., A2558-1.
[277] Wits, SAIRR, ZA HPRA AD1912A-S236.5.
[278] Wits, Rob. Coll., A2558-16.

Student Union for Christian Action, 1981. 'Resolution,' 30 January 1981, proposed by Stephen Granger and seconded by Chris Swart, about Peter Moll.

Moll, Peter G., 1981a. 'Special interview: Peter Moll after one year in D.B.' *Varsity*, March 1981, pp. 10-11. University of Cape Town.[279]

'Peter Moll one year later,' *Comment* (Christian student newspaper at the University of Cape Town), March 1981, p. 3.

Suzanne Lind, 1981. 'Diakonia accountant facing Detention Barracks,' *Diakonia News*, April 1981, pages 3-4.[280]

'Non-military service: "Let us work in the rural areas": Conviction of Moll and Steele sparked Yeats' return to Republic,' *Sunday Tribune*, 17 May 1981.

Rob Robertson, 1981. 'The trial of Charles Yeats,' typescript document duplicated by Gestetner, May 1981. 6 pages. Mainly about Charles Yeats, reference also to Peter Moll.[281]

'Tailpiece,' in *Non-violence news* (Justice and Reconciliation Division of the SACC, Braamfontein, produced by Rev. Rob Robertson), Second Quarter 1981.[282]

Moll, Peter G., 1981b. 'Peter Moll interview,' *War Resisters' International Newsletter* (London), no. 183, July 1981.[283]

Editorial, *Resister: Bulletin of the Committee on South African War Resistance*, no. 14 (June/July 1981). Page 2.[284]

'SACC support,' *Resister: Bulletin of the Committee on South African War Resistance*, no. 14 (June/July 1981). Page 7.[285]

---

[279] Wits, Rob. Coll., A2558-9.13.
[280] Wits, Rob. Coll., A2558-9.25.1.
[281] Wits, Rob. Coll., A2558-1.
[282] Wits, Rob. Coll., A2558-1.
[283] Wits, Rob. Coll., A2558-1.
[284] Wits, Rob. Coll., A2558-7.
[285] Wits, Rob. Coll., A2558-7.

David Breier, 1981. 'Anatomy of a South African draft dodger,' *The Star*, 11 September 1981. Refers to Peter Moll, Richard Steele and Chris Boshoff.[286]

'Court turns down objector case,' *Rand Daily Mail*, 15 September 1981. Refers mainly to Charles Yeats, also to Peter Moll and Richard Steele.[287]

'Peter Moll and Richard Steele,' in *Non-violence news* (Justice and Reconciliation Division of the SACC, Braamfontein, produced by Rev. Rob Robertson), Third Quarter 1981.[288]

Rob Robertson, 1981. 'Charles Yeats' 'Trial by ordeal''. Mayfair, Johannesburg: duplicated by Gestetner. 2 pages. Attached to *Non-violence news*, Third Quarter 1981.[289]

Lehman, Melvin H., 1981. 'The story of a South African conscientious objector,' *The Christian Century* (Chicago, USA), 4 November 1981, pp. 1128-1130. Refers mainly to Peter Moll, also to Richard Steele.

Richard Steele, 1981. 'Interview,' in *IFOR Report* (International Fellowship of Reconciliation), November 1981, pp. 10-14. Refers to Charles Yeats and Peter Moll.[290]

'I must obey conscience, says Yeats,' *Daily Dispatch*, 15 December 1981. Mainly about Charles Yeats, also refers to Peter Moll and Richard Steele.

'For Yeats the long struggle is over—now it's civvie jail,' *Daily Dispatch*, n.d. [but from the contents, 17 December 1981].

---

[286] Wits, Rob. Coll., A2558-16.

[287] *RDM* article reproduced on p. 72 in: Barry Streek, ed. *South African Pressclips: The SADF and conscientious objection*. Tamboerskloof, Cape Town: photocopied and stapled document, July 1982. 80 pages. Wits, Rob. Coll., A2558-16.

[288] Wits, Rob. Coll., A2558-1.

[289] Wits, Rob. Coll., A2558-1.

[290] UCT, Nathan Coll., BC912 A32 (2).

Mainly about Charles Yeats, refers also to Peter Moll and Richard Steele.

'Conscientious objectors,' in *Non-violence news* (Justice and Reconciliation Division of the SACC, Braamfontein, produced by Rev. Rob Robertson), Fourth Quarter 1981. 2 pages. Refers to Charles Yeats, Peter Moll, Richard Steele and Graham Philpott.[291]

'Alternative to military service demanded,' *Daily Dispatch*, 25 March 1982. Refers to Adi Paterson, Peter Moll and Richard Steele.[292]

'Conscientious objection,' in *Non-violence news* (Justice and Reconciliation Division of the SACC, Braamfontein, produced by Rev. Rob Robertson), First Quarter 1982, p. 1. Refers to Peter Moll, Charles Yeats, Michael Viveiros and Graham Philpott.[293]

' "If you believe it is an unjust war, it is your duty to refuse to fight,"' *Varsity,* 31 March 1982. Refers to Adrian Paterson, Peter Moll and Richard Steele.[294]

'Charles Yeats sentenced to another year,' *Resister: Bulletin of the Committee on South African War Resistance*, no. 18 (February/March 1982), p. 6.[295]

'Yeats: Political persecution,' *Resister: Bulletin of the Committee on South African War Resistance*, no. 18 (February/March 1982). Pages 16-17.[296]

---

[291] Wits, Rob. Coll., A2558-1.

[292] Wits, SAIRR, ZA HPRA AD1912A-S236.13.

[293] Wits, Rob. Coll., A2558-3.

[294] *Varsity* article reproduced on p. 57 in: Barry Streek, ed. *South African Pressclips: The SADF and conscientious objection*. Tamboerskloof, Cape Town: photocopied and stapled document, July 1982. 80 pages. Wits, Rob. Coll., A2558-16.

[295] Wits, Rob. Coll., A2558-7.

[296] Wits, Rob. Coll., A2558-7.

Rob Goldman, 1982. 'Another man of peace imprisoned,' *Diakonia News* (Durban), May 1982, p. 8. Refers mainly to Mike Viveiros, and also to Peter Moll, Richard Steele and Charles Yeats.[297]

Charlene Beltramo, 1982. 'Jail for objector Billy: the men who won't wear uniform: "I will not fight for apartheid and injustice,"' *Sunday Tribune*, 10 October 1982. Mainly about Billy Paddock, also refers to Anton Eberhard, Peter Moll, Richard Steele, Charles Yeats, Michael Viveiros and Neil Mitchell.[298]

'Military objector jailed 6 months,' *Daily Dispatch*, 13 October 1982. Refers mainly to Neil Mitchell, but also to Peter Moll and Richard Steele.[299]

'Why I object to service in the SADF: statement by Billy Paddock, October 1982,' booklet of eleven pages, including notes 'They stand together' and 'The Church stands with them,' published by C.O.S.G. (Durban).[300] Peter Moll's stand is briefly described.

Moll, Peter G., 1982a. 'The South African Defence Force Corps of Chaplains: a muzzled ministry,' paper for the Church History course in the B.A. Honours (Religious Studies), October 1982. 44 pages.

'Pacifists break the law—SADF,' *Pretoria News*, 5 November 1982. Refers to Peter Moll and Charles Yeats.[301]

Moll, Peter G., 1982b. '*Apartheid* the cause,' letter to the Editor of *The South African Baptist*, December 1982.[302]

---

[297] Wits, ECC Coll., ZA-HPRA AG1977-E1 (1.27).
[298] Wits, SAIRR, ZA HPRA AD1912A-S236.13.
[299] Wits, SAIRR, ZA HPRA AD1912A-S236.13.
[300] Wits, Rob. Coll., A2558-9.16.
[301] Wits, SAIRR, ZA HPRA AD1912A-S236.13.
[302] Baptist Theological College, Johannesburg.

CIIR and Pax Christi (1982). See References. Refers to Peter
Moll, Richard Steele, Charles Yeats, Michael Viveiros, Neil
Mitchell and Billy Paddock.

Moll, Peter G., 1983a. 'Outlook on the month: New laws for
objectors,' *South African Outlook*, vol. 113, no. 1340
(February 1983), p. 18.

Moll, Peter G., 1983b. 'Life in DB,' *South African Outlook*, vol.
113, no. 1340 (February 1983), p. 27-28. Reprint of a letter
to the *Cape Times*, 22 September 1982.

'12 objectors, 20 clergymen reject Bill,' *EP Herald*, 11 March
1983. Refers to Anton Eberhard, Peter Moll, Richard Steele,
Michael Viveiros, Adrian Paterson, Peter Hathorn, Stephen
Granger and Ivan Toms.[303]

' "Objector" Defence Bill full of thorns,' *The Argus*, 24 March
1983.[304]

'Objectors' Bill under attack,' *The Citizen*, 28 March 1983.[305]

'Conscientious objection: a brief history of the movement in
S.A.', *Objector: Newsletter of the C.O. Support Group*, no.
1, July 1983. Pages 2-3.[306]

Cape Town Conscientious Objector Support Group (CT
COSG), 1983. 'This was their choice,' typewritten
manuscript, September 1983. 4 pages.[307] Refers to Anton
Eberhard, Edric Gorfinkel, Peter Moll, Richard Steele,
Charles Yeats, Michael Viveiros, Neil Mitchell, Billy
Paddock, Etienne Essery, Adrian Paterson, Peter Hathorn,
Stephen Granger and Paul Dobson.

'Brett's solidarity night, 11.11.1983,' handwritten manuscript, a
speech delivered at the meeting at Rondebosch

[303] Wits, SAIRR, ZA HPRA AD1912A-S236.13.
[304] Wits, SAIRR, ZA HPRA AD1912A-S236.13.
[305] Wits, SAIRR, ZA HPRA AD1912A-S236.13.
[306] Wits, Rob. Coll., A2558-6.
[307] UCT, Nathan Coll., BC912 A32 (2).

Congregational Church; the speaker is not named. 16 (half-)pages. Refers to Peter Moll, Billy Paddock, Peter Hathorn.[308]

Centre for Intergroup Studies, 1983. 'Conscientious objection,' *Occasional Paper* no. 8 (1983). University of Cape Town, Rondebosch. ix + 71 pages.[309]

Report of the Commission of Inquiry into South African Council of Churches ('Eloff Commission'), RP 74/1983. Pretoria: Government Printer. 445 pages. Reference to Peter Moll and Richard Steele is on p. 195.

'COSG debates Board,' *Objector: Newsletter of the Conscientious Objector Support Group*, Vol. 2, no. 2 (April 1984). Page 2.[310]

Marion Whitehead, 1984. 'On the march—to religious objectors board,' *Sunday Express*, 8 July 1984. Refers to Anton Eberhard, Peter Moll and Richard Steele.[311]

Moll, Peter G., 1984a. 'Description of the Detention Barracks,' in: Louw, Ronald (1984), pp. 2-20. See References.

Moll, Peter G., 1984b. *A theological critique of the military chaplaincy of the English-speaking churches*. M.A. thesis, Department of Religious Studies, University of Cape Town.[312]

Moll, Peter G., 1984c. 'Controversy: chaplains in the army,' *Objector* (the newsletter of the Conscientious Objector Support Group (W. Cape)), Volume 2, no. 4 (July 1984).[313]

---

[308] UCT, ECC Coll., ZA-HPRA AG1977-E1 (1.3) Brett Myrdal.

[309] UCT, ECC Coll., ZA-HPRA AG1977-E1 (1.22) David Bruce.

[310] Wits, Rob. Coll., A2558-6.

[311] Wits, SAIRR, ZA HPRA AD1912A-S236.15.

[312] https://open.uct.ac.za/bitstream/item/16895/thesis_hum_1984_moll_peter_graham.pdf.

[313] Wits, ECC Coll., AG1977-B8-8.4.5.

'Conscription into the SADF—25 years of resistance,' *South African Outlook*, vol. 116, no. 1366 (April 1985), pp. 53-57. Refers to Peter Moll, Richard Steele, Billy Paddock, Peter Hathorn, and Brett Myrdal.[314]

'Peace in our time?' *Objector: Newsletter of the Conscientious Objector Support Groups,* vol. 3, no. 2 (May 1985), p. 6. Refers to Billy Paddock, Peter Moll and Richard Steele.[315]

Moll, Peter G., 1985a. 'Anglicans' break with the military,' letter to the Editor of the *Cape Times*, 23 July 1985.[316]

Moll, Peter G., 1985b. 'Military chaplaincy and unjust wars.' *Journal of Theology for Southern Africa*, vol. 53 (December): 13-21.

Moll, Peter G., 1986a. 'Conscientious objectors under renewed attack,' *South African Outlook*, October 1986, p. 113-115.[317]

Moll, Peter G., 1986b. 'A proposal for a civilianised chaplaincy', 1986. 10 pages, printed on the Sperry-UNIVAC computer at the University of Cape Town.[318]

'Wilkinson case put off 7 times,' *Out of step (Publication of the End Conscription Campaign Cape Town)*, April 1987, p. 1. Refers mainly to Philip Wilkinson, also to Peter Moll.[319]

'Conscientious objection,' *Non-Violence News* (produced by Rev. R.J.D. Robertson, Division of Justice and Reconciliation of the SACC), Second Quarter 1987, p. 1. Refers mainly to Philip Wilkinson, also to Peter Moll and Richard Steele.[320]

---

[314] UCT, Nathan Coll., BC912 B17.

[315] Wits, Rob. Coll., A2558-6.

[316] Wits, ECC Coll., AG1977-I3-I4.

[317] http://historicalpapers-atom.wits.ac.za/conscientious-objectors-under-renewed-attack-article-by-peter-moll-in-south-african-outlook-2 .

[318] Wits, Rob. Coll., A2558-9.13.

[319] UCT, Nathan Coll., BC912 A32 (3).

[320] Wits, Rob. Coll., A2558-3.

Moll, Peter G., 1987a. 'The "Brazil option"', *Non-Violence News* (produced by Rev. R.J.D. Robertson, Division of Justice and Reconciliation of the SACC), Second Quarter 1987, p. 2.[321]

Moll, Peter G., 1987b. 'Ministry in conflict situations,' Durban: typewritten manuscript, August 1987. 14 pages.[322]

Moll, Peter G., 1987c. 'Only religious pacifists can use options for CO's,' letter to the editor of the *Cape Times*, 15 September 1987.[323]

Law *et al.* (1987). See References.

'A history of objection,' article on page 4 of the pamphlet 'David Bruce interviewed: Facing six years in jail: Trial date 19 July 1988,' issued by Wits ECC. 4 pages.[324]

'Conscientious objectors to date,' in *PACSA Factsheet: conscientious objection*, no. 31 (July 1988), p. 2. Refers to Anton Eberhard, Peter Moll, Richard Steele, Charles Yeats, Michael Viveiros, Neil Mitchell, Billy Paddock, Etienne Essery, Adrian Paterson, Peter Hathorn, Philip Wilkinson, Dr. Ivan Toms and David Bruce.[325]

'Who are they? Physicians, physicists and priests…', about the 143 conscientious objectors, *Sunday Tribune*, 7 August 1988. Refers to Anton Eberhard, Peter Moll, Richard Steele, Neil Mitchell, Stephen Granger, Peter Hathorn, Dr. Mark Nel, Gary Rathbone, Saul Batzofin, David Bruce, Rev. Douglas Torr, Tam Alexander, David Schmidt.[326]

'The full list of the 143 names,' *The Star*, 11 August 1988.[327]

---

[321] Wits, Rob. Coll., A2558-3.
[322] Wits, ECC Coll., AG1977-24.10.1.14.
[323] Wits, ECC Coll., ZA HPRA AD1912AE-E93 (ECC).
[324] Wits, ECC Coll., AG1977-E1 (1.22) David Bruce.
[325] UCT, SCA/SCO Coll., BC1473 N6 (Part 2).
[326] Wits, ECC Coll., ZA-HPRA AG1977-E1 (1.22) David Bruce.
[327] Wits, Rob. Coll., A2558-16.

'Angola: the end of the war?' *Wits Student*, 12 August 1988. Refers to Gary Rathbone, David Bruce, Neil Mitchell, Peter Hathorn, Richard Steele, Peter Moll, Anton Eberhard.[328]

Moll, Peter G., 1989a. 'Public statement of conscience,' submitted to the End Conscription Campaign for inclusion in the 771-strong register of conscientious objectors in 1989, dated 14 June 1989. Filled-in form of 1 page.

Field (1989). See References. Refers to Peter Moll, Philip Wilkinson, Dr. Ivan Toms, David Bruce and Charles Bester.

Moll, Peter G., 1989b. 'Why I am a conscientious objector,' *Baptists Today* (published by the Baptist Union of South Africa), October 1989.[329]

Berat (1989). See References.

UNCAA and COSAWR (1989). See References.

'A short history of COSAWR,' *Resister: Journal of the Committee on South African War Resistance*, no. 67 (Fourth Quarter 1990). Pages 30-34.[330]

Moll, Peter G., 1990. 'Legislative change for alternative national service: past and future', in: Centre for Intergroup Studies, 1990. *Alternative National Service. Occasional Paper No. 14.* Rondebosch: Cape Town. Pages 227-234.

Pastor Joseph Barndt, 1991. 'The End Conscription Campaign in South Africa,' in *Peace Petitions: News for ELCA peacemakers* (published by the Commission for Church and Society of the Evangelical Lutheran Church in America), Fall 1991, pp. 10-12. Refers to Peter Moll, Richard Steele, David Bruce, Charles Bester and Saul Batzofin.

Frederick Hale, 1992. 'Romans 13:1-7 in South African Baptist ethics,' *The South African Baptist Journal of Theology* (Cape

---

[328] Wits, Rob. Coll., A2558-16.

[329] Baptist Theological College, Johannesburg.

[330] Wits, Rob. Coll., A2558-7.

Town), 1992. Pages 66-83. Refers to Peter Moll and Richard Steele.

Rob Robertson, 1994. 'Engaging the powers: some Presbyterian non-violence,' in *Non-Violence News*, First Quarter 1994. Refers to Anton Eberhard, Peter Moll and Richard Steele.[331]

Rob Robertson, 1995. 'The role of the International Fellowship of Reconciliation in South Africa's struggle: Part I: 1974-1982,' in *Non-Violence News*, First Quarter 1995. Refers to Peter Moll and Richard Steele.[332]

Collins (1995). See References.

Peter Moll (1997). See References.

T.A. Moll (1997). See References.

Truth and Reconciliation Commission of South Africa: Report: Volume Four. Presented on 29 October 1998. 318 pages. Quotations from Peter Moll on p. 232.[333]

Robertson (1999). See References.

Phillips (2002). See References.

Frederick Hale (2005 and 2009). See References.

Yeats (2005). See References.

Connors (2007). See References.

Jones (2013). See References.

Webster, Trevor, 2014. 'Resistance and activism,' in: Trevor Webster, 2014. *The Black and White: The Story of the Selborne Schools.* East London: Selborne Foundation Trust. 320 pages. Page 125.

South African National Museum of Military History, display 'Rebels and Objectors', 2023. Refers to Anton Eberhard, Peter Moll, Neil Mitchell, Paul Dobson, Philip Wilkinson,

---

[331] Wits, Rob. Coll., A2558-3.

[332] Wits, Rob. Coll., A2558-3.

[333] TRC Report: available at https://sabctrc.saha.org.za/reports/volume4/chapter8/subsection5.htm.

Ivan Toms, Rev. Douglas Torr, Saul Batzofin, Michael Graaf, David Bruce and Charles Bester.[334]

---

[334] http://militarymuseum.co.za/main.htm.

Appendix H. Motivations of conscientious objectors who refused a specific call-up or training

(The table below does not include exiles, evaders, people who refused call-ups for personal (non-conscientious) reasons, 'peace church' members such as Jehovah's Witnesses, men who did alternative service approved by the Board for Religious Objection, and the 143 objectors of 1988 and the 771 of 1989 etc. since the latter refusals did not necessarily involve a *specific* call-up but involved the refusal of a possible future call-up. The listing is by first court date. A court date in parentheses indicates that the court appearance did not materialise because the charges were dropped or the individual left the country. The motivations in the table are marked 'Yes' only if the objector mentioned them in his written or verbal statement, in or outside of court; otherwise it is marked '?' If you, the reader, fit the criteria of having openly refused a specific call-up for reasons of conscience, please inform me and I shall add your name in the next edition.)

	Universal pacifist	SADF war unjust	Apartheid is unjust	War is a civil war	Religious motive	Invokes 'just / unjust war' criteria	1st court date
Johan van Wyk[i]	Y	Y	Y	?	N	N	26/9/77
Anton Eberhard[ii]	?	Y	Y	?	Y	?	14/12/77
Peter Moll	N	Y	Y	Y	Y	Y	27/12/77

	Uni-ver-sal paci-fist	SADF war un-just	Ap-art-heid is un-just	War is a civil war	Reli-gious mo-tive	Invokes 'just / unjust war' criteria	1st court date
Edric Gorfinkel[iii]	Y	Y	Y	?	Y	N	5/1978
Chris Boshoff	N	Y	N	N	Y	?	17/1/80
Richard Steele	Y	Y[iv]	Y	N	Y	N	25/2/80
Charles Yeats[v, vi]	Y	Y	Y	Y[vii]	Y	Y[viii]	13/5/81
Graham Philpott[ix]	Y	?	?	?	Y	N	(8/81)
Michael Viveiros[x]	Y[xi]	Y	Y	N	Y	Y[xii]	23/2/82
Neil Mitchell[xiii]	Y	N	N	N	Y	N	20/7/82
Billy Paddock[xiv]	N	Y	Y	Y	Y	Y	5/10/82
Etienne Essery[xv]	Y	Y	Y	?	N	N	11/1/83
Adrian Paterson[xvi]	Y	?	Y	N	Y	N	20/1/83
Peter Hathorn[xvii]	N	Y	Y	Y	N	N	22/3/83
Stephen Granger[xviii]	Y	?	?	?	Y	N	24/5/83
Paul Dobson[xix]	N	Y	Y	?	N	N	17/9/83
Brett Myrdal[xx]	N	Y	Y	Y	N	N	(8/11/83)
Anthony Waddell[xxi]	N	Y	Y	Y	N	N	—

	Universal pacifist	SADF war unjust	Apartheid is unjust	War is a civil war	Religious motive	Invokes 'just / unjust war' criteria	1st court date
William Archer[xxii]	Y	?	?	?	Y	?	Late 84
Dr. Mark Nel[xxiii]	?	?	?	?	?	?	(20/2/85)
Alan Dodson[xxiv]	?	Y	Y	?	?	?	13/8/85
David Pijpers[xxv]	N	Y	?	?	?	?	Late 85
Philip Wilkinson[xxvi]	Y	Y	Y	Y	Y	N	23/5/86
Ivan Toms[xxvii]	Y	Y	Y	Y	Y	Y	12/11/87
David Bruce[xxviii]	N	Y	Y	Y	N	N	11/4/88
Ernst Tamsen[xxix]	?	Y	N	?	?	?	19/7/88
Jakobus Nel	?	Y	N	?	?	?	13/9/88
Charles Bester[xxx]	Y	Y	Y	Y	Y	N	3/10/88
Tam Alexander[xxxi]	?	Y	Y	?	?	?	(25/10/88)
Brendan Butler[xxxii]	?	Y	?	?	?	?	?
Richard Clacey[xxxiii]	N	Y	Y	?	N	N	7/11/88
Saul Batzofin[xxxiv]	N	Y	Y	?	N	N	<15/2/89
Michael Graaf[xxxv]	N	Y	Y	?	N	?	18/12/89

	Universal pacifist	SADF war unjust	Apartheid is unjust	War is a civil war	Religious motive	Invokes 'just / unjust war' criteria	1st court date
Douglas Torr[xxxvi]	Y	Y	Y	Y	Y	N	8/1/90
David Schmidt[xxxvii]	Y	—	—	—	Y	—	—
Andre Croucamp[xxxviii]	Y	?	?	?	Y	?	8/1/90
Gary Rathbone[xxxix]	N	Y	Y	Y	N	N	27/3/90
Louis Bredenkamp	N	Y	Y[xl]	?	N	N	—
Gavin Kirk[xli]	?	?	?	?	?	?	(16/5/90)
Alan Storey[xlii]	Y	?	Y	?	Y	N	15/4/91
Garth Damerell-Moss	?	?[xliii]	?	?	?	?	4/91
Peter auf der Heyde[xliv]	?	?	?	?	?	?	<6/91
Walter Rontsch[xlv]	?	?	?	?	?	?	17/6/91
Telford Vice[xlvi]	?	?	?	?	?	?	—
Clyde Wynter[xlvii]	?	?	?	?	?	?	(6/91)
Wayne Boshler[xlviii]	?	?	?	?	?	?	(6/91)
Cobus de Swardt[xlix]	?	Y	Y	?	?	?	—
Brendan	N	Y	Y	?	Y	N	—

	Universal pacifist	SADF war unjust	Apartheid is unjust	War is a civil war	Religious motive	Invokes 'just / unjust war' criteria	1st court date
Moran[l]							
Koos de Kock[li]	?	?	?	?	?	?	—
Warren van Rooyen[lii]	?	?	?	?	?	?	—
Francois Krige[liii]	?	Y	Y	?	?	?	—
Gerald O'Sullivan[liv]	?	Y	Y	?	?	?	—
Fritz Joubert[lv]	?	?	?	?	?	?	—
John Downie[lvi]	?	?	?	?	?	?	24/11/92
John Kelley[lvii]	?	?	?	?	?	?	24/11/92
Bruce Colin Schwan	N	Y[lviii]	Y	Y	N	N	—

---

[i] Johan van Wyk from Boksburg was called up on 6 July 1977 for basic training. He refused because he "did not believe in violence" and because he objected on political grounds (see 'Biography' in https://johanvanwyk.oblogs.co.za/). He admitted to being "the first white to refuse to go into the army for political reasons" (see literarytourism.co.za/johan-van-wyk/). He was arrested in early September 1977 by the military police and placed in the Detention Barracks for a night but after a breakdown was taken for psychiatric treatment at the Voortrekkerhoogte Military Hospital for two weeks (see 'Polisie vat digter: Belowende kunstenaar het beswaar teen diensplig', *Rapport Extra,* 11 September 1977). He refused a non-combatant position. He was tried on 26 September 1977 and sentenced to 15 months' imprisonment, suspended for three years, and returned home—see 'Johan se "dilemma" begin voor,' *Beeld*, 27 September 1977. He was later discharged

from military duty on account of his psychological condition. He continued to live in South Africa and pursued a career as a university professor in Afrikaans.

ⁱ Anton Adriaan Eberhard belonged to the Trinity Baptist Church in Port Elizabeth. Rev. E.D. Marshall, assistant minister, witnessed at the court case—see 'Guilty plea by objector,' *EP Herald*, 14 December 1977. (Wits, SAIRR Coll., ZA HPRA AD1912A-S236.5.) Eberhard stated to the magistrate's court that his stand was based on scripture, that he was a committed Christian, and that he attended church regularly—see 'Christian won't go into army', *Rand Daily Mail* (14 December 1977). The article was reproduced in full in: *South African Outlook* vol. 108, no. 1287 (September 1978), p. 142; see Wits, Rob. Coll., A2558-15.8. Rev. Rob Robertson asked his parishioners to pray for Anton Eberhard, who was a member of the church—see 'Pray for objector–minister,' *The Star*, 28 January 1978. (Wits, SAIRR Coll., ZA HPRA AD1912A-S236.7.) Eberhard's trial was on 14 December 1977; he wrote to the Officer Commanding, "I believe the current system of government to be totally unjust. Not only does it not govern with the consent of the majority of the people in South Africa, but it is only able to maintain its position through violence … These beliefs are strengthened by my Christian convictions."—see p. 8 of: Billy Paddock, 1982. 'Why I object to service in the SADF: statement by Billy Paddock, October 1982,' booklet of eleven pages, published by C.O.S.G. (Durban). (Wits, Rob. Coll., A2558-9.16 Billy Paddock.) Eberhard was a member of St. Anthony's United Church from 1977 to 1979, and led a service there in November 1978—Robertson (1999:76).

ⁱⁱⁱ Edric Gorfinkel: My own recollections from talking with him and from attending his court case. See also Anonymous, 1983. 'Conscientious objection in SA' (1983). (Wits, Rob. Coll., A2558-12.3.)

ⁱᵛ Richard Steele is quoted by Kearney (1980, p. 13) as writing: "… as far as I can see, the military is one of the central features of *apartheid* and what is maintaining its power, and so I see my stand as non-cooperation with the *apartheid* structure." Steele said, "The army is a very strong pillar of apartheid and by not signing up to help support that pillar I am also making my feelings known about apartheid"—Marian Shinn, 1980. 'Teacher faces court martial,' *Sunday Express*, 24 February 1980. (Wits, SAIRR Coll., ZA HPRA AD1912A-S236.9.) See also the summary of evidence to be presented by Richard Steele at his court-martial on 25 February 1980, where Richard stated, "central to my being a peacemaker is the pursuit of justice. I view the SADF as being a major pillar of a fundamentally unjust political, social and economic system: by co-operating with the military I would be

representing and perpetuating those injustices and I am unwilling to do so."
Reference: Richard Steele, 1980. 'Grounds for conscientious objection.'
Kempton Park: typewritten manuscript, dated 23 February 1980. 1 page.
(Wits, Rob. Coll., A2558-9.20.) See also David Jones (2013: 37): at the 25th
anniversary of the End Conscription Campaign, Richard Steele noted that the
early objectors were perceived as being religious rather than political
objectors. He stressed that these objectors' moral orientation had originated
in religious commitments. He commented, "The fact is we were using
religious language to help us understand what our values and principles were.
We were clear that we were making a political decision with political intent
and consequences." In turn quoted from *End Conscription Campaign 25*
(2009).

[v] Charles Yeats: See his autobiography (2005): pacifism, p. 76;
indefensibility of *apartheid*, p. 74; rejection of 'just war', p. 76. See also his
'Why I am a conscientious objector to war' (1981) (Wits, ECC Coll., ZA
HPRA AG1977-A24.4.3).

[vi] Charles Yeats's trial date: from p. 2 of: Anonymous, n.d.
'Conscientious objection in SA'. Typewritten manuscript, 1983. 5 pages.
(Wits, Rob. Coll., A2558-12.3).

[vii] Rev. Rob Robertson wrote, "[Charles Yeats'] view is that there is civil
war in South Africa and that the border war in SWA is part of that. SA's
presence there is illegal and confirms his objection to military service." See
page 1 of: Rob Robertson, 1981. 'The trial of Charles Yeats,' typescript
document duplicated by Gestetner, May 1981. 6 pages. (Wits, Rob. Coll.,
A2558-1.

[viii] Just/unjust war criteria: Charles Yeats distinguished between wars
"which appear to be avoidable by means of a negotiated settlement, and those
which do not. In wars where a negotiated settlement is clearly not possible, I
would be prepared to serve as a noncombatant." But he notes that in South
Africa it does appear possible to avert war by involving representative Black
leaders in a political settlement. Therefore he was not willing even to be a
noncombatant.

[ix] Graham Philpott: p. 6 of UNCAA and COSAWR (1989). Philpott was
a theology student called up to be a chaplain. After reporting for duty, he
refused to be trained in the use of a rifle in his basic training—*Daily
Dispatch*, 17 November 1981. Philpott wrote, "I am a conscientious non-
combatant. By this I mean that I am willing to be conscripted to do military
national service and be a member of the South African Defence Force, but
that I have conscientious objections to being trained for, and to serving in a
unit not recognised as non-combatant by the Geneva Convention on War.

This Convention recognises the Chaplaincy and Medical Corps as non-combatant units."—see Graham Philpott, 1981. 'My reasons for being a conscientious non-combatant,' Pretoria, typewritten manuscript (16 November 1981). 7 pages. (Wits, Rob. Coll., A2558-9.18 Graham Philpott. As of 16 July 1981, Chaplain Andrew van den Aardweg had become involved—see notes by Rob Robertson (Wits, Rob. Coll.,. A2558-9.18. Philpott appeared before a court-martial on 16 November 1981 but the trial was cancelled and he was advised he would be told later what the SADF required of him—see 'Conscientious objection,' in *Non-violence news*, First Quarter 1982, p. 2. (Wits, Rob. Coll., A2558-3.)

[x] Mike Viveiros: UNCAA and COSAWR (1989) quotes him as arguing that "By heeding the call-up of SADF, I would be required to defend the present system, a result of apartheid ideology, which is contrary to the teachings of Jesus Christ." In turn from *Resister* (London), no. 19, April/May 1982; and *Resister* (London), no. 20, June/July 1982. Mike Viveiros's trial date is from p. 2 of: 'Conscientious objection in SA'. Typewritten manuscript, 1983. 5 pages. (Wits, Rob. Coll., A2558-12.3.)

[xi] Mike Viveiros a pacifist: "Viveiros told the court he was a pacifist," according to the report 'Confidence is SADF eroded, court told,' *Argus*, 23 February 1982.

[xii] Criteria for a just war: he wrote that he would enter the military as a non-combatant if "all reasonable steps have been taken to avoid [the conflict]", among which would be "a national convention of all representative leaders." But so far negotiations have been undertaken "on the Government's terms with black leaders who have little or no grassroots support," so the conflict of the SADF is not a last resort. See Michael Viveiros, 1982a. 'Statement on conscientious objection—Michael Viveiros,' typewritten manuscript. 2 pages. (Wits, Rob. Coll., A2558-9.24.)

[xiii] Neil Mitchell: See 'Why I am a universal pacifist conscientious objector' in CIIR and Pax Christi (1982:89-93). Neil Mitchell's trial date of 20 July 1982 is from UNCAA and COSAWR (1989:6). BUT NOTE that in a letter from the Detention Barracks he wrote, "One thing that has bothered me is that at my court-martial, and in my statement, I did not give enough attention to the 'just war/political' aspect of my CO stand ... The South African political set-up is so fundamentally unjust and oppressive, and the SADF so clearly exists to uphold and keep intact this unjust set-up. To serve in the SADF would mean assenting to the very injustice which, as a 'peacemaker,' one should be endeavouring to eliminate..."—see p. 3 of: 'Neil Mitchell: Christian Witness for peace & justice,' printed pamphlet published by supporters, 1983. 4 pages. (Wits, Rob. Coll., A2558-9.12.)

[xiv] Billy Paddock: see 'Why I say no to collaboration with the SADF' in CIIR and Pax Christi (1982:95-102). Billy Paddock's first trial date is from UNCAA and COSAWR (1989:6).

[xv] Etienne Essery: Actor and writer. Concerning pacifism, he wrote, "I will not support any war and I will certainly not support this war." (Etienne Essery, n.d. 'Statement,' 3 pages. Wits, Rob. Coll., A2558-9.9.) Concerning the injustice of *apartheid*, he wrote, "This institutionalised violence has set brother against brother and deported whole families to 'pie in the sky' reserves ... This unequal society is violent ... using 'unjustifiable force' to perpetuate it." (Essery, *ibid.*) Jones (2013:43) notes that Essery said to the court that the lack of respect for human life that he saw in the operational area clarified his opposition to war. He wanted "to make a non-violent statement in the midst of all the violence". Another source referred to in Wikipedia is: *Mail & Guardian*, 28 August 2008 (re jail sentence). Etienne Essery's trial date of 'January 1983' is from Connors (2007:75). The date of 11 January 1983 appears in notes by Rob Robertson (Wits, Rob. Coll., A2558-12.3). Essery had been released by May 1983—see 'Minutes of Durban C.O. Support Group meeting held on 17th May, 1983' (Wits, Rob. Coll., A2558-12.3.)

[xvi] Adrian Paterson was named a "universal religious pacifist" by Jones (2013: 44). Paterson's trial date of 20 January 1983 is from p. 2 of: 'Conscientious objection in SA'. Typewritten manuscript, 1983. 5 pages. (Wits, Rob. Coll., A2558-12.3). He wrote, "I am a pacifist because of Christ and I hate and reject apartheid because of the Gospel. Therefore I identify myself with all genuine non-violent mechanisms of social transformation in South Africa that serve the interests of justice, peace, liberal freedoms and the redistribution of wealth."—see Adrian Paterson, 1982b. 'Reasons for Christian pacifism and responses to the South African dilemma—one person's view,' typewritten manuscript, 1982. 10 pages. (Wits, Rob. Coll., A2558-9.17.)

[xvii] Hathorn stated: "Since the conflict in this country is a civil not an external war, participation in the SADF is a profoundly political action. Participation does not act in the interest of the nation as a whole, but contributed only to the cause of the dominant minority....To go into the SADF is to take sides in the struggle in this country." Quoted by Jones (2013:50), in turn from 'Conscientious Objector Jailed,' *The Star*, 23 March 1983. Also, see his complete statement: Peter Hathorn, 1983. 'Dissension in the ranks: an argument for conscientious objection.' Ad Hoc Support Committee, SRC Press, University of Cape Town. 10 pages.

xviii Stephen Granger objected to a camp in 1983 on the grounds of Christian pacifism. The date of his court case, 24 May 1983, is from: 'Minutes of Durban C.O. Support Group meeting held on 17th May, 1983.' (Wits, Rob. Coll., A2558-6.) He was tried in Bloemfontein and owing to the change in the law in 1983, he was sentenced to 14 days of community work in the library of the Department of Land Affairs in Cape Town (personal communication, 1 February 2023). He was placed on reserve because he had done basics before 1973—see 'Minutes of Durban CO Support Group meeting held on 21 June 1983.' (Wits, Rob. Coll., A2558-6.)

xix Paul Dobson: see Jones (2013:52) where Dobson is quoted as saying that he could not be associated with the SADF "which serves to protect and reproduce an unjust society." In turn from 'Prison and discharge for army objector,' in *Daily News*, 10 September 1983. Paul Dobson's trial date: from p. 2 of: 'Conscientious objection in SA'. Typewritten manuscript, 1983. 5 pages. (Wits, Rob. Coll., A2558-12.3.) The trial date of Saturday 17 September 1983 is from 'Minutes of the C.O.S.G. meeting held at the Rondebosch Congregational Church on Tuesday 13th September 1983,' (Wits, Rob. Coll., A2558-12.3).

xx Brett Myrdal publicly refused a call-up for basic training at the Potchefstroom Medical Services Corps in July 1983 (Jones 2013: 44). He was charged and required to appear before a court-martial at Voortrekkerhoogte on 8 November 1983—Brett Myrdal, 1983. 'Speech delivered by Brett Myrdal 29 September 1983 at NUSAS UCT mass meeting: "Students reject the apartheid constitution."' Typed manuscript, 3 pages. (Wits, ECC Coll., ZA-HPRA AG1977-E1 (1.3)). He planned to argue in court that the SADF was waging a civil war (Jones 2013: 53). On 7 November 1983, the day before his trial, the charges were withdrawn and he was informed that he would be called up again in 1984; in terms of the new legislation of 1983, he would then face six years' jail if he refused— 'Solidarity night: Brett Myrdal: conscientious objector: R'bosch Congregational Church, 11 November [1983],' advertisement, published by Social Action for COSG, printed on UCT SRC Press. 2 pages. (Wits, ECC Coll., ZA-HPRA AG1977-E1 (1.3).

xxi Anthony Waddell: Called up for initial training in July 1984, he failed to report, was arrested on 12 October 1984, and taken to the Wynberg Detention Barracks. He knew he could be liable for six years in prison. After ten days he was taken to the Voortrekkerhoogte DB for a preliminary investigation. He was kept in solitary and in silence for ten days in Block Five. A procedural error was uncovered involving a mistaken address, so he was not brought to trial. His service was deferred and he was released—see

Louw (1984). He was then issued with call-up papers for January 1985—see Anthony Waddell, 1984. 'Letters to Objector,' Objector, Vol. 2 no. 7, issued by COSG, Woodstock, [December 1984], p. 12. (Wits, ECC Coll., AG1977-H9.4.) It is not known what happened subsequently.

xxii William Archer was a Jehovah's Witness. He started his training in the Reconnaissance Commando in January 1984. His application to the Board for Religious Objection was rejected on 8 August 1984 on grounds of insincerity because he had applied for alternative service only after having been refused a posting closer to home. Nevertheless he refused service, was court-martialled and sentenced to 75 months' jail. This was reduced to 63 months on review, of which 36 were suspended. The COSG declared its "solidarity and support with William in his courageous stand"—see 'Jailed for 6 years,' Objector, vol. 2 no. 7, issued by Conscientious Objector Support Group, Woodstock (Cape Town), [December 1984], p. 2; and editorial, p. 6. (UCT, Nathan Coll., BC912 B19 (2)). Also see 'Conscientious objection,' Non-Violence News, First Quarter 1988. (Wits, Rob. Coll., A2558-3.)

xxiii Mark Nel, a Wits medical student and a member of the NUSAS Health Directive, was charged for failing to report for a police camp. He had done his initial training with the police. He was to have appeared in a Durban court on 20 February 1985. Due to a technicality, charges were dropped.—'Legal technicality gives reprieve,' Objector: Newsletter of the Conscientious Objector Support Group, Vol. 3, no. 1 (March-April 1985), p. 2. (Wits, ECC Coll., AG1977-H9.4.) He intended to appeal to the Minister of Police—'Minutes of the Durban COSG held on February 21, 1985' (Wits, Rob. Coll., A2558-12.3.) It is not known whether he was called up again.

xxiv Alan Dodson, a Cape Town articled clerk, was on a one-month camp when he refused to go on a township patrol. He had explained his opposition to the use of conscripts to quell township anti-apartheid resistance. He was court-martialled in Durban and sentenced to a fine of R600—see UNCAA and COSAWR (1989: 9), Jones (2013:75), and 'Dodson defies,' Objector: Newsletter of the Conscientious Objector Support Group, Vol. 3 – no. 3 (August/September 1985), p. 3. (Wits, ECC Coll., AG1977-H9.4.)

xxv David Pijpers volunteered for service in the Cape Corps (the unit for coloured members of the Permanent Force) under a five-year contract. As he came to understand the SADF role during service in Namibia he decided to refuse further service and deserted repeatedly, each time being arrested and placed in the Detention Barracks. He was facing a court-martial in late 1985—see 'Some say no,' advertisement for a panel at the End Conscription Campaign Peace Festival, July 1985. (Wits, ECC Coll., AG1977-E1.2.) See also 'For peace and justice,' Objector: Newsletter of the Conscientious

Objector Support Group, Vol. 3 – no. 3 (August/September 1985), p. 3. (Wits, ECC Coll., AG1977-H9.4.) See also 'Support for a "just peace" is growing, ECC festival told,' *The Star*, 1 July 1985. (Wits, SAIRR Coll., ZA HPRA AD1912A-S236.16.)

xxvi Philip Wilkinson, from Port Elizabeth, applied to the Board for Religious Objection. His motive was judged by some supporters as "not pacifist."—see 'Conscientious Objectors Support Group: 19/2/86' (Wits, Rob. Coll., A2558-6.jpg.) But Wilkinson wrote, "I am committed to peace … I abhor all violence … all armies legitimise the use of violence … I must therefore follow the path of non-violence."—see 'Conscientious objector: Philip Wilkinson', pamphlet issued by the Philip Wilkinson Support Group, 1985. 2 pages. (Wits, ECC Coll., ZA-HPRA AG1977-E1 (1.1).) In the same pamphlet, Wilkinson wrote, "We are in a situation of civil war." His application for Category 3 was rejected; he was expecting a call-up and intended to refuse to report for duty—see 'Minutes of the CO Support meeting 16 April 1986' (Wits, Rob. Coll., A2558-6.) Wilkinson's first trial date was for Friday 23 May 1986—see 'Minutes of the COSG meeting (Durban), 21/5/86' (Wits, Rob. Coll., A2558-6.) Wilkinson's motives are summarised on p. 10 of UNCAA and COSAWR (1989). Wilkinson had another trial date of 29 July 1986, in Port Elizabeth—see 'Minutes of the COSG meeting of 1 August 1986' (Wits, Rob. Coll., A2558-6.) Wilkinson's final trial date of 'May 1987' is also from UNCAA and COSAWR (1989), p. 10.

xxvii Ivan Toms: see Jones (2013:115). Ivan Toms first appeared in the Goodwood Magistrate's Court on 12 November 1987, and was charged— Dale Lautenbach and Jeremy Dowson, 1987. 'Toms refuses to serve, arrested,' *The Argus*, 12 November 1987. (Wits, ECC Col., ZA-HPRA AG1977-E1 (1.2).) The case came to trial on 3 March 1988—UNCAA and COSAWR (1989:12). Universal pacifist: he wrote, "Later when I was sent to the operational area, I realised that to kill another person was impossible for me to reconcile with my conscience. I applied for and was given noncombatant status."—see Ivan Toms, 1988. 'Why I refuse to serve in the SADF: statement by Lieutenant Ivan Toms,' typewritten manuscript, no month or day [but from the contents, 22 February 1988]. 4 pages. (Wits, Rob. Coll., A2558-9.22.) Civil war: he said, "in a civil war you have to take sides,"—see Dale Lautenbach and Jeremy Dowson, 1987. 'Toms refuses to serve, arrested,' *Argus*, 12 November 1987. (Wits, ECC Coll., ZA-HPRA AG1977-E1 (1.2).) Religious motive: he wrote, "I have always tried to be true to my beliefs, especially since coming to a deep Christian commitment."—page 1 of *ibid.* 'Just war': he said he did not qualify for religious objector status because he would be willing to serve as a non-combatant in a 'just war'—see Dale Lautenbach, 1987. 'Objector willing to serve in 'just war',' *Argus*, 11 November 1987. (Wits, ECC Coll., ZA-HPRA AG1977-E1 (1.2) Ivan Toms.)

xxviii David Bruce: UNCAA and COSAWR (1989:15). Bruce referred to his family's experience in Nazi Germany in this way: "Being aware, as I am, of how European Jews and in fact the entire people of Eastern Europe suffered during the period of the Holocaust, I feel that I have no choice but to set myself against those who choose the path of increasing racial intolerance and racial hatred in the firmest way which is possible to me." In turn from *Resister* (London), No. 57, August/September 1988. David Bruce's final trial date of 25 July 1988 is also from UNCAA and COSAWR (1989). Bruce's first court appearance was at the Johannesburg Magistrate's Court was on 11 April 1988—see 'Minutes of the Johannesburg COSG meeting 30 March 1988' (Wits, Rob. Coll., A2558-6.) Unjust war: David Bruce said in court, "I would be willing to serve in an army which is involved in fighting for and defending all the people of this country. I am not prepared to serve in the defence of a racist political system." From Jones (2013:121f), in turn from 'Morals and the Law,' *Financial Mail*, 29 July 1988. Concerning civil war, he wrote, "The SADF is involved in defending the privileged position of a minority of South Africans in what is basically a civil war."—see David Bruce, 1988. 'Why I refuse to serve in the SADF: David Bruce on trial 19 July: Johannesburg: Waarom ek weier om in die SAW te dien.' Pamphlet issued by COSG, ECC, JODAC, NUSAS. 2 pages. (Wits, Rob. Coll., A2558-9.6.)

xxix Ernst Tamsen and Jakobus Nel: members of the right-wing Herstigte Nasionale Party, they were charged for not reporting to camps and given suspended sentences (Nel, 18 months suspended for 5 years, Grahamstown Magistrate's Court, 13 September 1988; Tamsen, 26 September 1988, court unknown, length of sentence unknown). Tamsen's first appearance was at the Johannesburg Magistrate's Court on 19 July 1988—see Jones (2013:216), and 'Conscientious objection,' *Non-Violence News,* Second Quarter 1988. (Wits, Rob. Coll., A2558-3), and 'Conscientious objection,' in *Non-Violence News*, Third Quarter 1988. (Wits, Rob. Coll., A2558-3.)

xxx Charles Bester's court case was originally scheduled for 3 October 1988—see 'Minutes of the COSG meeting held on 21 September 1988' (Wits, Rob. Coll., A2558-6). The date of Bester's final trial (5 December 1988) is from UNCAA and COSAWR (1989:16). Bester told the court that as a Christian he could have no part in the "evil perpetrated by the SADF." Quoted on p. 126 of Jones (2013). In turn quoted from 'Conscientious objector jailed for six years,' *The Star,* 6 December 1988. Pacifism: he wrote, "I must pursue the way of reconciliation and non-violence."—see 'Charles Bester: why I won't serve,' typewritten manuscript, n.d., 4 pages (Wits, Rob. Coll., A2558-9.4). Unjust war: Bester said, "In South Africa, we have lived and are living under a political system which belies the fundamental tenets of Christianity... The ideology of apartheid has been responsible for untold human suffering and humiliation in the pursuit of power by a small minority." From UNCAA and COSAWR (1989:16), in turn quoted from *New Nation* (Johannesburg), 29 September 1988. Civil war: he wrote "We have exported a civil war into our neighboring countries." (see pp. 2-3 of his 'Charles Bester: Why I won't serve'). Religious: see the poster at https://www.saha.org.za/ecc25/charles_bester_conscientious_objec tor_on_trial.htm saying 'Charles Bester: Conscientious objector: Christ's way - Yes! SADF – No!'

xxxi Tam Alexander, a member of the '143' and a member of the ECC, was called up for a twelve-day 'Dad's army' camp for 3 October 1988. He reported, refused to serve, and was held for a day by the Military Police before being released. His trial was set for 25 October 1988. He left the country before that date—Richard Steele, 1988. 'Conscientious objection—current trends (based on the case of Tam Alexander).' typewritten manuscript, Durban, October 1988. 4 pages. (Wits, ECC Coll., ZA-HPRA AG1977-E1 (1.23)).

xxxii Brendan Butler did his national service in 1977 and subsequently did seven camps. He was called up for a 60-day camp due to start on 30 November 1987. He wrote to the Officer Commanding of 4 Parachute Battalion on 26 November 1987, stating that his conscience dictated that he no longer serve in the SADF in any capacity, and that he would not report on 30 November. As his reason for refusal he cited the "atrocities committed by the SADF in various African countries"(Wits, ECC Coll., ZA-HPRA AG1977-E1.2).

xxxiii Richard Clacey, a field worker for the Association for Rural Advancement in Pietermaritzburg, referred to the "oppressive role that the SADF was playing in the townships," and "the irrationality, the brutality and the moral indefensibility of the apartheid system."— Richard Clacey, 1989. 'Statement of Richard Clacey: 16 January 1989,' typewritten manuscript. 7 pages. (Wits, ECC Coll., ZA-HPRA AG1977-E1 (1.34).) Clacey was originally called up for 11 December 1987—see his letter to the Officer Commanding, 15 Maintenance Unit, Durban, on 16 November 1987 (Wits, ECC Coll., ZA-HPRA AG1977-E1.2.) Clacey's first trial was scheduled for 7 November 1988 in Pietermaritzburg—see 'Minutes of the Conscientious

Objectors Support Group meeting, held on October 19, 1988' (Wits, Rob. Coll., A2558-6.) He had 3 charges pending: fraud, failing to report and refusal to serve—see 'Minutes of the Conscientious Objectors Support Group meeting, held on 21 September 1988'. Finally, prior to May 1990, all charges against Clacey were dropped after representations were made to the Minister of Defence by the Democratic Party—see see 'Minutes of the Durban Conscientious Objector Support Group meeting, held on Wednesday 16 May'.

[xxxiv] Saul Batzofin did his initial service as a corporal in the SADF in Ovamboland. He was one of the 143 resisters of 1988. He wrote, "I came to see that the SADF was being used as a part of a repressive strategy to uphold the apartheid system, and was not acting in the interests of the broad South African community." See UNCAA and COSAWR (1989:17). He claimed that the violence of the SADF against ordinary people led him to object, according to Jones (2013:127), in turn from 'Why I refused call-up,' *City Press*, 19 March 1989. Batzofin appeared in court for the first time on 15 February 1989—see 'Minutes of the Conscientious Objectors Support Group meeting held on the 15 February 1989' (Wits, Rob. Coll., A2558-6.) Batzofin's final trial was remanded to 12 April 1989—see 'Minutes of the March 21 1989 meeting of Durban COSG.'

[xxxv] Michael Graaf was a second lieutenant in the SADF citizen force in 1980. He refused a camp call-up on Friday 15 December 1989, and appeared in the Pietermaritzburg Magistrate's Court the following Monday, viz. 18 December 1989—'Press conference: Tuesday 15 May, 1990: Profile on objectors who have been imprisoned: Profile of objectors awaiting trial,' provenance not cited. 4 pages. (Wits, ECC Coll., ZA-HPRA AG1977-E1 (1.26) Douglas Torr.) Graaf appeared in court again on 13 February 1990 in Pietermaritzburg— 'Minutes of the Durban Conscientious Objector Support Group, held on Wednesday 17 January 1990' (Wits, Rob. Coll., A2558-6.) Graaf was sentenced on 28 November 1990 to one year in prison, suspended for four years on condition that he perform 2,400 hours of community service. He refused by stating that one should make one's individual decision based on informed understanding and one's own conscience—see 'Michael Graaf testifies about SADF activities in Namibia,' *Objector* (November/December 1990), p. 1. (Wits, Rob. Coll., A2558-6.) By June 1991 he had been granted political indemnity and the community service came to an end. See 'Update on South African war resistance issues,' *The Objector* (September 1991), page 5.

[xxxvi] Rev. Douglas Torr, an Anglican priest, was a universal pacifist and also argued, "From an ideological point of view, apartheid is a heresy.

Because SADF supports apartheid policy by maintaining the state of emergency, I can have nothing to do with it."—see p. 19 of UNCAA and COSAWR (1989); the quote is in turn from *The Weekly Mail* (Johannesburg), 18 August 1989. On civil war, he wrote: "The SADF, in fact, is a key agent in creating and maintaining a civil war."—see Douglas Torr, 1990. 'Statement of conscience: Reverend Douglas Torr,' included with the order of service for the vigil of support at Christ the King church; 13 May 1990. 4 pages. (Wits, Rob. Coll., A2558-9.23 Douglas Torr.) On universal pacifism, he wrote, "My role as a celebrant, or assistant, in [the Lord's Supper] makes it impossible for me to participate in acts of aggression and violence."—see p. 3 of *ibid.* He was sentenced to twelve months' imprisonment, but was released on bail while making an appeal. He was eventually sentenced to community service (Jones 2013:135). Torr's call-up was for 30 July 1990—see "A new wave: profile of objectors awaiting trial," *Objector: Newsletter of the Conscientious Objectors Support Group* (April/May 1990), p. 7. (Wits, ECC Coll., AG1977-H9.4 The Objector). Torr's first trial date of 8 January 1990 is from 'Minutes of the Durban Conscientious Objector Support Group, held on Wednesday 17 January 1990' (Wits, Rob. Coll., A2558-6).

xxxvii David Schmidt was accepted by the Board for Religious Objection as a religious objector in 1984, and commenced a six-year stint of alternative service. On 31 October 1989 he declared his intention to discontinue alternative service in a letter to the Minister of Defence. His reasons were that the sentences for conscientious objectors had not been reduced *pari passu* with the reductions in national service obligations; and that conscientious objectors such as David Bruce were being treated more harshly than common criminals, who could receive remission and parole of up to two-thirds of their sentences. By ceasing to perform service he exposed himself to a possible twelve months' imprisonment—see 'Community server says no to further service,' *The Objector* (December 1989), p. 5. (Wits, ECC Coll.. AG1977-H9.4.)

xxxviii Andre Croucamp: a theologian by training who refused to do a camp on 18 December 1989—'Press conference: Tuesday 15 May, 1990: Profile on objectors who have been imprisoned: Profile of objectors awaiting trial,' provenance not cited. 4 pages. (Wits, ECC Coll., AG1977-E1 (1.26) Douglas Torr.) Croucamp was charged in December 1989—Jones (2013:132). He first appeared in court at the same time as Rev. Douglas Torr, on 8 January 1990. His stand was not explicitly political. His trial was remanded to 26 March 1990—see 'Minutes of the Durban Conscientious Objector Support Group, held on Wednesday 17 January 1990' (Wits, Rob. Coll., A2558-6.) In June 1990, charges were withdrawn because the Board for Religious Objection accepted his application for C.O. status—see 'War resisters update,' *Resister: Journal of the Committee on South African War Resistance*, no. 67 (Fourth Quarter 1990). Page 27 (Wits, Rob. Coll., A2558-7.)

[xxxix] Gary Rathbone was charged for refusing service in January 1990—see 'Update on South African war resistance issues, May 1990,' *Objector: Newsletter of the Conscientious Objectors Support Group* (April/May 1990), p. 2. (Wits, ECC Coll., AG1977-H9.4.) Rathbone was tried for the third time in May 1990 but was acquitted because the military was unable to prove its case; he had already served three years in the Permanent Force and thus could be deemed to have completed his obligations—Jones (2013:133). See also Gary Rathbone, 1990. 'My trial as an objector,' *The Objector* (August 1990), p. 3. (Wits, Rob. Coll., A2558-6.) For the date of the first court appearance, 27 March 1990: see 'Gary Rathbone—conscientious objector,' typescript, press release by the Gary Rathbone Support Group, n.d. 1 page. (Wits, ECC Coll., AG1977-E1 (1.28).) On civil war: Gary Rathbone stated "By serving in the SADF I feel that one is taking sides in a war being waged against fellow South Africans"—see 'Gary Rathbone: conscientious objector on trial,' pamphlet issued by the Gary Rathbone Support Group (Troyeville), n.d. 2 pages. (Wits, Rob. Coll., A2558-9.19.)

[xl] Louis Bredenkamp, a student at the University of Pretoria, sent an affidavit to the Exemption Board on 21 June 1990, refusing to attend an 18-day camp to start on 18 June 1990, and requesting exemption. His refusal was based on "conscience and … political affiliations," that the SADF played "an oppressive role" and given the intimidation that it practised against people in Mamelodi township, and intimidation against himself, he found it "morally impossible to render service in the SADF"; and his membership of the ANC would be compromised if he were forced to serve in the SADF. He was later told that his call-up to the camp was cancelled—see Louis Bredenkamp, 1990. 'Affidavit: application for exemption,' letter to the SADF Exemption Board, 21 June 1990, signed at Johannesburg. 9 pages. (Wits, ECC Coll., AG1977-E1 (1.30) Louis Bredenkamp.) Also see: Philippa Garson, 1990. 'Call-up cancelled for ANC objector,' Daily Mail, 27 June 1990.

[xli] Gavin Michael Kirk, a student at the Baptist Theological College in Johannesburg from 1989 to 1990, had by May 1990 already appeared in court four times on a charge of refusing to serve in the SADF. The charge related to a call-up for a one morning parade. He was next to appear on 16 May 1990—'Press conference: Tuesday 15 May, 1990: Profile on objectors who have been imprisoned: Profile of objectors awaiting trial,' provenance not cited. 4 pages. (Wits, ECC Coll., AG1977-E1 (1.26) Douglas Torr.) See also

a letter of support from the Western Cape Branch of the Fellowship of Concerned Baptists, signed by Peter Steinegger, dated 15 May 1990. (Wits, ECC Coll., AG1977-E1 (1.34).)

[xlii] Alan Storey, a Methodist minister, could have applied to the Board for Religious Objection, but said he did not want to take advantage of a soft option that was not available to non-religious people. He refused military service on the basis of religious pacifism—see 'Community service ... the Rev. Douglas Torr: No more jail for objectors?' *Weekly Mail*, 24 May 1991. (Wits, ECC Coll., AG1977-E1 (1.26) Douglas Torr.) On *apartheid* as a reason for objecting: Storey wrote, "Apartheid is a violent system maintained by the use of force and over the years it has produced a 'culture of violence' in which human life has been cheapened. The use of force in resisting Apartheid has also contributed to this 'culture of violence'... I believe that all violence in South Africa–whether intended to maintain or change the status quo–needs to be challenged by a radical refusal to use this means."— see 'Statement of conscience: The Rev. Alan Storey,' typewritten document, 7 pages, unsigned, n.d.) (Wits, ECC Coll., AG1977-E1.2.) Storey was arrested in March 1991 and first appeared in court on 15 April 1991—see 'Reverend Alan Storey: conscientious objector: On trial for non-violence... The Methodist Order of Peacemakers Pledge,' pamphlet issued by the Conscientious Objectors Support Group with the Methodist Order of Peacemakers, Johannesburg, n.d. 2 sides of 1 page. (Wits, ECC Coll., A2558-9.21 Alan Storey.) Storey's trial was postponed to 17 June 1991—see 'Imprisonment for refusal to serve is virtually a thing of the past,' *The Objector* (February/March 1991), p. 2 (Wits, Rob. Coll., A2558-6). Jones (2013) says that in June 1991 charges were withdrawn.

[xliii] Garth Damerell-Moss, an ANC member, appeared in the Magistrate's Court in Port Elizabeth in April 1991, charged with failing to report for a camp in 1990. The case was postponed to 3 June 1991—'Update on South African war resistance issues,' *The Objector* (June 1991), p. 5 (Wits, ECC Coll., AG1977-H9.4). The outcome of Damerell-Moss's trial is unknown.

[xliv] Peter auf der Heyde was charged in 1989 for not registering. The charges were subsequently withdrawn, but in 1991 he was charged again— see 'Minutes of COSG meeting Wed. 17/4/1991' (Wits, Rob. Coll., A2558-6). In early 1991 he was tried in the Johannesburg Magistrate's Court, which found that failure to register was not a criminal offence in terms of the Defence Act—see 'Update on South African war resistance issues,' *The Objector* (June 1991), p. 5 (Wits, Rob. Coll., A2558-6). See also 'Update on S.A. war resistance,' *The Objector* (June 1992), p. 4.

[xlv] Walter Rontsch was charged for refusing to serve in the SADF. The date of Rontsch's call-up is not known. At the Johannesburg Magistrate's Court on 17 June 1991 the charge was withdrawn— see 'Wally Rontsch ...', The Objector (September 1991), p. 3. (Wits, ECC Coll., AG1977-H9.4.)

[xlvi] Telford Vice, an ANC member, wrote to his unit, the Kaffrarian Rifles, that he refused to serve in the SADF in a camp that was due to start on 2 July 1991. On 24 June 1991 he was informed by his unit that the camp had been cancelled—see 'Update on South African war resistance issues,' The Objector (September 1991), p. 5. (Wits, Rob. Coll., A2558-6.) See Vice's letter in: 'Telford Vice's call-up cancelled,' The Objector (December 1991), p. 4. (Wits, ECC Coll., AG1977-H9.4.)

[xlvii] Clyde Wynter was charged with refusing to serve in the SADF. He was to be tried in the Johannesburg Magistrate's court; charges were withdrawn in June 1991— see 'Update on South African war resistance issues,' The Objector (September 1991), p. 5. (Wits, Rob. Coll., A2558-6.)

[xlviii] Wayne Boshler was charged with failing to report for duty in the SADF. He was to be tried in the Johannesburg Magistrate's court; charges were withdrawn in June 1991— see 'Update on South African war resistance issues,' The Objector (September 1991), p. 5. (Wits, Rob. Coll., A2558-6.)

[xlix] Cobus/Kobus de Swart was a sociology lecturer at the University of the Western Cape, and was one of the 771 resisters of 1989. He refused to attend a 30-day camp which was supposed to start in December 1989. He presented himself for the call-up at the Navy's SAS Unitie base at Duncan Docks and then announced his refusal to serve, only to be told that the camp had been cancelled—see Jones (2013: 132) and 'Defiance bid fails after cancellation of call-up,' The Star, 28 December 1989. (Wits, ECC Coll., AG1977-E1 (1.34).) Reasons for refusal: he said he was opposed to "the structural and physical violence of the Government against the people of South Africa, as well as the role of the security forces in upholding this violence."—see 'Objector arrives for cancelled camp,' The Citizen, 28 December 1989. (Wits, ECC Coll., AG1977-E1 (1.34).)

[l] Brendan Moran had a call-up for 30 January 1990—'Press conference: Tuesday 15 May, 1990: Profile on objectors who have been imprisoned: Profile of objectors awaiting trial,' provenance not cited. 4 pages. (Wits, ECC Coll., AG1977-E1 (1.26) Douglas Torr.) Moran presented himself for the call-up and then announced his refusal to serve—Jones (2013:132). Moran said he refused to serve on political grounds—see Terry van der Walt, 2016. 'End conscription activists recall the past: brave young men's acts will be preserved for the future.' Pressreader, 21 February 2016. Available at https://www.pressreader.com/south-africa/sunday-tribune-south-africa/2016

0221/281779923191622. Moran was never summoned to appear in court—see 'War resisters update,' *Resister: Journal of the Committee on South African War Resistance*, no. 67 (Fourth Quarter 1990). Page 27 (Wits, Rob. Coll., A2558-7.)

[li] Koos de Kock, from Durban, wrote a letter to the SADF in late 1990, refusing his call-up—'I wrote a letter to Pretoria and on the way...' *The Objector* (November/December 1990). Page 3. (Rob. Coll., A2558-6.) It is not known whether he was charged.

[lii] Warren van Rooyen, a Uitenhage resident, reported in early January 1991 to the Forest Hill Command base, and then refused to render service, saying that he was prepared to go to jail as he was opposed to military conscription for political reasons—see ' "We won't serve in SADF," ' *Weekly Mail*, 11 January 1991. (Wits, ECC Coll., AG1977-E1 (1.34).) As of May 1991, van Rooyen had not been charged—see 'Community service ... the Rev. Douglas Torr: No more jail for objectors?' *Weekly Mail*, 24 May 1991. (Wits, ECC Coll., AG1977-E1 (1.26) Douglas Torr.)

[liii] Francois Krige was one of the ten COSAWR members who returned to South Africa on 1 December 1990. He was one of three who were promptly called up; his call-up date was 7 January 1991. He reported first in Cape Town, and then in Potchefstroom, and then refused to render service—see ' "We won't serve in SADF,"' Weekly Mail, 11 January 1991. (Wits, ECC Coll., AG1977-E1 (1.34).) Krige cited "political reasons" for refusing service and when reporting was wearing a T-shirt with the inscription 'No more apartheid war.'—'Conscientious objectors declare refusal to serve,' *Daily Dispatch*, 8 January 1991. As of May 1991 Krige had not been charged—see 'Community service ... the Rev. Douglas Torr: No more jail for objectors?' *Weekly Mail*, 24 May 1991. (Wits, ECC Coll., AG1977-E1 (1.26) Douglas Torr.)

[liv] Gerald O'Sullivan was one of the ten COSAWR members who returned to South Africa in November 1990. He was one of three who were promptly called up; his call-up date was for July 1991— Francois Krige, 1991. 'My return from exile,' *The Objector* (February/March 1991), p. 3. (Wits, ECC Coll., AG1977-H9.4.) It is not known whether O'Sullivan was charged.

[lv] Fritz Joubert was one of the ten COSAWR members who returned to South Africa in November 1990. He was one of three who were promptly called up; his call-up date was for July 1991— Francois Krige, 1991. 'My return from exile,' *The Objector* (February/March 1991), p. 3 (Wits, ECC Coll., AG1977-H9.4.) It is not known whether Joubert was charged.

[lvi] John Downie from Vanderbijlpark refused to turn up for a camp. He was arrested after writing a letter to the press, and released after being charged with refusing to serve; he was due to appear in court on 24 November 1992—see 'Update on S.A. war resistance,' *The Objector* (November 1992), p. 3. (Wits, ECC Coll., AG1977-H9.4.) Downie appeared in court again in April 1993, when his case was remanded to 28 June 1993. It was then again remanded to January 1994—see 'Update on S.A. militarism and resistance,' *The Objector* (September 1993), p. 8.) The outcome of the court case is not known.

[lvii] John Kelley refused to attend a camp and appeared in court in Vanderbijlpark in April 1993. The case was remanded to 28 June 1993 and then remanded again to January 1994. The outcome of the court case is not known.

[lviii] Bruce Colin Schwan wrote to the Registering Officer of the SADF on 6 July 1993, refusing to report for initial training that was due to start on 8 July 1993. He argued that the conscription system was racially discriminatory and hence immoral, and that by rendering military service he would be prolonging *apartheid*. He said that white soldiers were being sent to black townships to quell violence which itself was caused by *apartheid*; the SADF did not have the support of the majority of the population, and was engaged in a "civil war" (Wits, ECC Coll., AG1977-E1.2. It is not known whether Schwan was charged.

Appendix I. References

Amnesty International, 1982. 'Namibia: a country under control of South Africa'. Pamphlet. New York, September 1982. 6 pages. Available at http://kora.matrix.msu.edu/files/50/304/32-130-2743-84-namibia%20ai%20usa.pdf .

Berat, Lynn, 1989. 'Conscientious objection in South Africa: Governmental paranoia and the law of conscription.' *Vanderbilt Journal of Transnational Law*, 22/1, Article 2. Pages 126-186. Available at https://scholarship.law.vanderbilt.edu/cgi/viewcontent.cgi?article=2070&context=vjtl.

Boyce, Arnold Napier, c. 1965. *A history for South African high schools*. 2nd edition. 707 pages.

Budge, Thomas E., 2013. *It is what it is: grace through acceptance*. Johannesburg, Namasté Press. 277 pages. Documents relevant to the book are available at http://www.iiwii.co.za/web/pages/home.aspx/ .

Callister, Graeme, 2007. 'Patriotic duty or resented imposition? Public reactions to military conscription in white South Africa, 1952-1972.' *Scientia Militaria, South African Journal of Military Studies*, vol. 35, no. 1, 2007. Pages 46-67. Available at https://journals.co.za/doi/pdf/10.10520/AJA10228136_127.

Cape Town Conscientious Objector Support Group (CT COSG), 1983. 'This was their choice,' typewritten manuscript, September 1983. 4 pages.[335] Refers to Anton Eberhard, Edric Gorfinkel, Peter Moll, Richard Steele,

---

[335] Wits, ECC Coll., AG1977-E1.2.

Charles Yeats, Michael Viveiros, Neil Mitchell, Billy Paddock, Etienne Essery, Adrian Paterson, Peter Hathorn, Stephen Granger and Paul Dobson.

CIIR (Catholic Institute for International Relations) and Pax Christi, 1982. *War and conscience in South Africa: The churches and conscientious objection*. London. 112 pages.

Chikane, Frank, 1988 and 2009. *No life of my own: an autobiography*. Eugene, OR: Wipf & Stock Publishers and Orbis. 132 pages.

Christian Citizenship Department of the Methodist Church of Southern Africa, 1980. *Church and conscience: a collection of church and other statements on conscientious objection in South Africa*. Durban: Unity Publications.

Collins, Brian F., 1995. *A history of the Committee on South African War Resistance (COSAWR) (1978-1990)*. M.A. thesis in history, University of Cape Town. 231 pages. Available at https://core.ac.uk/download/185421470.pdf .

Connors, Judith Patricia, 2007. *Empowering alternatives: A history of the Conscientious Objector Support Group's challenge to military service in South Africa*. M.Com. thesis in the subject 'Conflict Resolution and Peace Studies' at the University of KwaZulu-Natal. October 2007. 260 pages.[336]

'Conscientious objection in SA.' Typewritten manuscript, no provenance cited, no date cited [but from the contents, 1983]. 5 pages.[337]

de Victoria, Franciscus, n.d. *De Indis, de jure belli: The second relectio of the Reverend Father, Brother Franciscus de Victoria, on the Indians, or on the law of war made by the Spaniards on the barbarians*. Edited by James Brown Scott

---

[336] Available at https://www.yumpu.com/en/document/view/13918358/view-open-university-of-kwazulu-natal/128.

[337] Wits, Rob. Coll., A2558-12.3.

in c. 1917 and prepared for international publication by Ernest Nys in c. 1964. Available at https://en.wikisource.org/wiki/De_Indis_De_Jure_Belli/Part_3 .

Detention Barracks Regulations (1961-1976). Referred to by GN R1190/61, published under Government Notice R1190 in Government Gazette Extraordinary 131 of 8 December 1961, as amended by GN R1949 in GG 5317 dated 22 October 1976 and GN R569 dated 1984. See Michelle Nel, 2012. *Sentencing practice in military courts.* Ll.D. Thesis at the University of South Africa, January. 556 pages.

Field, Roger, 1989. 'Exile or imprisonment—Conscription in South Africa,' *Socialist Lawyer* (London), No. 8, Summer 1989, pp. 9-11.[338]

Fowler, C. de K., and G.J.J. Smit, c. 1965. *History for the Cape Senior Certificate and Matriculation.* 6th edition. Cape Town: Maskew Miller Ltd. 547 pages.

Grundy, Kenneth E., 1983. *Soldiers without politics: blacks in the South African armed forces.* Berkeley: University of California Press. 297 pages.

Hale, Frederick, 2000. *South African Baptist social ethics: the captivity of the church in a multiracial society.* South African Historical Society. 411 pages.

Hale, Frederick, 2005 and 2009. 'Baptist ethics of conscientious objection to military service in South Africa: the watershed case of Richard Steele.' *Acta Theologica,* 2005:2, pp. 18-44; and 14 December 2009.[339]

Isaacs, Sedick, 2010. *Surviving in the apartheid prison: Flash backs of an earlier life.* United States: Xlibris.

---

[338] *Socialist Lawer*: available at https://static1.squarespace.com/static/562e7d33e4b0da14ad6d202f/t/566dcbe90e4c116bdc0eb6ca/1450036201325/SocialistLawyer08.pdf.

[339] Hale: available at https://www.ajol.info/index.php/actat/article/view/49013/35361 .

Jones, David, 2013. *Objecting to apartheid: The history of the End Conscription Campaign.* MA thesis in history at the University of Fort Hare, January 2013. 159 pages.

Kaempf, Markus E., 2002. 'Detention Barracks 1976: A somewhat different SADF experience.' 2 January 2002. About 5 pages. Available at https://sadf.sentinelprojects.com/bg1/dbmek.html.

Kathrada, Ahmed, 2004. *No bread for Mandela: Memoirs of Ahmed Kathrada, Prisoner No. 468/64.* Lexington, KY: University of Kentucky Press. 400 pages.

Kearney, Paddy, 1980. 'Conscientious objection: a Christian perspective: a lecture delivered at the University of Natal, Pietermaritzburg.' *Reality: A journal of liberal and radical opinion* (Pietermaritzburg), September 1980, pages 9-14.

Law, Lois, Chris Lund and Harald Winkler, 1987. 'Conscientious objection: the church against apartheid's violence,' pp. 281-297 in: Charles Villa-Vicencio (ed.), 1987. *Theology and violence: the South African debate.* Grand Rapids: William B. Eerdmans Publishing Company, 1987. 309 pages.

Lehman, Melvin H., 1981. 'The story of a South African conscientious objector,' *The Christian Century* (Chicago, USA), 4 November 1981, pp. 1128-1130. Refers mainly to Peter Moll, also to Richard Steele.

Lewin, Hugh, 1974-1989. *Bandiet: seven years in a South African prison.* Cape Town: David Philip. 228 pages.

Louw, Ronald, 1984. *Detention Barracks.* Observatory: Mission of the Churches for Community Development, 1984. 38 pages. Refers to Peter Moll, Peter Hathorn, Andrew Orpen and Anthony Waddell.[340]

---

[340] Wits, ECC Coll., AG1977-E1.2.

337

Mandela, Nelson, 1994. *Long walk to freedom: The autobiography of Nelson Mandela.* Boston: Little, Brown & Co. 656 pages.

Moll, Peter, 1978b. 'Why I am a selective conscientious objector,' typewritten and printed 300X by Gestetner, December 1978. 11 pages.[341] Reproduced in this volume in the section of original documents.

Moll, Peter, 1979a. 'The non-combatancy option and the disobedience option,' Mowbray: typewritten and duplicated 300 times by Gestetner, 2 March 1979. 6 pages.[342]

Moll, Peter, 1981c. 'Conditions in the Detention Barracks: A short report, for attention Maj.-Gen. Fourie.' Johannesburg: carbon copy, 16 March 1981. Wits, Rob. Coll., A2558-9.13.

Moll, Peter G., 1984b. *A theological critique of the military chaplaincy of the English-speaking churches.* M.A. thesis, Department of Religious Studies, University of Cape Town.[343]

Moll, Peter, 1984c. 'Controversy: chaplains in the army,' *Objector: Newsletter of the Conscientious Objector Support Group (W. Cape)*, vol. 2 no. 4 (July 1984), p. 6-7.[344]

Moll, Peter G., 1985b. 'Military chaplaincy and unjust wars.' *Journal of Theology for Southern Africa*, vol. 53 (December): 13-21.

Moll, Peter G., 1986b. 'A proposal for a civilianised chaplaincy', 1986. 10 pages, printed on the Sperry-UNIVAC computer at the University of Cape Town.[345]

---

[341] Wits, Rob. Coll., A2558-9.13.
[342] Wits, Rob. Coll., A2558-9.13.
[343] https://open.uct.ac.za/bitstream/item/16895/thesis_hum_1984_moll_peter_graham.pdf.
[344] Wits, ECC Coll., AG1977-H9.4.
[345] Wits, Rob. Coll., A2558-9.13.

Moll, Peter G., 1987b. 'Ministry in conflict situations,' Durban: typewritten manuscript, August 1987. 14 pages.[346]

Moll, Peter G., 1990. 'Legislative change for alternative national service: past and future', in: Centre for Intergroup Studies, 1990. *Alternative National Service. Occasional Paper No. 14*. Rondebosch: Cape Town. Pages 227-234.

Moll, Peter, 1997. *My experience with conscription: Submission to the Truth and Reconciliation Commission*. Washington, D.C., mimeo, 29 June 1997. 62 pages.

Moll, Theodor Arthur, 1997. *My memoirs*. Gaithersburg, MD: Signature Book Printing, April 1997. 278 pages.

Mureinik, Etienne, 1977. 'Conscientious objection: the United States and South Africa.' *De Jure et Legibus* (Journal of the Law Students' Council of the University of the Witwatersrand), vol. 4, October 1977.

Paton, Alan, 1979. *Towards racial justice: Will there be a change of heart?* The Alfred and Winifred Hoernlé Memorial Lecture. South African Institute of Race Relations. 21 pages.

Phillips, Merran Willis, 2002. *The End Conscription Campaign 1983-1988: A study of white extra-parliamentary opposition to apartheid*. M.A. thesis, University of South Africa, November 2002. 245 pages.[347]

Report of the Commission of Inquiry into South African Council of Churches ('Eloff Commission'), RP 74/1983. Pretoria: Government Printer. 445 pages. Reference to Peter Moll and Richard Steele is on p. 195.

Robertson, Rob, 1999. *St. Anthony's activists: turning dreams into deeds. The story of St. Anthony's United Church, Pageview and Johannesburg, 1975-1990*. Cape Town: 1990. 205 pages.

---

[346] Wits, ECC Coll., AG1977-24.10.1.14.

[347] Available on the web at https://uir.unisa.ac.za/handle/10500/15771.

SAMRAF, viz. South African Military Refugee Aid Fund, 1979. *The right to say no to a crime against humanity: A report on the militarisation of South Africa and the right of conscientious objection.* Published by SAMRAF, Brooklyn, New York. 24 pages. Authors Don Morton and others. Available at https://projects.kora.matrix.msu.edu/files/210-808-8528/african_activist_archive-a0b2q2-a_12419.pdf .

Smail, Andrew, 1980. *South African law and the conscientious objector (Revised Edition).* Durban Ad Hoc Committee on Alternative National Service, c/o Diakonia, Durban, April 1980. 57 pages.

Steele, Richard, 1983. 'Suggested procedure for non-"peace church" members to follow in becoming a conscientious objector in South Africa: written by a pacifist conscientious objector'. Typewritten manuscript, 19 pages. Wits, Rob. Coll., A2558-9.20.

Steele, Richard, 1997. *My experiences as a conscientious objector to conscription into the SADF, and as an End Conscription Campaign activist: Statement submitted to the Truth and Reconciliation Commission.* Cape Town: mimeo, 30 June 1997. 193 pages. Includes Appendix 2 which is a listing of the media coverage of Richard Steele's case.

Survey of Race Relations in South Africa 1979, ed. Loraine Gordon (Johannesburg: 1980). Available at http://psimg.jstor.org/fsi/img/pdf/t0/10.5555/al.sff.document.boo19800300.042.000.pdf .

Truth and Reconciliation Commission Final Report (1998). The Commission's Volume 4, chapter 8 focused on military conscription. See https://www.sahistory.org.za/archive/trc-final-report-volume-4 .

UNCAA and COSAWR (viz. United Nations Centre against Apartheid and Committee on South African War Resistance), 1989. *The Issue of Conscientious Objection in Apartheid*

South Africa: Growth of the Anti-Conscription Movement. Available at http://psimg.jstor.org/fsi/img/pdf/t0/10.5555/al.sff.document.nuun1989_09_final.pdf.

Watch Tower Bible and Tract Society of New York, 1977-80. *Pay attention to yourselves and to all the flock (Acts 20:28): Kingdom Ministry School Textbook.* Watch Tower Bible and Tract Society of New York, International Bible Students Association, Brooklyn, New York, 1977-1981. 150 pages. This is an internal document and is not available for sale. A copy may nevertheless be seen at https://www.childabuse royalcommission.gov.au/sites/default/files/WAT.0013.002.0001.pdf.

Webster, Trevor, 2014. *The Black and White: The Story of the Selborne Schools.* East London: Selborne Foundation Trust. 320 pages.

Yeats, Charles, 2005. *Prisoner of conscience: one man's remarkable journey from repression to freedom.* London: Rider, 2005. 210 pages.

Index